MADELEINE
L'ENGLE

GENESIS TRILOGY

Also by Madeleine L'Engle

The Glorious Impossible
An Acceptable Time
Two-Part Invention
A Cry Like a Bell
Many Waters
A House Like a Lotus
A Severed Wasp
Walking on Water
The Sphinx at Dawn
A Ring of Endless Light
The Anti-Muffins
A Swiftly Tilting Planet
The Weather of the Heart
Ladder of Angels
The Irrational Season
Dragons in the Waters
Summer of the Great Grandmother
Prayers for Sunday
Everyday Prayers
A Wind in the Door
A Circle of Quiet
The Other Side of the Sun
Lines Scribbled on an Envelope
Dance in the Desert
The Young Unicorns
The Journey with Jonah
The Love Letters
The Arm of the Starfish
The Twenty-four Days Before Christmas
The Moon by Night
Meet the Austins
A Winter's Love
Camilla
And Both Were Young
Isla
The Small Rain
Penguins and Golden Calves
Mothers & Daughters
Bright Evening Star

MADELEINE L'ENGLE

GENESIS TRILOGY

COMPRISING

AND IT WAS GOOD

A STONE FOR A PILLOW

SOLD INTO EGYPT

Northstone

Cover and interior design: Margaret Kyle
Cover photos: courtesy of Theodore Vouladakis
Consulting art director: Robert MacDonald

Northstone Publishing Inc.
is an employee-owned company, committed to caring for the environment
and all creation. Northstone recycles, reuses and composts, and encourages
readers to do the same. Resources are printed on recycled paper and more
environmentally friendly groundwood papers (newsprint), whenever possible.
The trees used are replaced through donations to the Scoutrees For Canada Program.
Ten percent of all profit is donated to charitable organizations.

Canadian Cataloguing in Publication Data
L'Engle, Madeleine
Genesis trilogy
Previously published in 3 separate vols.
ISBN 1-896836-12-7
1. Bible. O.T. Genesis – Meditations. 2. Christian life. I. Title.
II. Title: And it was good. III. Title: A stone for a pillow.
IV. Title: Sold into Egypt.
BS1235.4L46 1997 222'.11 C97-910443-2

Printing 9 8 7 6 5 4 3 2 1

Printed in Canada by
Transcontinental Printing, Inc.,
Peterborough, Ontario

Contents

Publisher's Note

In the midst of a resurging interest in biblical myth, and in the book of Genesis in particular, Northstone Publishing is pleased to be releasing a one-volume collection of Madeleine L'Engle's classic works *And It Was Good, A Stone for a Pillow*, and *Sold into Egypt*.

And It Was Good, the first book in the trilogy, was written over ten years ago. But it might have been written an hour ago. These books are amazingly current; like the book of Genesis itself, they have stood the test of time.

And it may be said that these books were, in fact, ahead of their time. Long before the "new interpretations" of Bill Moyers and Elaine Pagels and Karen Armstrong, there was Madeleine, quietly writing her own reflections on the most ancient of biblical stories, enhanced by her own experience. By sharing her life with us, Madeleine succeeds in making Genesis personal – with her trademark grace, elegance, humor, and fiercely keen mind.

Why does Genesis matter today? No matter who took the first bite of the apple or how the world came to be, stories are important. Each of our own life stories is important. And we can learn from the wisdom of those who came before us.

The people of Genesis were a complex mix of grief and glory, of failings and triumphs, of the mundane and the holy. And, Madeleine reminds us, so are we. May this book serve to comfort, provoke, and enlighten you.

– *The Publisher*

Preface

How pleased I am that my Genesis trilogy is going to be one book, because of course Genesis is one book, the beginning of scripture. It is the story of God's creating, making the heavens and the earth, and joyfully affirming that it is good, very good. Then we move on to the great stories of Adam and Eve, Abraham, Sarah, and Isaac, and God's continuing to be part of our story, our obedience, our stiffneckedness. We move through the terror of the flood and the joy of the rainbow, God's covenant with us. The story continues with Jacob and Esau, Rachel and Rebekah, a wrestling angel, and on to Jacob's sons, the 12 tribes of Israel. The book ends with the story of Joseph, and already in the first book of the Bible we are given the wonder of creation and God's loving concern for us, God's fascinating, frustrating, extraordinary creatures.

– *Madeleine L'Engle*
Crosswicks Cottage

AND IT WAS GOOD

1

Beginnings

A SMALL SHIP – a freighter – on a very large sea.

A cloudless blue sky, and the sun lighting an ocean which changed from blue to purple to steel grey as the wind rose and the waves lifted their crests.

We were caught in an unusual nautical event, a fair weather storm.

The crew strung ropes along all the walkways which did not already have rails. In the dining room the tablecloths were soaked with water to keep the dishes from sliding. People who travel on freighters are likely to be good sailors, so most of us made it in to dinner.

During the night we felt the wind continue to rise. We had to hold on to the sides of our bunks to keep from being thrown out, and sleep was out of the question. That morning it just happened that we had been given a sheet of paper explaining the Beaufort scale, which measures the severity of storms on a ratio of one to twelve. Where on that scale were we? As the wind rose, and the waves, we felt more than mere curiosity about it.

Our ship, though heavily laden with cargo at both ends, was rather light in the middle where the cabins and the public rooms were situated. Neither my husband nor I spoke the thought aloud, but later we confessed we both had had visions of the ship breaking in two. It was not that we rolled or hawed. It felt as though the ship was crashing into stone as it hit one mountainous wave after another.

We had been at sea only about a week, rejoicing at first in balmy weather, where at home in Connecticut there was snow and ice. We were both beginning to relax after weeks of very heavy work schedules. And I had turned back to Genesis as well as John's gospel for my Scripture reading, using the Gideon Bible in our cabin.

Something about the wildness of the weather started those great verses moving strongly through my mind. I was not really frightened by the storm, but I was, to put it mildly, ill at ease and uncomfortable, and so I rested on the great story of the Beginning.

In the beginning God created the heaven and the earth.

In the beginning was the Word, and the Word was with God, and the Word was God. And the earth was without form, and void; and darkness was upon the face of the deep. And the Spirit of God moved upon the face of the waters.

In the beginning was the Word, with God; and the Spirit was in the beginning. Always there are all three faces of our trinitarian God. Always. The past – before time and space. Always. Now – during quiet. During storm. And the word always also looks forward, beyond when time and space will end.

The same Word was in the beginning with God. All things were made by him, and without him was not anything made that was made.

One is very aware of time in the middle of a storm. I kept looking at our travel clock, faintly luminous at two o'clock in the morning. But outside, not a glimmer of light. Only the dark violence of wind and wave. How long would it go on? How long could it go on?

It is difficult for us who were born in time, into time, and whose mortality will die in time – to time, to understand that before that extraordinary beginning, that first act of creativity, that first epiphany, when God took nothing and made something, there was no time, no space. Everything began at the same moment. In the beginning.

And God said, Let there be light. And there was light.

And God saw the light, that it was good, and God divided the light from the darkness. And God called the light day, and the darkness he called light. And the evening and morning were the first day.

There's something of the feeling of that first day on a ship, especially a small ship. Caught up as most of us are in the complexities of daily living, we forget that we are surrounded by the creative power of Love. Every once in a while we need to step aside from the troubles and pleasures of our lives, and take a fresh look, a time to feel, and listen to our Source. Ever since my husband has been on the TV series, "All My Children" and gets a real vacation, we have done our stepping aside by boarding an ocean freighter. In mid-February, whenever possible, we embark on a small ship in a large sea. (Having been married for twenty-five years before we had spent more than two nights away from home together only heightens our delight in having a real holiday.)

The day before we sailed into that extraordinary fairweather storm, as our freighter moved down the east coast of South America to what is called "the Bottom of the World", our captain spoke to us. "As we get near the Strait of Magellan," he said, "be sure to look at the horizon. You'll never see it so clearly. There are no towns or cities to pollute the atmosphere."

It was true. Down there, when we looked at the horizon we saw air, air as it was meant to be when it was made. We saw clearly the beautiful curve of the earth. And at night we saw the Southern Cross in an absolutely black sky. I was astounded and awed at its blackness. Pure. Clear. With the stars blazing from out of it. There was none of the pinkish tinge we are used to seeing around the horizon from the city lights; even if we are as much as a hundred miles from the city, those lights still stain the sky of the "civilized" world.

And so, even before we moved into the wildness of the unexpected storm, we had a feeling of Genesis. The day after the storm was over and the ropes were taken down and we were able to balance as we stood or walked without legs wide apart, my husband asked the captain where we had been on the Beaufort scale. He replied laconically, "Eleven."

I stood at the rail and looked at the sea, which felt smooth again, though there were still whitecaps breaking the surface, and kept on with my thoughts. The first day. The beginning of time. Time, which, like matter, was created in that first great shouting of joy, of making nothing into something, time, a part of nature, which, like space, like all creation, will have an end. (All created things die. Before the seed can grow, it must be planted in the earth, and so die to itself before it can become a tree. Or a wave. Or a flying fish.)

But in the beginning, when all things were first shown forth, the light and the dark danced together; in the fullness of their time they comprehended each other; they knew each other, and it was good. It was very good.

God created. God *made*.

Night and day – that first flashing rhythm which marked the birth of time. Water and land. Galaxies and suns and planets and moons, all moving in the joyous dance of creation. Matter and time making music together.

God made. Fish and sea animals and birds. Land and land animals, every kind of living creature, ants and auks and aardvarks. Dromedaries and dragons and dinosaurs.

And God saw that it was good. And God said, let us make man in our image.

Our image, said the Trinitarian Creator, the Maker.

"Our" image, as it is translated in the *King James Bible*, is more in harmony with the original than some of the newer translations which say "my" image, completely missing the point.

If Christ suddenly appeared in Bethlehem two thousand years ago, as a surprising number of people seem to believe, how can there be unity in Trinity? Yes, for all three persons were there, always, inseparable, whole and holy.

So God said, Let us make man in our image ... male and female.

Both male and female go to make the image of God, not a singleton, not an independent entity. Not one: how could one be *our* image? *Our* image, said God, not my image. Our image, male and female.

That it takes both male and female to complete the image of God is not a new thought for me, but neither is it a static one. My own thinking about the balance of love and tension between male and female changes with each encounter. As a woman, I deny my own free will if I blame men for the patriarchal society into which I was born. Males cannot take over unless females permit it. And in permitting it, we erode male wholeness as well as our own. And our image is an image of wholeness – what we are meant to be.

In the beginning of the space/time continuum, night and day (female and male, according to Greek thinking) understood each other, as we need to understand each other now, if, in this time, we are not to destroy time, and ourselves along with it. I, as a woman, need to understand not only the men I encounter in my life, but the masculine in myself, just as men must seek to understand not only the women they meet, but the feminine in themselves. This is perhaps easier for women than for men, for through the centuries women have often had to be both mother and father, when their husbands were at sea, or at war, or, in my case, when my actor husband had to be on the road for months at a time with a play. Women have been allowed to affirm the nurturing and the intuitive in themselves, whereas more often than not men have been forced by society to limit themselves to the rational, fact-finding-and-proving part of their personalities. Women must be very gentle with men as they, as well as women, seek to regain the lost wholeness for which they were destined.

It takes two to make the image of God, not necessarily a male and a female, though this is the most obvious example. It takes all aspects of ourselves to be part of that image. And "our" image is an image of community, community which was in trinity in the beginning, and which will be after the eschaton, the end of time, when night and day and all of us will know each other again in the coming of the kingdom.

In that first epiphany, when matter was formless and space was empty, God created. How marvellous that there should be something rather than nothing! How marvelous that there is, rather than that there is not.

God created, and it was joy: time, space, matter. There is, and we are part of that is-ness, part of that becoming. That is our calling: co-creation. Every single one of us, without exception, is called to co-create with God. No one is too unimportant to have a share in the making or unmaking of the final showing-forth. Everything that we do either draws the Kingdom of love closer, or pushes it further off. That is a fearful responsibility, but when God made "man in our image, male and female," responsibility went with it. Too often we want to let somebody else do it, the preacher, or the teacher, or the government agency. But if we are to continue to grow in God's image, then we have to accept the responsibility.

God's image! How much of God may be seen in me, may I see in others? Try as we may, we cannot hide it completely.

A young reader knowing of my love of new words, sent me a beautiful one: namasté: I salute the God within you.

The words which have taught me most richly come in logical progression: *ontology*: the word about being, *ousia*: the essence of being, that which is really real; *ananda* (also sent me as a gift by a reader): that joy in existence without which the universe will fall apart and collapse. And now: namasté.

If we accept that God is within each of us, then God will give us, within us, the courage to accept the responsibility of being co-creators.

We live in a world which has become too complex to unravel, there is nothing we can do about it, we little people who don't have big government posts or positions of importance. But I believe that the Kingdom is built on the little things that all of us do. I remember my grandmother was fond of reciting:

Little drops of water,
Little grains of sand
Make the mighty ocean
And the pleasant land.

A single drop can't make even a puddle, but together, all our little drops and God's planning can make not only a mighty ocean but a mighty difference. Alone, there's not much we can do, but when Peter healed a cripple it was made very clear that it was not by his own power, but by the power of Christ, the creating Word, that the healing was accomplished.

This power is available to all of us. Indeed, with everything we do, we either use or reject it, for we do nothing in isolation. As the physicists who study the microcosm are discovering, *nothing* happens in isolation, nothing *exists* in isolation. Quanta, the tiny subatomic particles being studied in quantum mechanics, cannot exist alone; there cannot be a quantum, for quanta exist only in relationship to each other. And they can never be studied objectively, because even to observe them is to change them. And, like the stars, they appear to be able to communicate with each other without sound or speech, *there is neither speech nor language, but their voices are heard among them*, sings the psalmist.

Surely what is true of quanta is true of the creation, it is true of quarks, it is true of human beings. We do not exist in isolation. We are part of a vast web of relationships and interrelationships which sing themselves in the ancient harmonies. Nor can we be studied objectively, because to look at us is to change us. And for us to look at anything is to change not only what we are looking at, but ourselves, too.

And our deepest messages of love are often conveyed without words. In my writing I have used the word *kything*, found in an old Scottish dictionary of my grandfather's, to express this communication without words, where there is "neither speech nor language." To kythe is to open yourself to someone. It is, for me, a form of intercessory prayer, for it is to be utterly vulnerable.

To some people it smacks of ESP. They are wary of such things, not being able to understand them. Kything is indeed a kind of ESP although it goes much further, for it takes a deep faith in the goodness of creation and the power of love to open oneself in love and hope and faith. So it came as a shock to me when I received a letter asking me, with great sincerity, if kything was satanic. Evidently, to the writer, any form of extrasensory perception was of the devil. Of course, wherever there is good in comes the devil at a gallop. But to kythe to be with someone in that deepest communication which is beyond words, is of God not of the devil. When I was a child, my test for real friendship was the test of silence: could I and my friend be together without speaking and be comfortable with each other? If the answer was Yes, then I could trust the friendship.

We do not love each other without changing each other. We do not observe the world around us without in some way changing it, and being changed ourselves. To listen to the news on radio or television is to be part of what is going on, and to be modified by it. But how on earth – or heaven – can that be reciprocal? *We* are changed by war and rumor of war, but how can we in turn change what changes us?

There are some obvious, small ways. We can join, if we are female, the League of Women voters. We can do volunteer work (despite a nine-to-five job) in the hospice movement. We can write our senators and congressmen. In the Greek play *Lysistrata* the women were so outraged by war that they banded together against the men to stop it. We are not as helpless as we may seem.

Those are a few of the obviously active ways. But there are less obvious ones that are equally important. I was asked how we could pray for our planet, with the devastating wars which are tearing it apart, with greed fouling the air we breathe and the water we drink. And I replied that the only way I know how to pray for the body of our planet is to see it as God meant it to be, to see the sky as we sometimes see it in the country in wintertime, crisp with stars, or to see the land with spring moving across it, the fruit trees flowering and the grass greening, and at night hearing the peepers calling back and forth, and the high, sweet singing of the bats.

In the spring, the early spring, during the height of the Falkland crisis, I knelt on the damp earth planting onion sets, and smelling the rich growing odor of the freshly turned garden, and the pungency of the onions. Planting onions that spring was an act of faith in the future, for I was very fearful for our planet. It has long seemed likely that if there is atomic devastation, it will not come from one of the great powers. (Russia does not want war any more than we do. The land of Russia is still not healed from the terrible wounds of World War II. The scars are still visible. Nor is China hungry for war.) If we blunder into the folly of atomic warfare it is more likely to come from something seemingly as absurd as the battle over the inhospitable Falklands than from something predictable.

So I planted onions, and hoped, and prayed, and suddenly I was aware of being surrounded by the song of the birds, making an ecstasy of melody, and their joy was a strengthening of hope. As I sat back on my heels, the better to listen, the birdsong was an affirmation of ultimate all-rightness and also of immediate all-rightness, despite the news to which we were anxiously listening. The birds know. We sophisticated people have forgotten what the "primitive" people have always known, that the birds *know* and that a change in their song is a portent of change to come, usually terrible change. But this singing of the birds was their own spring song, which I have heard year after year, and so my heavy heart lifted.

That evening Hugh and I saw something we had never seen before, two robins in a mating dance, and that, too, was affirmation. It may seem that the beauty of two robins can do little to heal the horrors of our planet, but I believe that in their dance they were not only following the call of spring, but healing – or helping to heal – all that has gone wrong with the sweet green earth on which they live.

A year ago a family of robins made their nest in our garage. We are used to having barn swallows come in and try to set up light housekeeping, but not robins. However, one day we noticed that on the back of a bicycle which hangs on the wall was a robin's nest. By standing on a box, we could see the eggs, naturally a beautiful robin's-egg blue! And of course we could not use the garage until the eggs were hatched and the fledglings had learned to fly. That was the spring that the gypsy moths devastated the land, defoliating a tree in an hour. Mountainsides were as bare and brown as in winter. And it was our son's theory that this particular robin family had "known" that the trees were going to lose their protecting leaves, and so they had come into the garage, contrary to pattern, to keep their babies safe.

This spring the robins were back in the newly-dressed trees in their recreated green, and in our area of the countryside the gypsy moths have done little damage.

* * *

The Falkland crisis ended, but the fear of war does not.

With each onslaught of terror it hits us anew. Why do we tend to forget that this has been a century of fear, when the second half of the century has been gripped in the fear of atomic horror?

A reminder of how long this fear has been with us came to me when I turned to some old journals to type out for my children the stories of their births, and some of the things they did and said when they were little. I don't go back to those journals very often, and I was surprised at the many entries which showed my anguish about the possibility of atomic warfare.

One time in the fifties when we were listening in anxiety to every radio newscast, trying not to let our small children see how anxious we were, I recorded putting them to bed. Our youngest was four. His prayers were dictatorial to God (as only a four-year-old can be dictatorial), and intimate. That night, in the middle of his long "God blesses," he said, "God please don't let there be any more wars. Please just let everybody die of old age." And, a few months later: " ... and God, please remember about do unto others as you would they do to you. Please make them do these words. Make them think. Make them think, and not destroy this world."

So we all continue to pray for the planet, visualizing the pussy willows turning furry in the spring, listening to the songs of the insects and tree toads in the autumn, hearing the rain fall on the thirsty gardens, seeing the unique blue of the robins' eggs.

The robins affirm, for me, the validity and vitality of creation. The robin's song is as important to the heavenly harmonies as is the turning of the galaxies. And it is all, all held in the love of God.

One of the early words by which the ancient Hebrews knew God was El. El – the Lord. Beth-el, for instance, means the house of God. So I find it helpful, wherever and whenever possible, to call God El, or el, rather than using the masculine or feminine pronoun, because the name *el* lifts the Creator beyond all our sexisms and chauvinisms and anthropomorphisms.

We human creatures, made in the image of God, in church as well as out, too often reject instead of affirming the Word which has proven to be the cornerstone. And we worry, too often, about peripheral things. (Like baptism: is dunking more valid than sprinkling?) And we are continuing to worry about sexist words to the point where we are coming close to destroying language. To call God either him or her, he or she, is in both cases to miss the wholeness of the Creator. And so we lose all sense of proportion, and try to clamp God once again within our own broken image.

And so I return to the reality of our trinitarian God of creation, el.

El. That power of love. That holy thing. Do we believe that it was a power of love which created everything and saw it was good? Is creation purposeful? Or is it some kind of cosmic accident? Do our fragments of lives have meaning? Or are we poor human beings no more than a skin disease on the face of an unfortunate planet? Can we see the pattern and beauty which is an affirmation of the value of all creation?

On the cover of the May, 1982 *Scientific American* is a beautiful photograph of a "pattern of radio emission from the gigantic elliptical galaxy IC 4296. (There are so many quadrillions of galaxies that the scientists, alas, have run out of names and resorted to numbers. I am grateful for the psalmist's affirmation that God knows *all* the stars by name.) The galaxy, probably a member of the Centaurus cluster of galaxies, is 120 million light years away. It is nonetheless the closest of the 'classical' radio sources: the sources consisting of two symmetrical lobes of radio emission ... the patch is really two jets of ionized gas emerging in opposite directions from the center of the galaxy ... The distance between the lobes is almost a million light years."

The macrocosm. Too enormous for our finite minds readily to comprehend.

And then the microcosm. The distances between the parts of an electron are proportionately as vast as the distance between those lobes of radio emission from a galaxy.

What does that do to our concept of *size*? It either makes us throw up our hands in horror at the over-awesome incomprehensibility of creation, or it makes us cry out in joy at the total unimportance of size, for all, all of it is held in God's loving hand. "See, I will not forget you," el assures us in the book of the prophet Isaiah. "I have carved you on the palm of my hand."

* * *

I am grateful for our freighter vacations which provide stress release from the normal strains of daily living. But though there are no phone calls, no interruptions, nothing that *has* to be done, even a vacation on a freighter does not offer a safe and placid world. Creation is still wildly beautiful, and it is still wild. Eleven is mighty close to twelve on the Beaufort scale, and twelve is disaster.

If I affirm that the universe was created by a power of love, and that all creation is good I am not proclaiming safety. Safety was never part of the promise. Creativity, yes; safety, no. All creativity is dangerous. Even with the advances of science, women still die in childbirth. Babies are born with distorted limbs or minds. To write a story or paint a picture is to risk failure. To love someone is to risk that you may not be loved in return, or that the love will die. But love is worth that risk, and so is birth, its fulfillment.

This is no time for a child to be born,
With the earth betrayed by war & hate
And a nova lighting the sky to warn
That time runs out & the sun burns late,

That was no time for a child to be born,
In a land in the crushing grip of Rome;
Honor & truth were trampled by scorn –
Yet here did the Saviour make his home.

When is the time for love to be born?
The inn is full on the planet earth,
And by greed & pride the sky is torn –
Yet Love still takes the risk of birth.

Anyone embracing Christianity for the sake of safety is going to distort the broken body even further. The desire for safety at any expense ultimately leads to death. It is the desire for safety which has made some people take refuge in religions which provide all the answers, make their members feel more saved than people who don't belong to their group, and promise freedom from danger. Insistence on static answers has brought about the recurring conflicts between science and religion.

At a writers' conference I was asked by a young man, "Do you believe in evolution?"

I had been talking about structure in fiction, not about science, and the question was asked in the sort of belligerent manner that told me he was waiting to pounce on any answer, no matter what, as "wrong."

A crowded lecture room during a lecture on techniques of fiction was neither the time nor the place to get into an argument about evolutionism versus creationism, and in any event I find little to argue about. So I replied that I thought that God could create in any way which seemed good to el.

And that, indeed, is what I think. The only reason I can find for all the shouting about *how* God created is that it allows some people to stop thinking, to settle back into the safety of their rut, to stop thinking about what it is really all about.

What it is really about is that creation is God's. It is el who has made us, and not we ourselves. To argue about how God made us is to argue about nonessentials. As far as I am concerned, it doesn't matter a whit how God created. The important thing is that creation is God's, and that we are part of it, and being part of creation is for us to be co-creators with el in the continuing joy of new creation.

That is a great calling, and when we argue about how God created us, we forget our vocation, and the tempter rejoices. I'm all for genuine scientific research, but when we argue about *how*, rather than *if* or *why*, we miss the point. In a world where fewer and fewer people believe in God at all, where life is for so many an unimportant accident with no meaning, where we are born only to slip back into annihilation, we need to stop arguing and affirm the goodness of creation, and the power of love which holds us all.

❁ ❁ ❁

As far as the evidence of science shows today (and the evidence of science is always open to change with new discoveries), evolution seems a likely explanation of how all the galaxies, solar systems, planets, creatures, human beings came to be. There are holes in this theory, things left out, things left unresolved, but that we "thinking reeds" have evolved slowly, the original unicellular creature becoming ever more and more complex, until brains were developed which were complex enough to ask questions, seems consistent with present knowledge. One of the still open questions in the debate is the extraordinarily rapid development of the brain pan from something tiny to the much larger one which contains and protects our complex brains. Why this development came about more swiftly than the ordinarily slow process would account for is one of the still unexplained mysteries. But the rapid development of the cranium and the cranial cavity happened, and with our complex brains we think, and we ask questions, and often we want them answered before we have gathered enough evidence.

If new evidence should prove that evolution is not how it all happened, that won't do anything to change the nature of God, any more than Galileo's discoveries changed the nature of God. Nor would it shatter my faith. The Lord of Creation makes as el chooses, and only el knows how. "I'll be what I will be," God replied to Moses when asked about his name. The options are all open, free. Free of all the restrictions we human beings try to impose on our Maker. Free to offer us an example of freedom which we hardly dare contemplate.

Creation continues lavishly, and we are part of it. Not only are stars and people and fireflies born, not only do they die, but what we as creatures do during our lifespan makes a difference. We are not just passive, acted upon; we are also actors in the great drama of creation. As to the passionate arguers about creationism versus evolutionism, I still think they're missing the point. The more hotly they argue, the more widely do they miss the point. The more zealous they grow in defending their cause (like the church establishment of Galileo's day) the less are they able to sit back calmly and observe the evidence and say, "This, too, is the Lord's."

When I am most defensive about something, arguing hotly that I am right, it is time for me to step back and examine whatever it is I am trying to prove. When I am refusing to listen to anyone else, intractably defending some position or other (like doctors refusing Semilweisse's radical suggestion that they wash their hands before touching open wounds) then I am incapable of being a co-creator with God. God urges us to be willing to change, to go out into the wilderness, to wrestle with angels, to take off our shoes when we step on holy ground.

And to listen. God asks us to listen, even when what el asks of us seems most outrageous.

* * *

It has long struck me with joy and awe that the theory of evolution is not contrary to the teaching of the Bible. One of the many extraordinary things about those first passages in Genesis is that they so nearly describe what has come to be recognized as the order of evolution. What matter if, in the language of great poetry, a few billenia are the first day, and a few more the second?

The amazing thing is that at the beginning there was darkness, formless and empty, and the Spirit brooding, brooding almost as though getting ready to hatch creation, and then the Word shouting for joy, and here we are! The Word spoke, and from nothing came the glory and music and pattern of a universe.

And how long, in cosmic time, were the billenia which made up each of the days of creation?

Hugh and I lay on the top deck of our little ship at night and looked at the stars, the nearest one in that hemisphere perhaps seven light years away, and the next one seventy, and others seven hundred, seven thousand, seven million.

We were looking not at a one-dimensional sky, but a four-dimensional one, a multidimensional one, seeing out to the furthest reaches of space and time as we lay on one small spot on the top deck of a freighter; and that small spot in the space/time continuum was moving at approximately ten knots an hour. The planet, too, was moving, as it turned daily on its axis and yearly in its journey around the sun. And the sun was moving in the great turning of the galaxy, our Milky Way. In that magnificent immensity we realized, suddenly, how limited our view of time usually is.

We were looking at the brilliantly lit sky not only in our own present, but in the long past of most of the stars. Perhaps one of those sparkling diamonds was no longer there, we were seeing it so many million light years ago, perhaps it had gone out long before there was human life on this planet, and we were just now seeing its fire. How much time we were seeing, as well as space!

On a small ship the ability to be aware of our tiny, yet significant part in the interdependence of all of God's creation returns, and one's mind naturally turns to cosmic questions, rather than answers. Seeing the glory of the unpolluted horizon, the brilliance of the Southern Cross against the black velvet sky, opened up questions about creation and the Creator.

And laughter, too, for though we cannot take ourselves seriously enough, we can also take ourselves far too seriously.

One of the sailors remarked casually as he was swabbing down the deck, "It's a short walk from the womb to the tomb," and jolted us back from cosmic time to mortal time.

But mortal time is part of cosmic time, and during that short walk we are given glimpses of eternity, eternity which was before time began, and will be after time ends. The Word, who moved into time for us and lived with us, lives, as Christ, in eternity; so, when we live in Christ, when Christ lives in us we, too, are free from time and alive in eternity.

On the ship we moved from time zone to time zone, resetting our clocks, a reminder that our time follows the movement of the planet. And within one time zone there are probably a million different perceptions of time.

Every summer we watch eagerly for the hummingbirds to come sip the nectar of delphinium and bee balm outside our kitchen windows. They hover by the flowers, seeming to achieve a stillness in the air, their wings moving so rapidly that we cannot see the motion. I have been told that their perception of time is so much faster than ours that to the tiny birds we human beings, moving at fewer rpm (or mph) do not even appear to be moving. So, according to our human perception of time a century may seem long, but all that has happened since that first moment of creation is no more than the flicker of God's eye. In the lifespan of a star, an ordinary star like our sun, our lives are such a fragment of a fragment as to seem practically nonexistent, even if we live four score years and ten, like my mother, or even five score, like my grandfather. So, according to one perception of time, the zealous creationists are right – God created everything in an instant – or, rather, seven days; and according to another perception of time, the pragmatic evolutionists are right, and life has evolved slowly over our chronological millennia. And, according to *any* perception of time, we human creatures with our brief, mortal lives are nevertheless so important to the Creator that el came to live with us; we are so beloved!

Since we live in time, it is almost impossible for us to understand that eternity is not a time concept, that it has nothing to do with the passage of time. The astrophysicist's concept of time has changed radically in the past half century. Time is not, as the old hymn suggests, a never-ending stream. Time, like the rest of us creatures, is complex and paradoxical and full of quirks and surprises.

Sandol Stoddard in *The Hospice Movement*, quotes Dr. Cicely Saunders: "We learn, for example, that time has no fixed meaning as such. An hour at the dentist seems like forever, but an hour with someone you love flies past. And yet, wait a little and look back on it. The hour of discomfort and anxiety is totally forgotten. What we remember forever is the hour of love."

The hour of love is the hour when God's creature, time, and el's human creatures, like us, collaborate with each other.

In New York, where we must live most of the year, we are aware of time largely because we are too busy; we have too many appointments. Like the White Rabbit we constantly cry out in distress, "I shall be late!" But in the days before timepieces, when the rhythm of the seasons was essential to survival (as it was to the ancient nomadic Hebrews, to Abraham and Sarah) people were far more conscious of time than we are. Right timing was an integral part of prayer and of life. If the crops were not planted and harvested at the right time, there would not be enough to eat. Understanding the rhythms of nature was literally essential to survival, physically and psychically, and there was not the brokenness between the two that has come about in our time.

Scripture is constantly breaking through chronos into kairos. All those hundreds of years before the birth of Jesus, Job cried out of the intensity of his pain and grief an incredible affirmation:

I know that my Redeemer lives, and that he shall stand at the last day on earth, and though worms destroy this body, yet in flesh I shall see God, whom I shall see for myself, and whom my own eyes shall behold, though my reins be consumed within me.

For at that last day we shall truly understand the meaning of creation and the story of Genesis. We shall truly understand what it means to be co-creators with the Lord of creation. God's time is always *now*, and in this eternal *now* our Redeemer lives, and we shall see him, face to face.

2

Calling God Abba, Daddy

ONE DAY SHORTLY after we'd crossed the equator, heading north, we saw a pod of what the captain guessed was between one and two *thousand* dolphins sporting about our little ship. There before our eyes was the joy of creation. It was all Hugh could do to keep me from climbing the rail and diving overboard to join their joy. Our joy. Our leaping and diving and pirouetting. Our ocean. Our sky. Our joy in our Creator.

The anonymous author of *The Cloud of Unknowing* writes: "There are helps which the apprentice in contemplation should employ, namely, lesson, meditation, and orison or as they are most generally called, reading, thinking, and, praying."

Good advice, which I try to heed during my daily times with the Bible, so that sometimes after only a few verses my mind will move into "free fall" and sometimes the thoughts stray far from the words I have just read, and yet lead me into prayer. On a ship, time stretches beyond the boundaries of chronology, into real time, kairos, where it is possible to read more slowly, think more deeply, and pray more naturally, than during the usual over-scheduled days of chronos.

But something else, even beyond those excellent words of help for Scripture reading, made me go back to book 1, chapter 1, verse 1, of the Gideon Bible. That was the Lenten lections I was reading morning and evening, and which made me ask anew:

Who is this el, this Creator? Who was it to whom Jesus was always referring, and to whom he was always faithful? Who was it to whom Jesus prayed?

There are so many preconceptions encrusting our idea of the Father to whom Jesus turned in prayer, in joy, in anguish, that it is almost impossible to remove all the barnacles of tradition and prejudice which have accumulated over the years, and see and hear el freshly.

Each time I come to the story of Jesus' baptism it hits me with renewed force. After his baptism, during which the Holy Spirit descended upon him, that same Holy Spirit led Jesus into the wilderness to be tempted. That never ceases to shock me. It was not an evil spirit who led Jesus into the wilderness. It was not a fallen angel. It was the Holy Spirit.

And this story is as crucial to the New Testament as the Exodus is to the Old.

Jesus insisted that his cousin, John, baptize him. And though John proclaimed that he was merely the forerunner of one whose sandal strap he was unworthy to unloose, he did as Jesus asked. And as Jesus came up out of the water, he saw the heavens opening, and the Spirit, like a dove, descending upon him. And there came a voice from heaven saying,

"You are my beloved Son, in whom I am well pleased."

Whom do we pray to? If we are to pray, we must know where our prayers are directed. Jesus prayed to his Father. And here again we have, in this century, a source of confusion. It was my good fortune to have a father I could respect and honor as well as love. But there are many people who are not granted this blessing, who have fathers who are domineering, or weaklings, or incestuous, or alcoholics, or sadists, or anything but models of a true father. Jesus called the Master of the Universe *Abba*; daddy. Jesus' earthly father, Joseph, was a man he could admire, a man with enough sense of his own self to be able to accept Mary for his wife under the most unusual of circumstances. But what about the rest of us, living in this time of extreme sexual confusion? There was plenty of sexual confusion in Jesus' world, too, especially in the Roman culture where license and perversion were the order of the day. Nevertheless Jesus constantly referred to his heavenly Father, and he taught us to pray: Our Father.

Praying to the Father is easy for me, since my image of a father is of someone with total integrity. Not that my father was perfect – anything but. He had a volatile temper – which I have inherited. He had wildly fluctuating moods. Before he died (I was seventeen) he often made me angry and now I understand him better than I did then. But he never gave an answer to a question to which he had no answer. If he promised me anything, I knew that I could trust that promise, and it gave me a sense of the meaning of promises which helps me to this day.

Jesus calls the Creator *Father*, and for him it is a valid image. For those of us who are only confused or hurt by this image it is not as easy. Perhaps it helps to remember that it is an image, and an image is only a way of groping toward the real. Yet some of us may find in the image of the Father the parent that we always longed for, and needed, the parent that our human father never was. We have to look at, and take seriously, Jesus' image, whether or not it is one which is creative for us. What is it that we trust most? Is it the turning of the stars in the heavens? That, for me, is another image of the Creator. Julian of Norwich called Christ her sister. John of the Cross and John Donne used the powerful language of romantic love. Recently a young friend wrote to me about her reading the Bible in French. "I wanted to share with you one of my discoveries – it's one that Julian of Norwich would have liked. The other day I was reading the beginning of the Gospel of John. It goes,

Au commencement était la Parole, et la Parole était avec Dieu, et la Parole était Dieu. Elle était au commencement avec Dieu.

" '*She* was with God from the beginning.' Although I think too much fuss is made regarding sexist language, it was a real treat to see Jesus – la Parole – spoken of in feminine terms."

It is Jesus of Nazareth, the Word as human being, who calls God *Abba*. It is the Word, willingly and lovingly limiting itself in the form of what, as Word, Word had created – a sacrifice far beyond our comprehension. But if the Word, as Jesus, could call out, "Abba!" so can I.

We all have our own images, and they nourish us, but ultimately the Lord to whom we pray is beyond all images, all imagining.

The Holy Spirit came upon Jesus in the form of a dove – another image – and then that same Holy Spirit led Jesus into the wilderness to be tempted. Why? Why tempt us? Why tempt Jesus?

It was at the moment of his baptism that Jesus was recognized as Messiah, the Promised One. If, as Jesus, he was fully man as well as fully God, there had to come a time of recognition of his vocation. And a vocation must be tested. That is why, in a monastery or convent, there is a period of postulancy, of novitiate. Is this vocation real? Its reality must be tested.

So Jesus fasted. And he played. And at the end of his long period of fasting, when he was weak with hunger, the tempter attacked. "If you're really the Son of God," he urged, "turn these stones into bread."

And Jesus wouldn't. He could have, but he wouldn't. He simply quoted from Deuteronomy:

"Man shall not live by bread alone, but by every word of God."

Then the devil took him to Jerusalem and set him on the highest pinnacle of the temple and suggested that he jump off, just to prove that he really was the Son of God. And the devil, being very clever, and knowing Scripture better than most of us, quoted the Psalms:

"He shall give his angels charge over you, to keep you, and their hands they will bear you up, lest you dash your foot up against a stone."

And Jesus knew that if he jumped the angels would hold him up and he would not be hurt. And since he knew Scripture even better than Satan he quoted Deuteronomy right back:

"It is written: you shall not tempt the Lord your God."

But Satan, still hopeful, took him to a high mountain, and because Satan was an angel, even if a fallen one, he still had great power and used it to show Jesus all the kingdoms of the earth in a moment of time. And he said, "I can give you all this." And he could. And Jesus knew that he could, for Satan is the prince of this world, and in the world he has proven far too often how powerful he is. He said to Jesus, "I can give you all this, and all the world's glory, without any suffering on your part, for it is mine to give."

And it was. And it is.

But Jesus said,

"Get away from me, Satan."

and again he quoted:

"You shall worship the Lord your God, and him only shall you serve."

And the devil left him, and angels came and ministered to him.

One by one Jesus turned down the world's great temptations. Satan still uses those three; he doesn't need any others, we still fall for the same ones, over and over again.

When we pray,

"Lead us not into temptation."

we are asking the Holy Spirit not to test us as Jesus was tested, for we have seen that we are not immune to all that Satan offers us, as individuals, as churches, as the establishments of science and medicine and education and any other human establishment we can think of. We fall into one or another of the temptations, often deluded into thinking that what we are doing is for the best. We want short cuts to the Kingdom. We want it to be easy. We want to be pleased with ourselves – which is very different from loving ourselves. And so we heed the temptations. But Jesus didn't, because his whole being was rooted in his Father, the God who created heaven and earth and saw that it was all good.

It is impossible to understand the New Testament without a firm grounding in the Old. Jesus quoted again and again from Hebrew Scripture (and not just when he was getting rid of the devil). The writers of the Gospels assumed that those who heard them would be familiar with Hebrew Scripture. The quotations are not credited or cross referenced because as a part of daily prayer they were a familiar part of living. The God of the Old Testament is the God in and with and through whom Jesus lived, the God he refused to tempt, the God he served, even unto death.

I tend to stray from that God. All my false preconceptions get in my way, and these preconceptions surely please Satan, for they turn me from the Creator to the tempter who is much more "reasonable" and who, in *worldy terms*, has more power. Power is what Satan offers us, whereas God keeps pointing out that we serve el best in our weakness, so that we can acknowledge that it is the Creator choosing to work through us, his fragile creatures. It is God who has made us, and not we ourselves. But because we enjoy feeling powerful, we accept Satan's offers.

And look what happens. Just turn around. Watch the news on TV. Read the daily papers. Walk along a city street.

And so as I turned to Genesis, chapter 1, verse 1, I tried to read without all the preconceptions which have been built up over the centuries – a task I understood was not completely possible, but which could nevertheless be attempted. And at sea it was made easy, for the ocean and the sky were there to help and to encourage. And to pray for me.

I stood at the rail looking down at the ocean and saw the foil-like flickering of flying fish, and it struck me that knowledge is always open to change; knowledge, not wisdom. If it is not open to change it is not knowledge, it is prejudice.

* * *

One day in very early spring I spent several hours autographing and answering questions at a delightful bookshop in a college town. In the late afternoon a young man who had been standing around, listening, came up to me and said, "I've really enjoyed what you've been saying to people, but I haven't read any of your books because I hear they're very religious."

At that, all my little red flags of warning unfurled and began flapping in the wind. "What do you mean by religion?" I asked. "Please define it. Hitler was very religious. Khoumeini is very religious. The communists are very religious. What do you mean by religion?" And then with astonishment I heard myself saying, "My religion is subject to change without notice."

And I felt that I had received a profound revelation.

As God has revealed elself throughout history, our concept of the Creator has changed and deepened. If we close ourselves off to revelation we are, in a real way, silencing God. If God is *I will be what I will be*, (which is what el replied when Moses asked "who are you?") then our understanding of el's ways has to be open, too. A few years ago a popular lapel button read, *Please be patient with me, God isn't finished with me yet.* Did we really understand what that button was saying? If I discover that my concept of God is becoming limited, then I am beginning to shut myself off from revelation. And if I assume that my concept of God is final, I have fallen for Satan's temptations, because if I decide that my concept of God is final, then I am falling into hubris.

Faith and religion are not the same thing. Although my faith may falter, it has to do with the constancy of God's love. Religion, which is the expression of faith, may find different expressions appropriate in different times and places and to different people, and the variety of these expressions can enlarge our perceptions and deepen our faith.

John Wesley Watts, who lived in West Virginia in the nineteenth century, wrote his own epitaph as he lay dying, and subsequently it was engraved on his tomb; *John Wesley Watts: A Firm Believer in Jesus Christ, Jeffersonian Democracy, and the Methodist Episcopal Church.*

I respect his conviction, but it is conviction, not faith. I come closer to defining and describing faith when I remember the great preacher Phillips Brooks, who was asked by an earnest questioner why he was a Christian. He thought seriously for a moment, then replied, "I think I am a Christian because of my aunt, who lives in Teaneck, New Jersey."

Or, as my friend Canon Tallis puts it, "A Christian is someone who knows one."

If I have faith, it is because I have met faith, I have seen it in action. And this faith is never a vague, pie-in-the-sky kind of thing. Heaven is not good because life is bad; the quality of our lives while we live them is preparation for heaven.

3

Protecting God

IN THE BEGINNING God looked at creation and called it good. Very good.

There was nothing, and then came the mighty acts of creation, darkness and light, sea and land, fish and birds and, beasts and finally man – man made in the image of God, male and female.

And of course as soon as this glorious creature appeared on the scene, along came confusion and conflict. And story.

No matter what else can be said about human beings, we do provide good stories. One of my favorite Hassidic tales ends, "God made man because he loves stories." And story is where we have learned to look for truth.

Time is God's. We are God's. Creation is God's. Yet even as we attempt to regulate our dogmas in the church we adopt a proprietary attitude. In fact, we tend to try to protect God. For example, we explain exactly how el created everything, as though we knew better than el how the Creator chose to create. When we try to protect God, all we do is stop our understanding of God from growing and deepening, because if we are open to new discoveries in the world within or without, it might change our comfortable image of God. In a fairly recent issue of *Christianity Today*, a magazine for which I have deep respect, the entire issue was taken up with issues of creationism, with theologians and scientists trying to explain, without doubt, exactly how God started it all. Though the magazine tried to be fair, to publish more than one point of view, the whole thing left me exhausted and frustrated. Some of the articles were so defensive about exactly how it all happened, that I found them difficult to read. I am not comfortable in a closed system where there are no questions left to ask, or where questions are shunned as heresy.

In *The Meaning of Persons* Dr. Paul Tournier points out that scientists are a great deal more humble now than they were half a century ago. It is a pity that more theologians do not also have this humility before God's mighty acts of creation.

Why do people who are Christian feel so zealously that they have to protect God from truth? How can a scientific discovery, no matter how radical, be upsetting to a Creator who made all things, who is all Truth? God never promised us that truth would be easy, but he never warned us to shun it; he urged us to seek it, in order to be free. Often when we wrestle with truth we are reflecting Jacob's night of wrestling the angel.

Simone Weil writes, "For it seemed to me certain, and I think so today, that one can never wrestle enough with God if one does so out of pure regard for truth. Christ likes us to prefer truth to him because, before being Christ, he is truth. If one turns aside from him to go towards the truth, one will not go far before falling into his arms."

But we keep on trying to protect God, in order to keep him in our own little corner. When our eldest child was baptized in the Episcopal Church, my beloved Mrs. O' defied her Roman Catholic Church in order to go to the baptism.

Now things have changed so that when I am at Mundelein College I stay in the convent with the sisters and go to Mass with them in the morning, and that is great joy.

Only a decade or so ago in the Episcopal Church my Southern Baptist husband was – at least in a good many churches – not welcome. And I would not, could not, go to a Lord's Table which excluded Hugh. Why did we ever fear that God could not protect his own table? He is the Host – why did we feel that we had to check over the guest list for him?

That, too, has changed. Our religion is not closed from revelation; we are beginning to trust creation to the Creator, and to understand that our own awareness of the *hows* of creation truly must be subject to change without notice. But we cannot have this openness unless our faith in God as Lord of all is bedrock under our feet.

How we need this rock!

Paul, in his first letter to the Christians in Corinth, emphasizes the firmness of the rock, and the eternal *is*-ness of Christ, when he writes:

All our ancestors were under the cloud ... and all passed through the sea; and were all baptized into Moses in the cloud and in the sea; and did all eat the same spiritual meat; and did all drink the same spiritual drink; for they drank of that spiritual Rock that followed them: and that Rock was Christ.

Christ with us always, before the journey, during it, after the end. That is the rock under our feet, the rock which springs forth with healing, thirst-quenching water. The Trinity has always been a unity; the Father, who will be what el will be, the Holy Spirit, before creation, brooding over the universe. And then the Word shouting for joy.

And it was good. We have done much to distort and wound that good – that distortion and pain are results of the gift of free will. But that does not make the original good any less glorious.

And I turn to story, for enlightenment. Some of the stories Jesus tells about our places at the table say a good deal to me here.

Story is paramount throughout Scripture, beginning with the beginning. In the Book of Genesis alone is all the material for a flaming best seller – sex, incest, virtue, violence, greed, conflict, lust, love, murder – it's all there.

The first human characters in this amazing drama are Adam and Eve, who were expelled from Eden. In order to understand this story, we have to recognize that it is told from the point of view of the fall of this planet, whereas this planet was falling for something which had already taken place in more cosmic terms.

There was war in Heaven.

That fact was part of the revelation to St. John the Divine.

Michael and his angels fought against the dragon, and the dragon fought, and his angels, and prevailed not; neither was their place found any more in heaven. And the great dragon was cast out, that old serpent, called the devil, and Satan, who deceives the whole world; he was cast out into the earth, and his angels were cast out with him.

And Satan and his angels are still here. When the Lord, in the beginning of the Book of Job, asks Satan what he has been doing, he answers that he has been walking up and down, to and fro over the earth. (Looking to see what he could do? He finds plenty to do, then and now. Alas.)

The war in heaven is still going on, and we are a part of it. It is easy to see wickedness here on this planet, in every newscast, newspaper, magazine; a little less easy, perhaps to perceive that it is not limited to our earth, or our solar system, or our galaxy.

As we think about this vast, cosmic battle, it is far too easy to fall into dualism, to think of darkness and light battling each other from the beginning, as some of the eastern religions proclaim. But if God created everything and saw that it was good, then something must have happened to this good, to change and distort it. The problem is not from without; it rose from within. And we have within each of us some of this wrongness, and too often we refuse to see it, and don't understand why we are not happy, nor why our faith seems a dim thing, nor why our prayers are like dead ashes.

But what is faith? We all know people who are convinced of the rightness of their faith, and yet seem to be narrowminded and sometimes downright vicious. People who are convinced of the rightness of their religion are quite literally burning the books they have decided are not Christian, urged on by their ministers. Anything that mentions ghosts, witches, spirits, has to go, and if that is taken literally, the Bible will have to be added to the pyre: because of Saul and the witch of Endor and Samuel's ghost. It reminds me a little of the hysteria during Joseph McCarthy's wild attempt to point his trembling finger at communists in this country. Not that there aren't communists in this country, working for our overthrow; there are. But when we get hysterical about it, we tend to start looking under the wrong beds; we ignore the dangerous people and begin to persecute the innocent. We seem to have learned nothing from Salem.

Recently I was sent a clipping from a midwestern newspaper listing ten books which were to be removed from the shelves because of their pornographic content. One of them was my own novel, *A Wind in the Door*. This has me both frankly fascinated and totally baffled. I have thought seriously about this, looking at the book to see if there is anything which could possibly be interpreted as pornographic, and haven't found anything. Another of the books cited was C. S. Lewis's *Narnia Chronicles*. This is the first time Lewis and I have been listed together as writers of pornography. Of course, if teenagers get hold of this list, the sales of our books will soar!

And that itself says something sad, not about the children but about the world presented to them by the adults. We tend to find what we look for. If we have prurient minds, no matter how pure we delude ourselves into thinking we are, we will find pornography everywhere. If we are looking for dirt, we will find it, or worse, we will soil things which are not in themselves dirty. If we are looking for meaning, for order in complexity, for the love which heals, then we are less apt to find filth, seeing instead something which God has created, and is therefore valuable.

Some books, movies, paintings, are, in fact, destructively pornographic, and pornography is on the increase, in a world which we can no longer look on with loving eyes, seeing the goodness of it all. But C. S. Lewis pornographic? Should I laugh or cry?

Far worse than this absurdity is the sorry fact that across the planet people who are convinced of the rightness of their religion are killing people whose religion differs from theirs. There seems to be a terrible confusion between faith and prejudice.

A young friend told me of an East Indian Christian who had suggested to her that we are not called to be Christians; we are called to be Christs. I find this both challenging and freeing when I am confused by all the things which Christians are doing all over the planet, in the name of Christ, which seem incompatible with all that Jesus taught.

I distrust the word *Christian* as an adjective; it has become less an adjective than a label, separating those who call themselves Christian from the rest of the world. How can those who would follow Christ assume that they are more beloved of the Creator than any other part of his creation, when God created *everything*, and saw that it was good? And if God created man in his own image, male and female, then all, *all* of humankind is part of that image, known or unknown, served or betrayed, accepted or denied. God loves every man, sings the psalmist. Perhaps it is more blessed to be aware of our part in the Image than not, but Jesus made it clear that sometimes it is those who are least aware of it who serve the image best. It is truer to that image to be like the publican, aware of his unworthiness, than like the pharisee who was puffed up with the pride of his own virtue; it is truer to the image to say, "Lord, I believe, help thou my unbelief," than to dismiss the crucifixion by saying, "It is good for one man to die for the sake of the nation."

Faith consists in the acceptance of doubts, the working through them, rather than the repression of them.

Faith is beyond literal definition. If we could define it, or give a recipe for it, we could make a Fanny Farmer Cookbook of Faith and all we' d have to do is check the index for the kind of faith we needed at the moment. But faith, like prayer, is a gift, a gift of knowing that the light shines in the darkness, of knowing that the light cannot be put out, no matter how diligently the tempter tries to snuff it. The gift, when it comes, frequently alters our perception of reality, and the manner in which we pray. Prayer, like faith, is a much misunderstood, much abused word. Sometimes we pray most honestly when we pray in ways which are considered childish, when we give ourselves to God just as we are, with all our imperfections, prejudices and faults. Is it really prayer when someone who cannot force us to change our honest point of view says, piously, "I'll pray for you"?

* * *

Throughout recorded history there have been totally different perceptions of reality. To the ancient Hebrews, a hierarchy of gods did not, for a long time, seem inconsistent with their *God is one and God is all.* The earth was the center of the universe, and the sun by day and the moon by night were put there entirely for our benefit. Community was not only understood, it was essential for survival, and when the ancient Hebrew said "I" it was seldom clear whether he meant himself as an individual or the community. There are examples of this equating of the person with the community in many of the psalms.

Communication with God was simple and direct and often startling. It would not have seemed as astounding then as it would be today to have the angel Gabriel appear to a young girl, hand her a lily, and tell her that she was going to become pregnant by the Holy Spirit.

But even by the time of this amazing event, the world view was far more complicated than it had been only a few centuries earlier; but we human beings, on planet earth, were still, and would continue to be for a good many more centuries, the prime focus of God's concern.

The mediaeval world, having gone through the harsh purification of the Dark Ages, had its own clearly-diagrammed perception of reality. Heaven was up, earth was here; hell was down. God' s mysteries were taken for granted, and the relation between God and the creature was forthright. People were not afraid to ask God, *Why*?

In the Renaissance world the question became less *why* than *how*? This persistent asking of *how* can be seen in the notebooks of Leonardo da Vinci, although Leonardo, being a genius, often asked *why* and *how* at the same time.

As astronomy became a more and more sophisticated science, it was finally conceded that the earth was not, after all, the center of all that God had created, but a very small part of a greater whole – a difficult transition for many people. It is not easy for any of us to step out of the limelight.

With the coming of the industrial revolution and a focus on experiments which could be confirmed by laboratory testing, perceptions again shifted radically. When I was a school girl, probably the majority of scientists were atheists because God was no longer needed. Humanism rode high. It was assumed that what science had not yet discovered, it would shortly accomplish. We were, we thought, on the verge of knowing everything. The eating of the fruit of the tree of the knowledge of good and evil was about to pay off. The scientists in their labs, serene in the white coats of their priesthood, were the new gods.

I would like to think that it was my realization of this falseness that made me dislike math and science while I was in school, though if I had any such awareness it was purely intuitive and unknown to me. I loved geometry, because it dealt with questions, even when one was able to write Q.E.D. at the bottom of the paper. The rest of it I disliked because I was no good at it. During chemistry classes I tried to amuse myself by pretending that I was Madame Curie, and all I accomplished was blowing up the lab, which was in an old greenhouse. So when I am asked by interviewers about my "great scientific background," I have to reply that I have none. The magnificent theological mystery of science did not burst upon me until well after I was married and had three children.

Science changed, irrevocably, with the splitting of the atom, and our perception of reality has not yet caught up with this change. We discovered that for every question we have answered, a hundred new questions have been uncovered. For all our knowledge, all our technical advances, we have learned to our chagrin (and sometimes delight) that we know practically nothing.

We are still in the process of tiptoeing over the sill of this new perception of the universe which is, strangely, far more like the universe in which Abraham and Sarah found themselves when they left home and went into a strange land, than it is like the exalted individualism of Renaissance man, or the technocratic smugness of the late nineteenth and early twentieth centuries.

Our contemporary mystics are the astrophysicists, the cellular biologists, the physicists who study quantum mechanics, for they are dealing with the nature of being itself. Like Abraham and Sarah they are continually discovering the extraordinary mystery of being, and the charting of the worlds within us as well as the worlds beyond us. And we, too, are being asked to leave our comfortable home and go out into the wilderness, like Abraham and Sarah, into the mysterious world of unknown spaces, where there may be famine, drought, hostile inhabitants.

Only one thing was certain in Abraham's and Sarah's uncertain world, only one thing stands sure in ours, and that is that the universe is God's. Out of nothing el created us, and called us into being that we might go out into the unknown and become co-creators with our Creator, in this new and uncharted land where our concepts of space and time are radically different from what they were half a century ago.

So, as always in the face of the unknown, I turn and return to story. The first of the great stories in the Bible is that of Adam and Eve. The point is not which came first, the chicken or the egg, but that it is not good for the human being to be alone. Each of us needs others. Any single one of us, alone, cannot be the image of God; discovering that image within us is not a do-it-yourself activity. Before I can be an icon of the image of God, I must be with someone else, hand in hand.

As there are two creation stories in Genesis, so there are two stories of the making of Adam and Eve, and both make the same point. Despite the proliferation of do-it-yourself books, we can't do it ourselves. We need each other. As to who came first, Jesus makes it very clear that this is a matter of unimportance. He emphasizes this by stating that the first shall be last, and the last shall be first. Adam is not better than Eve because he arrived on the scene first; nor is Eve less than Adam because she came second. (Often the butler and the maid begin the play.) It was the storyteller's realization that it is not good for the human creature to be alone that is important. God has called us to be co-creators, a corporate activity. Dean Inge of St. Paul's says, "God promised to make you free. He never promised to make you independent."

We are most free when we are most willing to acknowledge our interdependence. Adam and Eve were free until they saw each other as separate and autonomous, and afraid of their Creator.

* * *

We never pray alone. Ever. Even if there is no other human being around us who is willing or able to pray with us, we are in the company of angels and archangels. We are surrounded by a glorious cloud of witnesses. And, even when we feel most isolated, there are other human creatures, somewhere, who are praying with us. It used to be required in my church that we read morning and evening prayer, and although it is no longer required, not even for those who are ordained, I am grateful that many of us still find comfort in this daily structure, so that when I am praying in this manner I know that many thousands of people are praying with me. A quiet listening to the words of the Psalms, to the readings from both Old and New Testaments, to the great prayers of the collects and canticles, is often a prelude to the prayers which go beyond words, go deeper than words, leading us from reading to thinking to prayer. And the practice of morning and evening prayer provides a structure to the day which keeps everything in proportion and perspective.

In the spring of the year I am among those who give the oral examinations to candidates for ordination who have already gone through most of the process. They have finished seminary, taken their General Ordination examinations, and are nearly ready for ordination in the Episcopal Church. Our job, in my diocese, is to examine these young men and women in whatever subject they have shown the greatest weakness.

This spring I was examining with two priests who are friends of mine, and with whom I am easy and comfortable and can speak spontaneously. Among those who came to us for examination was a personable young man who had done well throughout seminary and on his exams, but who showed a slight weakness in pastoral concerns. I asked him something I usually ask: "What are your own personal disciplines of prayer?" He replied that whenever it was possible he liked to read morning prayer, but that often he was so busy that there was no time. "All it takes is ten minutes!" I exclaimed. "Why don't you read it on the john?" To my amazement, I had shocked him. He asked, "But isn't that sacrilegious?"

Almost equally shocked by this response, I said, "That is a very unincarnational question."

One of my priest friends reminded him that Luther had done some deep theological thinking on what, in his day, was called the jakes, and all three of us tried to get over to him that life cannot be separated into secular and sacred that if God created everything, and called it good, then all of life is good, and only we can see it as sacrilegious. There is nothing which is, of itself, sacrilegious. Just as the act of making love can be sacramental, so can all aspects of our lives, even the most lowly. If we cannot pray in the bathroom, it is not likely that we will be able to pray anywhere.

My suggestion came not out of thin air but out of my own experience. Sometimes when I am on a lecture tour I am so tightly scheduled that there is certainly no programmed time for my reading of morning and evening prayer. But I need the affirmation and the structure they give me, and often the only time and place is in the bathroom. How can it be sacrilegious? God is the Lord of all of my life, and there is no place where it is not proper to turn to my Maker.

Paul said it so cogently in his first letter to Corinth:

Those parts of the body which seem to us to be less deserving of notice we have to allow the highest honor of function. The parts which do not look beautiful have a deeper beauty in the work they do, while the parts which look beautiful may not be at all essential to life!

In the Garden of Eden there was no separation of sacred and secular; separation is one of the triumphs of the devil. All of creation is God's, and therefore it is all sacred. And when everything is sacred, then we can understand something about freedom.

Part of the meaning of the incarnation is that Jesus enChristed everything, giving it again the sacredness it had when the Word first spoke all of creation into being.

God created Adam in a sacred world in which it was truly possible to be free. God made Adam, and saw that it was not good for this creature to be alone, and so God gave Adam a helpmeet. It is a marvelous story, and it tells us a great deal about the nature of ourselves and our relationship to God.

Story, unlike theories of science which are always open to change, is timeless. The story of Adam and Eve may have different things to say to different generations in different places, but it always has something to say. Therefore it touches on the nature of reality.

Once again we come to the old question: what is real? I look at my hand, at the bones and veins and skin, at the fingers which can touch the keys of the typewriter and so put words on paper, or touch the keys of a piano, and bring the sounds of a fugue or a sonata into the room. I rub them together and I can feel them generating a healing electricity.

I take a whisk in one hand, hold the pot with the other, and stir eggs and butter and lemon juice to make hollandaise sauce. My hands are very real to me. And yet I know that they are also a whirling dance of electrons, and that there are vast spaces between the parts of the electrons. There is energy in my hands, and energy and matter are interchangeable. The movement of my hands is not contained within the skin and bone, muscle and nerve, but is triggered by that part of my brain which is focused on the movement of my hands, my fingers. There is far more that I do not know about my hands than that I know. But they are real. I don't understand their reality, but neither do I doubt it.

If Pontius Pilate did not know what truth was, neither did he know reality, and most of us aren't much further along the way than he. God creates from nothing, *ex nihilo*, but we, el's creatures, can create only from what el has already created and given us. Therefore our reality must be part of God's reality if it is to have any validity. Could Shakespeare have created Hamlet if such a character were not possible? Isn't the perennial fascination with Hamlet partly because we all see something of ourselves in this questioning creature, and partly because Hamlet, like the rest of us, is so complex that he can never be understood? But is Hamlet unreal?

I had a delightful letter from a woman who expressed her hope that after death she would meet some of her favorite fictional characters. I agree with her that this would be a delightful aspect of heaven. There are so many I would like to meet – Emily of New Moon, Ivan Karamazo, Mole and Rat, Viola and Duke Orsino, Mary Lennox, and even, I hope, some of the characters who have come to me in my own books.

So story is real. And music is real, and what is real is an icon of our Creator, even if some of us who have been wounded balk at the use of the word, *Father*. A Bach fugue is for me an icon of this reality, and so with my often inadequate fingers I struggle at the piano, in order to get myself back into reality.

And when I go to a museum I am not going just to look at an exhibition of painting or sculpture in order to be *au courant* with the latest cultural fashion; I am going in order to look for that reality which will help me to live, my own life more fully, more courageously, more freely.

So there is no doubt in my mind that Adam and Eve are real.

And one of the first things their story points out is the importance of Naming.

(Here we go again: Madeleine and Naming. She's like a dog with a bone. True. But anyone who has had a name taken away, as happened to me in boarding school when, at age twelve, I was numbered, 97, not Madeleine, is likely to be overconcerned on the subject of names. Can we be overconcerned? Granted, naming seems to crop up in everything I write, but that is because it cannot, in this day of uninvolved anonymity, be overemphasized.)

All the animals, all the fish and fowl and land beasts had to be named in order to be. And we cannot name ourselves alone. Before we can love each other, before we can dialogue, each one of us has to be named by the other and we have to name in return.

While Adam and Eve were naming the animals, the story is that Adam asked, "Hey, Eve, why are you calling that creature a hippopotamus?"

And Eve replied, "Because it *looks* like a hippopotamus."

Are we going to be able to remain God's creatures who are known by name? On our little ship we could not become friends with any of our fellow passengers until we had exchanged names. "Hello, we are Hugh and Madeleine." Until we were Hugh and Madeleine we were not quite real. Can you imagine saying to someone, "Hello, I'm 061-12-5619"? That's Hugh's social security number, which he has memorized, so when anyone asks, "what's your social security number?" he is able to rattle it off. But it's not his name. I call him Hugh.

I do not know my social security number. I have no intention of ever knowing my social security number. I can look it up if absolutely necessary. But if we don't take care, if we don't watch out, society may limit us to numbers. I wonder if I could pray if I lost my name? I am not at all sure that I could.

If we are numbered, not named, we are less than human. One of the most terrible things done to slaves throughout the centuries, from Babylon to Rome to the United States, was to take away their names. Isn't one of the worst things we can do to any prisoner to take away his name or her name and call them by numbers? If you take away someone's name, you can treat that person as a thing with a clear conscience. You can horsewhip a thing far more easily than a person with a name, a name known to you. No wonder the people who were put in Nazi concentration camps had numbers branded on their arms.

When Adam named the animals he made them real. My dog is named Timothy and my cat is named Titus. Farmers do not let their children name the animals who are going to be slaughtered or put in the pot. It is not easy to eat a ham you have known as Wilbur or a chicken called Flossy.

When we respond to our names, or call someone else by name, it is already the beginning of a community expressing the image of God. To call someone by name is an act of prayer. We may abuse our names, and our prayer, but without names we are not human. And Adam and Eve, no matter what else they were, were human.

At first there was nothing but joy, joy in being created, and in worshiping the God who had created them. And wonder: wonder at sunrises and starfish and dolphin and even dandelions. My husband, who mows the lawn at Crosswicks, hates dandelions, but they are indeed wondrous things, and not to be taken for granted. In early June the big hay field north of our house is white with dandelion clocks, and the prevailing northwesterly winds blow those incredibly productive dandelions clocks right onto our lawn. My husband takes this insult so personally that I am not allowed to put delicious young dandelion greens into the salad. But he does not take dandelions for granted.

Abraham Joshua Heschel says: "The surest way to suppress our ability to understand the meaning of God and the importance of worship is *to take things for granted*. Indifference to the sublime wonder of being is the root of sin." Were Adam and Eve beginning to take the image of God in themselves and the loveliness of Eden for granted? Is that why they fell for Satan's temptations?

When we take things for granted, then what we have is not enough, and we are rendered vulnerable to the wiles of the tempter. We tend to take our own democratic freedom for granted, and every time I leave this country, especially if I am going to Asia or to South America, I am jolted to a fresh awareness of just how fortunate we are, despite all of the things which are wrong and getting worse. And I wonder anew at our funny, fumbling system, which nevertheless gives us freedoms unknown to people in countries with restrictions we find it hard to conceive of.

If Adam and Eve had remained satisfied, joyous and grateful for all the wonders of creation, for the creatures they had named, for the beauty of Eden, they would not have listened to the tempter, who came to them with the same temptations he offered Jesus: if you do what I say, you can be as God. You *can be God*.

When we lose our sense of wonder we become dissatisfied with who we are (just as the tempter became dissatisfied with who he was, the most luminous of all the angels); like the tempter, we are no longer content to be created. To love God and enjoy him forever begins to be dull. We are ripe for temptation.

* * *

It is my great good fortune to have for a close friend a woman who is as tall as I am, who was as gawky an adolescent as I was, who sees herself, as she says, as a mouse, but who is the chief health officer of a great city. We have known each other since we were in our late teens, and we have done a lot of growing up together, falling over many of the same stumbling blocks, and picking ourselves up out of the mud, wiping off the blood, and stumbling on. In the late summer she visits us at Crosswicks, and we go into a massive applesauce factory production. A couple of summers ago we were in the midst of the sauce pot and the Foley food mill when our corner of Connecticut was hit by the fringe of a hurricane. The rain and wind were lashing the house when the power went out and we ran out of apples. Without even consulting each other we ran upstairs, put on our bathing suits, and dashed out into the storm to pick more apples, exhilarated by the deluge of rain against our skin and the apples falling from the trees as the wind whipped the branches. Later on I thought how marvelous it is to have a friend, also in her sixties, with whom I can be so foolish and so gloriously happy, full of wonder at the marvel of being. And this sense of wonder is also prayer.

It is this awareness of the marvelousness of creation which helps to keep dissatisfaction away, rejoicing in and being wholly satisfied with being God's co-creators is a prayer of protection.

To be dissatisfied with who we are is not the same thing as that divine discontent which Plato talks about. Divine discontent is to accept to our sorrow that we are not what we have been created to be. We have fallen far short of our small part in the image of God; we are *less* than we are. Once we are aware of this we can open ourselves to our Creator, saying, Help me to be what you want me to be.

Whereas being dissatisfied with who we are involves being dissatisfied with being created. We have been given a marvelous role in the great drama, and suddenly it is not enough. But we become discontented with our roles and want our name up on the marquee in brighter and larger lights than anybody else's.

Adam and Eve lost their joy, their radical amazement at the wonders of being, simply being, being Adam and Eve, being Namers. They no longer looked at the world around them and said,

This is the Lord's doing; it is marvelous in our eyes.

And in came the tempter.

"It' s all right," he said. "You can do anything you want to, you know."

When you've stopped being delighted with who you are, it' s very nice to be told you're special. Even if there's nobody else around to be more special *than*, it's still a pleasurable feeling.

After that we are ripe for the real temptation. "Do as I tell you: eat the apple, jump from the highest pinnacle of the temple, worship me, and you shall be as God."

Hubris. Usurping the prerogatives of God.

"Go on then," the tempter urged. "You won't die if you eat the fruit of the forbidden tree. The only reason el doesn't want you to eat it is that el knows that if you do, you'll be able to tell right from wrong, and then you'll be as God."

So they ate of the fruit of the tree of the knowledge of good and evil, and the timing was all off; they weren't ready, and so the result was confusion.

Ever since that first disastrous mistiming, we have grown in knowledge without being aware that we have not grown equally in spirit. Children are pushed, and themselves push, to grow up earlier and earlier. We have forgotten that time is a creature like us, and that our relation with time is of the utmost importance. Adam and Eve knew too much before they had grown enough to be ready for knowledge. It was something like offering a double martini to a two-year-old, urging a five-year-old to read Freud, giving unleashed electricity to a ten-year-old. Adam and Eve were incapable of assimilating all that they suddenly knew. They saw that they were naked, and in their beautiful, created bodies they were embarrassed, not because they were cold, but because without preparation they suddenly knew more than they could possibly understand. And of course Satan sees pornography everywhere.

He must have known that when they ate the forbidden fruit they weren't going to be like God at all. They weren't even going to be like the human beings they were.

4

The Light in the Darkness

HOW WAS IT THAT the Prince of Light became the Prince of Darkness?

We are all meant to be light-bearers, but for Lucifer it was not enough to bear the light. Long before the Garden, Lucifer wanted to *be* the Light, and, in that passionate desire he lost the light by falling into the darkness of hubris. Now there is a touch of it in all of us, for we bear, as a wound, the sins of our ancestors.

We are not willing to bear the light. We want to be the Light. We want to be God. But what kind of God? Like Lucifer? Full of earthly power and grandeur, able to wave wands and work magic, reaching out greedily for the things of this world?

This is the god that Jesus rejected when the Holy Spirit led him into the wilderness to be tempted. And so he went not to a royal, temporal throne, but to the cross.

Adam and Eve did not live long enough to understand that the cross is the gateway to heaven. Most of us don't understand that, either, and so, like Adam and Eve, we bicker, we quarrel, we alibi, we jostle for power and glory.

A news letter was distributed on our freighter every morning, and every morning it was bad news, hijackers, assassinations, wars accumulating all over the planet in the name of religion: Islam, Judaism, Christianity, Communism ...

There is little difference between communism and some of the extreme sects which demand the total subservience of their followers. Questions are forbidden. Life is easier when no questions are asked, when all behavioral patterns are dictated. Within the structure that restricts rather than the structure that frees we lose our ability to make choices. But if we make no choices, we lose our creativity, we lose touch with real life, we lose more of the image of God, we abdicate our own human nature.

Granted, the ability to make choices does not automatically mean that we will make the right choices, otherwise what kind of real choice would it be? Since that first wrong choice made by Adam and Eve, when the timing of the human psyche got out of sync, we have continued to make disastrously wrong choices. For all our technocratic advances we have not been able to control terrorism, which grows worse daily. We have not stopped war. We see all around us the results of corruption and greed.

Sometimes we see in small ways, almost more clearly than in the great, the sick results of the accumulation of wrong choices. When I am in New York I start the day by filling my thermos with coffee, taking my old Irish setter, Timothy, and heading for the Cathedral library. As I walk I say my memorized alphabet of prayers, which helps clear my mind of trivialities. In the morning as I come to the words " ... because in the mystery of the Word made flesh ... " I look at whomever is nearest me so that I may see in that person, for that moment, Christ. The upper west side of Broadway is a heterogeneous neighborhood, and I may see a wino, a child going to school, the young, the old, the indigent.

That morning I saw an old black man carrying a large, plastic bag. When he saw me and my dog, this "Christ" took the plastic bag and began hitting at the dog and me with it. I said, as I might have said to one of my children, "Please, don't do that," and then, in a loud voice, without thinking, just saying it, "Christ help you." At that point his bag broke and bottles flew all over the sidewalk, shattering, and he careened away from the frightened dog and me. I walked on, soothing the quivering setter, my legs stinging from the assault, and a doorman, who was out hosing his sidewalk and who had been about to intervene, asked, "Is he mad?"

"Out of his mind," I replied, and walked on, too shaken even to talk. But, no matter how crazed he was, that man had to be Christ for me. If I cannot see Christ in the maimed, in those possessed by devils, I cannot see Christ in the whole and holy. But that was, in its own way, a small act of terrorism. And the greater acts of terrorism increase, too, as all the little gods in South America or South Africa or behind the iron curtain or in our own country play the game of god more and more frantically.

We can't undo what Adam and Eve did. We have more knowledge than the human mind can cope with, and we can't make it go away – and we don't want it to go away. It is not the knowledge which is the problem, but our misuse of it.

How ironic it is that we're still far from having the knowledge of good and evil, and it is more difficult to distinguish between them today than it was in Eden. Daily the nations' leaders, and we ourselves in smaller ways, are faced with decisions, with choices where there is no clear-cut answer. Should a baby conceived in rape be carried to term or aborted? To the fourteen-year-old girl who has been brutally raped, is the psychological damage greater if she has to carry the child of this horror for nine months, or if it is taken from her body as soon as possible? Abortion is murder, but there are times when the death of the fetus would seem to bring less evil than if it were not sent back to God as quickly as possible.

Children are always hurt by divorce. Yet sometimes they are more hurt if parents with an unendurable marriage stay together. There are no easy answers. Often we are put in positions where all of our choices are wrong, there is no *right* thing to do. At that point we must pray that we choose that which is least evil, and then ask for forgiveness for that inevitable evil which we have done.

Satan cannot make us like God. He promised it in Eden, he promises it now, but he cannot fulfill that promise. He can only make us like himself, carrying hell with him, being, in himself, hell.

We are not meant to be like Satan; we are meant to be like God, to be God's creatures, bearing el's image, making that image visible as we come together in community, the community of friendship, of marriage, of the church – the body of Christ. We are far more than we know, and even when we fall desperately short of that which we were meant to be, we are children by adoption and grace. When Adam and Eve left Eden, they were God's children. Even bickering, blaming each other, rationalizing and alibiing, they were still God's children. They could no longer walk and talk with their maker when el walked in the evening in the cool of the garden; but even though they could not see el, the Lord was there, watching them, caring.

Knowledge without wisdom can be a terrible thing. Now when Adam and Eve knew each other, they knew that they knew.

They knew each other, and Eve became pregnant and bore Cain.

That first birth has always fascinated me. When I was just out of college and living alone in Greenwich Village in New York, struggling to make a living as a writer and making it mostly as a general understudy and assistant stage manager in the theatre, I wrote the following tale:

THE FIRST BIRTH

"Adam," she said, "I'm afraid. Something strange has happened to me." She lay under the tree, staring up into his eyes. The roots of the tree were old and round, and seemed to be holding her body in strong, impersonal arms.

Adam dropped to his knees and held out a handful of berries. "Eat. Maybe you'll feel better then."

She sighed deeply in her fear and shook her head at the berries. "I'm not hungry. Only thirsty. What I want is some coconut milk. Would you ... "

Still down on his knees Adam looked at her. "You forget," he said. "There are no coconut trees here. Only there ... "

"But I want coconut milk. If only I had some I think I'd feel better."

"It's not my fault you can't have coconut milk, you know," Adam said.

Tears welled in her eyes, her fingers tightened on the round coarse arm of tree root; she dug her toes into the rough, dry moss. For some reason she did not want Adam to see her cry. After a long time, when she was sure her voice would come steadily, she said, "Something very strange has happened to me. Something I don't understand. Something we didn't learn when we had to leave home. Perhaps this is learning about death. I don't want to learn about death."

Adam bent over her, slipping his fingers under the antelope skin she was wearing, and felt her round, distended stomach. "It seems even larger," he said.

"Sometimes when I am holding it I feel something moving inside, as though something were striking me. Is this another way of His showing His anger?"

"No," Adam said. "I don't think He would punish us twice for one thing."

"Please, Adam," she whispered, "if I could only have some coconut milk."

"All right," he said "I'll try. I'll try and slip in somehow. But if I don't get back you'll know He has killed me."

"Don't get killed, Adam!" she almost shrieked, clutching at his tunic of elk-hide and pulling him towards her.

"You can be so unreasonable . . ." he sighed. "First you want me to go get you coconut milk then you don't want me to get killed when you know perfectly well what He said about our trying to get back. Well, I'll try to get the coconut milk and I'll try not to get killed, and if that doesn't satisfy you I don't know what will." And he got up from his knees, the little bits of moss and twig sticking to them making a fine tracery on his brown skin. But before he had gone more than a few yards he turned and came back. She was lying there with her eyes closed, paying no attention to a dry green leaf of the tree that had floated down and lay tickling against her bare right shoulder. Tears were slowly streaming from under her heavy lids. Again Adam got down onto his knees, bent over her, and pressed his lips against hers. Without opening her eyes she reached out and held him to her, her fingers as strong as though she were clutching him in pain.

"I hurt," she whispered.

Against his tongue he tasted the salt wetness of her tears. Her hair was moist where the tears had rolled unchecked, and he pushed it back from her face, clumsily, trying to dry her cheeks with the palm of his hand, but succeeding only in leaving streaks of dirt. "I'll hurry," he said, stood up, and ran off through the trees.

After the trees came a field of waving yellow grasses and after the grasses a river. This he swam, then clambered up a stony hill. Up, up, until the stones gave way to green clumps of bushes, until the bushes gave way to stones again, and the stones in their place to snow. From the top of the hill where ice cold rock had taken the place of the snow he could see their old home. A pang of desire went into his heart that was similar to the pang he had felt when his lips first touched Eve's that night they left home; and they had fallen together, rolling over and over on the ground. That had been a feeling that had momentarily made them forget that they must leave their home forever, that had made their life as eternal refugees seem bearable and even preferable to the old. Now as he saw the green peace of home again he forgot everything else, forgot even Eve, forgot everything but the great tidal wave of homesickness that swept over him and threw him down sobbing on the icy grey coldness of rock. The rock was so cold that it froze his sobs in his throat, kept the tears from coming out of his anguished eyes. He pulled himself up onto his knees, stretched his arms out until every muscle in his body was tightened to its utmost extreme, and cried out in a voice so deep that if he had been able to hear it, it would have made him afraid,

"Please!" Then with a great struggle he managed to scramble back onto his feet and start running, tumbling, plunging down the mountainside.

But when he had come near enough to home to feel in his lungs and against his cheek the difference in the air, to smell and almost to taste the difference, he saw, in a great flash of lightning, the angel with the flaming sword at the gates. Then there was a crash of thunder and he was flat on the ground, the dirt grinding against his teeth. When the thunder finally stopped reverberating in his ears he realized that he was in darkness such as he had never known. This was not the darkness he and Eve had found the night they left home and lay in each other's arms the whole of that first night. This was not a darkness tempered by stars, or even a night of clouds with a moon hidden somewhere in the depths. This was not a night of fireflies darting or of glow worms' slow light. This was a darkness such as he had never known. If it had not been for the taste of dirt in his mouth he would not have known that it was the familiar earth that he was lying on; he would have thought that this darkness that was so intense somehow had shape and solidity, had the power to hold him up, or perhaps he was falling through it, plunging downwards headlong like an unlighted comet.

Only the grating of dirt against his teeth reassured him that the world was still there, that he was still alive. Even if the sun or moon or stars had been near he felt that their light could not possibly have penetrated this darkness that lay upon him with such heaviness that it seemed as though it was breaking his bones, pressing his ribs together.

Nothing could pierce this darkness but sound, and out of its depths came a voice:

"Move On!"

It was a voice of many trumpets, a voice of the singing of stars, of the clashing of armies, and storms of the skies, a voice that was light dispelling the darkness.

At first as the blackness was slow in lifting he crawled along on his stomach like the snake. Then as he began to see through a thick grey fog, on his hands and knees; and at last as he neared the top of the mountain on his homeward journey and the sky lay streaked with blood on the horizon, he stood and began to run.

When he got back Eve was still lying under the tree, dirt streaked on her face where he had tried to dry her tears, but she was no longer on her back in languid weariness. She had rolled onto her side, with her hands she was clutching the tree roots and she was writhing back and forth, moaning.

Adam dropped beside her. He did not tell her of the angel with the flaming sword or the night that had come on him like a thunder clap. "I couldn't get the coconut milk."

But she had forgotten the coconut milk. When she realized that he was there she loosed her grasp on the tree roots and transferred it to him. Once he felt her teeth sink into his shoulder but somehow it didn't hurt and he felt only a strange satisfaction as he saw the red blood running down his arm. Then her grip slowly relaxed and she lay exhausted in his arms. Her antelope skin was wringing with cold sweat and when he laid his hand on her distended stomach she screamed because the pains were starting again.

They had never seen a baby before. It lay there between them in a bed shaped by the roots of the tree, and screamed at them angrily. It was very red and wrinkled. Its open mouth from which issued such ferocious yowls held no teeth. The eyelids which were squeezed close shut were seamed with a thousand wrinkles. They knew that it looked older than anything they had ever seen before.

"This is what we will look like when we are to learn about death," Adam whispered.

Eve suddenly snatched up the little starfish and held it to her. She had lost the antelope skin somewhere in the midst of her pains but she was unconscious of this now. She only knew that she must hold this little thing to her and somehow keep it safe.

"But what is it?" Adam whispered.

"I don't know, but you had better go get it a skin to keep it warm at night."

Adam stood undecidedly looking down at them. "You don't hurt any more?"

She laughed. "I had forgotten all about it!"

"You had forgotten!" he exclaimed in astonishment. He could never forget the feeling of her teeth sinking into his shoulder, her antelope skin wringing wet with cold, her face dead white with a circle of transparent green about the mouth, the nostrils pinched, the eyes glazed and sightless, and bestial animal sounds issuing from deep in her throat.

All this he would remember when he was an old man with white hair.

"I had forgotten all about it!" she laughed. "And then said in a voice that was tremulous with ecstasy, "But Adam, it was wonderful! I would do it again!"

He looked at her, disgust and anger rising in him. "You hurt and you forget it," he said heavily. "Something that it seems to me must be bad you say is good. How can something good come of hurt and badness?"

She laughed again. "I don't know, but this is good."

He scowled down at the little thing in her arms and strode off. Eve hardly noticed his going. She sat there, leaning back against the trunk of the tree, for she was exhausted with an exhaustion she had never known before, quite different from the feeling she had had the night they left home and set out to find a new place for themselves. This was an exhaustion that was wholly pleasant. She lay back against the tree, and the little screaming starfish in her arms suddenly became quiet and relaxed, drooping against her. She rocked it back and forth, her eyes closed, singing, murmuring over and over again, "Little old age, little old Adam, little knowledge of death," without realizing that she was using words or tune.

By and by she became conscious of a hissing. Opening her eyes slowly she saw the serpent, his hood spread, his little forked tongue quivering, stretching towards her. She snatched her child away, but not before the serpent had licked one small hand with its tongue, leaving a long red mark. Terror sprang into her heart.

"You go away!"

The serpent coiled around and writhed at her insinuatingly. "You thought me beautiful once. Let me just see your child. I can tell you all about your child."

"Go away, snake!" she shrieked. Still holding the baby in one arm, with the other she picked up the largest stone that she could manage, a boulder much greater than she would have attempted to lift with both arms ordinarily, and heaved it at the serpent, who writhed out of its path and slid away through the underbrush while the stone pounded down hill. When Eve was certain he was not coming back again, she sank down against the tree, exhausted. The child had begun to cry, raising its voice in a long, thin wail, and she sat clutching it to her until her heart had ceased its pounding and she could sing to it again without a tremor of terror in her voice.

When Adam returned with the skin, a very small skin, the child was sucking at her breast, while she rocked back and forth ever so slightly, ever so gently, singing. He threw the skin down at her feet, then, as she looked up at him, smiling, with an expression he had never seen on her face before, he flung himself down beside her, pressing his face against her thigh because he knew she would not allow him to disturb the little creature at her breast, and burst into a perfect passion of tears because of this day which had been the most terrible day of his life.

* * *

Thus far. For surely Cain was to give Adam far greater pain later on than he did on the day of his birth.

When Abel was conceived it must have been easier. Eve would have understood what was going on inside her body. She would have realized that her swollen breasts held milk for the infant.

If it was difficult to bear the first child, it must have been even more difficult to *be* the first child. And to be the cause of the first death.

Cain killed Abel. And that was the beginning. Brother against brother. Yankees killing Southerners and Southerners killing Yankees. Puritans killing Roundheads and Roundheads killing Puritans. Protestants killing Catholics and Catholics killing Protestants. Moslems. Christians, Jews, Cain killing Abel ... will it ever stop?

5

Intersecting Circles

WHEN I WAS WRITING that old story of Adam and Eve, I was both Adam and Eve. And I am also Cain and Abel. Scripture is not only the living Word of God, it is also my story, and your story. In the pages of Genesis, and all through the Bible, we recognize ourselves. It is God showing us who we are, and who el wants us to be. If we are to have the courage to recognize ourselves, we must have the courage to face ourselves, not only the parts which we like or of which we approve.

The story of Adam and Eve, of their making, of their expulsion from the Garden of Eden into a world so much less real that it was almost unendurable, of the birth of their children, is in its symbolic way a blueprint of our own personalities. Each of us will recognize something different, but, if we are honest, each of us will recognize something of ourselves.

In a book on Jung by Laurens van der Post I read with awe of Jung's feeling that we have completely misunderstood the Roman Catholic doctrine of the Assumption of the Virgin Mary. We have interpreted it literally instead of mythically. For, Jung points out, what this doctrine is really doing is attempting to return the feminine to the Godhead.

And I thought: How stupid I've been! Falling for the old trap of literal-mindedness again.

Perhaps this urge to literal-mindedness is why we pay so comparatively little attention to the Holy Spirit as an equal part of the unity of the Trinity, even in the most charismatic settings. Somehow it does not help to affirm the feminine aspect of the Godhead, or the Holy Spirit elself, by saying "she" – because the concept is far deeper than a personal pronoun.

Though the Holy Spirit calls forth from us all that is nurturing and intuitive, there is also a wildness of which we are afraid, and so we tend to suppress it. The wind of the Spirit can be balmy and tender, but it can also be fierce, can lash waves to mountainous heights, can become a tornado which creates destruction in its path. We rightly equate the Holy Spirit with wind – the word for spirit is the same as the word for wind in Hebrew: *ruach*.

This wildness is the maternal aspect of the Trinity!

Some people (and I have encountered this feeling in both the male and female of the species, but more often in the male) see the maternal being as totally devouring. The mother wants to eat the child, they say, and so the mother must be killed.

What must be killed, I think, is the false image of the mother we have created. Needing something to blame, we invent an image of the parent which often has no resemblance to reality. And we do need to kill this image in order to be able to love whomever is the real mother.

Let us not blame this image-making and mother-killing entirely on the male. One young woman told me that her relations with her mother were not good, yet her mother always knew when something was wrong, and would call her. She would try to pretend that everything was all right, because she didn't want her mother to be worried; she felt that she had to protect her mother. I told her that perhaps she needed to "kill" her mother, in order to be able to share with the real person, whose intuitive love did not need to be protected from whatever was troubling her daughter.

As both a daughter and a mother, I know how dangerous our images of our mothers can be. But we are hardier than we realize.

I am grateful for Jung's insight. It caused me to remember that Meister Eckhart, and many other mystics, have the same disregard for the limitations of sex. Eckhart writes: "The soul will bring forth Person if God laughs into her and she laughs back to him."

We need a little more merriment and considerably less brittleness as we come face to face with the problems of human and divine sexuality.

Since we are sexual human beings, we cannot avoid thinking about the Adam or the Eve in us. I doubt that it is possible for us to think about God without at least a touch of anthropomorphism (at least as long as our humanity limits as well as releases us). Throughout the centuries all people have wanted to know what God looks like. I am frequently amazed at how many people visualize God as looking like Moses – and Moses in a bad temper, at that. But the God of the Old Testament, the God to whom Jesus remained true, was, and is, slow to anger, quick to forgive, caring about recalcitrant human beings, longing for us to turn to our Maker, to love our Creator, to receive el's compassionate love. All through the Old Testament el participates in creation, and in the destiny of each of el's creatures. So the ultimate participation, God's becoming one of us in Jesus, is no surprise.

We're in it together, and God is in it, with us.

When our children were little, we had long bedtimes, stories, songs, prayers. And when things happened which were hard for us to comprehend like a sudden and unexpected death, I would pile the children into the station wagon and drive up to the top of Mohawk Mountain, to the fire-lookout tower, and we would lie on the great, flat glacial rocks and watch the stars come out, and talk about whatever it was that had shocked or hurt us. I'm not sure where the idea came from that all of creation is God's body, but if we must have an analogy, it is not a bad one.

When I look at the galaxies on a clear night – when I look at the incredible brilliance of creation, and think that this is what God is like, then, instead of feeling intimidated and diminished by it, I am enlarged – I rejoice that I am part of it, I, you, all of us – part of this glory. And so, when we go to the altar to receive the bread and wine, we are taking into our own bodies all of creation, all of the galaxies.

And our total interdependence is an astounding glory.

We are whatever we eat – junk foods, well-balanced meals, the books we ingest, the people we listen to – but most marvelously we are the eternally loving power of creativity. Does it sound incredible to say that when we receive Communion we are eating the entire universe? Of course it does, but it is also incredibly possible, and I rejoice in it.

As for size – as the old southern phrase has it, size makes no never mind. Those two sources of radio emission, sending their messages across millions of light years, are as close together as the eyes in a beloved face. A grain of sand commands as much respect as a galaxy. A flower is as bright as the sun. But all, all are part of creation. So, as there is nothing we can do that does not affect someone else (we can never truthfully say "it's my own business"), there is nothing we can do that does not affect God. This is an awesome responsibility, and one which we offer and accept whenever we receive Communion, asking that we may dwell in God and he in us.

This is not, as some people have wrongly assumed, magic. It is faith that God made everything, and that el saw that it was good. Nothing can be separated from God's love, or from the Word without which nothing was made that was made.

* * *

When I look at the stars to help me find perspective, I am seeking an alternate reality, one which is deeper and more real than the world of immediate consciousness.

Different people have different perceptions of reality, and our own perceptions change as we move from infancy to childhood to adolescence to adulthood. As Americans, as people whose background is from the Judeo-Christian tradition, the terms of our reality are very different from that of a fundamentalist Muslim whose presuppositions involve bloodbaths and the ritual killing of anyone who disagrees. But to someone within the framework of this reality, his is right, and ours is wrong. Can we be sure we are right? What about the Spanish Inquisition, the burning of anyone accused of being a witch, even if the accusation was false?

We have strayed far from the reality of those peoples of the world who live close to the land, who listen to the language of the birds, the singing of the trees, the message of the clouds in the sky. Our loss.

We are far from the reality of many of the people we encounter every day. I am light years away from the perception of reality of people who find that story is a lie, who believe that to act in a play is a sin, because it is to "make believe," and who have fallen for one of the devil's cleverest deceptions, that myth is not a vehicle of truth, but a falsehood.

Like it or not, we each live within our own perception of reality which makes each one of us the center of our particular universe. Some of the thoughts I have just been expressing have come from the overlapping of my own reality with that of the authors of two books I have been reading, *Alternate Realities*, by Lawrence le Shan, and *A Story Like the Wind*, by Laurens van der Post. The idea that we are each one the center of the universe has been haunting me for a long time, not because it seems a selfish idea of reality; it need not be; but because it can sometimes narrow our understanding of interdependence, and the necessity for the circles of our realities to overlap. I had even written this down, thinking it was a wholly original idea of mine, and then, as so often happens, the next morning I came to a question in le Shan's book by Thomas Mann: (I have used language somewhat more contemporary than the translator.)

The world has many centers, one for each created being, and about each one lies his own circle. You stand but half an ell from me, and yet about you lies a universe whose center I am not, but you are. . . And I, on the other hand, stand in the center of mine. For our universes are not far from each other so that they do not touch; rather, God has pushed them and interwoven them deep within each other.

One of the greatest problems besetting the world today is that across the continents the circles are moving further apart, just at the time when it is imperative that we move closer together so that our realities may once more overlap.

Within Christendom I see signs that our circles are coming closer together. But until the circles once more truly merge we belong to a failed church, a still failing church. It was surely not part of Jesus plan that the church, the body of Christ, should be broken into opposing and inimical factions. And I find it difficult to believe that condemning others as being incapable of reflecting the message of the Gospels because they belong to the wrong denomination is in any way Christian. What about the story of the Lord Jesus who asked water of the Samaritan woman at the well, or who ate with tax collectors, or who drove seven demons from Mary of Magdala?

One of the sorry results of this brokenness is a loss of understanding that the Trinitarian God we profess is indeed the God who is One, the God who is all. I am shocked at the number of people who seem to think that the second person of the Trinity didn't appear until Jesus was born in Bethlehem, or that the Holy Spirit never existed before Pentecost. Surely those who accuse us of polytheism are right unless we believe that the Trinity has always been whole, the Spirit moving over the waters in the beginning, as the Word shouted out the galaxies and the ancient harmonies. This fragmenting of the Trinity is reflected in the fragmenting of our own personalities, our fear of our subconscious minds, our intuitive selves. We are crying out with fear against healing with our extolling of youth and our limiting of love to the merely physical. Physical love is a great joy when expressed in a healthy way, but it is far from being the only kind of love.

Despite all the visible signs of brokenness, all the sharp edges, healing is going on today with something of the same radiance as when Jesus brought Jairus' daughter to life, or gave sight to the blind man on the road to Jericho, or drove demons from a pain-wracked body. It is my hilarious joy to be so clumsy that not only do I fall over furniture, but stumble into and knock down denominational barriers, shoved into them by gracious gusts of the Holy Spirit; and it is a mistake to think that the Holy Spirit is without humor!

I spent a gloriously happy week at the Baptist Bethel Seminary in Minnesota, I have a second home at Mundelein College, where I stay with the Roman Catholic sisters and go to Mass with them (something which was not possible when I first knew them), and an equally happy second home at Wheaton College, which is known as "the Harvard of the Evangelicals." I have spent happy weekends with the Presbyterians ... oh, and so on. But nowhere have I attempted to alter my own voice, to accommodate, to try to speak in a foreign language. Our circles overlap closely, we discover to our mutual pleasure that we are far closer than we realized, and that many of the harsh arguments going on around us are about peripheral things. And so, through the gift of grace, we are given glimpses of that which is really real.

Reality is not something we observe; something *out there*, as some people used to think that God was something out there. Reality is something we participate in making, as co-creators with God. Making reality is part of our vocation, and one of the chief concerns of prayer. And it is an affirmation of interdependence.

When I turn to the piano and a Bach fugue, I compose it along with Bach as I hear it and attempt to play it. A writer, alone and with great struggle, writes a book. That book becomes real only as someone reads it and creates it along with the author. Each one of us, reading Genesis, will begin to create a new reality. The important thing is that our realities intersect and overlap.

One way of overlapping is to identify with someone else, for instance, in intercessory prayer. To have compassion (com = with, passion = suffering) means to share with another whatever it is that circumstances are bringing to bear on that other. It does not mean to coerce or to manipulate or to dictate ("Of *course* you must sell your house first thing. After that there is nothing for you to do but leave him. What you *really* need is a new wardrobe"); when we coerce or manipulate or dictate we don't have to be involved with the one we are hoping to help. Compassion means to be with, to share, to overlap, no matter how difficult or painful it may be.

And compassion is indeed painful, for it means to share in the suffering of those we pray for, to love is to be vulnerable, and to be vulnerable is to be hurt, inevitably, yet without vulnerability we are not alive, and God showed us this when he came to live with us, in utter vulnerability, as Jesus of Nazareth.

Preparation for this kind of sharing comes with story. When I identify with Adam or Eve, with Cain or Abel, with Abraham or Sarah, this is practice in identifying with all the people around me, in helping our circles overlap. And it is sometimes practice in recognizing the dark side of myself, the side I would rather not acknowledge. Until I can bring myself to acknowledge it, I cannot offer it to God to be redeemed.

If I am both Adam and Eve, so also am I Cain and Abel.

Parables and fairy tales make much of older and younger sons. Joseph, for instance, is a younger brother whose ill advised bragging deserved the animosity of his elder siblings. And Gideon is a younger brother, who by his humble obedience, succeeded in rescuing the exiled Hebrews from their powerful enemies.

We're a mixed lot, but what a rich mix we are, and what material we provide for story – story which gives us glimpses of truth which otherwise might remain hidden!

6

The First Death

ABOUT A DECADE AGO I tried to work out my identification with Cain by writing another story:

THE WAGES OF INNOCENCE

If one has had an unhappy childhood, then all of the naughty acts one commits during adolescence and young adulthood, or even later, are explained, understood, and condoned: forgiveness doesn't really come into it, at least not for me, because I have no idea what it means, or even if I am forgivable.

My childhood was, in any event, odd. I'm not sure whether it was happy or unhappy, because those were new concepts in our world. My brother and I played from dawn to dark. Sometimes we helped our parents, he more than I. He was the younger of the two of us boys, and I think it made him feel big and important to be told he was a help. If our mother was annoyed with our father, she would praise my brother all the more for any little thing he did for her, so he began to get the idea he was better than anybody.

Our parents, I am sure, are largely responsible for what I did. Ought not parents to shoulder the blame for their children's acts? Our mother and father quarrelled constantly, each one blaming the other for our present low estate. Since my brother and I might very well not have been born in their other estate (though nobody is quite sure about this), they frequently shouted at or hit us because we reminded them that they had known better days. In cold weather my brother's nose ran constantly, and our mother would wipe it distastefully and tell us that in the old days it had never been cold and had rained only at night. There had been enough to eat and to spare, and they didn't have to worry about clothes and nobody knew the difference between work and play and the giants didn't come lumbering around to steal dinner just as it was ready.

When my brother and I were very little we liked the giants and the odd winged creatures who weren't men, being immortal. We, they told us, were mortal, but nobody yet knew what being mortal meant. The giants, like us, were mortal, but they lived in a different chronology, or so we were told, and their life span was longer than ours. What was a life span? We did not know. Some of the giants had only one eye in the middle of the forehead, and six fingers on each hand. They were gentle with small things, and would play games with my brother and me, tossing us back and forth like living balls, and we would squeal with excitement and pleasure. Of course our parents had forbidden us to play with the giants for fear they would harm us, if only by accident, but they never did. With large things they were not so gentle, and we saw them kill dragons and dinosaurs with one blow, though we did not at first know what it meant, to kill. The dragons and the dinosaurs would fall over and twitch and then stop moving and sometimes their blood would come out of them.

The giants told us that this was mortality, but one of the winged men told us not to pay any attention because we, being human, were neither like the giants nor like the dragons and dinosaurs, nor like the beasts of the field.

One particular winged creature took a special interest in us and taught us a great deal. He seemed to be the leader of the others, because they all deferred to him. First of all he showed us how wise it was not to tell everything to our parents, if they didn't know we had been playing with the giants, for instance, they couldn't scold us.

This special winged one was tall, not as tall as the giants but taller than our father, with great dark wings which he could spread like a cloud so that they covered the sun. Once, as he was thus hiding the sunlight, he told us that we must be particularly careful not to tell our parents when we had seen him. "They do not understand me," he said, sadly. "They blame me for what should have been a blessing. I was certainly bored in that Garden."

My brother could not keep his mouth closed. While we were eating our pottage that evening he let slip to our parents what the winged one had said.

"That snake! That serpent!" my mother hissed furiously, putting her arms around both of us and pulling us close to her. "Trying to seduce innocent children. Stay away from him, that evil one! If you go near him again I'll have your father beat the living daylights out of you."

I knocked my brother around a bit at bedtime, not to hurt him, you understand, just to teach him to keep his mouth closed next time.

When I saw the winged man again I could see why my mother called him a serpent. His shape seemed to be changing until now there was something sinuous about it that was unlike our bodies, a rippling and a darkness that was no longer shining. "Why does my mother hate you?" I asked him.

"Hate," he mused, smiling. "It's only the other side of love."

I tossed this aside. "Yes, but what does she blame you for? Were you in the Garden when they were there?" He nodded, stretching his wings and then folding them in much the same way that I stretched my arms above my head when I got up in the morning. "Oh, long before they were there. I can go back any time I want to," he added, "though I don't want to very often. Dull place. They don't know when they're well off, your parents."

"Why can you go back if they can't? What about the cherubim with the flaming sword?"

"Only man was thrown out of the garden," he said. "It's different for me. I threw myself out, so it's still open to me and my friends." He indicated some of the other winged creatures. He grinned "I've been thrown out of better places than that."

At this point my brother came leaping up behind us and scared me half out of my wits. He was like that, full of jokes and surprises and roarings of laughter. He laughed at all kinds of things that weren't funny to me at all. Once when we were kneeling by a still pond to drink and saw our faces reflected in the water, he threw a pebble at our watching faces, and laughed and laughed as our expressions changed and rippled in the moving of the water. He used to sing, too, and whistle, enough to deafen you, and run and leap and prance.

My father would shout, "Can't you keep still for a minute?"

My mother would answer him, "Let the child be happy if

he can." My mother used to sing, too, but it was a different kind of singing from my brother's. It was a tuneless humming, and usually came when she was annoyed with my father, or with the Lord El, or with herself, and we learned early that it meant that she was telling us, "*I* don't care. *I'm* all right. I don't need you. Go away."

When the humming went on for too long I would leave the home fire and go. Sometimes my brother would come running after me. "She doesn't mean it. She *does* need us. She really doesn't want you to go."

"You're too young to understand." I told him out of the darkness into which her humming had pushed me.

"Come on home. She's cooking dinner. Father brought home a mammoth and she's broiling mammoth steaks and they smell marvelous." That was my brother for you: he accepted anything our parents said or did. Mammoths, like the dinosaurs and the dragons which the giants killed, were mortal.

What was mortal? I did not understand, so I asked the great winged one.

But he did not answer the question. Instead he said, "Your father was given all the animals of the earth and air and water to name, and so he has power over them and may do with them as he will."

Why is he telling me this instead of answering my question? I wondered. But I was interested. "My father named me. Does he have power over me?"

"I'm glad you brought that up," the winged one said. "It is significant that this realization should come to you at this point when you are going through a crisis of your identity."

My mind was on power. "Who named my father?"

"The One who shut him out of the Garden."

"So the One has power over my father?" I thought about

this for a moment. Then I asked, "Who named you? What is your name?"

The winged one spread out his great leather pinions, darkening the sky so that a few confused drops of rain spattered on the ground at our feet. "I have no name. I am NoName."

Why did this frighten me? "Then if you have no name –"

He folded his wings calmly and smiled at me. "Then I am Not. And no one has power over me."

"I don't understand." How could he Not Be? There he was, standing right in front of me, larger than life – oh, he was taller than my father by far.

"Why don't you go hunting with your father?" he asked, as though he were answering all my questions. "You're old enough now. It would be a significant experience. You might learn a great deal."

"About what?"

"Not-ness." He laughed. His laugh was not like my brother's laugh. It was more like my mother's humming.

I went back to the home fire. My mother was there, stirring something in a clay pot, and she was singing instead of humming. Her singing was as different from my brother's singing as was her humming. My mother's singing came usually when she was preparing something for us, a special meal, or a new skin coat for cold days. I remembered her singing most when my brother and I were very little and she would hold us in her arms and sing and then kiss us as she put us down on our beds of skin for the night. She sang when she was holding us together in the circle of her song: herself, my father, my brother, and me: not pushing us away. She sang when she had forgotten the Garden.

"No," my brother said. "She has not forgotten it. When she sings she is still there."

"What nonsense," I said, "with that ferocious cherubim at the gates keeping us out, all she talks about is not being there."

Our father talked less than our mother about the Garden and the old days. Perhaps it was because he had less time. Food which had been theirs for the taking he now had to sweat for, struggling with thorns and thistles, drought and rain. Unlike our mother he seldom complained. Perhaps he didn't have time for complaints, either. Sometimes in the evenings he would play with my brother and me. Once when we were very small he woke us up and took us to see the night sky. Because we slept from sundown to sunup, we had never seen darkness before, and we were awed and frightened. The sky was hidden behind a black covering, which was filled with thousands of little holes through which the light shone.

"No," my father told us. "They are not holes, my sons, they are stars, and the Lord God knows them all by name as I know the animals, and as I know you."

"Does the Lord have power over the stars, then?" I asked. I was frightened. I thought perhaps the Lord God might decide to throw one of the stars at us if we angered him.

"Who is the Lord God?" my brother asked.

Here at least I could show him that I knew more than he did. "Idiot. The Lord God is the one who threw our mother and father out of the Garden and put the ugly cherubim there to keep everybody out." Then I remembered winged NoName. "Almost everybody, that is." Was it because he had no name that he could go past the flaming sword and into the Garden?

"Is the Lord God bad, then?" my brother asked.

"No," our father said. "The Lord God is not bad. But he is not to be understood."

"But if he made you leave the Garden then why isn't he bad?"

Our father stood looking up at the night sky, and at the flaming lights called stars. "God made the night and the day; he made the sun and the moon and the stars. Look at the sky, my sons, and ask yourself if the one who made the stars can be bad."

– Why not? I thought. The stars frightened me.

But my brother gave his pleased and happy laugh. "I see! The Lord God is Good. And he is not to be understood."

After that night my father included us when he made offerings to the Lord God.

"Why do you make the offerings?" I asked.

"In gratitude."

"For being thrown out of the Garden?"

"For food and sleep. For rain and sun. For you, my beloved children."

"And what else?"

"For forgiveness."

"But how can you forgive the Lord God when he threw you out of the garden?"

"No, no," my father said. "I ask him to forgive me."

I went to winged NoName for explanation and instruction. He sat down on a rock and drew me to him, unfolding his wings just enough to protect me from the east wind which had risen, bringing with it a stinging of sand from the desert. "I'm glad you've come to me for further orientation," he said. "Your father is, of course, old-fashioned in his dwelling on guilt. It's morbid, and morbidity is unhealthy. In the first place, he didn't do anything wrong –"

"But what did he do?" I interrupted. "They've never told me."

"They ate an apple," NoName said "That's all."

All I knew about apples was that my mother wouldn't let us eat them, and my father got angry when we teased.

"And then," NoName continued, "they learned the difference between good and evil, and so they became a threat to the powers that be, and had to be got rid of."

The difference between good and evil? My mother had called the winged NoName the evil one. To me he was the question-answerer. Perhaps it is evil to answer too many questions?

"You must understand," NoName said, "that your father belongs to the older generation and his attitudes are no longer relevant. What you must do is establish a meaningful relationship with this world. I must go now, but come see me again soon. I enjoy our dialogs."

As we grew older, my brother and I, we had less time to run about and play. We had to help our parents. Our father took us hunting with him occasionally, but mostly he set my brother to keeping the sheep, and me to tilling the ground, because I was older and stronger. Superior. I still went to see NoName whenever I had the opportunity. My brother seldom went with me. Instead, he often used to talk to the horrible cherubim with the flaming sword. And he got into the habit of talking with the Lord.

"But the Lord doesn't answer your questions," I said, "and NoName answers mine."

My brother laughed. "The Lord answers my questions. The sun rising in the morning is an answer. The stars at night are an answer."

I tried to talk to the Lord God, too, but I found it quite hopeless. First of all I tried to establish a dynamic relationship, like the one I had with NoName. I introduced myself, and then I asked, "What is your name?"

At that moment a storm started to blow up and there was a tremendous crash of thunder, so loud that it silenced the birds. In this thundering silence the Lord God said, "I will be that I will be."

This didn't make any sense, and I wasn't sure I'd really heard him because of the strange silence, so I asked again, "Yes, but do you have a name?"

"I am."

This was as confusing as NoName saying he was Not, and I certainly didn't regard it as an answer. It also made me think of my identity crisis, so I asked him. "Who am I?"

And the Lord God said, "Certainly I will be with thee."

I gave up and started to go. Old-fashioned language confused me. He called after me, "Where is your brother?" I shrugged. "I should know? He's always hanging around you. You see more of him than I do."

The rain started then, so I left. I was glad of the rain. The ground was dry, and we needed it for the grain.

The next time we made our offerings my brother brought his best lamb, and I brought some of the fruit of the ground that was a bit wilted. As usual, they started talking, the Lord God and my brother. I might not have been there.

"Oh, Lord, my Lord," my brother said, "my heart is ready, my heart is ready, blessed be your Name from the rising of the sun unto the going down of the same. Who is like unto the Lord God who humbleth himself to behold the things that are in heaven, and in the earth!" It was like singing, the way my brother spoke.

"How can he bless your name," I asked the Lord God, "if he doesn't know what it is?" At least NoName had No Name, I thought, and didn't play tricks like saying *I will be that I will be*.

As usual the Lord God gave an answer which wasn't an answer: "The earth is given daylight by the fire of the sun, but neither can you look directly at the brightness of the sun without dark coming to your eyes, nor can you understand it;

nevertheless it is by the sun that you see." I left them and went to seek NoName and some proper answers.

NoName was waiting for me by a large rock, and he opened and lowered his leather wings in greeting.

"This Name person," I said, "pays more attention to my brother than to me."

"He's just copying your parents," NoName said. "Too much is demanded of the first child. And yet you are not appreciated nor understood. No wonder you are an underachiever. Just because your brother has a pretty face and a nice voice is no reason for discrimination. They should try to have a deeper involvement in your self-fulfillment, and help you to realize your potentialities. Now, if your brother were out of the way, of course, things would be different. As long as he's under foot you are going to suffer trauma and distress."

I went to find my brother. He was holding a new born lamb in his arms and he paid more attention to the lamb than he did to me. So I took a stick and hit him with it the way the giants hit the dinosaurs and the dragons.

Still holding the lamb, he fell, and red blood came from his head. I looked at him, and then I told him to get up. But he did not move.

"Get up," I repeated. "You are not a dinosaur or a dragon. NoName said we were different. Come on. Get up."

Still he did not move.

I knelt down beside him. The lamb began bleating and I pulled it out of my brother's arms and pushed it away. "Get up!" I shouted in his ear. He did not stir. Then I saw that there was no breath in his nostrils, no rise and fall of his chest. The only motion was the slow stream of blood from his temple. His eyes were open as though they were looking at me, but they were not. They were empty, as though there was no one behind them.

Perhaps we were not, after all, so different from the dinosaurs and the dragons.

NoName stood beside me. "So we witness the first human death."

I continued to kneel beside my brother, beating at his chest to make it rise and fall again. "Is this mortality?"

"Yes," NoName said, "also known as death. You are not to blame. Make this quite clear to your parents. It was not your fault. It was theirs. There is no such thing as corporate guilt. They are the ones who sinned, not you. Remember that. It will be very bad for your personality development if they make you feel guilty."

I was not, at that moment, interested in my personality development. "Can't you make him get up?"

"He is dead." NoName snapped his fingers. "Finis."

I blew into my brother's mouth to try to blow breath back into him. But all that happened was that I lost breath myself. I drew back, panting, and NoName was gone.

I ran away from that place and from my brother. If I stayed away for a while and then returned, perhaps he would be singing to the sheep again.

The Lord God said to me, "Where is your brother?" I answered, "If you don't know, how should I? Am I my brother's keeper?"

I left his Presence and went back to the home fire and told my parents that something had happened to my brother. They both began to run, run, to the place where the sheep grazed. I ran after them. "Perhaps he's all right now," I panted. "I was told that we, being men, were different from the dragons and the dinosaurs. I didn't know he would fall down and not be able to get up. It is not my fault."

We reached the field and the sheep and my brother lying where I had left him, his blood drying on the grass.

My mother flung herself upon my brother, covering his body with hers, crying to him to get up, to move. "O my son, my son" she cried, "my son, my son."

"I didn't know about death. I didn't know," I said loudly. "I am not guilty. Therefore I am innocent."

My father stood very still. All about him there was a kind of terrifying quietness. I shifted my weight from one foot to the other, but my father did not move.

"I am innocent," I said again.

At last my father spoke, slowly, heavily. "Innocence is not enough. When your mother and I chose to eat of the tree of the knowledge of good and evil, innocence was lost. You were ignorant, perhaps, but not innocent."

"Then it was your fault. It wasn't mine."

"We are responsible for our actions," my father said. "This is what it means to be human. In this we *are* different from the dragons and the dinosaurs."

My mother still covered my brother with her body, crying out to him. My father left me and went to my mother. He knelt beside her and beside my brother. He did not look at me again, or speak to me. It was as though I was not there.

He held my mother, at first gently, then, as she began to scream, roughly.

My father knew my mother. He took my mother away and knew her.

After a time I had a baby brother. They called his name, Seth.

How sweet he was, how tiny, tender, and soft. I did not remember my other brother that way. But I was not allowed to touch this little one. Every once in a while as we squatted around the fire at dinner, my mother would reach out her hand almost as though she were going to touch me. But then instead she would reach into the bowl of food, or put the baby to her breast. My father was no longer angry; he was, instead, sad, except when the baby laughed. But he said that I was no longer to be trusted. After a while I left them and went off to live my own life away from them. The Lord God set a mark upon me so that no one would kill me for bringing death to the world. And NoName laughed at me and said that now all my questions were answered.

O Lord, my God. I think I could have loved my baby brother.

7

The God Who Is Free

AS CHAPTER FIVE of the Book of Genesis begins, Adam and Eve have left the Garden; Cain has killed Abel; and Adam and Eve have a third son, Seth. Seth had a son named Enos, though there is no mention of who Seth's wife is. But there must have been people around, for the last verse of chapter five reads:

And to Seth, to him also was born a son, and he called his name Enos; then began men to call upon the name of the Lord.

Not until then? Was it because the memory of Eden was becoming dim, and the easy communication with the Lord who walked in the Garden in the cool of the evening was no longer possible? Was it a longing cry of homesickness? As the Lord had called out when Adam and Eve had eaten of the fruit of the forbidden tree, "Where are you?" in wounded love, so were el's people now beginning to ache from their wounds and to call out to their begetter? Was that the beginning of conscious, verbalized prayer? In the Garden, prayer had been all of life, eating, knowing each other, sleeping, all were part of prayer. So wasn't the Fall the breaking of life into fragments which needed to be put together again by prayer?

Chapter five begins:

This is the book of the generations of Adam. In the day that God created man, in the likeness of God made he him, male and female.

The ancient Hebrew lived in a completely patriarchal society, so this reiterated insistence on male and female as the image of God is all the more extraordinary, and all the more wonderful.

Seth was probably the child who gave Adam and Eve the most pleasure and the least grief, though we do not know a great deal about him, beyond his genealogy. He had a son, Enos, who was important not only because it was after he was born that men (male and female) began to call upon the name of the Lord, but because he was an ancestor of Enoch. Enoch walked with God; that is far more important than that he begat sons and daughters, including Methuselah.

Enoch walked with God, and he was not, for God took him.

God took him. He didn't die, like other people. He walked with God, and God took him, as el later took Elijah the prophet.

In terminology which barely overlaps my own circle, Enoch was raptured.

I sometimes see a bumper sticker which I find disturbing. It reads: IN THE CASE OF THE RAPTURE, THIS CAR WILL BE

UNMANNED. That strikes me as being highly irresponsible. I have a vision of a VW bug careening along while the occupants are wafted out through the roof, paying no attention to the other cars on the highway being smashed by their abandoned vehicle.

(When my Anglican priest son-in-law, Alan, first visited my husband's family in Tulsa, my mother-in-law asked him barely before he had time to get in the door, "Alan, do you believe in the Second Coming?" "Yes."

That was only the beginning. Later on that day he and Josephine were taken on a drive around Tulsa. Josephine had visited there a good many times, so the focus of showing off the beautiful city was on Alan. A friend of my sister-in-law was driving and suddenly she asked, "Alan do you believe that at the Second Coming our feet will have left the ground before Jesus's feet touch down?"

My sister-in-law interjected quickly, "Alan, that's the courthouse over there. I do want you to have a good look at it. Dad spent a lot of time there."

To worry about whose feet are where at the Second Coming strikes me as trivializing the Parousia, and yet the questioner was utterly serious. Another case of circles not overlapping. What appears irrelevant to me was important to her.)

However it happened, Enoch walked with God, and God took him. Already, in chapter five of Genesis, God is trampling on death, telling us that death is not going to have the last word.

And, by the end of chapter five, Noah has been born, and so have Shem, Ham and Japheth.

Five short chapters, and already this Book of Books has outdone the best sellers: sex, the supernatural, violence, murder, and the strange, almost science-fiction story of Enoch, simply vanishing from the face of the earth, after a full life, of knowing his wife and begetting children, Enoch was taken by God. Perhaps, if we walk with God our sense of wonder is untouched, we retain our joy at being simply who we are, faulted and flawed, but God's. Perhaps if we walk with God, our lives are truly nothing but prayer.

For outrageous imagination, chapter six outdoes chapter five. And yet – is it imagination? (Can we imagine anything which is not real?) In the beginning of chapter six we read:

And it came to pass that the sons of God saw the daughters of men that they were fair, and they took them wives ...

Who were these sons of God? One theory is that they were fallen angels, which is why things went from bad to worse with poor, fallen human nature. Another theory is that they were an advanced race from a distant galaxy whose space ship was crippled perhaps, forcing them to land on this backwards planet. In any event, they married with us natives, and that is why we have our Leonardo da Vincis and Shakespeares and Beethovens ...

And perhaps ... but who knows what really happened? The Bible does not tell us, and thus far we do not know.

And then we read,

There were giants in the earth in those days.

Giants? All folk-lore includes stories of giants. In almost every culture there is some version of the story of *Jack and the Bean Stalk* – Jack, the naughty boy, who ends up outwitting the even naughtier giant.

But is it only folk-lore? What about the outline of the great chalk horse in England, a long, running horse which can only be seen from a distance? Or, even stranger, in Peru there are extraordinary markings which are visible as patterns only from the air. From the ground they appear random, but from the air it is apparent that they are not random at all, nor are they accidental patterns of nature, they are deliberate design. What they mean, and who made them, we do not know, just as we do not know more than a fragment of the complex and sophisticated culture of ancient Peru, a strange country, a frightening country, a country of ghosts and unknowns.

❊ ❊ ❊

There were giants in the earth in those days,

says verse 4 of chapter six, and it continues:

When the sons of God came unto the daughters of men, and they bare children to them, the same became mighty men which were of old, men of renown.

And then, immediately following in verse 5, we read,

And God saw that the wickedness of man was great in the earth, and that every imagination of the thoughts of his heart was only evil.

What happened? What turned the people's hearts to wickedness?

We don't know. Very likely it was the same things which turn people's hearts to wickedness today, discontent with who they were and what they had, so that they were easy prey for the temptations of hubris, selfish pride and greed and envy; boredom, lust, violence – all of which result in other people being treated as things, rather than the wonderful creatures, the children of the Creator which we really are.

So verse 6 goes on to say,

And it repented the Lord that el had made man (male and female) on the earth, and it grieved el in the depths of the heart.

Repent is a word used frequently in connection with the Lord of the Old Testament.

The Greek word for repent is *metanoia*, meaning to turn completely around, to reverse directions. The thing which may seem strange to us today is that the word repent, as used by the ancient Hebrew, referred not only to us creatures, but to the Lord: We have done evil in the sight of the Lord, perhaps if we amend our sinful ways el will repent and take away the harshness of the divine judgment. God, in other words, was as free as we are to have a change of mind.

After David had lusted after and taken Bathsheba, after she had conceived a baby by him, and he had planned that her husband be deliberately killed in battle in order that he might marry her, the baby of this illicit union became ill. While the baby had sickened and lay dying, David put on sack-cloth and ashes and fasted, praying that the child might be spared. But when the baby died, he took off the sack-cloth and ashes and asked for food. And he was asked why he wasn't wearing sack-cloth and ashes and fasting now, now that the child was dead. And he replied: What for? As long as the baby was alive there was a chance that God might repent, change el's mind. But el did not, and the baby was dead, so there was nothing to do but get on with life.

There is considerable contemporary argument about the possibility of God's changing. I was sent a sermon recently in which the preacher (whose name was not included) talked about the inadvisability of believing in a "God who is always changing, and therefore, inevitably, becoming what we want him to be." What's inevitable about that? The God to whom David prayed for the life of his son did not change as David would have wanted. The writer of the sermon said, "I am not sure I can worship a God who gives me what I ask for and who is always changing according to the way in which the world changes." But who is to say that if God chooses to change, he chooses to change in the way in which the world changes? It may be completely the reverse, I do not know whether or not, or how, God changes, only that el will be what el will be, and that is what el wills, not what I will. Perhaps there are people who see God changing according to their own manipulation of him (the masculine pronoun again, it gives me an idea of how I feel about this). Manipulation is idolatry, not faith. My faith tells me that God is utterly trustworthy, and that el's love of us is infinite and unfathomable. As long as the Lord will be what el will be, a living Lord still involved in creating, it is always possible that el will repent, either to forgive us when we are truly sorry for our sins, or to punish us when we are discontented, and often don't even know we are sinning, unless there is a prophet to point it out.

And prophets frequently aren't listened to. The great prophets did not concern themselves overmuch with foretelling the future. Instead, they pointed out to the people that they had turned away from the living Lord and were worshiping false gods (mammon, sex, self-righteousness, holier-than-thou-ness, greed, lust, avarice, destructive criticism, judgmentalism ...). So, when

God saw that the wickedness of people was great on the earth ... it repented the Lord that he had made these creatures, and el said, I will destroy man (male and female) whom I have created from the face of the earth.

But – and why on earth?
Noah (of all people)

found grace in the eyes of the Lord.

Noah: the first of the great Old Testament heroes. An ordinary man, with wife and children, enjoying the legitimate pleasures of the flesh, and enjoying wine rather too much.

Noah found grace in the eyes of the Lord.

The Lord gave Noah specific directions as to how to build the ark, and as I read these directions, I'm not sure how seaworthy the ark sounds, but that doesn't matter, because the Lord is the Director of the heavens and the earth and the seas. Noah listened to the directions, and he did what the Lord told him to do. That's the first thing the Old Testament heroes have in common: when God spoke to them, they recognized the Lord's voice, and they listened, and they obeyed. They might argue, they might obey reluctantly, but they obeyed.

And here we come to a mighty question: How did Noah, and those to come after him, Abraham and Sarah, Isaac and Rebecca, Jacob and Rachel, how did they know that it was the voice of the Lord they were hearing, and not the voice of the tempter? We human beings have often, with the best will in the world, confused the two.

When the crusaders, believing in the holiness of their cause, slaughtered orthodox Christians in Greece, whose voice did they hear? I have a beautiful Jerusalem cross, but I would never wear it in Greece, because it is a symbol of the massacre of Christians by Christians.

In our own daily lives, in smaller but nevertheless significant ways, how can we tell whose voice it is we are hearing?

Sometimes we can't, for the tempter is extremely clever, and is a superb mimic. But he always slips. If there is even a touch of any of the temptations offered Jesus after the baptism, then it is not the voice of the Holy Spirit we are hearing. If we are gently patted on the back and told that we have a particularly devout and effective prayer group, if we are complimented, ever so gently, on the depth of our spirituality, if we are set apart, even a little, from the rest of creation, then we can make a reasonable guess as to whose voice we are hearing.

When I ride the subway; when I think of the angry man who swung his plastic bag full of bottles at my old dog and me, when I read about drug pushers and rapists, it is not always easy to see these people as my brothers and sisters; but they are, and if I draw my skirts aside then I am drawing away from part of all that God has created. The hem of Jesus' garment must often have been dirty.

If anyone says, loftily, that so-and-so is not saved because so-and-so is a Roman Catholic – or an Episcopalian or a Seventh-Day Adventist – we are equally setting ourselves apart, and this setting apart is always a sign of the presence of the tempter. If we look down from the heights of our theological sophistication on the enthusiasm of the hymn-singers and alleluia-and-praise-the-Lord shouters, we are setting ourselves apart or, even worse, above – another sign that the tempter is breathing sweetly upon us.

John Wesley was a brilliant preacher, and one day after he had preached a great sermon, he was approached by someone who told him what a magnificent sermon it was.

"Yes I know," he replied. "The devil has already told me."

It is very disturbing to some people to accept that Satan and the fallen angels speak in tongues. Of course they do. After all, an angel is still an angel, even if fallen. We've all heard of churches which have been visited by the Holy Spirit, where the people have praised the Lord in tongues, where joy has abounded in the loveliest possible way. But, as so often happens, if these gifted people begin to think that they are even slightly more gifted and slightly more saved than the rest of the congregation, then it is no longer the Holy Spirit who is speaking through them, though they may not have noticed the takeover.

Of course Noah was special. I am special. Each one of us is special. It is when we begin to feel *more special than* that the trouble begins.

Noah found grace in the eyes of the Lord. God didn't dwell on that, but told Noah how to build the ark, and then told him to bring all the beasts of the earth and fowls of the air into the ark, by sevens, not by twos, as the old song has it. Building the ark cannot have been easy for Noah. Not only did it call for great physical labor, but it must have evoked the laughter and scorn of his friends and neighbors, who probably thought of him as no more than a doom mongerer.

But as the Lord told Noah it would happen, so did it happen, and water covered the face of the earth, and all life that was not in the ark perished.

When finally, after forty days, the torrents of rain stopped and the sun came out, God set a rainbow in the sky as a covenant between the Creator and el's fragile creatures.

And how fragile we are! The end of chapter nine, from verse 21 on demonstrates this. Here Noah and his family have been chosen from among all the people of the earth to survive the flood and repopulate the planet. Noah planted a garden and a vineyard, and grew grapes, and made wine, and got drunk, and one of his sons "saw" his father's nakedness, as we euphemistically translate it.

Human, frail, faulted, flawed – out of this sorry clay God produces the people, male and female, who are to do el's will, to be el's image. How strange and wonderful that the image of God is not made from an accumulation of perfection and virtue, but from blundering creatures who nevertheless struggle to listen, and to love.

So the earth was repopulated, and life went on much as usual. People were perhaps no worse, but there's no evidence that they were much better. Shouldn't they have been better, after all that had happened? But they weren't.

And so we come to the story of the Tower of Babel, the reverse story of the great day of Pentecost, which was the redemption of Babel, the great day of Pentecost when once again people understood each other when they spoke.

It was not the building of the tower that was wrong, but the reason for it: hubris, once again. If the tower reached to heaven, the builders reasoned, they would be as God.

And, as always when we fall for this particularly effective temptation of Satan, disaster followed, and the Lord said,

Go to, let us confound their language, that they may not understand each other's speech.

And suddenly the people began to speak in different languages, and they could no longer understand one another. The effects of this fragmentation are frighteningly visible today, among the nations, and (more surprisingly and less excusably) within the church.

Of all the roles my husband has played, one of my very favorites is that of Cardinal Cajetan in John Osgood's play, *Luther.* Cajetan has a long, impassioned speech in which he begs Luther not to leave the church. Among other cogent reasons he gives is that we would no longer have one language if the church were divided into denominations, each speaking the language of a different country. Whereas, if the church stayed together, there was always the *lingua franca* of Latin, understood whether one were in France or Germany or Serbo-Croatia. It would be a sorry fragmenting of the body.

It was either Emerson or Thoreau (from either of them it would have been an extraordinary statement) who said that the worst thing to happen to Western civilization was Luther's leaving the church. This statement, considering who made it, cannot be tossed aside. I'm still thinking about it.

Hugh was fascinated by the role of Cajetan, and did a good deal of research into the character of this complex man.

It so happened that, during the run of the play, friends of ours went to Rome with their two daughters, who were friends of our children. These little girls had not seen the play, and were probably not aware of Hugh's role in it. But one day when they were in Saint Peter's Basilica, the younger of the two girls stopped in front of a statue, pointed, and said, "Look! There's Mr. Franklin!"

The statue was of Cardinal Cajetan.

I have no explanation for this kind of marvelous synchronicity. I simply rejoice when it happens.

And synchronicity weaves and interweaves throughout Scripture.

***

After the disaster at Babel there's a long column of genealogy, until we come to the begetting of Abraham, Lot, and Sarah. For simplicity's sake I'm going to call them by their familiar names, though as so often happens in Scripture, part way through their lives their names are changed by God, Abram becomes Abraham, and Sarai becomes Sarah. One of the many reasons I wish I knew Hebrew is the importance of the meaning of names. For instance, the Hebrew for Isaac is Itzak, and Itzak means *laughter* (though Isaac had a singularly unfunny life). But I'm getting ahead of the story.

Abraham and Sarah were old. They'd probably used up their social security benefits. They were candidates for a Retirement Village or an Old People's home – had there been such things. Sarah was long past menopause, and Abraham his equivalent thereof. They had lived a full, if childless life, and surely deserved some peace and quiet in their old age. You would certainly think that they were the last people God would pick as pioneers.

But the Lord from whom Jesus refused to turn away when the Spirit led him into the wilderness to be tempted, doesn't pick the logical people to do the work which needs to be done, and that's one of the most important things to know about God. Each one of us, el's creatures, is going to be asked to do things we don't think we can do, and el is going to expect us to do them.

Perhaps that is the meaning of the strange story of the fig tree which did not give figs to Jesus. Nikos Kazantzakis wrote:

I said to the almond tree,
Sister, speak to me of God.
And the almond tree blossomed.

When God asks us to do something, el expects us to do it, whether we think we can do it or not.

Many great things have been accomplished by people the world didn't think adequate to do them. The pages of history are filled with heroic people who have had epilepsy, club feet, were stutterers, short of stature, blind, one-armed ...

In a much less sensational way, I was a tongue-tied, shyness-frozen adolescent and young woman. In any public gathering I backed into a corner and tried to become invisible. When I was first asked to give a talk in front of an audience, I had to hold onto the podium, quite literally, in order to stop my knees from buckling under me. It was only when I realized that my shyness and awkwardness were a form of self-centeredness, and that I, myself (or what I thought of as myself) didn't matter, that I began to be able to open my mouth and speak, to look at the other person's needs instead of my own, to be able to reach out instead of drawing back.

We do occasionally learn from our mistakes. When I am enabled freely to throw my arms around someone in spontaneous pleasure at meeting, I am reminded of an occasion in my young womanhood when I was in my mother's hospital room (she was there for some minor surgery), and a friend of mine came in, to see me, as well as to visit my mother. We hadn't seen each other in a while, and she held out her arms in greeting and I, the Yankee cousin frozen into shyness in the midst of all the southern kin, did not return the gesture, not realizing until later that this reticence could well have been interpreted as rebuff.

It wasn't till long after that experience that the human touch became a joy to me, but the acute awareness that I had not returned love with love was a lesson I will never forget. It was not a lesson I learned that day, once for all. It is a lesson I never stop learning.

Slowly I have realized that I do not have to be qualified to do what I am asked to do, that I just have to go ahead and do it, even if I can't do it as well as I think it ought to be done. This is one of the most liberating lessons of my life.

The qualifications needed for God's work are very different from those of the world. In fact, when we begin to think we are qualified, we have already fallen for the tempter's wiles. Not one of us has to be qualified in order to employ lesson, meditation, and orison, to read, think, and pray over Scripture. We do not need to have gone to a theological seminary, or to have taken courses in Bible in or out of college. We do have to be willing to open ourselves to the power of the living Word. And sometimes that can be frightening.

But we are in good company. Surely Abraham and Sarah were frightened when the Lord said to them,

Leave your country, leave your family, and go to a land which I will show you. And I will make from you a great nation, and I will bless you, and make your name great, and you will be a blessing.

The story of Abraham and Sarah is many-layered, and over the centuries we have barely scratched the surface of all that it means. But we turn back to it, again and again, because it gives us glimpses of the nature of the God who was called *Abba* – Father – by Jesus. God's calling of Abraham and Sarah demanded a response which was not action alone, but action which was prayer.

And God continued,

And I will bless them who bless you, and curse them who curse you, and in you shall all families of the earth be blessed.
All families, not just a few here and there, separated from the rest of the population, but all families of the earth shall be blessed, whether we deserve it or not.

Would we listen if the Lord asked of us what he asked of these old people? I hope we would, but I'm not sure, Nor am I sure that if we listened, and heard, we would have obeyed. But Abraham and Sarah, and Abraham's nephew, Lot, and all their retinue,

went forth to go into the land of the Canaan.

All was going well with the journey for these intrepid voyagers, and then there was a famine so severe that Abraham went into Egypt for food. But he was afraid that if he admitted that Sarah was his wife, he might be killed, for Abraham, suddenly looking at Sarah with fresh eyes, said to her,

I'm aware that you are a fair woman to look upon, therefore the Egyptians will kill me, but they will save you and keep you alive.

So he asked Sarah to pretend she was only his sister because, according to the custom of that time and that part of the world, it was all right for a stranger to sleep with a man's sister, but not with his wife. If one of the noble Egyptians looked upon Sarah, and wanted her, and knew that she was Abraham's wife, they would have to kill him first to have her.

Pragmatic, our father Abraham.

So they left Egypt when the famine was over and continued on their way. Abraham's and Lot's servants quarrelled, and because Abraham did not want dissension between himself and his nephew, they agreed to go their separate ways. Lot went to Sodom, where he was taken captive, whereupon his uncle *armed his trained servants, born in his own land, three hundred and eighteen*

to rescue Lot.

Scripture is often specific about numbers. Numbers are their own language, and it has been suggested that if and when we make contact with a culture from another galaxy, we should try to communicate with a binary code using numbers, rather than words. Nevertheless, numbers have their own magic, and musicians, such as Bach, are very aware of the importance of them.

After Abraham had rescued Lot he was blessed by Melchizedek. In spite of the conjectures of theologians and historians, he remains a mysterious figure. He was

a priest of Salem, and also a priest of the most high God.

And the psalmist foretold of Christ that he would be

a priest forever, not in the Aaronic priesthood, but after the order of Melchizedek.

Of course, Melchizedek was a priest long before the Hebrew temple was built, or the ark of God, long before the Lord gave the stone tablets of the commandments to Moses, long before Aaron became high priest, long before the tabernacle and the Holy of Holies. But Melchizedek was a herald of things to come, because he brought bread and wine to Abraham, thereby prefiguring the Eucharist.

Abraham continued the journey after this refreshment, but he was still unhappy because he had no children, and he complained to God about this.

That's another thing the heroes of the Old Testament have in common: whenever they are disturbed or upset they complain to God, loudly and uninhibitedly.

I am often surprised at the number of people who think it is somehow wrong to complain to God. When I complain to God, I don't take it out on my family and friends. And when I complain to God, I am often shown what it is that I am really complaining about, and that I am being silly, or trivial, or selfish, or cowardly. Or that I am in deep trouble and it is right to turn to my Maker. When I vent my feelings on God, el will give me the courage, or other gifts I need that I might very well not have received if I had been too reticent to complain.

Abraham was not afraid to complain. So God took him out one night and said,

Look now toward heaven and tell the stars, if you are able to number them . . . so shall your seed be.

What an extraordinary promise to make to an old man! But Abraham

believed in the Lord.

God does not ask us to believe the reasonable things; why should el? Believing in what is reasonable is no problem. El asks us to believe that which is not so much unreasonable as that which exists on the other side of reason. So that all that I base my life on is beyond reason, beyond proof.

Believing is never easy, and it is not cheap. Yet Abraham believed, and he did what the Lord told him to do.

And when the sun was going down, a deep sleep fell upon Abram, and lo, a horror of great darkness fell upon him.

I think that most of us have known something of this horror. *Terror anticus*, it is called. It is part of the price of faith. The greater the jewel we seek, the higher the price. But it is worth it. It is worth it.

* * *

In those days, if a woman were childless, she could bear her husband a baby through the body of her maid. It is difficult for us on our overcrowded planet to understand the vital importance of children for the nomadic peoples of those days. Children were a matter of life and death, not only for the individual family, but for the preservation of the tribe, the community. If there were not enough hands to bring in the crops, to protect the tribe from the enemy, disaster would follow.

So Sarah sent her maid, Hagar, in to Abraham, and she conceived, and when she saw that she had succeeded where Sarah had not, she despised the older woman. How bitter that must have been for barren Sarah. So she sent Hagar away, and in due time Hagar bore a son, Ishmael, and Ishmael means *bitterness*.

The story might well have been different if Hagar had not scorned her mistress. But she did, and there are depths below depths in the story of Hagar, and of Ishmael, too. Their story, being part of Abraham's and Sarah's story, was a familiar one to the people of Jesus' time; it was part of their mythic language, which runs in the bloodstream. When the child of the slave was compared to the child of the free woman in Paul's Galatian epistle, there were probably few people who did not remember Hagar's scorn of her mistress. And Hagar, in looking down on Sarah, had fallen into the trap of the tempter, and bitterness followed.

* * *

Chapter fifteen begins

The word of the Lord came to Abraham in a vision.

Scripture is full of visions, and they are to be taken seriously and tested very carefully. It may be appalling to us to accept that Satan can speak in tongues, mimicking the Holy Spirit angelically; so also can he send visions, and all visions must be tested against the temptations in order for us to know who has sent them, and whether or not we can trust them. People have had visions where they were told to murder, and they have obeyed these terrible visions, and the result has been sorrow on earth and in heaven.

Anything good (kything, visions, physical love) is immediately imitated and distorted by the tempter, but that does not make the original good any less good, or change or alter the original good which God made.

When the Lord of heaven and earth sends us a vision it is for a good reason. God often speaks to us at night, when we have let down our defences and are quiet enough to hear his voice. When we try to take control of our lives, and perhaps the lives of some of the people around us, our eyes and ears are closed to God's visions.

Scientists and artists both know that visions and inspiration come when least expected. Often we will worry over a problem, brooding fruitlessly, and when we have let it go, suddenly the answer will be there, just when we have stopped looking for it. Sometimes when I am walking my dog at the end of the day, and my mind and body are tired, I will simply walk without thinking, letting my mind roam free. And then I am often given unexpected and beautiful gifts. And sometimes I am given horrors.

As a story teller I have been trained to think of every possibility that can happen to my characters, and this training seeps off the page into what is happening in my own life, and the lives of my family and friends. And so, as I can imagine all the good things, so can I imagine the terrible. And, if I am open to the good things, I am also, as a consequence, open to the bad.

In *The Time Trilogy* there are evil creatures called the *echthroi*. The singular is *echthros*, a Greek word which simply means *the enemy*. It is an enemy-sounding word, and I have come to understand that the enemy rejoices whenever I project a fearful vision. If someone is late driving home, I have immediate visions of all kinds of terrible accidents, and there have been enough accidents in our lives so that I know that they do happen. But I try to shut off each bad projection, superimposing a lovely one instead. If there is too much talk of nuclear warfare, again I pray for the planet by visualizing it as whole and beautiful, perhaps in the autumn, when gold and scarlet sweep across the landscape. Or I visualize my family during a time of happiness, a festival dinner, with all the candles lit, and all of us holding hands around the table.

If the ugly visions persist "Lord!" I cry, "Protect me from echthroid projections!" And "Send your holy angels to cleanse me, mind, body, spirit. Send your angels to banish the echthroi." And I say the prayer from the office of Compline:

Visit this place, O Lord, and drive far from it all snares of the enemy; let your holy angels dwell with us to preserve us in peace, and let your blessing be upon us always, through Jesus Christ our Lord. Amen.

And I sing the ancient monastic hymn:

From all ill dreams defend our eyes,
From all nightly fears and fantasies.
Tread underfoot the ghostly foe
That no pollution we may know.

Some of these words seem even more applicable now than they did when they were written, centuries ago. No pollution? How do we escape the pollution of greed, and lust for power, and hardness of heart? And the more modern pollutions of noise and filth and contaminated air and water?

However, if I am totally immune from the projections of the ecthroi, from the horror of great darkness, from terror anticus, then I immunize myself also from the visions which the Lord sends. And I must trust the Lord and el's angels to guard and protect me.

Rainer Maria Rilke said that he was afraid that if he vanquished his demons, his angels would leave him, too. So here we are, once again caught in paradox. And we often refuse to accept the paradox by calling visions unreal, figments of the imagination, delirium, madness, hysteria. We don't want to let go our control.

So it is not surprising that it is during sleep ("Samuel!

Samuel!") that our manipulative selves let go their rigid authoritarianism, and our dreams come to us, with messages sometimes quiet and beautiful, sometimes terrible, so that we wake up, trembling. Most of us have recurring dreams. I go, periodically, to a beautiful house, a house I have never been to, but whose many rooms are well known to me, and whose beautiful views rest the troubled spirit.

Then there is the waking dream. I hope I never outgrow my need for daydreams, for they are a part of the healthy psyche – as long as we do not confuse them with reality.

* * *

Far different is the relaxing control which comes as a gift. It is the goal of contemplation, and although it can be sought consciously, it cannot be attained consciously. When it happens it is given to us. And sometimes it is given to us in surprising ways and in surprising places and when we are not even looking for it.

One Sunday in July each summer, Hugh and I take the worship service for the Congregational church in the village, and to be asked to do this, and to do it, is a special privilege.

Our two younger children were baptized in this church. I have cried, laughed, learned, questioned in this church. To work on a sermon to be preached from the old wooden lectern is probably a more demanding task than to prepare one to be preached from the great stone pulpit of the Cathedral in New York.

Last summer after the church service I said to Hugh, "Go on and get the paper. I want to walk home down the lane." We were having friends in for dinner and I wanted to pick wild flowers.

It was a perfect July day, the sky high and blue with a few fairweather clouds, warm, but not humid, with a gentle, northwesterly breeze. I ambled down the lane, pausing to pick flowers as I saw them, daisies, buttercups, and my mind happily drifted with the breeze. And I was not thinking at all. And then I moved, was moved, into what I suppose would be called an altered state of being. It is, when it happens, a far deeper state of being than the one we live in normally. Everything is more real. The sheer beauty of creation has something of the fresh miraculousness of Eden. Wonder and awareness are heightened. Friendship and love are deeper and richer than anything we encounter in ordinary living, and that is indeed a strong statement, for friendship and love are what make the wheels go round.

When I am returned to myself, as it were, then the glory fades, and once it is over it cannot really be recalled nor described. But it is glory, and it is a way of being that I believe we were meant to know. The loss of it is one of the results of the Fall. These glimpses of reality are not given frequently; we could not often bear such intensity. I suspect that this gift of reality is a gift of the deepest kind of prayer. I know that it cannot be sought consciously, that like all prayer which is out on the other side of words it comes from the infinite grace of God. It is not easily talked about, not only because it is impossible to describe, but because in this frenetic world it is neither easy nor customary to pause and listen to God, and when we talk about people having visions, we're more apt to think they're ready for the mental institution than that they are receiving a message from the Lord.

But we live by revelation. Paul writes in his second letter to the people of Corinth about being taken up to the third heaven, whether in his own body or out of it he is not sure. And immediately after this glorious experience he complains that he has a thorn in the flesh, and that he has asked God not once, but three times, to take it away from him. And the answer is, "No, Paul. My strength is made perfect in your weakness."

Ecstasy is frequently followed by pain, and perhaps it is the joy that gives us the courage to bear the pain, and to experience the pain as birth pain, and to offer our weakness to our Maker, knowing that it can be turned to el's strength.

We were meant to be finely-tuned receivers, but we have created our own static, the messages are no longer clear, we are losing our ability to tune in, an ability we desperately need to renew.

But sometimes the gift is given, as it was as I walked down the old dirt road and my human feet trod glory.

8

Paradoxes in Prayer

AND THE LORD came to Abraham in a vision, saying, Fear not, Abraham. I am your shield and your exceedingly great reward.

And Abraham said, Lord God, what will you give me, seeing I go childless?

And the Lord brought him out and said, Look now toward heaven, and tell the stars, if you are able to count the number of them: and he said, so shall your seed be.

God does not hesitate to repeat something if it is important.

And Abraham believed in the Lord, and el counted it to him for righteousness.

Abraham believed, and Abraham did not believe, because, later on, God spoke to Abraham about his wife, Sarah, and said,

I will bless you, and give you a son of her; yes, I will bless her, and she shall be a mother of nations, kings of people shall come from her.

Then Abraham fell upon his face and laughed, and said in his heart, Shall a child be born to him that is a hundred years old? And shall Sarah who is ninety, bear a child?

And God said, Sarah, your wife shall bear you a child indeed, and you shall call his name Isaac.

Isaac. Itzak. Laughter. Where was the Joke?

The story flows on. One day Abraham

sat in the tent door in the heat of the day, and he lifted up his eyes and looked, and lo, three men stood by him.

Abraham and his three angelic guests. For the ancient Hebrew an angel was not only a messenger of God, an angel was an aspect of God, was God. So those angels were an icon of the Trinity, the Trinity which was, from the beginning, before the beginning, and will be at the fulfillment of all things.

One of the greatest thrills for me was to see in Saint Basil's Church in Moscow that magnificent icon of Abraham and his three guests. There was the Trinity, sitting at the table, with bread and wine, an affirmation of the dignity of all creation, and the magnificent mystery of the Creator.

And the affirmation was all the more poignant because Saint Basil's Church, with its multicolored onion domes, like something out of a fairy tale, stands in Red Square, in a state which denies the existence of God. (I did not know until we reached Moscow that *red* and *beautiful* are the same word in Old Russian, and that Red Square was so named in the fifteenth century.)

So I looked at the icon of the Trinity and thought of Sarah, who was summoned from the tent. She, too, is told that she is going to bear a child, and she, too, thinks that the idea is hilarious. It cannot have been happy laughter. Sarah had wanted a baby for a long time, so long that a baby was no longer even a possibility. It must have seemed a cruel joke indeed that now that it was too late, now that she had given Abraham a child by Hagar, her maid, and had been scorned, now, after all these years of hope and disappointment, she is told the incredible – that her withered womb is going to ripen and open and she is going to have a son.

And she does. For man it is impossible, for God, nothing is impossible.

("I didn't laugh," Sarah protested. "Oh, yes, you did," insisted the Lord.)

And so, despite incredulous laughter, Sarah conceives and bears a child, and his name is called Isaac.

God's ways are not our ways. Often we would like them to be our ways. Each generation in turn creates its own god in its own image, thereby hoping to tame all Glory in order to make it comprehensible. It is the attempt to make a poor photocopy of God which produces all the confusion about God's sex, thereby further confounding us about our own sexuality. And we are as confused as were the ancient Romans in the frantic centuries before Rome fell. To bear a child is considered by some people to be degrading (like reading the Morning Office in the bathroom?). Pleasure becomes more important than joy. Transitory thrills are offered as the cure for boredom, restlessness, and that discontent which is surely not divine.

Abraham and Sarah were simpler than we are in many ways, as a nomadic people, close to the rhythms of the earth, dependent on community, one did not make it alone in the desert.

There the stars at night were like the stars at sea, undimmed by city lights. They must at times have been overwhelming.

I like my creature comforts, my stove and refrigerator and washing machine, and certainly, oh, most certainly, my electric typewriter, and even the black felt pen I used on the ship as I began to set down these thoughts on the back of the ships daily newsletter. But technology, for all its obvious advantages, has its limitations, and has dimmed our sense of the numinous. At Crosswicks when the power goes out, as it does in winter ice storms or summer thunder storms, and the rooms are lit only by firelight and candlelight, then the darkness comes alive, as it must have been alive for Abraham and Sarah. Shadows move, stretch up the walls, shrink down again. We cannot quite see what that dark shape is, lurking in the corner. The fear of darkness is supposed to be an acquired fear, but I suspect that we acquire it early, inheriting it from our father, Abraham. The old Scots were totally serious when they included these words in their litany: "From ghoulies and ghosties and things that go bump in the night, the good Lord deliver us."

Abraham and Sarah knew the fear of ghoulies and ghosties and things that go bump in the night (they'd never have denied their existence by banning books which mention them), and they had absolute trust that the good Lord would deliver them, even when they laughed at el's outrageousness. For even when God spoke to them in the form of three angels, el was present, tangibly present, giving el's creatures free will, and then poking a celestial nose in, poking a finger in the pie, being part of the story, which is, after all, God's story.

But if it is el's story, where do we come in? What happens to our free will?

There are many people who believe that we have no free will at all, that everything is predetermined. Each event leads to another, unchangeable event. Ultimately everything will wind down. We will die. The universe will flicker out.

Then, among those who tolerate the thought of free will, there is an increasing tendency to believe that free will dooms us to failure. That when God created us free, free to make wrong choices, as Adam and Eve made wrong choices, el made our failure inevitable.

But why? If we are free to fail, we are also free not to fail. We are free to love God, and to be obedient to el's will. Our free will is most evident when we are being co-creators with God. We may have little free will about outward events, granted. There was nothing most of us could do with our free will to stop the eruption of war in the Falklands. We cannot stop the fighting in the Middle East. Our free will lies only in our response. To be able to respond is to be human, and I learn about this human free will from the great characters in Scripture.

Genesis is a book of contradiction and paradox, just as our lives and thoughts are full of contradiction and paradox. Indeed I am beginning to feel that without contradiction and paradox I cannot get anywhere near that truth which will set me free.

Abraham and Sarah, leaving the comforts of home and going, in their old age, out into the wilderness, were following God's way, definitely not the world's way. In the New Testament it is spelled out even more clearly: we are to be *in* the world, but not *of* it.

In New York, far more than when we are at Crosswicks, we cannot escape being surrounded by the world, and we are constantly offered the world's temptations, sometimes in extreme forms. When someone asked Hugh where the hot new night spots were his response was laughter, the hot night spots are no temptation for us. But there are other, subtler temptations. The more brittle women's libbers (who have lost a view of true liberation) are terrified to accept their fair share of man, made in the image of God, male and female, and abdicate their responsibility by insisting on being their "own woman," and fulfilling their potential by seeking pleasure, or success, or money, at any cost. I am seriously advised that I have really not been fulfilled because I have limited myself to one man, and that any personal problems I may have are the result of this limitation. Or, they may be the result of my parents' overprotectiveness; or, perhaps, their underprotectiveness. If I listen, my free will becomes undermined. Or rather, if I listen without selectivity. Women *are* supposed to be themselves. Her true self is what Jesus made Mary Magdalene when he freed her of possession by seven devils. She became her own woman by completely surrendering herself to the Lord, and it was to Magdalene that Christ first showed himself after the Resurrection.

Keeping myself for one man does not mean that I do not have deep and fruitful friendships with other men. These friendships strengthen rather than lessen, my love for the one man with whom I made my promises. And the same thing which is true for me is true for him.

We *are* supposed to free ourselves from unhealthy ties to our parents, childish overdependencies. But we are not supposed to free ourselves from genuine love and concern.

Pleasure in itself is not a bad thing; it is a good thing. But when we seek it frantically, we lose it. One of my favorite pleasures is soaking my weary bones in a hot bath. It is particularly a pleasure because when our children were very young, and we were living in Crosswicks year round, running the general store in the village, we didn't have enough money to pay for the oil to heat the water for regular tubs for the entire family.

So about twice a week I would fill the tub and put one of the children in with me. As soon as we could afford private baths, it occurred to my children that this was one time when they could be with me alone, and frequently one of my daughters would ask, "Mother, can I come talk to you while you take your bath?" And now my grandchildren do the same thing. So when I get into a hot bath, all by myself it is a privilege, and one I have never yet taken for granted. And it is all the more special because it has not always been my privilege. It is, I trust, an innocent pleasure, but it is surely a pleasure.

It reminds me of a young woman I met at a writers' conference. She was a successful writer for magazines all across the country, and was leading the nonfiction workshop. In awe and amazement, the second day of the conference, she said, "Last night was the first night I have ever spent in a room all by myself." She had slept in a room with her sister until she was married, and ever since then in a room with her husband, whose work did not take him away from home. To spend a night all by yourself for the first time! What a pleasure! So is ice cold lemonade on a hot day, or running across the sand into the water, or curling up under the eiderdown on a cold night.

Seeking pleasure as the ultimate good, however, leads to all the porno houses on Times Square in New York, which once was the glamorous Great White Way of the theater, but which is now ugly and shoddy. The pursuit of pleasure when pushed to the present extremes leads to perversion and violence. Instead of affirming the dignity of human beings, pleasure misused turns us into things to be used and tossed away.

Abraham and Sarah had no time for this kind of pleasure, nor did our forbears. Staying alive took all the energy the human creature possessed. The people who built our home, Crosswicks, around two hundred twenty-five years ago, worked from morning to night. The great beams of the house were hewn from forests of virgin pine. About four miles from the house is the last stand of the old trees left in the state, and it makes me understand Longfellow's lines:

This is the forest primaeval,
The towering pines and the hemlocks.

Both men and women were essential to survival. Candles had to be made; meals cooked, wool spun, meat salted. Simply living was a full-time job. Pleasures did not have to be frenetically looked for; an evening of singing and dancing for the entire community brought great joy.

Let me not sentimentalize our forbears, for they were human beings, as pragmatic as Abraham passing Sarah off as his sister, as shaken by terror of great darkness, as stubborn and self-centered as the men and women of Scripture. But perhaps they were blessed in not having time for massage parlors and adult bookstores and nervous breakdowns, nor time to spend on worrying about self-fulfillment and all the other self-indulgences which come with too much spare time; we all need some time for ourselves, some quiet be-ing time, but too much time, like too much of anything brings trouble.

The paradox is that self-surrender instead of being a denial of personal pleasure brings with it the gift of joy which is to be found in true pleasure. Sarah had to let go her bitter laughter and surrender herself before she could conceive Isaac and receive God's gift of true laughter.

But paradox and contradiction were no surprise to Abraham and Sarah. They were not surprised to see angels, even though they laughed at their messages. They knew how to get themselves out of the way in order to listen. What we call contemplative prayer was an ordinary and essential part of their lives.

In the Western world in the past several centuries we have denied ourselves this kind of total communion with the Creator because we have been afraid of it. Not just we, as individuals, but we in the corporate body of the church, where the tendency has been to sweep the numinous under the rug and pretend it isn't there. Many students ask me about Zen methods of contemplation, about Hinduism, about Sufi, and are astonished to hear that we Christians have a heritage of contemplative prayer without our own scriptural tradition.

The methods of contemplative prayer are similar in all traditions. Sit quietly, preferably comfortably, so that your body works for you, rather than against you. The fourteenth century mystic, Richard Rolle, said that he liked best to sit, "because I knew that I longer lasted ... than going, or standing, or kneeling. For ... sitting I am most at rest, and my heart most upward."

One of my most-loved places for this kind of prayer is a large glacial rock on which I stretch out, flat on my back, so that I can feel that I am part of the turning of the planet, so that rock and I merge, becoming part of the energy of creation.

Having found the physical context, breathe slowly, rhythmically, deeply. Fit the words of your mantra to this rhythm. And don't be afraid of the word, *mantra*. One young college student came to me full of self-righteous indignation, saying that the use of a mantra was forbidden in the Bible.

"Where?" I asked.

She did not know. But it was there.

Jesus warned us against *vain* repetition. But allowing the name of Jesus to be part of our life rhythm is never vain unless we try to take credit for it.

"But the Bible says a mantra ..."

"*Please* go home and check the Bible and see if you can find out where it is forbidden, and come back and bring me chapter and verse," I suggested.

If she looked it up, she didn't find it, not in a concordance, not in the text.

Mantra is simply a convenient borrowed word for the kind of prayer that is constant, which helps us to pray at all times – which the Bible does tell us to do. For the Christian, the mantra can be any short petition from the Bible, preferably one which includes the name of Jesus. The most frequently used petition is the cry of the blind man on the road to Jericho, *Lord Jesus Christ, Son of the Living God, have mercy on me, a sinner*, or the shorter version, *Lord Jesus Christ, have mercy on me.*

This is familiarly known as the Jesus Prayer, and I am uncomfortable whenever anyone says, "I use the Jesus Prayer," for we never "use" the Jesus Prayer. It uses us.

And far too often we take the name of Jesus casually, or, even worse, possessively. I do not want to be what my husband calls "a bumper-sticker Christian." Recently we were parked behind a car with two bumper stickers. The one on the left said I LOVE MY PEKINGESE. The one on the right said I LOVE JESUS. Somehow I do not put much stock in that kind of love! Perhaps I was turned off by I LOVE MY PEKINGESE and I LOVE JESUS side by side because there was something possessive about those messages, something separating the owner from those who have neither pekingese nor Jesus as pets. That scares me. The Word is not a pet. The Word is the wildness behind creation, the terror of a black hole, the atomic violence of burning hydrogen within a sun. (Christ is both lion and lamb, and lions are not domesticated.) A minister friend of mine in the midwest was parked beside a car, at a red light, and the other car had the familiar bumper sticker HONK IF YOU LOVE JESUS. The car behind them began to honk insistently, and the man in the car with the bumper sticker got out, went to the honking car, leaned in the window and said, "You goddam fool, can't you see there's a red light?"

The man who had been honking replied mildly, "But I just love Jesus!"

Remember what Jesus had to say about someone who called his brother a fool?

A friend of mine, an old and holy man, occasionally talked about people he felt were "bejeezly." The people in the above two stories were bejeezly, using the name of Jesus trivially, thoughtlessly, smugly. Anyone saying the Jesus Prayer with such an attitude is tampering with the incredible Power of the Word which created all things. We must approach the name of Jesus humbly, in the same way that we approach the table to receive the bread and wine.

"But doesn't the Jesus Prayer seem selfish?" I am sometimes asked. "Isn't it selfish to ask it for *me*?"

We must learn that we never ask it for ourselves alone. *Me* is always the Body. And when I am praying for someone, holding onto the Jesus Prayer, *me* is whoever I am praying for.

When I was given this prayer by my spiritual director two decades ago, I, too, asked if it wasn't selfish, and he didn't even bother to answer my question, knowing that the Jesus Prayer itself would inform me. And it did. When we have been with this prayer long enough it becomes part of our life rhythm. When I wake up at night it comes bubbling up into my conscious mind like a little fountain – somewhat like the fountain in the wilderness which the Lord made to spring up for Ishmael. When I am frightened or in pain I hold onto it like a drowning sailor holding onto a rope. When I was going under anesthesia for some scary surgery (well, all surgery is scary) I held tightly to the life line of the Jesus Prayer, and there it was, holding me up out of the deep waters as I came back to consciousness.

A friend of mine who had a frightening series of episodes where her heartbeat raced alarmingly, clutched at the Jesus Prayer to calm her panic, and her heart beat, and then wondered if it was all right to say such a prayer in order to slow down the out-of-control rhythm of her heart, for the Jesus Prayer did indeed alleviate the wild acceleration. And I could only say that God wants us to be healthy, and that she was not "using" the Jesus Prayer, but holding onto it faithfully, so that she could offer herself to God and allow her body to respond according to el's will.

I do not understand the radiant power of the Jesus Prayer, but I am grateful for it every day. And perhaps it is just as well not to understand, because if we did, we might indeed be tempted to "use" it, to treat it merely as a tool.

One time, more than thirty years ago, after I had come very close to death, I had a terrible dream which recurred to haunt me for a good many years. I would wake up from it in a cold sweat of terror. There were various settings for the dream, but the constant element was that I could not light the lamps in whatever room I was in. I would reach for a light switch, or a lamp pull, and the light would not come on. It would not come on because there was evil in the room, keeping it in darkness. It was the evil which was so terrible, and I would rush frantically from light to light, but the light was under the power of the evil. Sometimes I knew where the evil was, coiled like a snake, and I could not pass it. One time when I was visiting my mother in the South, it was in the hall between her room and mine, coiled around a small bookcase which held a set of encyclopedias, and it would not let me by to get to my mother. Another time it was in our apartment in New York, possessing the kitchen. The setting varied, but the terror was the same, and I would wake up from the dream cold with terror. It was Abraham's horror of great darkness in its most extreme form.

One night, after I had been given the Jesus Prayer, and it had been deep within me for quite some time, I dreamed this dream again. This time the setting was a house in London. I was in a room on the top floor, and as usual in the dream I was rushing from lamp to lamp, but the evil had control of the light. The evil was coiled across the door sill, so that I could not get out of the room to get down the stairs, and the evil possessed the stairs. And then, suddenly, in the dream, I was holding onto the Jesus Prayer, and the strong rope of this prayer took me through the miasma of evil, all the way down the stairs, and out into the brilliant sunlight.

I have not had the dream since, and that is twenty years. I may have it again, I do not know. But I do know that the evil cannot permanently quench the light, that the light shines in the darkness, and that it will be there for me, bright and beautiful, forever.

I do not always say the Jesus Prayer well, but that is all right, it helps me, not the other way around. And it has helped to show me the aim of contemplative prayer.

The aim of the oriental method of contemplative prayer is total loss of self – nirvana. My son-in-law, Alan, tells me that *nirvana* means "where there is no wind." For the Christian the wind of the Spirit is all-important, that Spirit which brooded on the face of the waters in the beginning, which spoke through the prophets, and which came to us as our Comforter after the Ascension. We do not seek to go to that place where there is no wind, where there is nothing.

Rather than the total loss of self which comes with nirvana, the aim of the Christian contemplative is discovery, our discovery of God and by God. We seek God not in order to find but to be found. When God discovers me in the deepest depths then I am truly Named, and rather than ceasing to be, I *become.*

It is a meeting of lovers.

John of the Cross wrote:

Let us rejoice, beloved,
And let us go forth
to behold ourselves in your beauty,

And he wrote again:

... that I may resemble you in your beauty, and you resemble me in your beauty, and my beauty may be your beauty, and your beauty my beauty; wherefore I shall be you in your beauty, and you will be me in your beauty, because your beauty will be my beauty; and therefore we shall behold each other in your beauty (Spiritual Canticle, *stanza* 36, *no.* 5).

It *is* a mountain-top experience (as the cliché has it), but we must remember that for one Mount of Transfiguration there were multiplied days of fishing, ploughing the fields, walking the dusty roads. The daily duties must be done before we are given a glimpse of glory. As an old southern woman said, "I don't mind cookin', 'cept hit's just so damn daily."

We can get hooked on too many mountain-top experiences, and this is as dangerous as drugs. Our love of God, and God's love for us, is most often expressed in dailiness.

The incarnation is an affirmation of the value and richness of dailiness, and of the rhythm of work and play.

We get out of rhythm, out of synchronization, and a Quiet Day, a retreat, a place and time apart from the regular round of dailiness can help us to reestablish the rhythm.

My annual birthday present to myself is a retreat at the convent of the Community of the Holy Spirit, just a few blocks from our apartment – but it might be half way around the world. I move into silence slowly, but also with a feeling of homecoming. The Sisters still eat in silence, except on special days, and since they are a teaching order, the silence must be a welcome relief. During the day most of the Sisters are teaching at school, and I can be in the chapel by myself (but never alone), or in the peace and privacy of my room. In the early morning, at noon and in the late afternoon and evening, I share in the Offices. I am nourished in all areas of myself, and then am better able to return to the dailiness of the ordinary working day.

Simone Weil writes, "The key to the Christian concept of studies is the realization that prayer consists of attention. It is the orientation of all the attention of which the soul is capable towards God."

(Orientation: "Eastward-ness." Fascinating.)

"The quality of the attention counts for much in the quality of the prayer. Warmth of heart cannot make up for it."

Warmth of heart is often emphasized in essays on the Jesus Prayer, such as *Unseen Warfare*, or *The Way of the Pilgrim.* I think that Simone Weil is warning against prayer as a pleasurable, self-satisfying emotion, rather than total attentiveness to God and his will, no matter how startling that may sometimes be.

Sometimes the Jesus Prayer does surprise and turn me around, but mostly it is a beautiful part of that rhythm which is with me not only when I am on retreat, but during that "damn dailiness" which is the largest part of our lives.

William Johnston writes in *The Mirror Mind* that "we must carefully distinguish between a word that is truly religious and one that is magical. In authentic religion the power of the word resides not in the sound itself but in the faith of the speaker. In magic, on the other hand, the power resides in the word itself – hence what counts is the use of the correct formula, correctly pronounced, and this formula must be kept a dark secret, since anyone who knows it automatically possesses the power. It is this magical use of words (as well as the mechanical repetition of sounds) that Jesus castigates when he says, 'And in praying do not heap up empty phrases as the Gentiles do, for they think that they will be heard for their many words.' ... I emphasize this because magical formulas have been used in certain forms of oriental meditation that have been introduced to the West, and magic is to be avoided by anyone who would practise authentic religion."

Certainly I have never attempted to count the number of times the Jesus Prayer repeats itself within me during the day and night. There is no more virtue to be found in saying it a million times than half a million. I share Father Johnston's sensitivity about turning religion into magic (If I say the Jesus Prayer ten thousand times then God will give me thus and so); but I also believe that there is more power in the words of the Jesus Prayer than in my own fragile faith. When my spiritual director gave me this prayer I was still trying (and failing) to understand the incarnation with my intellect. Jesus is wholly God and wholly man?!? Jesus is exactly like us, except sinless?!? Jesus came to save us from our sins and from the Father?!?

My mind was running into intellectual brick walls. But I had been trained in college to use my mind. Even though I had majored in English literature, I was trained to be suspicious of anything which was beyond the realm of logic. And so I was suspicious of the incarnation; I was suspicious of accepting Christ as Lord.

My spiritual director knew this when he gave me the Jesus Prayer. He offered it to me not as an easy solution to my problems, but gently, tentatively, as a gift. And because I trusted him I was willing at least to open the gift, look at it, try it on. And so, not really believing in Jesus, I started to live with the Jesus Prayer. And the power of the prayer itself moved from beyond the limitations of the intellect and into my heart.

I never stumbled into the error of thinking of the prayer as some kind of magic formula. I knew only that I was lost and that I needed to be found. My finding was not magic, it was miracle. And miracle comes from God. Human beings can use magic, sometimes for good, sometimes for evil, it has great power. But miracle is wholly God's, and miracle, the particular miracle of the Jesus Prayer, made me understand as never before that all power belongs to God.

With man it is impossible. With God nothing is impossible.

Magic: I find I'm not really sure what magic is. An old woman growing healing herbs in her backyard and brewing them into tea for ailing children is not practising magic, she is practising an old and valid form of medicine. People who do not know the virtue in healing herbs can wrongly confuse the posset with magic. Magic is simply using what God has created, using it to do the things God created it to do. The problem arises when people forget that the power is God's and give it to a human being, or to whatever the human being is using. Magic becomes bad when a human being takes the credit for it. The focus should be on God, the Giver of the gift, otherwise something which is intrinsically good will be turned into something which is at the least dangerous, and at worst downright evil.

The Old Testament prepares us for the gift of the Jesus Prayer. In Deuteronomy we read:

And these words which I command you this day shall be upon your heart; and you shall teach them diligently to your children, and shall talk of them when you sit in your house, and when you walk by the way, and when you lie down, and when you rise. And you shall bind them as a sign upon your hand, and they shall be as frontlets between your eyes. And you shall write them on the doorposts of your house and on your gates.

God's Word shall be everywhere in your life, in all parts of your living, in your downsitting and your uprising. The continual trust in the Word of God is not limited to the Jew or the Christian. It is part of the longing of the human psyche in all cultures. The Kalahari bushmen listen for it in the tapping of the stars. The Buddhist believes that the "proper recitation of the sutra is a way of salvation not only for the one who recites but also for his relatives and friends", writes William Johnston in *The Mirror Mind.*

And in all cultures it is made clear that the recitation of the holy words is never for the individual; it is for the salvation of all people, the redemption of the entire universe. The interrelationship is so total that at the death of a single person the galaxies quake. And the laughter of one child is part of the singing of the stars.

* * *

Nevertheless I would like all the answers re my prayer life, my spiritual life, handed me all tidily wrapped up. But I have learned that if I want neat, unconflicting answers, I would have to go to some rigid sect where my free will would be denied. And so I have learned to rejoice in questions.

I left the Episcopal Church, the church of my birth, after six years of Anglican boarding schools. In college I opted for the world of the intellect, where mind alone was going to conquer all. I read philosophy, taught by a brilliant atheist, and found that I still longed for God, and so did the philosophers.

My return to the church was not easy. It was a difficult journey of painful questions and painful happenings. I had to live through illness, and through the death of some close to me. I had to live through more than a decade of rejection for my work. And a near decade of living year round in a rural setting, while we had our family, ran a general store in the village, and I was forced to face all the questions to which I found no answers, and which I learned, agonizingly, *had* no answers. Not in mortal terms.

At a writers' conference a young woman stood up and said, "I read *A Wrinkle in Time* when I was about eight, and I didn't understand it. But I knew what it was about." And that remark, too, was a revelation to me.

At a church conference recently someone asked, "You have referred to your agnostic period. What happened to get you out of it?"

And I reply, joyfully, that I am still an agnostic, but then I was an unhappy one seeking finite answers, and now I am a happy one, rejoicing in paradox. *Agnostic* means only that we do not *know*, and we finite creatures cannot know, in any intellectual or ultimate way, the infinite Lord, the undivided Trinity. Now I am able to accept my not-knowing – and yet, in a completely different way, in the old biblical way, I also know what I do not understand, and that is what my agnosticism means to me now. It does not mean that I do not believe; it is an acceptance that I am created, that I am asked to bear the light, knowing that this is the most wonderful of all vocations.

When I returned to the church of my birth it was not to discard the intellect, but now I know that to depend on intellect alone is not enough. Perhaps it is because I am a story teller that I need sign, symbol, sacrament, that which takes me beyond where my mind can go alone.

I discover that I am most certain of who I am when I am paying least attention to myself, that I most enjoy the legitimate pleasures of this world when they are not uppermost in my mind. My prayer life is very up and down. I go through long dry periods, and although I know that these are part of faith, when I am lost in the dark night of the soul I fear that it is never going to end. I do know that I need to do my daily finger exercises of prayer, reading Morning and Evening Prayer and meditating on psalter and Scripture even when the words seem empty and my thoughts stupid. Sometimes the Jesus Prayer is like a slack rope. But if I do not do my finger exercises regularly, when the time comes for the words to be filled, they will not be there.

I wish that the church demanded more of us. The human psyche thrives on creative demands, and if we aren't given real ones, we fall for illegitimate ones, like those imposed by some of the sects and which can sometimes lead to horrors such as ritual suicide in Guyana. In order to receive and fulfill legitimate demands, I am an associate of the Community of the Holy Spirit, and following that rule is, far from being restrictive, wonderfully freeing. It is shape and pattern when the days are overbusy, or when I look for definitive answers and find none.

I don't think there are any. There certainly weren't for Abraham and Sarah.

9

Love's Hardest Lesson

SARAH BORE A SON, and his name was Isaac, and he was, not surprisingly, the apple of his parents' eye.

But before we get into the story of Isaac, we come to Sodom and Gomorrah. Since I was born in, and live for a good part of the year in the modern Sodom, I have a certain feeling for the destruction of great cities.

It was immediately after the laughter of Sarah, and while the three heavenly visitors were getting ready to leave Abraham and Sarah, that

the Lord said, Because the noise of Sodom and Gomorrah is very great, and because their sin is very grievous, I will go down now

and see if they are truly as wicked as they seem to be.

So the three heavenly visitors turned away from Abraham and Sarah on the plain of Mamre, and looked towards Sodom.

But Abraham stood in front of the Lord and said, Will you also destroy the righteous along with the wicked? Possibly there are fifty righteous people within the city. Will you go ahead and destroy? Or will you spare the place for the sake of the fifty righteous ... Shall not the judge of all the earth do right?

Powerful language for Abraham to use before the Lord of the universe, but the prophets, for all their faults and flaws, had the courage of their convictions, and Abraham's conviction was that the Lord had to do what is right, that what el did must *be* right. Perhaps this encounter with divine judgment over Sodom and Gomorrah stood him in good stead later on.

And the Lord said, If I find in Sodom fifty innocent people, I will spare the city for their sake.

Abraham continued to push. "Forgive me – but what if there are only forty-five innocent people?" and then forty, and then thirty, and then twenty, and then ten – and each time the Lord said that el would save the city for the sake of the innocent people.

A wonderful conversation, a freeing conversation. There is nothing we need be afraid to say before the Lord.

* * *

So I continued to read, to think, to pray. And by the time our freighter holiday was over, I was so deep in Genesis that wherever I went I reached for whatever Bible, in whatever translation was available, and continued to read, to think, and to hope that what I read and thought would move me on into prayer.

* * *

After this remarkable conversation about the wicked inhabitants of Sodom and Gomorrah, God went along, and Abraham, having had his say about the innocent people, went home, and Jehovah left the two angels to complete the mission he'd given them. They left Mamre and went to Sodom, where Lot, Abraham's nephew was sitting at the city gate. He greeted the two angels, who were in the form of two beautiful young men, and after some persuasion on Lot's part they went to his house where he had a fine meal prepared for them, which they ate. Angels may be pure energy, but these angels made a point of eating so that people would understand that they were real (energy and matter are, we now understand, interchangeable; nevertheless this proof of reality for our sakes is amazing. And as the resurrected Christ made a point of eating fish and bread and drinking wine, so that his friends would know that he was real, even if they failed to recognize him by sight.

So the angels ate the meal Lot offered them. At bedtime all the men in the city, young and old, surrounded Lot's house and asked him to bring the two young men to them. According to the King James translation, the men of Sodom wanted to "know" the two young men, in the same sense that Adam "knew" Eve. The *Good News Bible*, which was the translation in my room when I came to this part of the story, puts it very bluntly. They wanted

to have sex with them.

Lot, of course, was horrified. It was his ingrained habit of hospitality which had caused him to ask the two young men home for a meal, nothing else.

He went outside and closed the door behind him. He said to them,

"Friends, I beg you, don't do such a wicked thing!"

The sacredness of hospitality, and of one's responsibility towards one's guests was far greater then than it is now. It is difficult for us to understand Lot's feeling of obligation towards these two strangers whom he felt he must protect at all costs. Of course, he didn't know that they were angels and well able to protect themselves; therefore he could not betray his sacred obligation. Even so, his response seems extreme. Lot offered the men of Sodom his two daughters, which may have been wily, rather than naive, under the circumstances, adding,

"But don't do anything with these men; they are guests in my house and I must protect them." But the men of Sodom said, "Get out of the way, you foreigner!"

Distrust of foreigners seems to be as old as the fear of great darkness, and probably came about because foreigners, if they were stronger than you, were apt to take your land and your wives and make you into slaves. However, Lot surely posed no threat to Sodom.

When the men of that city would have forced their way into Lot's house by breaking down the door, the two angels pulled Lot back into the house and shut the door. Then they struck all the men outside with blindness.

The two men said to Lot "If you have anyone else here, sons, daughters, sons-in-law or any other relatives living in the city, get them out of here, because we are going to destroy this place." ...

So Lot went to the men his daughters were engaged to and said, "Hurry up and get out of here! The Lord is going to destroy this place."

For by now he understood that the two men were angels.

Where were the ten just men for whom Abraham had begged the Lord to save the city? It seems that there were not even ten just men in that great city.

According to Hassidic tradition, there are always ten just men in the world (and once again I am using the word *men* in the generic, biblical sense of male and female). These ten just people do not know who they are. Only God knows. When one dies, the place is filled by another. So long as there are ten just men ...

But there were not ten just men in Sodom, and in the morning the angels took Lot,

his wife, and his two daughters, by the hand and led them out of the city. Then one of the angels said, "Run for your lives! Don't look back and don't stop in the valley. Run to the hills so that you won't be killed!"

God's people are ever argumentative. Lot thanked the angels for saving their lives, but argued that the hills were too far away.

"Do you see that little town? It is near enough. Let me go over there. You can see that it is just a small place. And I will be safe."

The angel answered, "All right, I agree. I won't destroy that town. Hurry! Run!"

And at last Lot ran. The sun was already beginning to rise when Lot reached the little town which was named

Zoar. Suddenly the Lord rained burning sulphur on the cities of Sodom and Gomorrah and destroyed them and the whole valley along with all the people there and everything that grew on the land. But Lot's wife looked back and was turned into a pillar of salt.

Sodom had been their home. It was a natural enough thing for her to want to take one last look. And if Lot hadn't argued with the angel, and so delayed their departure, she might have been all right.

In Pompeii one can see the petrified forms of people who had been caught in the grey ash of the volcano, perhaps also looking back for one last glimpse of home, and who were turned, not into salt, but into statues of volcanic rock.

Early the next morning Abraham hurried to the place where he had stood in the presence of the Lord. He looked down on Sodom and Gomorrah and the whole valley and saw smoke rising from the land, like smoke from a huge furnace.

The destruction of Sodom and Gomorrah, whatever caused it, sounds terrifyingly like the destruction which would be caused by atomic warfare.

At a dinner party I sat next to someone who works for the Army Corps of Engineers, and whose present job is planning the evacuation of New York city, and the feeding and housing of survivors, *after* the city has been hit by an atomic bomb. This person is receiving a government pay cheque for this effort in futility, and I could not help exploding, "The thing to do is to stop an atom bomb from falling on New York in the first place, not figure out how to feed and house people after they're dead, or dying of radiation sickness."

I still believe that atomic warfare can be prevented, as long as there are ten just men left in the world. As I continue to type out for my children some of the loveliness of their childhoods, trying to cull from my journals the delicate flowers from the overgrowth of rank weeds, and reliving the years of raising a family and struggling to write, I also live through the continuing series of past international crises. One spring back in the fifties when the serious news commentators did not think it likely that we would make it through the summer without hostilities breaking out between the Soviet Union and the United States, I walked down our dirt road picking pussy willows and wondering if this was the last time I would see the loveliness of spring trembling across the land. In school the children were taught how to hide under their desks, with their hands over their heads, and I was shocked at the folly of it, for how could the wood of a desk protect these little ones from even an ordinary bomb?

So I shudder when people link atomic destruction with the Parousia, the Second Coming. It seems to me that it trivializes Christ's Second Coming to assume that it involves this planet only, or could be caused by the folly of power-greedy man. If we take seriously that Christ was the Word who spoke creation into being, if we take seriously that

In the beginning was the Word, and the Word was with God, and the Word was God ... All things were made that was made –

all things, all of the galaxies with their countless trillions of solar systems – if we truly believe this, then the Second Coming is not for this planet alone. It is for all of creation.

When we concentrate on ourselves, on planet earth, we stumble into the old Greek flaw – a fatal one – of hubris. We play into the hands of Satan, and also of the various extreme sects which assume that they, and they alone, of all of God's creation, are to be saved. It is a presumptuous thing, and very seductive one, to decide that you and your group are the sheep destined for heaven, and all the rest, including Anglicans like me, are destined for hell fire.

My children and grandchildren have never known a world which was not under the shadow of the mushroom cloud. It is hard for them to realize that when I was a child there was no Pentagon. It is hard for me to realize that, too, as I look through those old journals, and decide that when I finish culling things for children and grandchildren they had better be burned.

If we continue our arrogant ways until we incinerate this planet, it will be we foolish creatures who are doing it, not God. We need to rid ourselves of the megalomania which focuses God's prime concern on this one minuscule part of creation. Not that we aren't important, we are. *All* of creation is important. If we blow ourselves up it will likely have negative effects on planets in distant galaxies.

Are we grown up enough to use the power we have discovered in the atom creatively instead of destructively? Are we capable of holding back on this use until we have learned how to dispose of atomic waste? And what about those containers of atomic waste which are already lying on the bottom of the ocean and which are beginning to rust, so that radiation is seeping out and spreading its contamination? We have discovered this incredible power at the heart of the atom, and we can't make it go away. And we, like Adam and Eve, are still out of synchronization. We know, with our intellects, much more than we can comprehend with our spirits. We are woefully, terrifyingly, out of balance.

I do believe in the Second Coming, the fulfillment of all things, but not that it is tied in with man's ability to turn the earth into a dead, dark satellite. I do not think that God collaborates with us creatures in destruction. That's Satans realm. God calls us to be co-creators with el. If we refuse this high calling, then we – in one way or another – destroy ourselves. Like the people of Sodom.

And what about those people of Sodom? Do I want even the most depraved sodomite to be destroyed forever?

There are crimes so vile that they are totally beyond my ability either to assess or to forgive. In ancient Hebrew times when someone was put outside the city walls it was because he had done something so terrible that the tribe could not punish it, and so the sinner was handed over to God. "This is beyond us, Lord. We're delivering him to you."

There is a club in New York, membership in which depends on the ability to find and produce a white man's testicles, and little boys are the easiest victims. I know about this only because it happened to someone we knew of. After my first murderous reaction, I realized that it is beyond anything I can understand or respond to. And the very perpetrators of this crime have had, or their ancestors have had, equally vile horrors done them by white men. Evil spawns evil.

A plague on both your houses! Mercutio cried. Outside the city walls! Only God can deal with this.

What can we human beings do with an Eichmann? Or the doctors in the concentration camps who made lampshades out of human skin, who turned children into soap?

There is *nothing* we could do which would be adequate punishment.

But what is punishment?

There is only one purpose for punishment, and that is to teach a lesson, and there is only one lesson to be taught, and that is love. Perfect love banishes fear and when we are not afraid we know that love which includes forgiveness. When the lesson to be learned is not love, that is not punishment, it is revenge, or retribution. Probably the lesson of love is the most terrible punishment of all – an almost intolerable anguish – for it means that the sinner has to realize what has been done, has to be truly sorry, to repent, to turn to God. And most of us are too filled with outrage at rape and murder to want the sinner to repent. We want the sinner to feel terrible, but not to turn to God, and be made whole and be forgiven. And so we show that we do not know the meaning of forgiveness, any more than Jonah did in his vindictive outrage at the people of Nineveh.

We are so familiar with the Parable of the Prodigal Son that we forget part of the message, and that is the response of the elder brother. As I read and reread Scripture it seems evident that God is far more loving than we are, and far more forgiving. We do not want God to forgive our enemies, but Scripture teaches us that all God wants is for us to repent, to say, "I'm sorry, Father. Forgive me," as the Prodigal Son does when he *comes to himself* and recognizes the extent of his folly and wrongdoing. And the father rejoices in his return.

Then there's the elder brother. We don't like to recognize ourselves in the elder brother who goes off and sulks because the father, so delighted at the return of the younger brother, prepares a great feast. Punishment? A party! Because the younger brother has learned the lesson he has, in a sense, already punished himself. But, like the elder brother, we're apt to think the father much too lenient.

When our children were little they used to do what I called "working up to a spanking." It usually took about two weeks, and quite a few warnings. One time our eldest child had worked herself up to a spanking and been given one, and that night she sat in her father's lap, twined her arms about his neck, and said, "Daddy, why is it I'm so much nicer after I've been spanked?"

Because it was a lesson of love, that's why. I did not spank my children when I was angry, when I was angry I was incapable of teaching that lesson of love. If I was really angry, I would say, "Go sit in your room until I have calmed down enough to talk with you. I don't want to talk while I'm angry."

And our younger daughter once asked me "Mother, are you mad *at* me, or mad *with* me?"

"I'm mad with you," I replied. She was right, there is a big difference.

So whatever punishment God gives us when we do wrong, it is to teach us a lesson of love. And, just as we do not enjoy punishing our children, God does not enjoy punishing us. But that hard lesson of love must be learned.

The Book of Common Prayer includes Manasseh's Song of Repentance:

O Lord and Ruler of the hosts of heaven
God of Abraham, Isaac, and Jacob,
and of all their righteous offspring:
You made the heavens and earth
with all their vast array.
All things quake with fear at your presence;
they tremble because of your power.

But merciful promise is beyond all measure;
it surpasses all that our minds can fathom.
O Lord, you are full of compassion,
long-suffering, and abounding in mercy.
You hold back your hand;
you do not punish as we deserve.
In your great goodness, Lord,
you have promised forgiveness to sinners,
that they may repent for their sin and be saved.
And now, O Lord, I bend the knee of my heart,
and make my appeal, sure of your gracious goodness.
I have sinned, O Lord, I have sinned,
and I know my wickedness only too well.
Therefore I make this prayer to you:
Forgive me, Lord, forgive me.
Do not let me perish in my sin,
nor condemn me to the depths of the earth.
for you, O Lord, are the God of those who repent,
and in me you will show forth your goodness.
Unworthy as I am, you will save me,
in accordance with your great mercy,
and I will praise you without ceasing all the
days of my life.
For all the powers of heaven sing your praises,
and yours is the glory to ages of ages. Amen.

How wonderful to know that God forgives us when we come to ourselves and understand whatever it is that we have done and ask for forgiveness. Perhaps it is the quality of repentance which counts, not the magnitude of the sin. I must bend the knee of my heart and beg God's forgiveness as fervently as did the Prodigal Son, though my sins may be far less flamboyant.

Perhaps the Sodomites had gone, in this life, beyond repentance. In any case, Lot probably felt that they got no more than their due.

But that's the elder brother syndrome. And it's a disease, a contagious disease.

So there's no avoiding my bumping headlong into the accusation of universalism.

And I am not, repeat, am *not* a universalist.

I used to think, when people worried about whether or not I am a universalist, that a universalist was someone who believes that Jesus is good, and Buddha is good, and Mohammed is good, and that all ways to Heaven are equal, and I wondered where on earth they had got this odd idea about me.

It took me nearly five years to figure this out. As far as I can gather, universalism means that all of a sudden, and for no particular reason, God is going to wave a magic wand, and say, "Okay, everybody, out of hell. Home free."

Now that I know what it means, I can, and do, reply, "No, I am certainly not a universalist. That plays trivially with free will." And about God's great and terrible gift of free will I feel very strongly indeed.

At one southern university one young man, who had asked the inevitable question, pushed me further. "But you do seem to indicate, in your writing, that you believe in God's forgiveness?"

That seemed to me an extraordinary question, considering that it came from a student in a Christian college.

Fortunately, he qualified it. "You seem to believe that ultimately God is going to forgive *everybody*?"

I said, "I don't believe that God is going to fail with el's creation. I don't worship a failing God. Do you want God to fail?"

He said, "But there has to be *absolute* justice."

"You're maybe nineteen or twenty years old. When you die, is that what you want – absolute justice? Don't you want the teeniest, weeniest bit of mercy? Me, I want lots and lots of mercy. Don't you feel that you're going to need any mercy at all?"

That had not occurred to him. So he started to quote Scripture. I stopped him. "I can quote Scripture, too. Let's start with Ezekiel. In the thirty-third chapter, the tenth verse, Ezekiel says:

"Son of man, say to the House of Israel, 'You are continually saying: Our sins and crimes weigh heavily on us; we are wasting away because of them. How are we to go on living?' Say to them, 'As I live – it is the Lord who speaks – I take pleasure, not in the death of a wicked man, but in the turning back of a wicked man who changes his ways to win life. Come back, come back from your evil ways. Why are you so anxious to die, House of Israel?'

"And you, son of man, say to the members of your nation, 'The integrity of an upright man will not save him once he has chosen to sin; the wickedness of a wicked man will no longer condemn him once he renounces his wickedness ... All his precious sins will no longer be remembered ...

"The members of your nation object: 'What the Lord does is unjust;' but it is what you do that is unjust. When an upright man renounces his integrity and commits sin, he dies for it. And when a wicked man renounces his wickedness and does what is lawful and right, because of this he lives."

These must have been comfortable words to Paul, who surely would not have done well when judged by men's standards of absolute justice. He had cheered on the stoning of Stephen, he had caused many Christians to be put to death. He had a great deal of blood on his hands. But he repented. He turned around completely, and served the Lord he had been denying and denouncing.

So I suggested to the young man that he go to Scripture, to Genesis 1, and read straight through to the end of John's revelation, and set down on a pad all that speaks of God's mercy and loving forgiveness versus all that shows el's anger and wrath, and see which came out most clearly. The sulkiness of the elder brother is pointed out to us again and again as being the opposite of God's loving forgiveness.

I don't know when or how it is going to happen, but don't give up on me: God is not finished with me yet. Nor with you. Nor – whether we like it or not, for we have hard hearts – the Sodomites. Nor any part of creation. For we are God's, a part of creation, a part of that which God made and called good. The story of Adam and Eve, and all the stories which follow, show us what we have done to that good, fouled and desecrated it; but that which God created is good, and, as John points out:

Anyone who fails to love can never have known God, because God is love. God's love for us was revealed when God sent the world his only Son so that we could have life through him; this is the love I mean: not our love for God, but God's love for us when he sent his Son to be the sacrifice that takes our sins away.

God's love is not easy for us elder brothers to accept. A party for the sinner! Horrors!

When I do something which is less than God expects of me I am miserable. Accepting that I have done wrong is excruciatingly painful. Often it is even more difficult for me to forgive myself than it is to accept God's forgiveness for me. My own acknowledgment of my wrongdoing is the most difficult punishment possible. Repentance is neither easy nor cheap. It hurts. It costs us all our pride and self-will. It means letting go completely and handing ourselves back to God. To hand

God our sins is far more difficult than any other kind of prayer and yet it is one of the most important parts of prayer. And when I can completely let it go, let God take it, and redeem it and transform it, then I, too, am ready for a party!

It is difficult to express a seriously thought-out point of view in an area where there are no final answers, without appearing to make a final answer, a definitive and lasting judgment. No one of us can read the mind of God. I know only that through a lifetime of reading and rereading Scripture I have come to believe that "mercy and truth have kissed each other" and that God's love is beyond our puny comprehension.

Job asked God the finite questions we all ask, and God replied,

Where were you when I laid the foundations of the earth? Tell me, if you understand it. Who measured it out, and stretched the line upon it? Where are the foundations of the earth? Who laid the cornerstone when the morning stars sang together and all God's children shouted for joy?

That was not the answer Job was looking for, but it was the answer God gave.

If eternal damnation is part of our mindset, it is far too easy to wonder if part of the joy of the saved in heaven is looking down on the tortures of the damned. How unlike the shepherd who left the ninety-nine saved sheep and went in search of the single one who was lost!

Most of the passages in the New Testament which imply eternal damnation (Dives and Lazarus, the wheat and the tares) are in parables, and parables are stories. Jesus often used hyperbole when he wanted to make a point. Are we to believe that someone actually had a plank of wood in his eyes, or that Jesus really recommended the dishonest wheeling and dealing of the unjust steward? Did he really expect a father to consider giving a scorpion instead of an egg to his child? "But if you, who are only a human father, are good to your children, how much more loving is the heavenly Father!"

Jesus did not speak in the language of proof, but in the language of story. We can neither prove nor disprove the existence of God. But if we examine human perception of God as it is revealed, bit by bit, through Scripture, the unqualified love of the Creator for creation and for all of us creatures is paramount. Is it unfair for me to equate the mind that looks for porn with the mind that looks for damnation? I'd much rather look for wonder and salvation! Is Gandhi to be excluded from heaven because he never made a formal commitment to Christ? Gandhi, who was thrown out of a Christian church because his skin was not the "right" color? We have much to answer for, we Christians, and excluding part of God's family from God's church is a big problem. How do we solve it?

Jesus walked and talked with those who, like Gandhi, were considered not quite good enough for the establishment of his day: the Samaritans, the wretchedly poor and ill, fallen women, lepers. It was of such "disqualified" people that Jesus said, "I have come not to heal those who are well, but those who are ill."

I am a flawed human being in need of this healing. I dread to think what I would be like if I felt much more saved than other people (often people far better than I, but who have not accepted Christ), that I could think I had a greater right to heaven than they. And those who are worse. I have never raped, murdered, committed adultery, the more spectacular sins. I think of God's words to Job, to Jonah. I think of the Good Shepherd who cannot rest until he has found the one lost sheep. I think of the Prodigal Son who ultimately repented of his folly, of his own free will. Perhaps he repented only because he was starving and thought of all the food his father's servants had to eat, but repent he did, and his father threw a party, and his elder brother stamped his foot and sulked because this repentant sinner was admitted to heaven.

Knowing that we cannot define God, why do we try to put limits on el? How can we limit el's love? It is we who are limited, not God. I cannot believe that God's unlimited love (and that limitlessness is shown in the incarnation), will not outlast all our rebellion and anger and independence and brutality and indifference and hubris and all that keeps us from turning to him.

I suggest Jonah as bedtime reading every night for a month or so. Jonah doesn't want God to save the enemy, the Ninevites, who aren't on "our side," even if they repent of their sins. And God reminds Jonah that Jonah spared a worm, so why should el not spare the Ninevites who do not know their left hand from their right, and also much cattle?

* * *

After the destruction of Sodom nobody is ready for a party. The scene is grim indeed. And then follows a passage so shocking it is often deleted, for public reading. Lot and his daughters

moved up into the hills and lived in a cave. The elder daughter said to her sister, "Our father is getting old, and there are no men in the whole world to marry us so that we can have children. Come on, let's make our father drunk, so that we can sleep with him and have children by him."

That's the *Good News Bible.* The *King James Version* has it: *Come, let us make our father drink wine, and we will lie with him, that we may preserve the seed of our father.*

"Preserving the seed" is closer to the intent of the thinking of the time. At moments of devastation the old taboos break down. The instinct for survival, for the propagation of the species, is stronger than the taboo. In our generation we remember the plane which crashed in the snow, high up in the Andes; the starving survivors ultimately had to eat the bodies of their dead companions to avoid starvation. Again, under such extreme circumstances the taboo no longer held.

So

That night Lot's daughters gave him wine to drink, and the older daughter had intercourse with him. But he was so drunk that he didn't know it.

I was in Covington, Louisiana, while I was reading about Lot and meditating upon his story, so I'll stay with the Bible in my room there, the *Good News Bible*, for a while.

The next day the elder daughter said to her sister, "I slept with him last night. Now let's make him drunk again tonight, and you sleep with him, Then each of us will have a child by our father."

Pragmatic, practical young women, like their great-uncle Abraham. They both had sons, who became the ancestors of the Moabites and the Ammonites, and we remember the Moabites because of the story of Ruth, who was from Moab, and through whom Jesus' genealogy is traced.

But where are the Moabites now? War. Holocaust. Genocide. What has happened to the Moabites and the Ammonites, the Hittites and the Amalakites? Gone, gone without a trace, a sad reminder that throughout earth's history civilizations rise and fall. Ozymandias is an example of the consequence of human pride.

* * *

One of the most fascinating aspects of reading the Old Testament is to see the perception of God changing throughout the ages, so that the Abba to whom Jesus prayed is seen as different from the tribal god who helped Israel's kings destroy entire nations and peoples in order to give the land to the Israelites. (Are *most* wars over land boundaries?)

God's anger with David for not killing *everybody* has always bothered me, and the explanation that it was necessary to keep the children of Israel from worshiping the gods of the enemy has never seemed quite satisfactory. Then I remember that people were then, as now, struggling with finite minds to comprehend an infinite God. Anything we can say about God is going to be inadequate, a groping for truths beyond our limited capacities.

And (paradox again) I believe in the Bible as the living Word of God. But this faith involves an acceptance that the Bible is not static, that at different times the living Word can speak in different ways to different ears, and that even the Bible itself can never fully express or manifest the glory of the Creator. That does not make it any less the living Word. It is because it lives that it moves.

Listen: this is the song of the great prophet, Moses:

The Lord is a mighty warrior;
The chariots of Pharaoh and his army has he hurled into the sea; the finest of those who bear armor have been drowned in the Red Sea.

The fathomless deep had overwhelmed them; they sank into the depths like a stone.
Your right hand, O Lord, is glorious in might; your right hand, O Lord, has overthrown the enemy.
You stretch forth your right hand; the earth swallowed them up.

"Is that vengeful God the Lord whom Jesus called Abba, and was faithful to?" I was asked.

Well, the song of triumph over the death of enemies, the praise to the Lord for killing our oppressors, upset even the oppressed, the children of Israel who were so ill-treated by Pharaoh and the Egyptians.

And, as usual, when something is beyond us, we try to look for understanding in story. This one comes, I think, out of the Hassidic tradition, but it says everything that needs to be said about the Song of Moses:

The Israelites flee Egypt, and the waters of the Red Sea open, and they go through on dry land, and are safe on the other side. The Egyptians in their chariots pursue them, and dash into the open path where the waters have rolled back, and as soon as they are all in the sea, the waters close over them, and they all drown.

And in heaven, joyful at the narrow escape of the Jewish people, the angels start to sing. And God stops them, saying:

"How can you sing when my children are dying?"

* * *

We must try to keep our receivers tuned finely so that we will not drown out revelation with static, and thus set our perception of God in concrete, unable to change.

The revelation given me when the words, "My religion is subject to change without notice," came unbidden from my lips, was not trivial. For this openness is what we should practice, with religion as well as science. Abraham and Sarah lived with this childlike ability to change, to leave the known, to go out into the wilderness, and God didn't give them much notice.

The discoveries of the quantum physicists have done nothing to change the nature of the universe, but they have changed, radically, our way of perceiving the universe.

There is nothing static. We change each other simply by observing each other. We are all part of something far greater than we can begin to comprehend, and to be part of the changing melody and the complexity of the dance is part of our vocation as co-creators.

In both Old and New Testaments, the institution of slavery is taken for granted. Now we could consider it intolerable in God's eyes, so far has our perception of God changed. We have moved from seeing God as one who favors one part of creation over the rest of it, to a God who is Lord of all.

In this century we are moving from an impassible God who cannot suffer to an Abba who shares all our pain with us, who hurts when we hurt, who not only notes but sees the fall of every sparrow. And who steadily and gently guides us to a wider understanding of love.

As our love for our Maker grows, so does our love for each other. In our society we can no longer tolerate having indentured servants. The idea of the "white man's burden" seems arrogant and self-serving, though there are still many who treat people of other races not only as inferiors, but as less important in God's eyes than they themselves are. We know that greed makes the skies and the seas more polluted than they need be, though we know how to clean up our wastes, since we have brought a dead Great Lake and the great Hudson River back to life. Why do things have to reach a desperate state before we do anything about them? In many ways we are as inturned and shortsighted as the captains and crews of the great whaling ships, though we see the wrong they did better than we see our own wrongdoing. We can guess that later generations will see our sins more clearly than they see their own. We all get trapped in chronology.

But in God's time, in kairos, all is *now*, is present. Part of the joy of silence, of meditation and contemplation, is to touch on this is-ness. In God's mind, nothing is lost. All acts of love are eternally present. And all that is not love can be redeemed and changed by that Love which created all.

* * *

Sometimes we human beings are allowed to touch on kairos.

While I was in Covington, reading the story of Lot, then moving on to Abraham and Sarah and Isaac, I was given one of these revelations of divine love. It came in a dream, the kind I call a Special Dream.

There are, by and large, three kinds of dreams. There is the dream which is easy to translate, which comes from something we have eaten, or some recent event. Then there is the regular dream, which is more difficult to understand. Dreams do have messages for us, which we do well to take seriously, but I don't want to get faddish about them. If I wake from a dream in the night and think it may have something to say to me, I ask my subconscious mind to surface it for me in the morning, and it usually does.

The Special Dream is different. It, like prayer, is a gift.

The retreat center at Covington is part of a much larger

complex. There is a seminary, a school, a church. As I was being driven through the grounds to the retreat center I could see that a service was about to begin at the church, for a large group of people of all ages was going up the steps and through the doors. And I was told that it was a funeral for a high school senior who had died in an inexplicable automobile accident, her car had been found slammed into a tree. As so often seems to be the case when someone dies young, she had been a popular and happy girl, with an excellent academic record, expected to be able to get into any college to which she applied. No one knew what had happened to make her car go out of control. And she was an only child.

A chill shadow was cast over the day.

Then I was being shown through the beautiful retreat center, the retreatants began to arrive, I joyfully met old friends, was introduced to new. Because I was fully in each present moment of the retreat, everything else faded.

At the end of the evening I went gratefully to bed, read for a few minutes, and went to sleep. Perhaps I had been thinking about God taking Abraham out at night and showing him the stars. I slept, and I dreamed. A Special Dream. Many such dreams are golden. This one was diamond.

It was a gorgeous night, and I was outside with many of the people who were on the retreat. I was joyfully looking at the stars which were clustered far more densely than usual, in brilliant, intricate patterns. Suddenly, in the east, there was a child of light, of dazzling light, and all the stars began to dance about the child in joy. And we were part of that joy.

That was the dream. I didn't remember it on first waking, but something brought it flashing up to my conscious mind. And I realized that I had been given the gift of a resurrection dream.

And I knew that the girl who had died was part of that glory and part of that joy. For the brief moments of a sleeping dream I had been caught up in that love which is eternal and knows no restrictions of time.

God is omnipotent. All time is in el's hand. Past, present, future.

So what (the question asks itself once again) does that do to our free will?

And again the astrophysicist, rather than the theologian (though I am well aware that there are many poor astrophysicists, just as there are many poor theologians) comes to my rescue. As God created time to be free, so el created us to be free. As we are capable of change, so is time. What we do is going to make a difference to the future, may change the future. And here we come to an astrophysical theory which is so extraordinary it is hardly conceivable: what we do may change not only the future; it is possible that it may change the past.

How? Well, there are many theories, such as alternate universes and time warps. But that time is free, past time as well as future, is being put forth as a serious theory, and it is the theory behind *A Swiftly Tilting Planet*.

Possibly I am reading more theology into astrophysics than the scientists intend, but if there is no dichotomy between sacred and secular, then everything is theological, from a solitary hot soak in the tub to the dance of the galaxies to the changing of a diaper. The new theories of time certainly leave us with more questions than answers; but allowing ourselves to move from question to question, knowing that in this life we are not likely to find all the definitive answers, is part of prayer.

10

Impossibilities That Happen

IN OUR DAILY READING of Scripture, when we move from reading to thinking and, if the gift is given, from thinking to praying, it is not surprising, nor is it bad that we often find ourselves far from the original verses which have triggered our thoughts.

Surely Sarah prayed for a child. Perhaps she argued with God, cried out to el in anguish and anger. Why was Hagar able to conceive when Sarah was not? Why was Hagar's response smugness and pride with herself, and scorn towards Sarah?

Perhaps Sarah even tried to bargain with God. Is that not one of the first things the tempter taught us? And one of the saddest?

But what were her prayers all about? Did God even hear them? And, if el heard, why did el not heed them? Why was the answer always *no*?

And then, of course, came the miracle.

And I think of some of the miracles of my own life.

Many happenings in my life are beyond reasonable understanding. But that they happened there is no doubt. One of the most amazing and the most glorious has to do with prayer, my prayer, bad prayer. At least, it was the kind of prayer I had been taught to believe was bad. If I learned nothing else in those Anglican boarding schools, I did learn that we are never, ever, to say, "This isn't fair. This shouldn't have happened to me." Especially, most especially, we are not to say this to God. Not ever. No matter what.

When my children complained, "It's not fair," I told them that nobody had promised them life was going to be fair. And I thought that I, myself, had learned this lesson.

One spring I had some complicated eye surgery, done by my marvelous ophthalmologist. I also had some nasty foot surgery. Each of these operations would have meant three months out of my life, and as I could not see taking six months off, I talked the doctors into doing the foot surgery first, and ten days later, the eye surgery. Preferably a short time of intense unpleasantness than dragging it out, I thought.

I went home from the hospital with everything going well, pins sticking out of the toes of my right foot, and a patch on my right eye which I was to take off when I bathed.

After I'd been home about two weeks, we went to the ballet to see our ballet-dancing son, a young man who had become part of our family a few years earlier. We went out to dinner first; the ballet was beautiful, and it was a happy evening. We went home and started getting ready for bed.

Because of the pins still sticking out of my toes, I had to get into the bathtub bottom first, the right leg hanging out of the side of the tub. (Fortunately we have a right-legged tub.)

While I was bathing, the phone rang. Hugh was in the shower down the hall, and I knew that he couldn't hear it.

But when the phone rings at eleven-thirty at night, we answer it. There have been enough accidents and unexpected crises in our family so that I never just let a phone go on ringing. With some effort I heaved myself out of the tub and limped toward the phone. It stopped, after only three rings, so I knew it was not one of our children. They would have let it go on ringing.

I turned back to the bathroom. Perhaps because I was wet and slippery, I slipped and fell, hitting my eye, right on the wound, on the corner of a chest.

I kept saying, childishly, "Don't let anything have happened. Don't let me have hurt my eye. Don't let anything be wrong."

But the world which, day by day, had been slowly coming back into view, had disappeared into a yellow fog.

Hugh came out of the shower and I told him what had happened. (All this in the space of a shower!) He called my doctor, who told us to get to the emergency room at St. Luke's, fast. We dressed hurriedly, and took a taxi to the hospital. The emergency room of a city hospital is a lot like hell. Out of a loud speaker rock music was blaring. This may have been comforting to some people, it made me ready to scream my way up the walls.

And Hugh was surrounded, by both patients and nurses. Everybody wanted Dr. Tyler's autograph. At any other time I would have thought it was funny, but being very aware of the grave damage to my eye, and being very, very frightened, I wanted to get to the ophthalmological department *as soon as possible.*

Nothing happens quickly in an emergency room unless you are spouting blood. Having "Dr. Tyler" with me did help, because he was able to cut through some of the red tape as though he were a "real" doctor, not simply one out of a soap opera.

By the time that my eye was examined, the pressure in the eyeball had dropped to zero, meaning that the eye could collapse at any moment. This was further complicated by the fact that the eye was hemorrhaging internally. The doctor was honest with me, I was admitted to the hospital and prepped for an operation in the morning which I knew well might mean the removal of the eye.

It was the early hours of the morning by the time I was left alone. I had been given a sleeping pill which was supposed to knock out an elephant. It might as well have been a bread crumb, I was so wide awake, and so very aware of the seriousness of the situation, and my adrenalin was pumping full force. I tried to lie quietly, to pray quietly. I was grateful to the night nurse for her gentle concern. I tried to offer everything to God, not to be frightened.

And suddenly I heard myself saying in a loud voice, "Lord, have I ever, in all these years, have I ever once said: This isn't fair? Have I ever once said: This shouldn't have happened to me? You know I haven't. Well, now I'm saying it!"

After that outburst I was able to lie quietly, to rest on the strong lifeline of the Jesus Prayer for the rest of the seemingly endless night.

In the morning when the doctor came, the pressure in the eyeball was up to normal. Half of the hemorrhage had already absorbed. And this simply is not possible. But it happened.

My doctor said with amazement, "You're all right, and I'm going to send you home, but just in case, I want you to lie flat on your back for ten days."

At that time I was working on the final revisions of *Walking on Water*, and Hugh called Harold and Luci Shaw to tell them what had happened, and to warn them that there would be a ten-day delay. Immediately, Luci called me back.

"Madeleine," she said, "I feel strongly that this was demonic interference."

The idea of demonic interference has not been part of the Episcopal tradition for a long time, though once again the possibility of it is being recognized. And I remembered that when I had been teaching at a writers' conference in Nashville, Tennessee, a lovely young woman I had never seen before came up to me and said earnestly "Madeleine, I want you to know that I pray for you every day. Your work has made you vulnerable to attack and you need protection." I lay there, flat on my back, and it seemed to me likely that the protection had somehow slipped, but then the angels came in and drove out the demon and undid his mischief. It is as reasonable an explanation as any.

When I went to the doctor to be checked, the eyeball pressure was still normal, and the hemorrhage had completely absorbed. That quickly? Not possible. But it happened.

Now every morning I put in my contact lenses and the world comes into view and I cry out, "Miracle!" and "Thank You!" There has yet to come a morning when I've taken restored sight for granted, and I doubt if there ever will, for the difference between seeing a vague, general blur, and seeing is not only quantitative but qualitative. Daily it is miracle, and awe, and joy.

I am grateful to the young woman in Nashville for her prayers of protection, and for the prayers of many others, for it is my firm conviction that it is these loving prayers which have kept me seeing and which go on keeping me seeing.

And the miracle of prayer is daily as fresh as the first daffodil in spring.

As to the phone call which was the superficial cause of all this: it was to tell me that *A Swiftly Tilting Planet* had won one of the National Book Awards.

* * *

A sensitive question was asked me. "In regard to intercessory prayer, if one prays for healing for someone, and the healing occurs, can we conclude that the healing would not have occurred had the prayer not been offered?"

Again, there is no easy answer, for if the healing would have occurred anyhow, why pray?

So we approach the mystery of intercessory prayer. George MacDonald answers one question with another: "And why should the good of anyone depend on the prayer of another? I can only answer with the return question. 'Why should my love be powerless to help another?' "

It is a beautiful question, and I believe that our love is never powerless to help. Thinking is powerful, and prayer is highly focused thinking, and it can be offered for good, and, alas, it can also be used for evil. The stories told about practitioners of the dark arts hurting and even killing people by the power of thought are not figments of the imagination, such things happen. But if the power of darkness is strong, the power of light is even stronger. In the physical world, the laser is a demonstration of the power of light. Love is power, and loving prayer is one of the greatest powers in the world.

As I was typing this page, the mail was put on my desk, and one of the letters was from a woman who questioned the prayers which are answered with a *No*, or, what is almost worse, with a hollow, echoing silence. I have had a great many *Yes* answers to prayers, but I have also had a great many *Noes*, including a decade-plus of my life which seemed to be nothing but *Noes*. I don't have any cut-and-dried answers to this. If I did, I could probably make a fortune as a psychologist.

The Book of Job is a struggle to understand this question: Why do terrible things happen to good people? Is it their "fault"? Is it part of something so great that we cannot understand it, or even our tiny role in the great drama? I have a friend who is a brilliant singer, and yet one event after another has kept her career from flourishing. Why? I have no answers. Only an offer of hope, of a tiny little flickering light of hope that cannot be extinguished no matter how many *Noes* we receive.

We do not like it that our love is often powerless to help in the way that we would wish. Sometimes our prayers for curing are answered with a Yes, sometimes with a No, and in the end, death comes for all of us. As I write this, a close friend of my own age is dying in great pain, dying of cancer. My love is powerless to save her life. But it is able to enter her suffering, as Jesus entered the suffering of all human creatures. It is not powerless to be part of the journey we all must take, from this known life into the unknown life of resurrection.

If our calling is to be co-creators, isn't the healing of all the brokenness and sorrow of the world part of that co-creating? Do we sometimes help in this great vocation in our dying as well as in our living?

George MacDonald writes:

" 'O God' I said, and that was all. But what are the prayers of the whole universe more than the expression of that one cry? ... He who seeks the Father more than anything He can give is likely to have what he asks, for he is not likely to ask amiss."

O God!

Lord Jesus Christ have mercy on me becomes more and more my deepest prayer, and the form in which I couch my intercessory prayer, and the *me* is never myself alone, for I, like quanta, cannot live in isolation, but only in relation to all others, to the Other.

We live not within ourselves but within God. In God we live and move and have our being. This is indeed mystery, but one which Jesus illuminated for us when he told the disciples to remember him when they broke bread and when they drank wine. Re-member. Make anew these members. Can these dry bones live again?

From Luke's gospel:

He took bread, and gave thanks, and brake it, and gave unto them saying, This is my body which is given for you: this do in remembrance of me. Likewise also the cup after supper, saying, This cup is the new testament in my blood, which is shed for you.

In God we live and move and have our being. God within us that we may be part of God, God's beauty our beauty, that we may be God's beauty. This is not magic. It is part of the miracle of the total unity of the universe.

Thomas Aquinas writes:

"The eucharistic food, instead of being transformed into the one who takes it, transforms him unto itself. It follows that the proper effect of the Sacrament is to transform us so much into Christ, that we can truly say: 'I live, now not I, but Christ liveth in me.' "

This is as gloriously true for those who view Communion as no more than a memorial service as for those who believe in the "real presence" in the transformed bread and wine. Transformed? Not into the actual corporeal body and blood of the dead Jew, Jesus of Nazareth, but into the risen body of the living Christ.

Lord Jesus Christ have mercy on me. May I be you. And you be me. May I be myself and my dying friend. Myself and my living friend, living in the new life of the risen Christ. May Christ have mercy on me and be in me as I grieve for my friend, for my parents, lovers, acquaintances, strangers dying in famine and flood and drought, all of creation groaning in travail until the redemption of all things, until the coming of the kingdom.

I learn my lessons slowly, seldom once for all. Continually they have to be learned and relearned, not with solemnity, but with awe and laughter and joy.

Grandfather George again: "It is the heart that is not yet sure of its God that is afraid to laugh in his presence." And William Temple: "It is a great mistake to think that God is only or chiefly interested in religion."

So I learn with laughter, sometimes rueful laughter, as the Spirit teaches me with a sense of humor I have not always appreciated. But the wind blows where it will, and the Spirit moves how and where and as the holy Wind chooses.

* * *

I, like most people, tend to make specific demands of God, not thinking them all the way through. And making specific demands thoughtfully is not a bad idea, for if we think seriously about what we are demanding, we may find out that it is not, in fact, something we want to ask for. Or we discover perhaps, that we do not want to ask it as unequivocally as we thought we did. Or, we may end up wanting simply, in our cloud of unknowing, to turn it over to God.

But sometimes – too often – we don't stop to think.

Because of faulty depth perception I have taken more than my share of falls, crashing down steps I have not seen. I have finally convinced my husband that when we are on vacation, in strange terrain, it is wise for him to walk slightly ahead of me, with me following a step behind, like a good Middle Eastern wife. If I see him going up, I know that I must step up. If he goes down, I know that I must step down. Often his hand comes out to warn, to guide me. But before this pattern was established, before he was convinced of the wisdom of what might superficially be considered discourtesy, there were two vacations in a row in which I had bad falls, damaging my psyche as well as my body, and losing a week of our vacation with bruises and pulled muscles and a body outraged at such violence.

The following year our vacation was on a freighter which left from Brooklyn and went to the great ports of Philadelphia, Baltimore and Newport News, and was then to head out into the Caribbean, we were to fly home after having traversed the Panama Canal. The first days of the trip were cold and rainy, but marvelously relaxing. There was nothing we had to do, nowhere we had to be. It was total release from dailiness. On the first warm, sunny day I was sitting in a deck chair, writing, minding my own business, when the first sign of a sudden squall made the little ship lurch violently and the deck chair, with me in it, was flung across the deck. I put out my arm to break the fall, and spent the rest of the trip with my arm in a cast.

I was very angry, and totally unamused when I seemed to hear gentle laughter, and the words, *"But you didn't fall!"* The following winter I left New York for a week of lecturing, first at Mundelein, then at Wheaton, then on to the Episcopal Diocese of Idaho – a very ecumenical jaunt.

As I was being driven from Mundelein to Wheaton, I felt a tightening in my throat, a hoarseness in my voice. All the signs said that I was coming down with a heavy laryngeal cold. "Please," I prayed, "I have eleven more lectures to give. Please, please don't let me get laryngitis." That evening I was a guest of honor at a small dinner party at Harold and Luci Shaw's. I had a wonderful time despite the fact that I definitely did not feel well. I went to the Lorentzens for the night, asked for a glass of orange juice for my throat, and went to bed, with apologies. The next day I felt miserable, but managed to get through the various assignments on my schedule.

That night I had to cut short my evening lecture. I was, fortunately, close to the end, when I realized that if I did not sit down I was going to faint. And when I wound down, rapidly, and sat down, I realized that I had to get to the bathroom, quickly. There was no way I was going to be able to attend the evening reception which had been planned to follow the lecture. I was driven back to the Lorentzens where I spent an exhausting night, rushing to the bathroom every few minutes. By morning I was expelling burning hot, clear fluid. It was, in fact, the worst attack of intestinal flu I had ever had.

But my voice was fine.

I was anything but amused by this turn of events. I said to myself, "If I was at home I'd go to bed for a week, and instead I have to go to Idaho."

I managed to give the Wheaton College chapel talk in the morning. Then Luci and two of my other friends drove me to O'Hare airport, broke all rules and carried my bags, and almost carried me, onto the plane where they prayed for me, with the laying on of hands. I'd never have made it otherwise. And only their sustaining prayers and amazing grace got me to Salt Lake City, where I had to change planes, and on to Idaho.

How should I have prayed? Are we never to ask for specifics? Of course we are. That is how we find out whether or not our prayers are appropriate. We may always begin our prayers like the small child with the Christmas list. Only after we have gone through the "gimme" prayers can we let them go and move on to true prayer.

Jesus asked for specifics. In the Garden of Gethsemane he begged, with anguish, to be spared the horror of crucifixion. According to Mark:

My soul is exceeding sorrowful until death: tarry here, and watch. And he went forward a little, and fell on the ground, and prayed that, if it were possible, the hour might pass from him. And he said, Abba, Father, all things are possible with you; take away this cup from me: nevertheless not what I will, but what you will.

And St. Luke adds:

And there appeared in angel from heaven, strengthening him.

Yet, despite the comfort of the angel,

being in agony he prayed more earnestly; and his sweat was as it were great drops of blood falling down to the ground.

What is true of the great things is also true of the little things (are galaxies larger than quanta?). It is all right for us to pray for the continuing full quality of life for those we love when they are ill. Sometimes it is given, sometimes it is not.

It is more than all right for my friends to continue to pray for my eyesight, and I accept this miracle with untellable joy, knowing also that at some time in the near or distant future this exterior vision may be taken from me. It is all right for me to pray for the small, silly things – Do not let me fall, Do not let me get laryngitis – as long as I hand the prayer, no matter how minor, no matter how foolish, to God. Your way, Lord, not mine.

Does Satan interfere in our prayer? Tempt us to plea-bargain, to try to manipulate? Or, more frightening, does he work for bodily death, for blindness, for self-centeredness? Probably. Satan does have tremendous power in this world. I cannot contradict Scripture. But his power is only temporal; it is not eternal. It may slow down the coming of the kingdom, but it cannot prevent its ultimate arrival. He may cause cancer and fire and obscenity and terrorism, but he cannot do so beyond a point. Love is always greater than hate, has more power than hate. The name of Jesus does make Satan shudder. The cross has the power of life over death. God's mercy is stronger than Satan's vindictiveness.

I doubt if I will ever unravel the mystery of intercessory prayer, for myself, for others. I know that there are powers of healing that Jesus tried to teach the disciples, and us, to tap. But the disciples could not throw out the unclean spirit from the possessed boy because their faith was not sufficient. If we had faith, we could indeed move mountains. And I learn faith, I deepen my faith, not only by exercising it but by reading Scripture, and contemplating the mighty acts of God. And perhaps most of all by being near people of faith, for faith is beautifully contagious.

I know that God does not want us to be ill, that el wants us to be whole. But sometimes our prayers for the cure of an illness belong to a transient, rather than an eternal wholeness. We are trapped in the now and cannot see the eternal picture. For God's good reason, Paul's "thorn in the flesh," which he begged the Lord to take away, was of more use in God's purposes than would have been his curing. I do not know why my friend is dying young, and in pain, but my faith is nothing if I do not believe that in kairos, in God's time, she will be made whole, and that even now she can be used by God – as, indeed, she has been, during this illness, as a witness to gallantry, laughter, and joy. But ultimately God's will for her is wholeness, and I do not have to know how or when or where God's purpose for her, and for us, will be achieved.

Sometimes when I have not understood why God has not answered my prayer *my* way, it has been made clear to me later. Sometimes when it has seemed that my way has been done, I have learned later that it was not the best way. I am gradually learning to turn everything over to God, sometimes grudgingly, often argumentatively (like my favorite Old Testament characters), but I am still learning.

11

A Fountain in the Desert

WE TEND TO SKIP over or disparage parts of Scripture, such as Abraham's passing Sarah off as his sister, or Lot's daughters sleeping with their father, because such distasteful events arose out of cultures vastly different from our own. We have damaged each other and ourselves in the name of Christ in our contempt for and ill-treatment of Indians and Africans and Asians; because they, too, have cultures different from our own, we are suspicious of them. Like the people of Sodom, who called Lot a foreigner, we assume that because foreigners are not "us" they are therefore not as good as we are.

F. S. C. Northrup in *The Meeting of East and West* writes:

Nothing is more evil and tragically devastating in actual consequence than one's own moral and religious ideals, fine as they may be, when they are accompanied by ignorance and resultant provincialism and blindness with respect to people and cultures different from one's own.

A careful and steady reading of Scripture helps free us from this insularism. Jesus spoke and ate not only with sinners, but with foreigners, with "them" – with Samaritans, who were looked down on with contempt by the good, middleclass people of his day, with a Syro-Phoenician woman, with the Roman enemy. He made it clear that people who are different are not therefore inferior. He knocked all our race and class distinctions to smithereens.

So. Lot and his daughters were saved from the destruction of Sodom and Gomorrah, and Abraham moved from Mamre to Gerar, and once again tried to pass Sarah off as his sister, this time to King Abimelech. But God warned the king in a dream not to touch her. Abimelech heeded the dream, and was, to put it mildly, annoyed at Abraham for his deception. Then,

The Lord blessed Sarah, as he had promised, and she became pregnant, and bore a son to Abraham when he was old.

With man such a thing is impossible. With God nothing is impossible. Sarah's prayers were answered, not in human time, but in God's time.

The boy was born at the time when God said he would be born. Abraham named him Isaac, and when Isaac was eight days old Abraham circumcised him. . . Abraham was a hundred years old when Isaac was born. Sarah said, "God has brought me joy and laughter."

Now she could acknowledge her laughter, could revel in it and share it and rejoice in it. She said,

"Everyone who hears about it will laugh with me... Who would have said to Abraham that Sarah would nurse children? Yet I have borne him a son in his old age."

I think often about Sarah's prayer, answered not in human time, but in God's time. In a way, the very outrageousness of the time in which Sarah conceived and gave birth is a reemphasis of the truth that God is not restricted by time;

The child grew, and on the day that he was weaned, Abraham gave a great feast.

How fathers love to give parties for their children! We can almost think of those first mighty acts of creation as the grandest party ever thrown, and ever since, God has thrown a party whenever possible.

And of course, as with anything good, Satan and the fallen creatures he has gathered around him, angelic and human, move in and distort the good, so we get the excesses of cocktail parties and sex orgies, parties which are not parties at all in the real sense of the word. How lovely real parties are! Every time one of the children has been away and comes home we have a party, candles on the table, and flowers, and maybe presents, and meals cooked with loving care, even if it's mostly vegetables from the garden. A party is a celebration of love, just as a punishment is a lesson of love.

* * *

One day Sarah saw Isaac playing with Ishmael, the son of Hagar – Hagar who had scorned Sarah's barrenness – Laughter playing with Bitterness. And Sarah still had bitterness over Hagar's scorn lodged like a splinter of ice deep in her heart, and when she saw the two boys playing together she was afraid.

So she went to Abraham and asked him to send Hagar and Ishmael away, so that Ishmael would not inherit anything that Sarah felt belonged rightfully to Isaac.

Abraham was troubled. Ishmael was his son, too. But God informed him that it was all right to do what Sarah had asked; el would take care of Ishmael. So Abraham gave Hagar

some food and a leather bag full of water. He put the child on her back and sent her away. She left and wandered about in the wilderness of Beersheba. When the water was all gone she left the child under a bush and ... said, "I can't bear to see my child die." And she began to cry.

So did her son.

God heard the boy crying, and from heaven the angel of the Lord spoke to Hagar: "What are you troubled about, Hagar? Don't be afraid.'

Don't be afraid! How often the Lord's angels start their conversations with us this way: Don't be afraid! Don't be afraid, the angel Gabriel said to Zacharias and later to the fourteen-year-old Mary. Don't be afraid, an angel told the shepherds on the hill outside Bethlehem.

We need this reassurance. Even for those of us who believe implicitly in angels, to be confronted by one is an awesome thing.

So the angel reassured Hagar and continued,

"God has heard the boy crying. Get up, and go pick him up, and comfort him. I will make a great nation out of his descendants." Then God opened Hagar's eyes, and she saw a well

where no well had been before. "Why are you troubled? Don't be afraid, " God's angel reminds us over and over again. "Let not your heart be troubled. You believe in me. It will be all right," Jesus told his anxious friends. *What* will be all right? If I put my arms around you and comfort you and say, "Let not your heart be troubled, it will be all right," what am I promising?

In the world's terms, nothing. In the world's terms I am being a lie and a cheat to give such empty comfort. There are miracles, indubitably. But there are other times when the answer is No, or silence. When we put our arms around someone to give comfort, we cannot bring the dead back to life, or keep the spouse from walking out in favor of someone else, or stop the course of debilitating illness. We cannot prevent flood or drought or war. So what does the promise that "it will be all right" mean? *What* will be all right?

God's purpose. God's purpose for us and for all of creation. In God's time. In kairos. El did not prevent Abraham from sending Hagar and Ishmael into the wilderness. And Hagar had no way of knowing that many generations later, when Joseph's brothers would sell him to some merchants, those same merchants would be descendants of Ishmael.

God's purpose. God's plan. The Great Dance, the ancient harmonies, weaving and interweaving to make the pattern perfect. Often it is difficult to see that there is any pattern. We are too small to see the richness of the whole. But all of creation is pattern, from the Great Dance of the galaxies to the equally Great Dance of the submicroscopic, subatomic particles, existing only because they are dancing together. Satan tried to make dissonances, to interrupt the rhythm, to distort the pattern. One of his most successful ploys is to make us believe that his distortions of the original good have destroyed that good. But they have not. It is only the distortions we must fear and shun, never the original good itself, kything, singing and dancing, loving.

God created, and saw that it was good. In the beginning was the Word, the Word which is the Light that the darkness can neither snuff out nor comprehend.

The Lord told Abraham that it was all right to give in to Sarah's fears and emotional wounds and send Hagar and Ishmael away, and then this God of creation produced a well where there had been no well before. The skeptic might say, "The well was underground all the time and just happened to break surface at that moment." But did not God choose to have the waters break surface at that moment? As he chose to allow the waters of the Red Sea to divide at the particular moment in which Moses needed to lead his people out of Egypt? If all of Creation belongs to God because el made it, el can do what el wills with it, and what el wills may, to us, be miracle.

But we never earn or deserve our miracles. Often the most deserving people don't get them. God always hears our cries, but sometimes el does not answer in a way we think fair, and because we are too small to see the whole pattern, we don't understand why. And not all the No answers come from God. Illness and accident and death can come from man in his fallenness, from the temporary victories of the enemy.

More people have been killed in automobile accidents than in all of the wars in all of our history. And surely those who invented the internal combustion engine and made cars and airplanes had no idea that it was going to cost so heavily in human life. It was an example of what we know with our intellects being far ahead of our wisdom to understand all the implications.

It was the desire to *know* which led us to explore the heart of the atom. The desire to know is part of what makes us human, and in its proper rhythm it is a creative desire. But, alas, it was the Second World War which accelerated the interest in splitting the atom and provided the enormous funds needed for research, which would not have been available in peace time: the rhythm distorted again. Surely if those first atomic scientists in New Mexico had had the slightest idea where their experiments were going to lead, if time had curved and they had seen visions of the victims of Hiroshima or Nagasaki, they might well not have exploded that first atom bomb.

But what we already know, we know. That's one of the messages implicit in the story of Adam and Eve. We cannot turn our backs on what we know, or bury our heads in the sand. We need to try to find wisdom enough so that our knowledge will serve us and the rest of the human race creatively and not destructively.

How, O Lord, do we learn wisdom as well as knowledge? It is somewhat like miracle and magic. Wisdom, like miracle, is yours, Lord, and to be received as gift. The enemy tries to keep us from it, by praising us for our great knowledge, our knowledge, and so shattering us into further fragments. But the Spirit who danced upon the face of the waters in the beginning and who came to us as Comforter after the Ascension will help to heal us, will help to mend our broken pieces with spiritual glue so that the break does not even show.

God can and does come into the most terrible things and redeem them. I do not believe that God wills cancer, or multiple sclerosis. I do not believe that we are ever to regard the brutal death of a child as God's will. I know only that el can come into whatever happens, and by being part of it, can return it to wholeness. This is a large part of the meaning of incarnation. Nothing ever happens to us alone. It happens to God, too.

This used to be considered heresy, but yesterday's heresy is today's truth. Within our own century it was taught in seminary that God is impassible, that he is inaccessible to injury, and therefore does not and cannot suffer. What does such teaching make of the Suffering Servant passages in Isaiah? What does it do to the Incarnation? To the Cross? If Jesus was fully man as well as fully God, surely he suffered. This impassibility of God makes no sense to me. If Jesus suffered, but God did not, what does that do to the concept of the Trinity, except split it into polytheism? The impassibility of God seems totally incompatible with everything I read in the Bible, and with all my experience.

God cared about Ishmael, crying with terror there in the wilderness.

God cares about us, for our Lord is in us and we are in our Lord, and el's beauty is our beauty and all of creation is an act of creative love.

Towards the end of her book, *Peter Abelard*, Helen Waddell writes:

"My God," said Thibault, "what's that?" From somewhere near them in the woods a cry had risen, a thin cry, of such intolerable anguish that Abelard turned dizzy on his feet, and caught at the wall.

"It's a child's voice," he said "Oh, God, are they at a child?"

Thibault had gone outside. The cry came again, making the twilight and the firelit hearth a mockery.

"A rabbit," said Thibault. He listened ... "It'll be in a trap ... Christ!" The scream came yet again.

Abelard was beside him, and the two plunged down the bank.

"Down by the river," said Thibault. "I saw them playing, God help them, when I was coming home. You know the way they go demented with fun in the evenings. It will have been drumming with its hind paws to itself and brought down the trap."

Abelard went on, hardly listening "Oh, God," he was muttering. "Let it die. Let it die quickly." But the cry came yet again. On the right, this time.

He plunged through a thicket of hornbeam.

"Watch out," said Thibault, thrusting past him. "The trap might take the hand off you."

The rabbit stopped shrieking when they stooped over it, either from exhaustion, or in some last extremity of fear. Thibault held the teeth of the trap apart, and Abelard gathered up the little creature in his hands. It lay for a moment breathing quickly, then in some blind recognition of the kindness that had met it at the last, the small head thrust and nestled against his arm, and it died.

It was this last confiding thrust that broke Abelard's heart. He looked down at the little draggled body, his mouth shaking. "Thibault," he said, "do you think there is a God at all? Whatever has come to me I earned it. But what did this one do?"

Thibault nodded.

"I know," he said. "Only – I think God is in it too." Abelard looked up sharply.

"In it? Do you mean that it makes Him suffer, the way it does us?"

Again Thibault nodded.

"Then why doesn't He stop it?"

"I don't know," said Thibault. "Unless – unless it's like the Prodigal Son. I suppose the father could have kept him at home against his will. But what would have been the use? All this,"

he stroked the limp body, "is because of us. But all the time God suffers. More than we do."

God is in it, too.

That was the great difference between the God of the nomadic Hebrew and the multiple gods of the other tribes. Abraham's and Sarah's God cared.

But when he told them to leave their comfortable home and go into an unknown country, he didn't coerce them.

They obeyed because they chose to obey, not because God forced them. They could have been like the Prodigal Son, choosing the fleshpots. But they listened, and they obeyed, and they went into the unknown, and God was with them.

God is in it, whatever it is, with us.

That is heresy, Abelard and Thibault were taught, heresy still being taught in some seminaries. But God, in it, with us, is the only God I can believe in. It was the tempter who thought up impassibility and labelled as heresy the idea that God is part of all of creation, and suffers whenever any part of creation suffers. But what else does the Incarnation affirm? How else do we pray, except to the Maker of ourselves who loves us enough to be part of us? What else do we affirm when we do as Jesus taught us to do and take the bread and drink the wine and affirm that el's beauty is our beauty and that we are in el and el is in us and all, all, is el's?

So God heard Ishmael crying, as only a small, thirsty, frightened little boy can cry, and in the dry desert wilderness the Master of the Universe brought up a fountain of water.

12

The God Who Cannot Fail

GOD BROKE OPEN a fountain in the dry, parched land of the desert in order to quench the thirst of a child. And after we read this evidence of God's loving concern for the lost little things of creation, we are taken back to the center of the story of Abraham and Sarah.

Everything is going pleasantly for them. Abraham makes a treaty with Abimelech, also about a well (wells are of crucial importance in any desert land) where Abraham plants a tamarisk tree and worships the living Lord.

It seemed that Abraham and Sarah in their old age had everything they wanted. And then God called, again:

Abraham!" And Abraham answered, "Yes, here I am!"

"Take your son," God said, "Your only son, Isaac, whom you love so much, and go to the land of Moriah.

There on a mountain that I will show you, offer him as a sacrifice to me."

There follows no cry of outrage or rebellion. Perhaps what God asked was beyond the bounds of outrage and rebellion. Other gods demanded human sacrifice, or displayed anger that could only be appeased by blood. But those were *other* gods, gods who didn't care about their people. The difference between the God of the Hebrews and the gods of the neighboring tribes was that God does care about el's people. They matter.

So how could God ask such a thing of Abraham?

Christians have been criticized by other theists for equating the sacrifice of Abraham with the sacrifice of God the Father when his son was crucified. I don't think God ever tells the same story twice. One story can help us understand another, we know more about human confusion because of Hamlet than we would otherwise, but no other story is the story of Hamlet. From Oedipus we know more about the terrible fact that even an unwitting sin must be punished than we would otherwise, but no other story is the story of Oedipus. The great drama of Jesus of Nazareth is unique, independent of the complex drama of Abraham and Sarah and their son. We may see a pattern that links them, but to equate the two is to show a misunderstanding of the Trinity.

The story of God's terrible demand of Abraham is unique and has unique things to tell us. How could a loving Lord, a Lord who cares about el's creatures, for whom the tiniest atom is of the utmost importance, the hair on a head, the fate of a sparrow, how could the Master of the Universe ask such an unnatural, impossible thing of Abraham?

How indeed? The question has haunted us for several thousand years. In the Middle Ages, God's demand of Abraham was often the subject of miracle and morality plays. In the beginning of *Fear and Trembling* Kierkegaard retells the story of Abraham and Isaac three different ways and still he reaches no conclusion, even today we cannot understand it unless God reveals its meaning to us. Our only proper response is silence, a silence that is echoed following the words from the cross, "My God, my God, why hast thou forsaken me?"

In Jerusalem, inside the old city, I went to the great gold mosque which the devout Jew cannot enter because the mosque is built over the place where the temple stood and no one knows exactly where the Holy of Holies was placed.

The Holy of Holies is so sacred that the place where it stood so long ago may not be stepped on, even inadvertently. I went in, with my shoes off, feeling deep awe (Moses took his shoes off before the burning bush, and so must we when we approach God's holy places), and I stood in front of a great spreading rock, the rock where Abraham laid Isaac and raised his knife to kill his son, and my skin prickled. In my bare feet I stood there, lost in wonder at the magnificent incomprehensibility of the Creator, who loves us so much that he came to live with us and be part of us and die for us and rise again for us and send the Holy Spirit to comfort us.

And I was, somehow, comforted by the very incomprehensibility of all that makes life creative and worth living.

The story continues:

Early the next morning Abraham cut some wood for the sacrifice, loaded his donkey, and took Isaac and two servants with him.

How must Sarah have felt? What kind of laughter was there in this? Did Abraham tell her what God had asked of him, tell her perhaps at the last moment in order to avoid her tears and protestations? Or did he just take the boy and go? Scripture says nothing, but Sarah was a mother. She had known Abraham for a long time, and there was no way he could have hidden from her the heaviness of his heart.

So perhaps she got it out of him. "Abraham, something's wrong. What is it? Tell me." And then perhaps he unburdened himself. It is not good for the human creature to be alone. And what a burden that was for Abraham to carry, much heavier than for the boy. He must have told Sarah, his helpmeet.

In my ears across the centuries I can hear the echo of Sarah's cry. "God! You know nothing about being a mother!" Our perception of God has grown and changed through the centuries, but we still have learned little about the mother in the godhead, we have focused so consistently on the father. I understand Sarah's cry, and the medieval mystics' radiant affirmation of Christ as sister, lover, All in all. We need that intuitive and casual knowing that as God is in all things, el is also in both sexes, the brittle insistence on God's femaleness is as limited as the old paternalism.

But Sarah knew about being a mother and, after all she had been through, I doubt if she would have hesitated to tell God where el was lacking.

Abraham started out for the place that God had told him about. On the third day he saw the place in the distance. He said to his men, "Stay here with the donkey while the boy and I go over there; and when we have worshiped we will come back to you."

So Abraham took the wood for the sacrifice and laid it on Isaac's shoulder; he himself carried the fire and the knife, and the two of them went on together.

Isaac said to Abraham, "Father!"

And he answered, "What is it, my son?"

Isaac said, "Here are the fire and the wood, but where is the lamb for the sacrifice?"

Abraham answered, "God himself will provide a lamb for the sacrifice, my son." And the two of them went on together to the place of which God had spoken.

There Abraham built an altar and arranged the wood. He bound his son Isaac and laid him on the altar on top of the wood.

What spareness in the telling of the story! Not an extraneous detail. Here I am quoting largely from the *New English Bible*, but in all the translations I have checked there is the same simplicity, the same control, enough to keep us wondering for centuries. Did Isaac realize what was happening? Did he scream with terror? Did he beg to be released? Did he try to resist, to escape, to run away? Abraham

took the knife to kill his son; but the angel of the Lord called to him from heaven, "Abraham! Abraham!"

He answered, "Here I am."

The angel of the Lord said, "Do not raise your hand against the boy. Do not touch him. Now I know you have obedient reverence for God, because you have not withheld from me your son, your only son."

You have not withheld from *me*. The angel is speaking in the voice of the Lord, elself.

Abraham looked up and there he saw a ram caught by its horns in a thicket. So he went and took the ram and offered it as a sacrifice instead of his son. Abraham named the place

Jehova-jireh; and to this day the saying is : "In the mountain of the Lord it was provided."

Then the angel of the Lord called from heaven a second time to Abraham, "This is the word of the Lord: by my own self I swear: because you have done this, and have not withheld your son, your only son. I will bless you abundantly and greatly multiply your descendants until they are as numerous as the stars in the sky and the grains of sand on the sea shore."

Perhaps this story tells us more about the nature of man's understanding of God than it does about God elself. The story is staggering in its simplicity. It never falters. Its very straightforwardness, its lack of explanation is one of the most difficult things about it.

But the Bible is for me – I repeat – the living Word of God, although I do not need to believe that it was divinely dictated by God in a long beard and white gown (a picture of Moses, again) and written down in a moment of time by an angel scribe. It is a great story book written over a great many centuries by many people. And when I call it a great story I am emphasizing that it is a great book of Truth. It is the truth by which I live. I do not understand it all, but that does not make it any less the truth.

During the writing of this I was asked to tell, during an interview for a Christian magazine, what Jesus meant in my life. I think I know what I was supposed to say, but though most of the things I was supposed to say are true, they don't sound natural to me, they sound out of context with the God who created everything and everybody and called it all good. So I answered that Jesus taught me about story, the truth of story, and that story is light.

Sometimes the light of the story seems veiled or shadowed, no matter how we struggle to seek for its meaning.

After his terrible experience, we may ask ourselves – could Isaac ever have trusted his father again? Was Abraham's response to God changed? What are we to understand? How does God's demand of Abraham fit in with el's love for all creation? Was Isaac's fear of as much consequence to God as Ishmael's tears?

I am still waiting for the telephone call which will tell me that my college friend is dead, and I know that even though those of us who love her deeply may not be near her hospital bed, we are nevertheless with her. And I think of a mutual friend who died a few years ago at ninety-three, a great lady of vision and laughter who never lost her ability to change and to go into the unknown, and I feel that she is waiting at the gates, to hold out her hand and say, "See! El has not forgotten you; you are carved in the palm of his hand. As am I, and all of creation. See! You can be with and pray for those you love even better here than you could before! See! El has created you to *be*, and it is good."

Today the great blue spruce which we planted as a tiny seedling, far, far from the house at Crosswicks, had to be cut down. In thirty years the little plant had grown into an enormous tree which not only shaded us from the glare of the hot, setting sun in summer, but whose roots were beginning to undermine the old foundations of the house. It is the spruce our son once used for a ladder when he came home from a late night swim with friends and did not want to disturb his sleeping grandmother. Now there is a great new space of air where the spruce stood, it seems the atoms have not yet gathered together within its outline.

And it is somehow all part of the story. Perhaps one day that rock I saw in the mosque in Jerusalem will be gone, that rock on which Abraham bound and laid Isaac, but the story will not be gone. And I do not have to understand, not Isaac's ultimate death, after Jacob had cheated Esau out of the blessing which should have been his, not the cutting down of the great spruce (it's only a tree, they said), not even my own lack of understanding.

In his second letter to the Corinthians, Paul writes (and now I am turning to the *Jerusalem Bible*):

He has said, "My grace is enough for you; my power is at its best in weakness." So [says Paul] I shall be very happy to make my weakness my special boast so that the power of Christ may stay over me.

And that, too, is what Christ means to me, that God can come to me in my weakness and poverty and still find use for it and say that this, too, is good, is very good.

In *Messengers of God*, Elie Wiesel writes:

And Abraham sacrificed the ram in place of his son.

Poor ram, said certain sages. God tests man and the ram is killed. That is unjust; after all, he has done nothing.

Said Rabbi Yehoshua: This ram had been living in Paradise since the sixth day of creation, waiting to be called. He was destined from the very beginning to replace Isaac on the altar.

A special ram, with a unique destiny, of whom Rabbi Hanina ben Doss said: Nothing of the sacrifice was lost. The ashes were dispersed in the Temple's sanctuary; the sinews David used as chords for his harp, the skin was claimed by the prophet Elijah to clothe himself; as for the horns, the smaller one called the people together at the foot of Mount Sinai and the larger one will resound one day, announcing the coming [the first? or the second?] of the Messiah.

Again we confront the problem of free will. Did the ram have to come, to play his part in the drama, to get his horns caught in the bushes, and to be killed in place of Isaac? Did he not have a choice to say yes, or to say no?

In the parable of the two sons, when the father asked them to go work in the vineyard for him, the elder said, "Of course, Father, I will," and did not go. The younger son said, "I won't" and then thought better of it and went.

There is also a legend that Mary was not the first young woman to whom the angel came. But she was the first one to say yes.

And how unsurprising it would be for a fourteen-year-old girl to refuse the angel. To be disbelieving. Or to say:

"Are you sure you mean –
but I'm unworthy –
I couldn't, anyhow –
I'd be afraid. No, no,
it's inconceivable, you can't be asking me –
I know it's a great honor
but wouldn't it upset them all,
both our families?
They're very proper, you see.
Do I have to answer now?
I don't want to say no –
it's what every girl hopes for
even if she won't admit it.
But I can't commit myself to anything
this important without turning it over
in my mind for a while
and I should ask my parents
and I should ask my –

Let me have a few days to think it over."
Sorrowfully, although he was not surprised
to have it happen again,
the angel returned to heaven.

Who could not understand such hesitation in a young woman – fear of the whole wild thing being misunderstood, fear that she would be considered an adulteress (for any woman taken in adultery was stoned to death)?

God will never force us. If we are to be co-creators with el, we must be co-creators willingly. Or maybe that's wrong. Unlike Mary, not all the prophets were immediately willing. They were often like the younger son who said, "I won't" but ended up doing what God had asked. Even if they had to spend three days in the belly of a great fish before they thought better of the Lord's request and went off grudgingly to preach repentance – whether they, personally, wanted the people to repent and be saved, or not.

So perhaps we need not be immediately willing. We can argue and protest that it's too difficult, that we aren't up to it, that we deserve a little rest for a change, that dying by stoning is a nasty way to die. And then we can say, still a bit grudgingly, "Here I am. Send me. Be it unto me according to your word." And then we will be given the strength to do whatever it is that God wants us to do, to bear whatever it is that God wants us to bear. If God wants us to bear figs out of season, el, the Creator, will give us the ability to do so.

Long before I read Wiesel's words, I had been thinking a good deal about the ram, as well as the human characters I was reading and thinking about. To help me think, I have, throughout the years, written poems in the voices of some of the characters in the stories in Scripture, in order to understand better what they have to say to me, that I may move from reading to thinking to prayer.

Here is one from the point of view of the ram.

CAUGHT IN THE BUSH

Asked to leave Eden
where I, with all the other beasts,
remained after the two human creatures left,
I moved to the gates.
The cherub with the flaming sword
drew aside to let me by,
folding his wings across his eyes.

I trotted along a path which led through the woods,
across a desert, made a long detour
around a lake, and finally climbed a mountain
till trees gave way to bushes
and a rock.
An old man raised a knife.
He stood there by the rock
and wept and raised his knife.
So these are men I thought,
and shook my head in horror, and was caught
within the springing branches of a bush.
Then there was lightning, and the thunder came,
and a voice cried out to me: My son, my son,
slain before the foundation of the world.

And then I felt the knife.
For this I came from Eden;

my will is ever his,
as I am his, and have my life
in him, and he in me.

Thus the knife pierced his own heart,
in piercing mine,
and the old man laughed for joy.

If God created everything, and saw that it was good, then we have much to learn from all that good, from the ram, from the robins who had the courage and the hope to build their nest outdoors in the trees this spring, to my old Irish setter, needing to be close either to the other dogs or to one of us, needing the assurance of touch. The other animals, instead of shunning him as old age leads him towards death, provide him with their own equivalent of handholding: Titus, the amber cat, continues his old job of cleaning Timothy's ears, putting one paw firmly on the old setter's head as he cleans and licks, as though the big beast were the size of a kitten. Tiye, the Ibezan hound puppy, a beautiful, galloping reproduction of the temple dogs in Egyptian friezes, licks the old dog's watery eyes. And this concern is part of the good which we human beings have lost, and are at last beginning to recognize that we have lost; and so there is hope that it may once again be recovered.

The telephone call that I have been waiting for, these last several weeks, has come at last. But before it came, my friend and I said our good-byes, and somehow the telephone was not between us. In the truest sense of the word we kythed, and I was able to tell her of the dream I had of her and our ninety-three-year-old friend, the two of them dancing together in a field of daisies, dancing in the joy that is part of the dance of all creation.

"Oh how beautiful, how beautiful," she said.

And we kythed our love and hope.

And at the same time I was cooking and cleaning and preparing for a houseparty to celebrate the double fiftieth birthday of two of our friends, with the attic once more turned into a dormitory, and the kitchen smelling of homemade pasta. And it is all part of the mighty act of creation and it is good.

We can recognize the holy good even while we are achingly, fearfully aware of all that has been done to it through greed and lust for power and blind stupidity. We forget the original good of all creation because of our own destructiveness. The ugly fact that evil can be willed for people by other people, and that the evil comes to pass, does not take away our capacity to will good. There may be many spirits abroad other than the Holy Spirit (the Gospels warn us of them), but they do not make the Holy Spirit less holy. Our paradoxes and contradictions expand, our openness to God's revelations to us must also be capable of expansion. Our religion must always be subject to change without notice – our religion, not our faith, but the patterns in which we understand and express our faith. Surely we would feel ill at ease today with people who had family morning prayers and Scripture readings daily, and yet kept slaves?

Our perception of faith in our Creator is of necessity different from Abraham's and Sarah's perception – neither better nor worse, but different. But since all, all, is part of God, then the differences are part of el, too, for el is All in all, and is loving us tenderly in order to redeem all that was made in the beginning, so that it may once again be called very good.

And I am convinced that not only is our planet ultimately to be freed from bondage to Satan, but with it the whole universe – all the singing, dancing suns and stars and galaxies –

will one day join unhindered in the great and joyous festival. The glorious triumph of Easter will encompass the whole of God's handiwork. The praise for the primal goodness of God's creation in the beginning will be rounded out with the final worship, as John has expressed it in the Revelation:

"Worthy art though, our Lord and God, to receive glory and honor and power, for thou didst create all things and by thy will they existed and were created." And I heard every creature in heaven and earth and in the sea, and all therin, saying, "To him who sits upon the throne and to the Lamb be blessing and honor and glory and might for ever and ever. Amen!

* * *

I look at the colors of autumn moving across the land, and even now creation is ablaze with glory. The oak trees are touched with purply-bronze. The maples flame scarlet and gold. We are harvesting vegetables from the garden, grateful that an early frost has not touched the delicate green peppers, the sweet corn, the tomatoes, or the zinnias and marigolds which border the garden and protect it from Japanese beetles. We have startled an enterprising rabbit sitting in the middle of the greenery, eating lettuce and green beans, bold as brass as long as the dogs are indoors.

Sometimes at dusk we see the loveliness of a doe and her fawn walking across the field, but they have stayed away from the garden, chewing instead the bark of tender new trees.

Broccoli, Brussels sprouts, carrots, don't mind the cold. We'll be picking them long after the ground is rimed with frost. We have discovered a new vegetable this summer, spaghetti squash, which we scrape out with a fork, after cooking, in long, spaghetti-like strands. Leeks are a delight, creamed, or in soup, and spinach salad. We glory in the goodness of creation every day. All that weed-pulling was worth it, though weeds have their own beauty, and, like mosquitoes and flies, are an inevitable part of the summer.

At night now the sky is clear, with no heat haze. One night we eat supper out on the little terrace which we have made with flagstones and lots of honest sweat. We linger at the picnic table through sunset and star rise, and suddenly someone says "How light it is on the northern horizon!" We blow out the lamps and there is the staggering beauty of the Northern Lights. There is something primal about those lights pulsing, in pale green and rose, upwards from the horizon. They give me the same surge of joy as the unpolluted horizon near the Strait of Magellan, showing the curve of the home planet; the same lifting of the heart as the exuberance of the dolphins sporting about the ship after we had crossed the equator.

I sit at the table as we all watch the awesome display of beauty, and there again is the promise of the rainbow covenant which God placed in the sky, and there, too, is the fulfilled new covenant of Easter, radiant, affirming.

And it is good.

In those northern lights, in the great river of the Milky Way, in the circle of family and friends around the table, and in the meal we have just finished and which came largely from the garden, I see God, and the joy we have jointly with him in creation.

My dear people, we are already the children of God, but what we are to be in the future has not yet been revealed; all we know is that when it is revealed we shall be like him, because we shall see him as he really is.

Not only do all our human hopes and dreams look forward to that time of reunion with God. Paul, writing to the Romans, tells us that

The whole creation waits with eager longing for the revealing of the sons of God. The creation itself will be set free from its bondage to decay, and obtain the glorious liberty of God's children ... We know that the whole creation has been groaning in travail together until now.

In writing to the people of Colossae, Paul goes even further in his hope for the future:

For in Christ all the fullness of God was pleased to dwell and through him to reconcile himself to all things, whether on earth or in heaven.

We, on our small planet, can either help with this cosmic reconciliation, or we can hinder it. Hardness of heart hinders the coming of the kingdom. Smugness, pride, self-absorption, hinders it. "You are a stiff-necked people," God chided the children of Israel, and we are still a stiff-necked people and that, too, hinders the coming of the kingdom.

But if I believe that God is not going to fail with me, I must also believe, with Paul and John, that el is not going to fail with anybody, or Satan has won. El will not fail with the gypsy moth caterpillar nor the encephalitis mosquito nor the rapist nor the warmonger nor any part of all that el has made for his own delight – and ours, too. El will not fail, otherwise el is allowing Satan to keep this planet forever. I do not believe that this can happen, for we are God's, and it is el who has made us and not we ourselves.

And as long as I have even a small splinter of unlovingness lodged in my heart, how can I look down on or judge anybody else? Jesus says that I must not. I know that I cannot throw the first stone, and I hope that, no matter how many sinful prodigal sons are invited, I will still want to go to the party.

If I believe in the loving Abba to whom Jesus prayed, then I must also believe that this loving father is not going to fail with creation, that the glorious triumph of Easter will ultimately be extended to the entire universe.

Namasté

In the beginning God created the heaven and the earth.
In the beginning was the Word, and the Word was with God, and the Word was God.
And the Spirit moved upon the face of the waters.
And God saw that it was good. It was very good.

At sea, on the S. S. Santa Mariana, 1981,
to Crosswicks, autumn, 1982

A STONE FOR A PILLOW

1

Separation from the Stars

IN THE LATE AFTERNOON, when the long December night had already darkened the skies, we opened Christmas cards, taking turns, reading the messages, enjoying this once-a-year being in touch with far-flung friends. There, incongruously lying among the Christmas greetings, was an official-looking envelope addressed to me, with Clerk of Court, New York County, in the upper left hand corner. A call to jury duty. Manhattan does not give its prospective jurors much notice. My call was for the first week in January To the notice inside had been added the words, *Must Serve*.

It wasn't the first time that my call had read *Must Serve*. A few months earlier I had written from Minnesota to the Clerk of Court, New York County, explaining that I was not trying to avoid jury duty, that I had previously served on a panel under a fine woman judge, and that I was ready and willing to serve again. But I pointed out, as I had already done several times before, that I do a good bit of lecturing which takes me far from New York, and I gave the Clerk of Court several dates when I would be available, sighing internally because bureaucracy never called me on the weeks that I offered.

This time they did.

So I relaxed and enjoyed Christmas in the country at Crosswicks, bitter cold outside, warmth of firelight and candlelight within, and laughter and conversation and the delectable smells of roasting and baking. One of the highlights came on Christmas Day itself, with the mercury falling far below zero, when my husband went out into the winter garden and picked brussels sprouts, commenting as he brought them in triumphantly, "Mr. Birdseye never froze them like this," and we had brussels sprouts out of our own garden with Christmas dinner.

And then, before Twelfth-night, I was back in New York again, taking the subway downtown to the criminal court to which I had been assigned. I took plenty of work with me, because I had been told that lawyers do not like writers. But just as had happened on my previous jury duty I got chosen as a juror on the second day The case was an ugly one, involving assault in the second degree, which means possession of a dangerous weapon, with intent to cause injury or death.

Two men were sitting in the courtroom as defendants. They looked at the twelve of us who had been told to stay in our seats in the jury box – looked at us with cold eyes, with arrogance, even with contempt. Later, as we jurors got to know each other, we admitted that we were afraid of them. And yet, according to our judicial system, we had been put in the position of having to decide whether or not, according to the law, these men were guilty as charged.

I was fortunate to serve again under a highly intelligent woman judge, who warned us that we must set aside our emotions. What we felt about the defendants should not enter into our deliberations. We should not form any preconceived opinions. "And remember" she told us, "these two men and their lawyers do not have to prove to you that they are innocent. They do not have to appear on the witness stand. The burden of proof is on the assistant district attorney. The American way is that these two men are innocent, unless it can be proved, beyond a reasonable doubt, that they are guilty This is the American way." She also pointed out that this assumption of innocence unless guilt can be proven is not the way of the rest of the world, of countries behind the Iron Curtain or in much of South America, where the assumption is that you are guilty unless, somehow or other, by persuasion or bribe, you can prove your innocence.

When I was called for jury duty I knew that I would be taking two long subway rides each day, and riding the subway in Manhattan is nothing one does for pleasure. So I picked up a small book from one of my piles of Books To Be Read Immediately. Why did I pick this book at this particular time? I don't know. But I have found that often I will happen on a book just at the time when I most need to hear what it has to say.

This book couldn't have been more apt. It was *Revelation and Truth*, by Nicholas Berdyaev. I didn't do much reading the first day because I was sent from court to court, but once I was on a jury and had long periods of time in the jury room, I opened the book, surrounded by my fellow jurors who were reading, chatting, doing needlework or crossword puzzles. There couldn't have been a better place than a criminal court in which to read Berdyaev's words telling me that one of the gravest problems in the Western world today is that we have taken a forensic view of God.

Forensic: *to do with crime*. I first came across the word in an English murder mystery. Forensic medicine is medicine having to do with crime. The coroner needs to find out if the victim has been shot, stabbed, or poisoned. Was the crime accidental, self-inflicted, murder? Criminal medicine.

And there I was, in a criminal court, being warned by a Russian theologian that God is not like a judge sentencing a criminal. Yet far too often we view God as an angry judge who assumes that we are guilty unless we can placate divine ire and establish our innocence. This concept seemed especially ironic after the judge's warning that this is not the American way of justice.

How did the Western world fall into such a gloomy and unscriptural misapprehension? Only a few weeks earlier I had participated in a teenage TV show on the topic of religion. When the master of ceremonies asked the group of twenty or so bright high school students on the panel what they thought God looks like, I was horrified to hear them describe a furious old Zeus-figure with a lightning bolt in his hand. A forensic god.

Would this angry god, out to zotz us, have cared enough about us to come to us as Jesus of Nazareth, as a human, vulnerable baby? Or was it anger and not love at all that was behind the Incarnation, as a forensic view would imply? Did Jesus have to come and get crucified, because only if he died in agony could this bad-tempered father forgive his other children?

We got into a good discussion, then. The teenagers did not really like their cartoon god. They were ready and willing to hear another point of view. We talked about astrophysics and particle physics and the interdependence of all of Creation. But I suspect there may have been in their minds a lingering shadow of God as a cold and unforgiving judge – not a judge who believes in the American way, but one who assumes our guilt.

But no, Berdyaev states emphatically, no, that is not God, not the God of Scripture who over and over again shows love for us imperfect creatures, who does not demand that we be good or virtuous before we can be loved. When we stray from God, it is not God's pleasure to punish us. It is God's pleasure to welcome us back, and then throw a party in celebration of our homecoming.

In Hosea God says,

All my compassion is aroused.
I will not carry out my fierce anger,
I will not destroy Ephraim again,
for I am God, not man:
I am the Holy One in your midst,
and have no wish to destroy.

The nature of God does not fluctuate. The One who made us is still the Creator, the Rejoicer, the Celebrator, who looks at what has been made, and calls it good.

* * *

After the guard summoned us from the jury room to the court room, I sat in the jury box and looked at those two men who were there because they were destroyers rather than creators. They had used sharp knives, destructively; their intention had been to injure, or kill. I wasn't at all sure I wanted to be at the same celebration with them. They both had long hair, one head dark and greasy, the other brown and lank. They looked as though they had strayed out of the sixties, hippies who had grown chronologically, but not in any other way. It was difficult to abide by the judge's warning and not form any opinion of them until all the evidence was in.

That evening I was tired, mentally as well as physically. I bathed, then sat in my quiet corner to read Evening Prayer. For the Old Testament lesson I was reading the extraordinary story of Jacob's ladder of angels ascending and descending, linking earth and heaven, the Creation and the Creator, in glorious interdependence. The story of Jacob is not a story that can be interpreted forensically. It is not a tale of crime and corresponding punishment. Jacob is anything but a moral or virtuous character. He is a liar and a cheat. Heavenly visions do not transform his conniving nature. The story of Jacob is unfair. He didn't get his just desserts. But do not turn to Scripture if you are looking for fairness!

When Jacob saw the ladder of angels he was fleeing Esau's legitimate outrage. He was afraid of his brother, and of God: that is, his father's and his grandfather's God. He had not yet made the decision to accept their God as his own.

But God stood above the ladder of angels, and said:

I am the Lord God of Abraham, your father, and the God of Isaac: the land that you are lying on, to you I will give it, and to your seed. And your seed shall be as the dust of the earth ...

And behold, I am with you, and will keep you in all the places where you go, and will bring you again to this land, for I will not leave you, until I have done that which I have said.

And Jacob woke out of his sleep, and he said, Surely the Lord is in this place, and I knew it not.

And he was afraid, and said, How dreadful is this place! This is none other than the house of God, and this is the gate of heaven.

For Jacob the house of God was not a building, not an enclosure, but an open place with earth for the floor, heaven for the roof. It would be several generations before the ark of God was built. For the early people of El Shaddai, the All Mighty One, any place where God spoke to them became the house of God.

So Jacob took the desert stone he had used for a pillow and upon which he had dreamed the angelic dream, and set it up for a pillar and poured oil upon the top of it. Oil – precious, sacramental. Today we can buy oils of all kinds, bath oil, olive oil, virgin oil, saturated and unsaturated oil. But to Jacob and his tribe, any oil was precious enough to make a significant sacrifice to El Shaddai and that sense of oil as sacramental and significant is retained today in my church as the healing oils are blessed each year.

Jacob called the place where he had set up the pillow-altar Beth-el – the house of God. Seekers and followers have sensed the Presence ever since, in circumstances that were often far from comfortable as Luci Shaw suggests in her poem "Disciple" based on Luke 9:57–58:

Foxes lope home at dusk, each
to his sure burrow. Every bird
flies the twilight
to her down-lined nest.
Yet come with me to learn
a stern new comfort: the earth's
bed, me on guard at your side,
and, like pilgrim Jacob,
a stone for a pillow.

A stone for a pillow. It sounds odd to us, until we remember that very few people on this planet go to bed at night on soft pillows. In Japan the headrest is often made of wood. In some countries it is simply the ground. I've tried a stone, not in bed, but late on a hot afternoon, when I call the dogs, and walk across the fields to the woods. Placed under the neck in just the right way, a stone can help me relax after a morning of typing – though I wouldn't want it for a whole night. But for a time to rest, to think, to let go and be, a warm, rounded stone can be a good pillow reminding me that I am indeed in the house of God, that wherever I call upon my maker is always God's house.

When I was writing *And It Was Good*, reflections on the first chapters of Genesis, I found it helpful, when talking about the Creator, to use el (the first name by which the ancient Hebrew called God), rather than the personal pronoun, she/he, him/her. I still find it helpful when thinking about the Maker of All Things. The personal pronoun was not a problem when it referred to the entirety of the human being, but we are presently living in a genitally-oriented culture, and I do not find it comfortable to limit God to the current sexual connotations and restrictions of the personal pronoun. Calling God *She* is just as sexist and limiting as calling God *He*.

It is fascinating that the conflict ever God's sexuality comes at a time when pornography and sexual license are rampant. Even small cities have their massage parlors and "adult" book stores. This emphasis on the male and female genitals seems to be everywhere, even in our vision of the Creator.

Of course God is mother, nurturer, generator, as well as father, ruler, lawmaker. But when we pound away with a sledgehammer at God's sexuality (ouch! but that is the image that comes to mind) we are seeing a God even more anthropomorphic than the God of the patriarchs.

In a universe which is becoming more and more varied as we discover more of the glories of the macrocosm and the infinite variety of the microcosm (are stars confined by gender? Or quarks?), this preoccupation with God's sex seems amazingly primitive. But then, I suspect that we are still a pretty primitive people.

For all our mechanical and electronic sophistication, our thinking about ourselves and our maker is often unimaginative, egocentric, and childish. We need to do a great deal of growing up in order to reach out and adore a God who loves all of us with unqualified love.

But all those thousands of years ago when our forbears lived in the desert of an underpopulated and largely unexplored planet, the God of Jacob was definitely a masculine God, the Father God of the patriarchs. So, when I am within Jacob's frame of reference, I'll return, for his story, to the masculine pronoun. But when I am lying on the rock in the late afternoon I am not in Jacob's time, or indeed not in any chronologic time at all, but in *kairos*, God's time, which touches on eternity.

I lie there quietly, lapped in peace, the blue of sky the ceiling, the stone under me the foundation, the trees forming arches rather than walls. The breeze is gentle, the sun not too hot; the stone is sun-warm and firm beneath me. Sometimes after dinner I go out to the rock known as the star-watching rock and wait for the stars to come out. There I can see all of Creation as the house of God, with the glory of the stars reminding me of the Creator's immensity, diversity, magnificence.

The stars are often referred to in Genesis. El Shaddai took Jacob's grandfather, Abraham, out into the desert night to show him the stars and to make incredible promises. How glorious those stars must have been all those centuries ago when the planet was not circled by a corona of light from all our cities, by smog from our internal combustion engines. Jacob, lying on the ground, the stone under his head, would have seen the stars as we cannot see them today. Perhaps we have thrown up a smoke screen between ourselves and the angels.

But Jacob would not have been blinded to the glory of the stars as part of the interdependence of the desert, the human being, the smallest insects, all part of Creation.

If we look at the makeup of the word disaster, dis-aster, we see *dis*, which means separation, and *aster* which means star.

So dis-aster is separation from the stars. Such separation is disaster indeed. When we are separated from the stars, the sea, each other, we are in danger of being separated from God.

Sometimes the very walls of our churches separate us from God and each other. In our various naves and sanctuaries we are safely separated from those outside, from other denominations, other religions, separated from the poor, the ugly, the dying. I'm not advocating pulling down the walls of our churches, though during the activist sixties I used to think it might be a good idea if we got rid of all churches which seat more than two hundred. But then I think of the huge cathedral which is my second home in New York, and how its great stone arms welcome a multitude of different people, from the important and affluent to waifs and strays and the little lost ones of a great, overcrowded city. We need to remember that the house of God is not limited to a building that we usually visit for only a few hours on Sunday. The house of God is not a safe place. It is a cross where time and eternity meet, and where we are – or should be – challenged to live more vulnerably, more interdependently. Where, even with the light streaming in rainbow colors through the windows, we can listen to the stars.

Stars have always been an icon of creation for me. During my high school years, when I was at my grandmother's beach cottage for vacations, I loved to lie on a sand dune and watch the stars come out over the ocean, often focussing on the brilliant grace of one particular star. Back in school, I wrote these lines:

I gaze upon the steady star
That comes from where I cannot see,
and something from that distant far

Pierces the waiting core of me
And fills me with an aweful pain
That I must count not loss but gain.

If something from infinity
Can touch and strike my very soul,
Does that which comes from out of me
Reach and pierce its far off goal?

Very young verses, but they contain the germ of an understanding of the interdependence of all Creation.

After I was out of college, living in New York and working on my first novel, I was so hungry for stars that I would take the subway up to the Planetarium and connect myself to the stars that way. My distress at being separated from the stars is not something esoteric or occult; it is a symptom of separation from Creation and so, ultimately, from community, family, each other, Creator.

* * *

That January evening after the first tiring day as a juror, after I had read the story of Jacob and the angels, I turned to the New Testament, to read from the ninth chapter of Matthew's

Gospel, where Jesus had called Matthew from collecting taxes. In Israel in those days, a tax collector worked for the hated Romans, rather than for an equivalent of the I.R.S. We don't have any analogy for the kind of tax collector Matthew was. But because they were employed by the enemy, all tax collectors were scum.

Nevertheless, incredibly, Jesus called Matthew to be one of his disciples, and that night he went for dinner to his house, where there were more tax collectors, and various other kinds of social outcasts, and the censorious Pharisees asked the disciples, "Why does your master eat with tax collectors?" Jesus heard the question and said, "It is not the healthy who need a doctor, but the sick. Go and learn the meaning of the words, *What I want is mercy, not sacrifice*." He was quoting from the prophet, Hosea. And he went on, "And indeed I have not come to call the virtuous, but sinners."

I'm uneasy about self-conscious virtue. It implies that the virtuous person is in control, keeps all the laws, has all the answers, always knows what is right and what is wrong. It implies a conviction which enables the virtuous person to feel saved, while the rest of the world is convicted.

Probably it was because I was on jury duty that I noticed the paradoxical connections between the words conviction, convince, convicted, *convict* (noun), and *convict* (verb). If we assume that we are virtuous, particularly when we set our virtue against someone else's sin, we are proclaiming a forensic, crime-and-punishment theology not a theology of love. The Pharisees who did not like to see Jesus eating with sinners wanted virtue – virtue which consisted in absolute obedience to the law.

The Pharisees were not bad people, remember. They were good. They were virtuous. They did everything the Moral

Majority considers moral. They knew right from wrong, and they did what was right. They went regularly to the services in the temple. They tithed, and they didn't take some off the top for income tax or community services or increased cost-of-living expenses. They were, in fact, what many Christians are calling the rest of us to be: good, moral, virtuous, and sure of being saved.

So what was wrong? Dis-aster. Separation from the stars, from the tax collectors, the Samaritans, from the publican who beat his breast and knew himself to be a sinner. The Pharisees, not all of them, but some of them, looked down on anybody who was less moral, less virtuous than they were. They assumed that their virtue ought to be rewarded and the sin of others punished.

If we twelve jurors found those two men guilty as charged, they would be punished by the state. They would likely be put in prison: forensic punishment. Necessary in our judicial system, perhaps, but Berdyaev warned that we should not think of God's ways as being judicial. God is a God of love.

When I looked at those two cruel-faced men I had to remind myself that they were God's children, and that they were loved. If they had committed the crime of which they were accused, it would cause God grief, not anger.

The three patriarchs must have caused El Shaddai considerable grief. If Jacob was a cheat, it ran in the family. Abraham, Isaac, and Jacob had much in common – long lives, many wives, children born late to the barren but beloved wife, and a shrewdness which did not shrink from cheating.

Jacob's grandfather, Abraham, who had been called by God from the comforts of home into the dangers of a strange land, pretended to King Abimelech of Gerar that his wife, Sarah, was his sister. According to the custom of that place and time,

Abimelech or one of his men could "know" the stranger's sister. But if they wanted his wife, then, according to custom, they would have to kill the husband.

Abimelech uncovered Abraham's deception, and then, a generation later, we have almost the same story with Isaac, Abraham's son, pretending that Rebekah is his sister, not his wife, in order to protect his own skin. And again Abimelech discovers the deception.

"Why did you do this to me?" he demands.

"So you wouldn't kill me," Isaac answers. Isaac, like Abraham, his father was willing to sacrifice his beautiful wife's honor to these powerful men in order to save his own life. Evidently both Sarah and Rebekah went along with the deception, but whether willingly or unwillingly we are not told. Many things were different in those days, particularly the position of women.

* * *

In order for us to know Jacob and to think about his story, it is helpful to remember his family tree. Jacob was the third of the three patriarchs. The first was Abraham.

Abraham and his wife, Sarah, had a son, Isaac.

Isaac and his wife, Rebekah, had twin sons, Esau and Jacob.

Isaac never seemed to question the fact that his father Abraham's God was also his God. But Jacob was a more complicated character than his father. It took him considerable time and several incredible encounters with the divine Presence before he decided to accept as his own God the God of his father, Isaac, and his grandfather, Abraham. He tried to bargain with God, but he found that his bargaining did not work. Ultimately he dropped all his deviousness and cheating and, naked before God, accepted El Shaddai.

Isaac, a far more direct person than his son, was acted on more often than he was allowed to act. Abraham actually raised the knife to offer Isaac as a sacrifice. He also chose Isaac's wife for him, and although Isaac came to love Rebekah, he had no say in the choosing of her. And yet Isaac knew himself to be singled out by God, and he remained faithful to this God who made promises as splendid as the star-filled sky.

The God of the Patriarchs belonged to a people, rather than to a place. El Shaddai, their God, was one god among many gods, the varied and various deities of the surrounding tribes. Throughout the Old Testament, there are numerous references to other gods, and to "our" God as the greatest of these. Whose God is like our God? There is no other God like our God. "Who is he among the gods, that shall be like unto the Lord?" asks the psalmist.

The chief difference between the God of Abraham, Isaac, and Jacob, and the gods of the other tribes, was that El Shaddai cared for, loved his people, and did not stand apart from them and demand constant blood sacrifices. It was the other gods who were forensic. Jacob's God was the God who was *in* the story It is only slowly, as we move through Scripture, that this God among many gods becomes the God who is One, the God who is All. The human being's attempt to understand the Creator is never static, it is constantly in motion. If we let our concept of God become static, and we have done so over and over again throughout history, we inevitably blunder into a forensic interpretation, and that does not work.

In a vain attempt to make people see God as an avenging judge, theologians have even altered the meaning of words. Atonement, for instance. A bad word, if taken forensically.

A young friend said to me during Holy Week, "I cannot cope with the atonement." Neither can I, if the atonement is thought of forensically. In forensic terms, the atonement means that Jesus had to die for us in order to atone for all our awful sins, so that God could forgive us. In forensic terms, it means that God cannot forgive us unless Jesus is crucified and by this sacrifice atones for all our wrongdoing.

But that is not what the word means! I went to an etymological dictionary and looked it up. It means exactly what it says, at-one-ment. I double-checked it in a second dictionary There is nothing about crime and punishment in the makeup of that word. It simply means to be at one with God. Jesus on the cross was so at-one with God that death died there on Golgotha, and was followed by the glorious celebration of the Resurrection.

Our legal system has to be forensic. We have laws, Paul points out, because we have sin. And what is sin? It is not frivolous to say that sin is discourtesy.

* * *

Discourtesy. I sat in the jury room with the radiators hissing and the January cold pressing against the windows, hearing the constant sound of taxis and buses and cars honking on the streets below, and thought of Crosswicks, our house outside a village so small that it doesn't have traffic lights. In New York, without lights, our traffic would be in an even worse mess than it is. I was amazed when I was at St. Scholastica College in Duluth, Minnesota, to find a city so small that there were few traffic lights, and at the intersections cars courteously took turns. By and large, drivers across the United States are not that courteous. So we need traffic lights.

Sin, then, is discourtesy pushed to an extreme, and discourtesy is lack of at-one-ment. If you drive your car without any thought for the other drivers on the road, you are separating yourself. To be discourteous is to think only of yourself, and not of anybody else. The result of this "me, myself and I"-ism leads to the horror of drivers who will hit animals – or human beings – and callously drive on. Dis-aster. Separation. Atonement reversed and shattered. And so crime increases in the anonymity of our cities, as does drunkenness and drug-taking and stealing and raping and killing, and as a result we have our judicial system, and the criminal courts. In that dusty little jury room I understood Paul's comment that we have laws because we have sin. Dis-aster. But the stories of Abraham, Isaac, and Jacob precede the coming of the Law, and there was for the patriarchs, despite their cheating and lying, an innocence in their encounters with God that got lost with laws, with crime and punishment.

If we on the panel found those two men guilty the state would punish them, but I'm not at all sure that this forensic type of punishment is punishment at all. It may be deterrence, or an attempt to protect the innocent. I have no desire to go all wishy-washy and bleeding-heart about the rapist who is let off with an easy sentence so that he can then go out and rape and kill again, as statistics prove is almost inevitable. Our jails may be deplorable, our courts overcrowded and years behind schedule, our lawyers are not knights in shining armor, but we do what we can, in our blundering way, to curb crime and violence, and our top-heavy system remains one of the best on the planet.

But our own need for law and our system of prosecution and sentencing does not produce true punishment, because true punishment should result in penitence. Real punishment produces an acceptance of wrongdoing, a repugnance for what has been done, confession, and an honest desire to amend.

Real punishment comes to me when I weep tears of grief because I have let someone down. The punishment is not inflicted by anyone else. My own recognition and remorse for what I have done is the worst punishment I could possibly have.

Jacob punished himself after tricking Esau. His terror of revenge made him run away from his brother, and it was to be many years before he could return home.

Perhaps the most poignant moment for me in all of Scripture comes after Peter has denied Jesus three times, and Jesus turns and looks at him. That loving look must have been far worse punishment for Peter than any number of floggings. And he went out and wept bitterly.

Jacob, too, learned to weep bitterly, but he was an old man before he came to an understanding of himself which included acceptance of repentance without fear.

This is something a criminal court is not equipped to cope with. The judge and the lawyers and the jurors are there to learn the facts as accurately as possible, and to interpret them according to the law. Forensically.

It is impossible to interpret the story of Jacob in this way. Jacob does outrageous things, and instead of being punished, he is rewarded. He bargains with God shamelessly: "*If* God will be with me, and will keep me in this way that I go, and will give me bread to eat, and raiment to put on, so that I come again to my father's house in peace; *then* shall the Lord be my God."

Jacob also agrees to tithe, but only if God does for him all that he asks. He cheats, but he knows that he cheats; he never tries to fool himself into thinking that he is more honest than he is. He openly acknowledges his fear of Esau's revenge.

And yet, with all his shortcomings, he is a lovable character, and perhaps we recognize ourselves in him with all his complexity. He has an extraordinary sense of awe – an awe which does not demand fairness, an awe which is so profound a response to the Creator that it cannot be sustained for long periods of time.

But whenever El Shaddai came to Jacob, he was ready for the Presence. That was why he took his stone pillow and built an altar. Jacob knew delight in the Lord in a spontaneous manner which too many of us lose as we move out of childhood. And because we have forgotten delight, we are unable to accept the golden light of the angels.

Three centuries ago Thomas Traherne wrote:

Should God give Himself and all worlds to you, and you refuse them, it would be to no purpose. Should he love you and magnify you, should he give his son to die for you, and command all angels and men to love you, should He exalt you in His throne and give you dominion over all his works and you neglect them, it would be to no purpose.

Should he make you in His image, and employ all his Wisdom and power to fill eternity with treasures, and you despise them, it would be in vain. In all these things you have to do; *and therefore all your actions are great and magnificent, being of infinite importance in all eyes; while all creatures stand in expectation of what will be the result of your liberty … It is by your love that you enjoy all his delights, and are delightful to him.*

As I live with Jacob's story I see that there is far more to him than the smart cheat, the shallow manipulator. There are many times when he so enjoyed the delights of God, that he himself became delightful.

How often are we delightful to God? How marvelous that we are called to be delightful!

We are not meant to cringe before God, or to call on Jesus to come and save us from an angry and vengeful Father. We are to enjoy all the delights which the Lord has given us, sunsets and sunrises, and a baby's first laugh, and friendship and love, and the brilliance of the stars. Enjoying the Creator's delights implies connectedness, not dis-aster.

And so there is hope that we, too, may so enjoy all the delights that God has given us, that we may truly be delightful.

2

The Butterfly Effect

ALMOST EVERY EARLY SPRING we have ice storms around Crosswicks. While the mercury hovers around the freezing point, the rain falls and as it touches the trees it coats the branches with silver, bending the birches like bows, drooping the delicate twigs of willow and maple with a heavy freight of ice. Inside the old walls of Crosswicks the wood stoves and the open fireplace keep us warm, and when the ice-laden power lines fall, candles and oil lamps are lit.

The power usually goes out during an ice storm, so since our pump is powered by electricity, at the first sign of freezing rain we fill the tubs, and several kettles of water. During our first ice storm we were not country-wise enough to prepare for waterlessness, and caught cold by having to go out into the icy rain to relieve ourselves. Since then, while the power is out, we flush the toilet once or twice a day by filling a bucket with water from the tub, and sloshing it down the bowl.

This used to fascinate the children, who wanted us to flush the toilet more often than we thought necessary After all, that tub of water had to last us until the power came back on.

One time, many years ago when the children were little, an ice storm came at the time of the full moon. We went to bed with nothing to see in the sky but thick clouds, and we listened to the progressive sounds of rain, the clicking of ice, and the sudden loud cracking of broken branches. During the night the wind shifted from the east to the northwest. The clouds had been ripped away and the full moon was revealed, bringing the ice-coated branches to life with silver and diamonds. It was a faerie land of beauty and we woke the children, so that they would not miss the extraordinary loveliness.

Ice storms are magically beautiful, but they also cause great damage to the trees, which cannot withstand the weight of ice.

Such storms are part of the normal expectations of wind and rain as the earth begins to thaw from the long winter freeze.

But the weather also does things which are not at all anticipated. On the last Monday of June a twister pranced by our house, which was neither expected nor usual. Throughout most of the area there was no more than an ordinary summer thunder storm, not particularly severe. But along one lethal path there was a tornado. Fortunately we were all out, and all the windows were wide open to catch the breeze. Otherwise, I am told, we might not still *have* a house.

On the little terrace outside our kitchen window are some fairly heavy chairs, deliberately heavy because a house on a hill is vulnerable to high winds. One of the chairs was tossed across the road, along with a couple of small tables. Branches of the old willow tree were found twisted in the limbs of a maple tree on the other side of the garden. In the orchard our favorite old winesap apple tree was snapped off at the roots and lay dying on the ground. A majestic maple was felled and crashed across the road. Another maple was split from top to bottom, sliced in half. Almost all the trees lost major branches. The ground was littered with limbs and leaves and with hail the size of golf balls. It was a scene of devastation.

And we ourselves were devastated. It was an abrupt reminder of the precariousness of this world full of the Creators delights. After the separation of the creature from the created when Adam and Eve were sundered from the Garden, the world has been unstable under our feet. There seems to be no spot on earth which is immune to the "natural disasters" of tornado, hurricane, earthquake. In northwest Connecticut we must often batten down against hurricanes, but a tornado in our part of the world seemed an unnatural disaster, leaving us bewildered.

The only reason we had a vegetable garden left was the unusually cold spring which delayed planting, and the tender shoots of corn and tomato, broccoli and green pepper, were still tiny. They were lashed to the ground by wind and rain, but they were young enough so that they could be lifted upright again, take deeper root, and grow.

All during the summer we stiffened nervously whenever we heard a rumble of thunder, and looked at the horizon to make sure there was no dark funnel of cloud rolling towards us. But the precariousness of the planet next manifested itself not in a storm but in the trembling of the earth. I woke up one early autumn morning just after dawn, feeling the bed shaking under me. Earthquakes are not common in the Litchfield Hills, but there was no doubt that this was an earthquake, rattling the windows, shaking the floors.

It was not a severe earthquake, though it was an unusually long one, and it again left us with a renewed awareness of the uncertainty of life. We never know from one moment to the next, what is going to happen.

The psalmist sings, "God is our refuge and strength, a very present help in trouble. Therefore we will not fear, though the earth be moved, and though the hills be carried into the midst of the sea: though the waters rage and swell, and though the mountains shake in the tempest."

On one level that is true. To know that we are one with our Maker gives us this deep understanding that el is indeed our hope and our strength. But there is another level in us that legitimately experiences fear when the earth is moved, or the hills fall, or the tempest rages.

Earthquakes were more common when the planet was younger, and the earth's crusts were still settling. In Jacob's desert world there was a newness and a harshness to the land, shrivelling under the fiery sun. Famine was more lethal than storm, and Jacob came to know famine in much the same way that it is being known in desert countries today, where the rains are not falling, and the sands move across and choke a once green and fertile land.

My mother, who was a very wise woman, used to say that when we abuse the planet overmuch, it will turn on us. Is that what is happening, with earthquakes, floods, droughts, volcanic eruptions devastating the earth? We have not wondered enough at the delights God has given us to appreciate them, and be good stewards. We have overworked the land, poured pollutants into river and stream, fouled the air we breathe with gas fumes and chemical smoke spiralling up from industrial chimneys. We have sown the wind. We are reaping the whirlwind.

Cleaning up after the tornado was a sad job. A fleeting thought crossed my mind: We have faithfully tended our little corner of field and forest, we plough compost back into the garden in the autumn, we use no chemical fertilizers or sprays, we try to keep the woods a safe haven for wild life. We plant and nurture trees and flowers and vegetables and herbs. But if we expect that to protect us from wind and storm, aren't we falling into forensic thinking again? Aren't we crying out, in effect, "But it's not fair!"

We cut and piled wood from the wind-felled trees, knowing that they would provide more than enough firewood for the winter, but still grieving for the death of those trees which had been our friends.

I like to take time out to listen to the trees, much in the same way that I listen to a sea shell, holding my ear against the rough bark of the trunk, hearing the inner singing of the sap. It's a lovely sound, the beating of the heart of a tree.

I couldn't stop myself from asking, Why the old apple tree? Why the grand maples? Why did the twister skip the ancient willow, fading with age, or a sapling which wasn't doing well, and attack the strongest and healthiest trees? If the tornado was not consciously evil, it was still evil.

I wrestle with these questions which do not have logical answers, wrestle with mysteries, much as Jacob wrestled with the angel. How do we even attempt to understand the meaning of tempest and tragedy, love and hate, violence and peace?

I struggle, and as always when I struggle to find the truth of something, I turn to story for illumination. And, as I grapple with the angels of difficult questions, I think of Jacob who saw a ladder of angels, reaching from earth to heaven, with the angels of God ascending and descending, linking heaven and earth, the creation to the Creator, not separated from each other, but participating in each other. Delight. At-one-ment.

For God is beyond all our forensic thinking. God is love.

During the first week of jury duty I got home one night as the phone was ringing. With no sense of foreboding I picked it up, and a cold and angry voice accused me of spreading abroad a terrible secret I had been told in deepest confidence. I had told no one. I do not know how the secret – so terrible I cannot even hint at it – leaked out, who else had been told. But I was blamed, and I was angry, very angry at the injustice of the accusation. How could the person who had trusted me enough to tell such a devastating story then turn around and think that I was the kind of person who would abuse and betray such trust?

In my outrage, I wanted justice to be done. I wanted to be exonerated. I wanted whomever it was who had viciously spread the secret to be caught and punished. Forensic thinking – and I needed to grapple with this, not angrily, but lovingly, compassionately. Jury duty and Jacob had pushed me into some hard thinking.

Jacob's brother, Esau, also went through outrage at the injustice which had been done him, but he did not remain in anger. He wept in anguish over the lack of justice, but he did not sulk.

Family stories are as complicated in the great dramas of Scripture as they are in real life. A few weeks ago, after a large family gathering, I wrote in my journal with a figurative sigh of relief that nothing untoward had happened, adding that with a family as complex as ours, that was no small achievement. But honest family relations are seldom simple. Isaac must often have grieved about his twin sons. And what kind of image did Isaac himself have of fathers? What did he think of his own father who had bound him and laid him on the wood for the holocaust, and lifted his knife to kill him? What did Isaac think of a father/God who would ask such a thing even if, at the last moment, this masculine God sent a ram in a bush for a reprieve? If Jacob was slow to accept Isaac's God for his own, it would surely be understandable for Isaac to be slow to accept Abraham's God, but there is no indication that he was reluctant. He was an extraordinarily accepting man.

I must learn to accept, too. To accept that life is not fair. That I must not remain in my hurt and anger over being falsely accused of betrayal. That I must let it go, and move on, as best I can. As the people of Scripture were willing to let go and move on, to go wherever it was that God called them.

Poor Isaac, Jacob's father. His life was not easy. Probably the best part of it was his love for Rebekah, even if Abraham chose her for him. But the meeting of Isaac and Rebekah is the first love story in the Bible – love story rather than romance, for "romantic love" was nonexistent in the harsh and practical realities of desert life when the nomadic Hebrews were wandering from oasis to oasis. That is just as well, for romantic love is not real love. The illusion of romantic love as something pure and undying kills the possibility of real love. Romantic love inevitably leads to death. Tristan and Isolde, Pelleas and Melisande, Héloise and Abelard: theirs was romantic love, magnificent romantic love, perhaps, but it led to death. There is also a creative death to romantic love, the death to the illusory love of romance, and a growing up to the true love of mature human beings.

The great teacher at Smith, Mary Ellen Chase, told our class that the novel begins where the romance and the fairy tale end.

The patriarchs and matriarchs, Abraham and Sarah, Isaac and Rebekah, Jacob and Rachel, had the real thing, despite their human foibles, and their human sins. Having seen the great Sahara desert, I understand something of the incredible physical demands made of husband and wife in that unfriendly climate. They had to be able to work together, to be good companions. A love which was romantic or merely erotic would never have survived.

Isaac had need of a good companion, especially after Sarah, his mother, died. In those days the genuine love of mother and son was not considered neurotic, nor need it be at any time. It was Isaac's father, not his mother, who bound him and laid him on the altar of the rock. It was the incomprehensible Father/God who gave the order for the holocaust. Perhaps Sarah would have refused?

Even after the substitution of the ram, Isaac may have had twinges of wonder about the reliability of fathers. Maybe fathers were expected to be unreliable. But Sarah, the mother, was to be counted on, in laughter, in tears, to accept even where she did not condone. Isaac must have missed her grievously.

And in those days people had not yet fallen into the "blame it all on your parents" syndrome, a misconception as fallacious as the illusion of romantic love. It insists that nothing is our fault, thereby denying us any share in the writing of our own story. Whatever we have done that is wrong is considered to be not our fault because of our parents. Or our teachers. Or somebody. When we refuse all responsibility for our behavior by blaming it on our parents (or anybody else), we are also abdicating free will. A lot of us (I, too), have had unhappy or strange childhoods, but this need not be lethally crippling. Isaac rose above all that had happened to him and became one of the trinity of patriarchs invoked as Israel's heroes.

And as helpmeet he had Rebekah.

The story of Abraham's search for a wife for Isaac emphasizes that there will be trouble if one marries someone who worships an alien god. Therefore Abraham did not want Isaac to marry someone from the land of Canaan, in which they had settled, and where the gods were not El Shaddai. So Abraham called to himself the eldest servant of his household and said to him, "I am asking you to put your hand under my thigh." (By this Abraham's servant and friend knew that he was being asked to make the most solemn oath possible, because special veneration was given the organs of generation.)

Abraham continued,

I ask you to swear by the Lord, the God of heaven, and the God of earth, that you will not let my son marry a daughter of the Canaanites, among whom we live. No. You are to go back to my country, and to my kind, and find a wife among them for my son, Isaac.

The servant said "But perhaps the woman will not be willing to come with me to this strange land. Then would you want me to bring your son back to the land you came from?"

Abraham said, "No! Do not take my son back there. The Lord God of heaven, who took me from my father's house, and from the land of my own people, and who spoke to me, and who swore to me saying, 'To your seed will I give this land,' this Lord my God will send an angel before you, and you will be able to bring back a wife for my son."

Arranged marriages continue in a good many parts of the world to this day; it is only in our century in the Western world that they have become a thing of the past. How could a marriage arranged by God and his angel fail? Isaac and Rebekah loved each other from the start.

Love stories in the Bible tend to begin at a well, the common meeting place for nomads. Abraham's servant went to the well in Aram-Naharaim – all the way back to Mesopotamia in the northwest. A young woman appeared, and drew water for the servant and for his camels. The servant asked her name, and when he learned that she was Rebekah, a young woman of Abraham's tribe, he gave her the jewels Abraham had sent with him, and she hurried home with the news of the stranger's arrival.

Laban, Rebekah's brother, came out to meet Abraham's servant, to give him food, and to make marriage negotiations.

Laban, the negotiator. Years later, when Jacob fled to him and fell in love with his daughter, Rachel, he was a party to many more elaborate negotiations.

Laban agreed to the marriage of his sister, Rebekah, with Isaac. Rebekah, too, agreed, although she had never set eyes on the young man, and she set out with Abraham's servant to go to the land of Canaan.

Isaac appeared to have had no objection to having a marriage arranged for him. One evening, while Abraham's servant had not yet returned from his mission, Isaac went out into the fields to meditate. To meditate on the strange events of his life. On the wonder of the desert stars, and the incomprehensible maker of them all. Dis-aster was not for him. He was connected to the stars, and to the land, and to the tribe. While he was alone, meditating, he lifted up his eyes, and saw camels coming toward him. And he saw Rebekah.

Rebekah, in her turn, saw Isaac, and asked who the young man was. Abraham's servant told her that it was Isaac, to whom she was betrothed.

Her heart must have lifted, for it was a brave thing for Rebekah to do, to leave her family and go to a strange land to be the bride of a young man she had never seen. Even though such was the custom of her people, it was still courageous. But as the story continues, it is apparent that Rebekah did not lack courage.

So Isaac took Rebekah for his wife, "and he loved her, and Isaac was comforted after his mother's death." Abraham, too, comforted himself: he married again, despite his advanced age, and had several more children. But, according to the story it was to Isaac that Abraham gave everything he had.

And then Abraham died.

Isaac, and his half brother, Ishmael, buried their father. Isaac, the legitimate son of Abraham and Sarah, was the favorite. Ishmael was the child of Hagar, Sarah's handmaid, according to the custom of the time. Hagar's scorn of barren Sarah began a bitterness which only death could heal, and it is comforting to think that these two alienated brothers were reconciled, and that together they buried their father. They had played together as children. They came together as men, with their father's death binding them, salving the old hurts. The schism caused by Hagar's arrogance and Sarah's resentment was finally healed.

There was no denial of death in those days of a sparsely-populated land. Now we hide it away in nursing homes and hospitals, prolong it, often painfully, with life-support systems. But for Isaac and Ishmael, birth and death were a natural part of life, and unless someone was killed by a wild animal or in an unforeseen accident, death was prepared for openly. I hope that the two brothers, together at last, were able to hold each other's hands as well as their father's. Now, in the bloody world of the Middle East, it is time for Isaac and Ishmael to clasp hands again. In the world of Islam, Ishmael is revered above Isaac but they laughed together as children, and God heard them both and loved them.

* * *

At Crosswicks we are dependent on a well for our water. But it was not until I stood on the sands of the Sahara that I consciously understood the importance of wells for the people of the desert, where the sun scorches the parched land and the sand blows constantly.

Before our trip to Egypt I read that people who wear contact lenses should leave them at home, the blowing sand is so pervasive. Since I do not see without contact lenses, leaving them at home was not an option for me, so I bought a pair of swimming goggles to wear over my contacts! On the day that we went to see the Sphinx and the great pyramids the wind rose, and we were caught in a sand storm. I was more than grateful for my swimming goggles: they protected my eyes from the stinging sand far more effectively than ordinary spectacles would have, and while everybody else ran for cover, I was able to watch the strange beauty of the storm until the force of the sand, blowing in horizontal waves, stung my legs like shot and finally drove me to shelter.

No wonder women wear veils in that part of the world. The veils protect them not only from men's eyes, but from the blowing sand.

A well provides not only water for drink, but irrigation for keeping an oasis green. A well is necessary for life.

When Abimelech sent Isaac away from Gerar, saying, "Go from us, for you are mightier than we are," Isaac's first priority was finding water. He pitched his tent in the valley of Gerar and his servants dug in the valley, and found there a well of springing water. And the herdsmen of Gerar fought with Isaac's herdsmen, saying, "The water is ours." So Isaac's herdsmen dug another well, and there was a battle over that one, too. So they went further and dug yet another well, and no one tried to take that one away from them, and Isaac called the name of it Rehoboth and he said, "For now the Lord has made room for us, and we shall be fruitful in the land." And the Lord appeared to him that night and said, "I am the God of Abraham, your father, fear not, for I am with you, and will bless you, and multiply your seed for my servant Abraham's sake."

'And Isaac built an altar there, and called upon the name of the Lord, and pitched his tent, and there his servants dug yet another well.'

Digging a well in the desert is no easy chore. Water is not always reached at the first dig, or the second, or even the third. And often the digging has to be very deep before a spring is reached. But they succeeded in digging a well.

Then Abimelech came from Gerar, with two of his chief warriors, and Isaac said, "Why have you come after me, after you have sent me away from you?"

And Abimelech and his warriors said, "We saw certainly that the Lord is with you. Let there now be an oath between us, and let us make a covenant together, that you will do us no hurt. We have not hurt you, we have done only good to you, and we sent you away in peace. And we see now that you are the blessed of the Lord."

And Isaac made them a feast, and they ate and drank together, and in the morning they rose early and swore to join each other, and Isaac sent them away, and they departed in peace.

Isaac wanted peace. When he married Rebekah he must have thought that at last his life was going to move in quiet ways of love, harmony, and prosperity. Their marriage was one of deep love, but Rebekah had no children. Since it was the woman who carried and bore the children, it was assumed that the woman was at fault if the marriage was not blessed by babies. Childlessness was a source of humiliation to a woman. Rebekah's childlessness must have seemed a bitter irony to Isaac, who had been born so late in his parents' lives that they could have been his grandparents. How amazing was this God who had brought Abraham and Sarah to this strange country, who had given Sarah a baby in her old age, and then almost taken him away in that extraordinary demand for blood sacrifice! Now what was this God going to do about that rash promise that Abraham's descendants, through Isaac, would be as numerous as the stars in the sky? What kind of a jokester God was this?

Perhaps Isaac had mixed feelings about the Creator of the universe, of the countless stars in the heavens, of the grains of sand in the desert, and of strange promises. But he entreated God, as the Hebrew patriarchs never hesitated to do, and at last he and Rebekah were given twin sons.

Rebekah had a difficult pregnancy:

The children struggled with one another inside her, and she said, "If this is the way of it, why go on living?"
So she went to consult the Lord, and he said to her,
There are two nations in your womb.
Your issue will be two rival peoples,
One nation shall have the mastery of the other,
and the elder shall serve the younger.

The descendants of Esau were to be the Edomites, and those of Jacob the Israelites, and there was indeed to be enmity between them.

I wonder if Rebekah was sorry she had consulted the Lord? This was a hard prediction to carry with her through the rest of her pregnancy.

When the time came for her confinement, there were indeed twins in her womb, and a rough birthgiving, two babies, one coming immediately after the other, the younger grabbing his twin's heel. Esau, the first born, was covered with red hair like a little animal. Jacob, the heel-grabber, was a fraternal twin, smooth-skinned and far from identical.

As they grew, Esau became a hunter, and Isaac's favorite son. Jacob tended the land around the home tent, and was loved by Rebekah.

In *The Parable of the Tribes*, Alexander Schmookler points out that the world of the hunter was moderately peaceable. It was a sparsely populated world. If the human being was to survive, interdependence was essential. It was only when one tribe grew stronger than other neighboring tribes, had more children, cattle, goats, and camels, that trouble began, as was the case with Isaac and Abimelech. "The rise of agriculture made possible a more settled life with far larger populations living in the same territory."

When wells were dug, and water made more available, the tribe tended to settle around the well. So, when Isaac's wells, animals, and retinue prospered and enlarged, he had to leave Gerar. He left peaceably, but far too often the ancient Hebrew praised God for helping his tribe take over another peoples' land.

The slaughter of tribes who worshiped alien gods, slaughter commanded by God, disturbs me. In Psalm 44, we read:

We have heard with our ears, O God, our fathers have told us
What you did in their time,
How you drove out the heathen with your hand, and planted our fathers in,
How you destroyed the nations, and made your own people to flourish,

For they did not get the land in possession through their own sword,
neither was it their own arm that helped them,
But your right hand, and your arm, and the light of your countenance,
because you favored them.
You are my King, O God,
send help to Jacob.
Through you we will overthrow our enemies,
and in your name we will tread under those who rise up against us.

This triumphalism is profoundly disturbing. But Scripture makes it clear that we are never to stay in one place, one way of thinking, but to move on, out into the wilderness, as El Shaddai moved Abraham, Isaac, and Jacob. As promised, they had many descendants and, alas, a large population seems to encourage war.

But on a planet where population has grown beyond bounds, this warring way of life does not work any more. Wars in the name of religion not only give religion a bad name, they are a warning that it is time for us to move out of and beyond the old tribalism. Not easy, for it would seem that some form of tribalism is inherent in human nature. Science fiction writers often cast their characters in the old tribal mode, even when the tribe is the people of this planet, and the neighbors, " them," are from other planets. In Star Trek, the tribe includes a Martian, so "us" is the solar system, and "them" (usually the bad guys) are from other solar systems. Sometimes it is this galaxy that is the tribe, versus other galaxies.

But everything we are learning about the nature of Being is making it apparent that "us" versus "them" is a violation of

Creation. Tribalism must be transformed into community. We are learning from astrophysics and particle physics and cellular biology that all of Creation exists only in interdependence and unity.

In a recent article on astrophysics I came across the beautiful and imaginative concept known as "the butterfly effect." If a butterfly winging over the fields around Crosswicks should be hurt, the effect would be felt in galaxies thousands of light years away. The interrelationship of all of Creation is sensitive in a way we are just beginning to understand. If a butterfly is hurt, we are hurt. If the bell tolls, it tolls for us. We can no longer even think of saying, "In the Name of the Lord will I destroy them." No wonder Jesus could say that not one sparrow could fall to the ground without the Father's knowledge.

Dr. Paul Brand points out that every cell in the body has its own specific job, in interdependence with every other cell. The only cells which insist on being independent and autonomous are cancer cells.

Surely that should be a lesson to us in the churches. Separation from each other and from the rest of the world is not only disaster for us, but for everybody from whom we separate ourselves. We must be very careful lest in insisting on our independence we become malignant.

If we take the whole sweep of the story, rather than isolating passages out of context, this is the message of Scripture. So now, as we take the next steps into the wilderness into which God is sending us; now, as the human creature has moved from being the primitive hunter to the land-worker to the city-dweller to the traveler in the skies, we must move on to a way of life where we are so much God's one people that warfare is no longer even a possibility. It is that, or dis-aster, and we must not let Satan, the great separator, win.

The phrase, "the butterfly effect," comes from the language of physics. It is equally the language of poetry and of theology. For the Christian, the butterfly has long been a symbol of resurrection.

The butterfly emerges from the cocoon, its wings, wet with rebirth, slowly opening, and then this creature of fragile loveliness flies across the blue vault of sky.

Butterflies and angels, seraphim and cherubim, call us earth-bound creatures to lift up our mortal dust and sing with them, to God's delight.

Holy. Holy. Holy!

3

Let the Floods Clap Their Hands

ESAU WAS A MORE PRIMITIVE personality than Jacob. He lived for the moment, with little thought of the morrow or the consequences of his impulses. When he came home from hunting, famished, and saw that Jacob had made pottage (a delicious stew of rice, lentils, and onions), the smell was too much for him, and he asked Jacob to give him a bowlful.

Jacob's response was hardly generous – surely he could have shared with Esau! But, no: he demanded Esau's birthright as the price of a mess of pottage. Because Esau was famished and because that moment was all he was thinking about, he let Jacob trick him, and to fill his immediate need he thoughtlessly gave away his birthright as eldest son. While this was merely imprudent of Esau, it was a thoroughly dirty trick on Jacob's part: but Jacob never hesitated to pull dirty tricks. And yet it was Jacob, not Esau, who became the third person in the trinity of patriarchs. Over and over in Scripture we hear the invocation: "the God of Abraham, Isaac, and Jacob." And God named Jacob *Israel* – one man as the icon of a nation.

Poor hairy Esau, more like a monkey than a man. Perhaps he compensated by becoming a mighty hunter, whereas Jacob, who was called to be Israel, stayed home with his mother. Jacob cooked the savory smelling pottage Esau was so hungry for. Jacob did many things which today are considered effeminate. It is almost as much of a shock to us to think of Jacob staying around the tent, cooking rice, onions, and lentils, as it is for us to visualize Jesus eating at Matthew's house with all those sinful people. Jacob, in a masculine world, had feminine qualities, and so, despite his cheating, he also had intuition and a willing suspension of disbelief.

Take a new look, these unexpected happenings seem to say Jacob may not be who you thought he was. You may not be who you think you are, or who you think you ought to be.

The glorious message of Scripture is that we do not have to be perfect for our Maker to love us. All through the great stories, heavenly love is lavished on visibly imperfect people. Scripture asks us to look at Jacob as he really is, to look at ourselves as we really are, and then realize that this is who God loves. God did not love Jacob because he was a cheat, but because he was Jacob. God loves us in our complex *is*ness, and when we get stuck on the image of the totally virtuous and morally perfect person we will never be, we are unable to accept this unqualified love, or to love other people in their rich complexity.

If God can love Jacob – or any single one of us – as we really are, then it is possible for us to turn in love to those who hurt or confuse us. Those we know and those we do not know. And that makes me take a new look at love.

It is not easy. The forensic attitude is deeply ingrained. I need the help of the Holy Spirit in order to turn my demands for fairness to love, as (for instance) when I think about whoever it was who was willing to allow me to take the blame for something I did not do. It is not easy to reject the forensic response, but it is essential. And does it make any difference if I try to think of those two horrid men on my jury duty case with love? If the world and all of us in it are as interdependent as the physicists tell us, yes. If the butterfly effect is true, yes, it does make a difference. They don't have to be perfect, or even repentant, to be loved. Of course they won't ever know that I am trying to love them, but that does not negate love. Not if it is part of the love of God.

And Jacob received the beneficence of that love.

Why Jacob?

The stories of the great scriptural characters are not stories about fairness. Life is not fair. Indeed, the idea of fairness and unfairness didn't come into being until after the Fall. In Eden there was no need to think about such things, because life was the joy of at-one-ment with the Creator. It is after the fracture of this union, this separation (the first apartheid), that we begin to get caught up in shoulds and oughts, and fair and unfair. Children tend to stamp their feet and cry out "It's not fair!" and very likely it isn't. When we think in terms of fairness and unfairness, we begin to want to "pay back" whoever has been unfair, we begin to want to get even, to punish. That is the beginning of forensic thinking.

Unfortunately, as many of us move on in chronology, we tend to stay stuck in the "It's not fair!" frame of mind, which, for the adult, is crippling. It takes great courage to live in a world where fairness simply doesn't play a part, and hasn't, since Adam and Eve ate of the fruit of the tree of the knowledge of good and evil. And one of Satan's most successful ploys is his insistence that things ought to be fair. The good should be rewarded; the bad should be punished. If we think forensically and earn enough merit badges everything will work out just as we would like. But that is not how grace works.

In a fair world, that tornado which devastated our trees would have gone some place where people didn't lovingly tend the land. But tornadoes don't have anything to do with fairness. It is easier to understand that the "natural" world operates on principles where fairness plays no part than it is to understand that we cannot dwell overmuch on fairness with human nature, either. In a fair world no child would be struck down by a drunken driver, no family would have to grieve; no one would have to carry the burden of killing. In a fair world there would be no crime, no violence in the streets, no body cells growing out of control with cancer. Fairness is devoutly to be desired, but it is not the way things are. In this world the wicked flourish and the innocent suffer, and the Lord of all is no respecter of persons, and may sometimes speak through the wicked even more clearly than through the innocent.

In our own cumbersome, unwieldy court system, which is nevertheless one of the better court systems in the world, those who can afford the best lawyers are more likely to be given a verdict of Not Guilty than those who have to take whatever lawyer the state assigns them. During my time on jury duty in January, I was very aware that the two arrogant men had managed to retain very clever lawyers, who were doing their best to clear them, according to the law, whether or not they believed them to be guilty of the crime of which they were accused. We jurors were not at all sure that justice was going to prevail.

And in my own life I was struggling to accept the fact that justice was not going to be done. I did *not* have to be exonerated over that spilled secret. I did *not* have to know who told, and then allowed me to be blamed. I had to let go thoughts of justice and vindication, and live with the situation as it was, as lovingly as possible. Which was not very.

Why is it so hard to understand that in this world everything is not going to turn out all right, all strings neatly tied, and justice triumphant? If we take the short view, it would be almost impossible not to drop into pessimism. It is not easy, in the midst of tragedy or trauma, to take the long view, to understand that ultimately there is meaning, meaning we may not in our lifetimes ever understand.

It is impossible for us finite creatures to understand the infinite Author of All in any definitive way. We can never say, This is God, Q.E.D. We would like to feel that we understand God, and the Creator's ways, but we can't. We never have. Not since the Garden. The important message, throughout Scripture, is that God understands us and loves us, and so frees us to keep our concept of el open to change as revelation comes to us in new and unexpected ways.

When Jacob tricked his twin brother, Esau was justly outraged. Outrage is an emotion we are all familiar with. When something horrendous happens we want the perpetrator of the crime to be punished. We look for justice, absolute justice, rather than mercy. The Psalms are full of outrage and demands for redress:

Let my adversaries be clothed with shame, and let them cover themselves with their own confusion, as with a cloak ... Break their teeth, O God, in their mouths, smite the jawbones of the lions, O Lord. Let them fall away like running water; when they shoot their arrows, let them be rooted out. Let them slime away like a snail, and be like the untimely fruit of a woman, and let them not see the sun. Or ever your pots be made hot with thorns, he shall take them away with a whirlwind, the green and burning alike. The righteous shall rejoice when he sees vengeance, he shall wash his footsteps in the blood of the ungodly.

No!

Not any more.

Now we have to move beyond that.

Am I only like my dog with her rawhide bone, chewing and chewing until there is nothing left? It has been pointed out to me that this vengeance against enemies was obedience to the Lord, and that this obedience is the highest law But is it? Didn't Jesus break the Mosaic law in order to obey the higher law of love?

It takes more maturity than many of us possess to want the monstrous criminal to repent, saying to God and to us, "Forgive me. I am horrified at what I have done. I am sorry, sorry, and I will never do it again. With your help I will turn my life to love."

Hate the sin and love the sinner is too easy. As long as there is any hate in us we are not ready for heaven, not as long as we're shutting the golden doors on anyone else.

I continued my own struggle during that time on jury duty Several evenings, when I was tired and wanted to relax, I received angry phone calls from people condemning me for telling that terrible secret I had not told. All I could say was that I had not breathed a word. Some people believed me. Some did not. It is a taint in human nature to like to see someone else do wrong so that we can affirm our own righteousness. My own wish to find out who had told the secret was a part of this taint. I was well aware that, as my friend Tallis points out, we cannot afford the luxury of hurt feelings. My head could get that all straight, but there was still hurt in my heart.

I thought of the heavenly banquet, where part of my job might have to be blowing up the balloons and setting the place for whoever it was who willingly dumped blame on me – a job which would have to be done, ultimately, with love. Not just forgiveness, but love. And I knew I wasn't ready, yet. And what was going on in the courtroom during the day helped me to see the situation more clearly than otherwise might have been possible.

But it still hurt.

And I had to let that hurt go. I could not hold on to it.

Ernest L. Boyer, Jr., in *A Way in the World*, writes, "Forgiveness is, then, a renewal, and for love to grow it must be renewed every day. This renewal is not one that seeks somehow to return to the past, however, rather, it seeks to revitalize the present. To carry a grudge is to live in the past, to live with the bitterness of disappointment of the expectation of a future that never was." To carry a grudge is to live in the past. That hit home. It helped me to move into the present so that there might be hope for friendship to be reborn.

Boyer continues, "Both of these – the past that is now gone and the future that never was – are illusionary worlds. Forgiveness frees a person to live in the reality of the relationship's present."

Esau has something to teach us here. He was willing to sell his birthright to satisfy his immediate desire for food, but he did not carry grudges. He did not live in the past. He had no expectations of impossible futures. Once his anger at Jacob was spent, he did not dwell on it. He let it go.

The two men who were being tried for assault in the second degree struck me as grudge keepers. Shouldn't that have taught me something?

The heavenly banquet cannot begin until we are all there, and I can greet with love the two resentful men, and everybody who has caused me pain, and call out a welcome to them all. The heavenly banquet cannot begin until all those whom I have hurt are ready to welcome me, in all my flawed and contradictory humanness.

Forgiveness which leads to welcoming, with open arms, the forgiven ones to the party, comes less from an act of will than from a gift of grace. Sometimes prayer opens the door to this gift.

Prayer is most real when it moves away from forensic demands, from a crime and punishment, eye-for-an-eye thinking, and into an open and vulnerable listening. It is not so much talking to God as being quiet and focussing on listening, so that perhaps we will be able to hear if God has something to say.

When I was a little girl I used to say my prayers, ending, "and God bless me and make me a good girl." As I grow older, I become less and less sure that it was a good prayer, as I become less and less sure what being a good girl actually meant.

I suppose in my case it meant that I was to honor my mother and father, and I can't fault that. It meant that I was to obey them which, as long as I was a child – accepting everything from them, food, clothing, housing, ideas, schooling – was right and proper, especially since they were reasonable and loving parents. It also meant that I was not to tell lies. That I was to keep clean. That I was to be courteous. To be considerate of other people.

So what's wrong with it?

Did it imply that being a "good girl" was in my control? Did it imply a degree of conscious direction of my feelings and actions which life has taught me that I don't have?

Sure, I want to be "good," but can I consider myself "good" in a world where a small proportion of the people have too much to eat while the rest of the world is starving? Where a small proportion of us live comfortably if not luxuriously, while the rest of the world is in favelas and barrios and ghettos or out on the streets? Can I closet myself in my "goodness" while there is injustice and prejudice and terrorism?

Perhaps I may not personally cheat the government, consider the poor expendable, murder, steal, mug, or rape. Perhaps I may not use a knife with the intent to injure or kill. Perhaps I try to eat a diet suitable for a small planet. But can I separate my own health from the rest of the world? My own good nutrition from the poor nutrition of billions? My longing for peace from the warring in the Middle East or South America or Ireland or anywhere else at all? In a universe where the lifting of the wings of a butterfly is felt across galaxies, I cannot isolate myself, because my separation may add to the starvation and the anger and the violence.

I am not burdening myself with a lot of guilts which are impossible for me to resolve. But to separate myself from the suffering of the world is dis-aster. If I call myself "good" is that not separation?

Jesus said, "Why do you call me good? Only my father is good."

Aren't we supposed to be good? Do we always have the wisdom to know what good is? If we truly understand what Jesus was saying, we know that what matters is not moralism, but understanding that God with infinite grace can work goodness through us. Goodness is of God; we cannot make ourselves good through an act of will.

Surely the Inquisitors thought they were being good, that they were doing God's will, when they tortured people (whether innocent or guilty is hardly the point). Terrorists think that they are being good, nay, holy, when they throw bombs and shoot guns in religious zeal. Those in South Africa who believe in apartheid think they are being good when they assume they are superior to anyone of another color.

Trying, of our own virtue, to be good, usually leads to disaster. If I, self-consciously, try to make myself good, I am unwittingly separating myself from those I love and would serve.

I learned this the hard way during our four summers of four generations living together under one not very large roof. I wouldn't have missed those summers. They were a kind of miracle in this day and age, and I have written about them in *A Circle of Quiet* and *The Summer of the Great Grandmother.* I learned that if I tried to be good, that is, if I tried to be the perfect wife, mother, daughter, grandmother, all I did was become exhausted and ill and humorless and help nobody. If I spent the morning at the typewriter; if, in the late afternoon before I cooked dinner, I went off with the dogs for a walk, the entire household was happier, there was more laughter and song. I learned that if I was what I had considered selfish, that is, if I took reasonable care of my own needs, we had a smoothly running household. Paradox, as always.

If I am ever good, it is not because I am trying to be, but because goodness is for a moment offered me as a gift of sheer grace. Jesus made it very clear that goodness comes from God, not from el's creatures.

Not that I want to wallow in my own sin and badness, or that I see myself as hated by God because I am human and often do wrong. Actions have consequences, but that is not what "original sin" means, and we need to rethink "original sin" just as much as we needed to rethink the impassible God who could not suffer. Does any mother, holding her newborn babe in her arms, see anything except innocence and purity and God's delight?

How did we get hung up on "goodness" as a criterion? If that were so, God would not have called Abraham, or Isaac, or Jacob.

Especially not Jacob. It is quite clear that Jacob was not "good."

Nor was he particularly religious: he was slow to accept the God of his fathers. But even before he had decided to call their God his God, too, he made altars, upon which he poured sacred oil. How many altars Jacob made! One day I'll count them, but I'm less interested in adding up numbers than in the need to make altars, to understand sacred spaces.

I, too, have my altars, such as the Star Watching Rock and the Icon Tree. Whether we acknowledge it or not, we all have our own altars (and a kitchen stove on which meals are cooked with love is not an unworthy one), altars which may be for us ladders of angels, joining heaven and earth, God and creature.

* * *

In this time of increasing stress and tension we need our altars of affirmation, our ladders drawing us to adoring awe.

Not easy. If, twenty-five years ago, I had somehow been allowed to see a few clips from almost any evening's news, I'd have found it impossible to believe. We've had assassinations, scandals, bombings, kidnappings, hijackings, and crisis after crisis among nations.

In my own neighborhood in New York, in twenty-five years I've seen stores previously only locked at night now protected with iron gates to keep out vandals. Private guards help the city police to patrol the streets. Not long ago my husband put me in a taxi to go downtown to give a talk, and told me to put my gold earrings in my pocket till I arrived, commenting "Isn't this a terrible way to live."

He was not being an alarmist. Only a few days before, a friend of ours had been walking along Broadway past Lincoln Center, when she felt an arm go about her neck – and her gold chain was gone. She said the thief must have been extremely professional, because she could not find a mark on her neck.

What has happened to our country in the past quarter-of-a-century would be incomprehensible to my grandparents, but it has all happened and is happening. We need to be aware of it, and to try to listen to God for what our part is in trying to change it, to bring terrorism to compassion, greed to generosity, lust to love. We don't have to succeed, single-handedly, in reforming the world, or in improving the morals of those around us by our own goodness. God-Within-Us-In-Jesus did none of these things.

But if we listen, we will be given the courage to do whatever it is that God wants us to do, big things or, more likely, small. This faith in God's gifts of courage and grace is like a foundation of rock under my feet, even as I help pile the wood from the trees ripped off at their roots by the twister, even as the bed shakes under me in the earthquake, even as I take the crowded rush hour subway down to Manhattan's criminal court.

* * *

How can we expect peace in the world, sanity in our cities, when as Christians we cannot live creatively together with all our wonderfully diverse ways of affirming our love of God? Why are we so concerned about those who do not express their faith in exactly the same way that we do? If I need a doctor, I am not going to ask, "What is your denomination?" any more than I am going to inquire about sexual preference. What I want to know is: Is this a good doctor? Will I be treated effectively? Can I be cured?

When we worry about someone's denomination, we sometimes forget that this person may be a superb surgeon, or pianist, or car mechanic. We sometimes forget that our own vocations are not limited by denominational boundaries. Our responsibility as faithful people of God is in every area of our lives, not only in our churchgoing.

If I am true in my living to what I proclaim in my writing it is because of grace, not virtue. It has little to do with my denomination. I pray for grace, knowing that it is not mine to grasp; it is a gift of love.

And of course I am not always true to what I proclaim. I am human and flawed and frequently fall flat on my face. All of us do, even the saints. But we struggle to be true. If we struggle honestly, humbly, the angels will help us.

When they do, it is usually when we least expect it, when we have to respond to something or someone immediately, and so don't have time to get ourselves in the way. I turned from the typewriter to answer the phone, and it was a young woman in Oregon. We'd met at a writers' conference, and corresponded sporadically. She's lively and bright and talented.

Her question came at me out of the blue. "Madeleine – all the things you've written, do you believe them?"

"Yes I do."

"You really do?"

"If I didn't believe them, I couldn't survive."

"I'm in the hospital. I had a hysterectomy. I can't ever have a baby."

To a young woman in her twenties this is a bitter blow. What she had expected to be a simple D and C (though she'd signed the release for further surgery if necessary) had revealed a malignancy.

"The doctor says the outlook is good, but he wants me to have chemotherapy, anyhow. Oh, God, Madeleine, I try not to say, *Why did this happen to me* – " She started to cry.

I wanted to put my arms around her and hold her, and did the best I could, long distance.

When she had stopped crying, she said, "I don't know why I had to call you and tell you all my troubles. I just need to be sure you believe what you say in your books."

"I do." God help me, I do. Even when I don't, I do.

(And that is the truth: even when I don't, I do.)

"You'll pray for me?"

"Of course." This means simply holding this young woman out (or in) to God's love, and visualizing her as whole and healthy and beautiful.

The important thing about this conversation was that I was given the grace of affirming all that my books say at a time when that affirmation was needed. And not only by my young friend, by me, too.

Now, this young woman was not in any conservative sense of the word, a "practicing Christian." But she asked for prayers, and that was enough, more than enough.

Jesus did not limit his love to those accepted by the establishment. He spoke with Samaritans, even making a Samaritan woman the protagonist of one of his parables, despite the fact that the Samaritans were the socially despised, the religiously untouchable. In that culture one didn't take water from a *woman* in the casual way that Jesus did, and even less from a Samaritan woman. But he did.

If we Christians truly love one another, that love spreads out to include all the Samaritans and the Canaanites and unbelievers and worshipers of Baal and the unorthodox and the heterodox and even the Shiites and Khomeini and Idi Amin and Muammar Qaddafi – and the two men on trial in criminal court.

Perhaps we have been giving too many answers instead of asking questions, of ourselves, of each other, of God.

Montaigne's "Que sais-je?" sits more comfortably with me than Descartes' "Je pense, donc je suis."

The most brilliant people really don't know very much. We will not move along on our journey if we are afraid to ask questions. What is my place in this glorious universe? Where shall I set my stone pillow to make an altar? Will there be a ram? Or a butterfly? What do you want me to do? How can I criticize less and love more? How can I show in my own life the loveliness of creativity? Can I call a Christian from another denomination less Christian than those in my own without further battering the broken bride of Christ? How do I help to heal and not to separate?

Never with pride. Never with being sure that I am right and everybody else is wrong.

There's an old story of a student who went to a famous old rabbi and said, "Master, in the old days there were people who could see God. Why is it that nobody sees God nowadays?" The old man answered, "My child, nowadays nobody can stoop so low."

* * *

Why are we afraid of stooping so low? Didn't the second person of the Trinity stoop lower than we can even conceive when he willingly relinquished all power and glory to come to earth as a human baby?

We find it difficult to understand that the magnificence and might of all Creation is also small and vulnerable. Isn't the Creator supposed to be invulnerable? Isn't that what used to be taught in seminary? If God can be hurt, what kind of protection can this suffering servant give us?

But God, in choosing to become incarnate, with all our human limitations, also chose the possibility of being hurt. Possibility? Probability? Inevitability? Those who are fully alive are also usually those who have been deeply wounded, and the God who came to us in Jesus of Nazareth was fully alive, with an awareness and a joy and a perceptiveness most of us can only wonder at. Along with the joy was a willingness to assume all of our human sufferings, which should make us look differently at our own pain.

Would I really be able to worship a God who was simply implacable power, and who was invulnerable? If I am hurt, I don't turn for strength and help to someone who has never been hurt, but to someone who has, and who can therefore understand a little of what I am going through. The people I know who are the most invulnerable also tend to show the least compassion.

The kind of person I turn to is someone who has been strong enough to face pain when it comes – and it does come. Someone who faces it, endures it, and tries as hard as possible to go through it and come out on the other side. Someone whose urge for health is strong enough to hold on to wholeness even in the midst of suffering. And someone who manages to retain a sense of humor, who has the gift of laughter.

As these are the qualities I look for in another human being when I am in need of healing, so these are the qualities I look for in God.

And it is God who promises the Heavenly Banquet, the banquet which is for all of creation, for every single one of us, all us members of the jury, the two arrogant defendants, and their clever lawyers. We will all be changed in the twinkling of an eye (though that may be many thousands of years in human time), come to ourselves, even if it brings us bitter tears of self-revelation before we can turn to love.

To be in a state of unforgiveness is to know hell, at least in a small way. I know, because I've been there. It's not easy to get out of hell, but it can be done, when we come to ourselves and turn to the source of all love.

Belief in hell is lack of faith, Berdyaev said to me in his book as I sat in the jury room. "Belief in hell is lack of faith because it is to attribute more power to Satan than to God."

I know what Berdyaev was trying to say. He was emphasizing Satan's ultimate downfall. In the meantime hell remains to be conquered. I believe in hell, but my faith in the power of Satan and the fallen angels is nowhere near as strong as my belief in the eternal and infinite power of the Creator. Paul, in his first letter to the Corinthians, asks, "O death, where is thy sting? O grave, where is thy victory?" But then he makes a marvelous affirmation – "Thanks be to God, who gives us the victory through our Lord Jesus Christ!" Though Satan cannot win the final victory, during our lifetimes we will all experience the sting of death, the dark power of hell and the grave. But it is not the last word. It is God who has the last word!

We are all going to face God's judgment, but we will not receive forensic judgment from the throne of heaven. Listen to the way judgment is referred to in these lines from the 98th Psalm:

Show yourselves joyful in the Lord, all you lands,
sing rejoice, and give thanks.

Praise the Lord upon the harp, sing to the harp
with a psalm of thanksgiving.

With trumpets, and with horns, O show yourselves
joyful before the Lord, the King.

Let the sea make a noise and all that is in it;
the round world and all that dwell on it.

Let the floods clap their hands, and let the hills
be joyful together before the Lord,
for he is come to judge the earth,

With righteousness shall he judge the world
and the peoples with his truth.

That sounds more as though we were preparing for a celebration than judgment, but isn't that what judgment is really about? For the judgment of God does not falter. God is not going to abandon Creation, nor the people up for trial in criminal court, nor the Shiites nor the communists nor the warmongers, nor the greedy and corrupt people in high places, nor the dope pushers, nor you, nor me. Bitter tears of repentance may be shed before we can join the celebration, but it won't be complete until we are all there.

The book of the prophet, Micah, ends with these words:

Who is a God like you, who pardons iniquity and overlooks the transgressions of us all. He does not hold on to his anger, because he delights in mercy. He will have pity on us, and will subdue our faults, and will cast all our sins into the depths of the sea. Grant Jacob your truth, and your mercy to Abraham, as you promised to our forbears from the days of old.

This is the God of Scripture, the God of forbearance, forgiveness, and unqualified love. We have been living in a world where we have viewed God and each other in a forensic way for too long, and it should be apparent that it is not working, and that it is not going to work. This forensic world is not a scriptural world, but a clever projection of the Tempter. It is not helping our traffic jams. It will not help the national debt. It will not help our peacemakers to keep the peace. Our planet totters on the brink of disaster. Our only hope for peace, within our own hearts, and all over our small green earth, is for us to open ourselves to the judgment of God, that judgment that makes the waters and the hills to sing. For God's judgment is atonement, at-one-ment, making us one with the Lord of love.

Let the floods clap their hands, and let the hills
be joyful together before the Lord,
for he is come to judge the earth,
with righteousness shall he judge the world
and the peoples with his truth.

4

What Are You Looking for?

WHEN I WAS A CHILD nobody told me that I should read the Bible piously, so I read it just as I read Hans Christian Andersen and George MacDonald and books of fairy tales. I read it as story, great story, about fascinating and complex people called by God to do amazing things.

Perhaps it was a blessing that as a child I was not taken to Sunday school. I have met far too many people who have had to spend years in the difficult task of unlearning bad Sunday school teaching, who have found it almost impossible to get rid of the image of an angry God, out to punish them.

My church teaches that the Bible contains everything necessary for salvation. What on earth do we mean by that?

I can affirm it only if I know what the Bible is, and what it is not. It is a living book, not a dead one. It urges us to go beyond its pages, not to stop with what we have read. It is a book not only of history and of the prohibitions of the commandments and laws, but of poetry and song, of fantasy and paradox and mystery and contradiction.

It is not the only book in which I will look for and find truth. There is much to inspire me, to widen my understanding of the Creator, in the works of Shakespeare, Dante, Dostoyevsky. There are important insights into the nature of God in the sacred books of other religions. When I was a child, my parents had these words framed and hung in the bathroom:

Listen to the exhortation of the dawn.
Look to this day, for it is life, the very life of life.
In its brief course lie all the verities and realities
of your existence,
the glory of action – the bliss of growth
the splendor of beauty
For yesterday is but a dream,
and tomorrow is only a vision,
but today, well lived,
makes every yesterday a dream of happiness,
and every tomorrow a vision of hope.
Look well therefore to this day.
Such is the salutation of the dawn.

Good words, those, good words to live by. They come from the Koran. Does that mean that my Episcopalian parents were flirting with Islam? Of course not. I've memorized those words, because they help keep me aware of the wonders of each day, even when they may be painful.

Hugh and I spent seven hours in the emergency room of a big New York hospital, a scene of pain, noise, fear, confusion. Hugh woke up with a pain in the chest. Our doctor was away for the weekend (of course this was Saturday), so it was off to the emergency room. Seven hours, mostly spent waiting, once the electrocardiogram was normal. But then there were hours spent facing the possibility that the pain might be from a pulmonary embolism. And at last, at the seventh hour, the welcome news that it was from pulled muscles, with perhaps a cracked rib, from the strain of trying to open one of the recalcitrant, ancient windows in our apartment. Oh, the joy of sitting down together at our own table, an hour after Hugh was released, to eat dinner together! The joy in the simple ordinariness of a simple meal in our own home! Indeed, look well therefore to this day.

It is not only in the religious writings of various peoples that I find truth. I find that my forbearance is widened, my understanding of human potential expanded, as I read fiction, even if it is only to disagree with a narrow or ugly view of life, or to turn away from discontent. The fiction to which I turn and return is that which has a noble understanding of God's purpose for all that has been created.

My theology is deepened and broadened as I study the new sciences. I do try to read with discrimination, to turn to writers whose vision is not mean or narrow or degrading. It was a sad moment when I had to admit to myself that I was not going to be able to read, in this lifetime, all the books I need to read!

I turn daily to the Bible because in it are the stories of my own tradition, of what Jung calls our racial memory. The story of Jacob is my story, too.

Karl Barth said, "I take the Bible far too seriously to take it literally." The Bible is a book which urges us to keep our concept of God open, to let our understanding grow and develop as we are illumined by new discoveries. If we stopped where Scripture leaves us, in the New Testament as well as the Old, we could still, with clear consciences, keep slaves. The apostle

Paul exhorts masters to treat their slaves well, and slaves to be obedient, with no hint that slave-owning may not be a good thing in the eyes of God. According to the law, a woman taken in adultery was to be stoned. To death. Not men. If we stopped, literally, with Scripture, we could keep on justifying going into any country we wanted, when we needed extra living space, and slaughtering the heathen natives, because God is on our side, and will help get rid of the pagans for us, so we can have their country.

Who are the pagans? A child, asked this question in Sunday school, replied, "The pagans are the people that don't quarrel about God."

It is terrifying to realize that we can prove almost anything we want to prove if we take fragments of the Bible out of context. Those who believe in the righteousness of apartheid believe that this is scriptural. I turn to the Bible in fear and trembling, trying to see it whole, not using it for my own purposes, but letting its ongoing message of love direct me.

The problem of extra living space for an overcrowded planet is one with which science fiction writers have honestly struggled in their depiction of space exploration, with few answers. The old legalism was, perhaps, behind the way the pioneers treated the Indians – not all the pioneers, thank God, but some of them. Did they justify giving the Indians blankets impregnated with smallpox virus because they knew God wanted the white man, not the heathen, to have the land?

Scriptural literalism has caused and still causes incredible damage. But I don't want to throw up my hands and toss out Scripture because we have constantly misused it.

How do those of us who are not seminary students or theologians read the Book creatively and not destructively? Not, I think, with volumes of interpretation – not, that is, for our daily reading. We must take it as it is. What a passage says to us today may not be what the same passage will say when we next encounter it. We must strive to be open to the deeply mythic quality, expressing the longings and aspirations and searchings of the human race.

After a tiring day on jury duty I sat in my quiet corner and picked up the Bible. In Matthew's gospel, I turned to chapter 11 where Jesus was speaking to the multitudes about his cousin, John. He asked,

"What did you go out into the wilderness to see? A reed shaken in the wind? But what did you look for? A man clothed in soft raiment? Look, they that wear soft raiment are found in king's houses. But what did you look for? A prophet? Yes, a prophet indeed, and more than a prophet."

And he continued, asking the people,

What is this generation like? It is like children sitting in the market place, and calling to their companions, saying we have piped for you, and you have not danced, we have mourned for you, and you have not grieved." John came, neither eating, nor drinking and the people accused him of having a devil. And the Son of man came eating and drinking, and they accused him of being gluttonous, and a wine bibber, and a friend of publicans and sinners."

"What are you looking for?" Jesus asked the people.

What are we looking for? Are we looking for things we can criticize, or are we looking for Christ, for love and compassion? Are we looking for evidence that our Christian group is *the* group, with *the* truth, or are we looking for at-one-ment?

I care very much about Christian unity, and therefore it gives me great joy when I am privileged to speak with many different kinds of Christian groups. I had the pleasure of being the keynote speaker in Boston at a gathering of two thousand United Methodist women. Shortly thereafter I had the joy of receiving an honorary doctorate from Wheaton College, in Illinois, and from there I went to Dallas, Texas, to teach at a Christian Writers Conference. Following that, I preached at the Episcopal Cathedral Church of St. John the Divine in New York; on to Immanuel Congregational Church (United Church of Christ) in Hartford, Connecticut. Back to Boston for the Catholic Library Association, and on, the next weekend, to Presbyterian Wilson College in Pennsylvania. I came home from all this ecumenical traveling, and I said, fervently, to my husband, "I've had it with Christians."

How could I possibly say such a thing?

Not because of the majority of loving, faithful people I met, but because of a minority, small, but growing, of people who seemed to think they were called to discover the devil in other people. (Believe me, when you look for the devil, you'll find him.)

Jesus was accused of casting out devils by the Devil. He was

casting out a devil, and it was dumb. And when the devil was gone out of the man, he was able to speak. And some of the people said, "He casts out devils through Beelzebub, the chief of devils." Jesus answered them, "Every kingdom divided against itself will fall. If Satan is divided against himself, how can his kingdom stand? You say that I cast out devils through the devil, well, if I cast out devils by the devil, by whom do your sons cast them out? They will be your judges. But if I, with the finger of God, cast out devils, then the kingdom of God is come upon you."

What are we looking for?

The people who accused Jesus of casting out devils by the Devil, frighten me. The people who are looking to see if they can accuse someone of being in league with the Devil frighten me, too. There aren't many of them, yet, but I met or heard one or two every place I went. They are powerful, and they claim to be Christians, to be even better Christians than those of us who are looking for Christ, for love, rather than Satan.

And they are dividing the kingdom, and Jesus warns that a kingdom divided against itself will fall.

There are times when I may have had it with Christians, but I do not want the kingdom to fall. My hope and my faith is that we can worship God in our different ways, and still be one body. My feet walk, my eyes see, my nose smells, but I am still one body. And that one body is a part of the body of Christ.

As Christians, we have a responsibility to love one another, not to be suspicious and judgmental. The early Christians were not divided into inimical factions. Jesus Christ, and him crucified, and risen from the dead, was what mattered. Anyone looking at the divided body of Christ today might be tempted to imagine Jesus gathering the disciples together and saying, "Hey, Peter, you start the Roman Catholic Church. John, why don't you get the Episcopalians going? James, do you want the Baptists? Andrew, what about Methodism? Philip, can you start the Presbyterians?"

Is that the kind of body of Christ Scripture talks about? How can we have an effective evangelism if we are a divided body? How can we even call ourselves Christian?

Many years ago I belonged to a group which put on a musical comedy each spring, the proceeds going to the two churches in the village – I won't bother to mention what denomination they were. One year the regular director was away; and I was asked to take over. I didn't want to immerse myself for several months in music I might get tired of, so with incredible naivete and a notable lack of common sense, I decided that we would do Smetana's *The Bartered Bride. The Bartered Bride*, I discovered to my rue, is no musical comedy. It is not even an operetta. It is an opera. Eventually we came up with an excellent production, but I was totally exhausted, and those of us involved called it not the *Bartered* Bride, but the *Battered* Bride.

That's us, the Christian church right now, the Battered Bride.

We are supposed to be the bride of Christ, but what kind of bride are we? Not very beautiful.

The terrible difference between us, the bride of Christ, and the tragic brides who are beaten by their husbands, is that it is we, ourselves, who are doing the battering. With our warring denominations we have scratched at each others' eyes, pummeled and punched each other and ourselves, and so disgraced our host. What kind of a bruised and bloodied face do we show to the world? What kind of a bride of Christ do we make visible?

We will not become beautiful again until religion becomes a unifying and not a divisive word. We will not be beautiful again until we look for love, rather than Satan. We do find what we look for.

A letter came to me from a woman who was in charge of taking photographs for a conference where I had recently been a speaker. She asked me if I had a picture I could send her, the snapshot she had taken of me was not usable because I was surrounded by an aura of light which, she wrote, was surely a mark of the presence of the Holy Spirit. And then she continued, sadly, that she had mentioned this to a friend, and the friend's response had been that perhaps I was worshiping Satan, and that was what had caused the light.

Such a reaction saddens me. And frightens me. Because we do find what we look for.

As to the picture of me, it was taken with one of those cameras which spit the picture out at you, and we've all seen what odd tricks of light result, blue eyes turned to glaring red, for instance. Or it could have been old film. But it certainly did not indicate Satan worship.

I sent the photographer another picture, and in her response she told me that she had talked to another friend, who had laughed, and commented of the woman who had suggested I might be worshiping the devil, "Oh, she's on that toot, now, is she?" And my correspondent continued, "As for the tooter, I bumped into her in the supermarket the other day, and she does not look happy. Positive, but not happy."

Can one be happy while looking for Satan? I doubt it.

There's another story of light in a photograph. In Malcolm Muggeridge's book, *Something Beautiful for God*, he is writing about Mother Teresa of Calcutta. She believes that each day we should do something beautiful for God. I'm a lot happier with that than with looking for Satan. Malcolm Muggeridge describes going to one of the houses where Mother Teresa and her Sisters take care of the dying people they have rescued from the streets of Calcutta. They are tenderly nursed until they die or, in some cases, recover because of the loving care they are given.

Muggeridge wanted to get a picture of the room, but Mother Teresa would not allow a flash bulb. She would not have her dying people disturbed as they were being led out of this life and into the waiting arms of Christ. Muggeridge told his photographer to take a picture anyway, without using the flash.

The photographer replied that it would be pointless; there wasn't enough light for a picture. Muggeridge said "Take one, anyway." When the picture was developed, it had indeed taken, and the room with the cots of dying people was bathed in a lovely golden light. And that, Muggeridge felt, was a sign of the presence of the Holy Spirit. He was looking for holiness, and so he found holiness.

In *Desert Wisdom, Sayings from the Desert Fathers*, "Abba Mios was asked by a soldier whether God would forgive a sinner. After instructing him at some length, the old man asked him, 'Tell me, my dear, if your cloak were torn, would you throw it away?' 'Oh, no!' he replied. 'I would mend it and wear it again.' The old man said to him, 'Well, if you care for your cloak, will not God show mercy on his own creatures?' "

One of the desert fathers says that a dog is better than we are, because a dog loves, but does not judge. Surely that is how Doc, my golden retriever, loves me, with unqualified love, without judging me and with no expectation that I will ever be less than lovable to her. If I am judgmental of the woman who has expectations of devil worship, I am falling right into the same trap she has fallen into.

One of my books was listed in a Midwestern newspaper as being pornographic. I reread the book, looking for pornography, and for the life of me could find none. Perhaps I do not know as much about pornography as the person who saw it in *A Wind in the Door*.

A beautiful letter came to me recently, in which the writer told me how much my book, *A Ring of Endless Light*, had helped her through her grief over the death of a friend. But, she said, someone had commented to her that I use swear words in the book, and how could I, as a Christian, do that? I wrote back saying that I wasn't about to go through my book looking for swear words, but as far as I could remember, the only word in that book which might be considered a swear word is *zuggy* a word I made up, and which means nothing, and is used by a spoiled young man who is far from being a Christian. I coined the word *zuggy* used by that same young man, in *A Moon By Night*, in order to *avoid* using the current swear words. Somebody had to be looking very hard for swear words in order to find them. (What an ugly way to read a book!)

Even when a writer does, in fact, use such words, because they seem appropriate within the vocabulary of the character using them, searching out four-letter words is no way to read a book. A librarian friend told me of a woman who attacked *Catcher in the Rye*, a frequent target, as having in it, say, four thousand eight hundred and thirty-two swear words. "How do you know?" the librarian asked. "I counted them," the woman said. "But did you read *the book*?" "No." How sad to pick up a book looking only for dirty words and thereby perhaps missing an encounter with Christ.

Catcher in the Rye does use the language the young protagonist would use. But that is not what the book is about. It is about the loneliness of adolescence, and some of the harder lessons which must be learned in growing up, and it has helped many thoughtful youngsters to accept themselves and the world as being less perfect than we would like.

I wonder if those who search out dirty words realize that this indicates how well they know them?

What are we looking for? We should be very careful, because that is what we are going to find.

I don't want to stop being a Christian because Christians can upset and confuse me, because I fear judgmentalism in others, and also in myself, or even because sometimes in Christian settings I have seen a lack of faith in a God of love, and seen instead a God of fear and hate.

"What are you looking for?" Jesus asked.

The Gospels tell us that the professionally good people weren't looking for Jesus, and when they did, it was tentative.

Nicodemus came to Jesus by night, so that he would not be seen approaching this radical teacher. Jesus was, and still is, a threat to the very establishment which proclaims him as Lord. He emphasized that he had not come to save the saved, but to save the lost, the sinners, the broken. To save the sinners, the lost, the broken, who *want* to be saved. It is possible to wallow in whatever our own particular misery is, almost taking a perverse pleasure in it. We must *want* to be healed, whole, and holy, before we can turn ourselves to Christ, and ask that we may be infused with the Spirit, and mended, so that God's image in us may become visible.

And I doubt if we can turn to Christ for healing while we are condemning anybody else.

If we, like some of the good people in Jerusalem and Nazareth and Bethlehem, are looking for people who disagree with us in order to put them down, we'll find them. If we look for people who may disagree with us, but who will challenge us to examine our own opinions and our own beliefs in a creative manner, we'll find them. And we may find some wonderful surprises, as did the wounded people who flocked to Jesus.

Recently I was shown a book said to be a Christian bestseller in which the author is identifying people who worship Satan – or people she suspects of worshiping Satan. When she included Teilhard de Chardin on her list I started to laugh, then realized it was not humorous. Instead of seeing a man so in love with God that he could express his love in a book such as *The Divine Milieu*, all this author saw was a man whose view of God and Creation differed from hers. This to her was a mark of a Satan-worshiper. She also cited a fondness for unicorns as a mark of the Satan-worshiper, which is equally hilarious and frightening. The unicorn is a creature of utter purity who will approach only a true virgin of complete innocence. Since to turn towards Satan is to relinquish all innocence, is it likely that a Satan-worshiper could get anywhere near a unicorn?

Do I believe in unicorns? Is a belief in a symbol of purity incompatible with belief in Christ? If so, wouldn't we have to stop having the loveliness and the family warmth of bringing in and decorating a Christmas tree, since the Christmas tree was originally a pagan practice? If a symbol leads us to a wider love of each other and of the Creator of us all, has it not in its truest sense become a Christian symbol? What would happen to my faith if I had to destroy all symbols – bread and wine, the cross?

Our faith is a faith of vulnerability and hope, not a faith of suspicion and hate. When we are looking for other people to be wrong in order that we may prove ourselves right, then we are closing ourselves off from whatever unexpected surprises Christ may be ready to offer us. If we are willing to live by Scripture, we must be willing to live by paradox and contradiction and surprise.

And what surprises! When the wonderful day of Pentecost, promised by Jesus, came, it was received with such joy that the disciples were accused of being drunk although, as it was pointed out, it was only ten o'clock in the morning! We are Christians through the power of the Holy Spirit, not through our own virtue. And the Holy Spirit is a Spirit of love and joy, not of hate and suspicion.

Witchcraft and the worship of Satan do exist. They are serious and dangerous phenomena. But when Christians look towards other Christians who worship Christ in a different manner and call them Satan-worshipers, they must please Satan. When someone accuses Teilhard de Chardin of being a Satanist, then whoever is making the accusation does not see the real Satan-worshiper who worships destruction and hate, and works for the annihilation of Christian love.

The Cathedral of St. John the Divine where I am the volunteer librarian backs onto Harlem. To the north is Columbia University. Spanish Harlem is south, and a melting pot of ethnicity to the west. One evening my friend, Canon Tallis, and I went into one of the larger chapels in the Cathedral to teach a class on preaching. There we saw pennies on the floor, arranged in the design of a pentagram. We picked them up, and I understood how my dog feels when the hair on the back of her neck prickles with apprehension.

I have been told that a chicken was found behind the altar, with its head off – a ritual, demonic blood sacrifice. I am afraid of the Satanists with their dark and secret rituals which include the shedding of blood. Sometimes, during a black mass, an infant is actually slaughtered and its blood shed. How different is this horror of shedding blood in order to appease Satan from the life-giving blood of Christ offered in the sacrament of the Eucharist. A black mass is a terrible mockery, a perverse imitation of Holy Communion, because the devil and his worshipers cannot make anything original: they can only foul and distort what God has designed with love.

As far as I know I have never met a devil worshiper (do Satanists ride the subway?) and I never want to. But I take them very seriously, and I fear them.

And I pray that we will listen to the promptings of the Holy Spirit, and not serve Satan's demonic purpose by accusing other Christians and confusing them with Satan's followers. I pray that we will learn to love one another, as the early Christians were recognized by their love, so that in all the richness of their diversity they were At One.

One of my favorite passages in John's first epistle is, "Anyone who fails to love can never have known God, because God is love. God's love for us was revealed when God sent into the world his only Son so that we could have life through him. This is the love I mean: not our love for God, but God's love for us."

It is not a simple thing to accept God's love, because if we do, we must return love. Jacob was tentative about accepting the love of his father's God, and he wanted to make sure that this tribal deity would keep his share of the bargain before he accepted him. It was not until Jacob was alone in the desert that his need overcame his wariness, and he was at last able to receive God's revelatory love.

Was it because Jacob knew himself to be a cheat and a fraud that he was able to receive the vision of God without being tempted to arrogance by it? He felt holy terror, not smugness. Self-satisfaction is what Satan offers us immediately after any manifestation of the Holy Spirit. For Satan is still a Spirit, still an angel, even if a fallen one, a negative angel eager to distort God's vision of love and turn it small and sour and selfish.

The early people of the risen Christ were not checking on other groups to see if they were less Christian than their own group, and when they did set themselves apart, Paul took them severely to task. They knew that love was what it is about, not an exclusive love, but an inclusive love, embracing all creatures, all corners of the cosmos.

When we are once more known for our love, we will be the hope of the world, and we will bear the light.

I don't want ever again to say, "I've had it with Christians," because, first of all, it isn't true. I've never *really* had it with Christians. What I'm fed up with is judgmentalness and coldness of heart. What I've had it with is those who would look for Satan, rather than Christ; who would sniff for the putrid odor of pornography rather than the lovely scent of love.

When I meet people who are truly Christian, which is often my privilege and my joy, I see people who are willing to bear the light, to *be* the light of the world – not just their own denominations, not just the light of Christians, or of Americans, but of the world. To love where love is not easy. To bring people to Christ not through fear and coercion, but through love.

What are we looking for? The love of Christ which comes to us through the power of the Holy Spirit, that Spirit who blew in the very beginning, before there was anything at all, who spoke through the prophets, who always was, is, and will be.

5

Rooted in Cosmos

IN THE BEGINNING OF GENESIS, God affirms that the Creation is good – very good. The Incarnation is a reaffirmation of the innate goodness of all that God has made.

Teilhard de Chardin says that "for a soul to have a body is *enkosmismene*."

Enkosmismene. To have our roots in the cosmos. We are like trees, drawing spiritual water through our rootedness in Creation. This is the affirmation of incarnation.

Even in time of tornado, earthquake, ice storm, our very roots are part of the entire cosmos. Surely Jacob, picking up the stone he had used for a pillow, and pouring oil on it as it became an altar, was making this same affirmation in his cry that *here* was the house of God. Jacob was indeed rooted in cosmos. At that moment he knew at-one-ment.

What actually happened to Jacob? Did God really speak to him in his dream of angels? Later, was it a physical angel who grappled with him? Is the word physical combined with angel a contradiction? Is any of this important?

As we are rooted in cosmos these images are part of the myth which the Creator gave us so that we may begin to understand something which is beyond literal interpretation by the finite human being.

On a TV interview I was asked by a clergyman if I believe that fantasy is an essential part of our understanding of the universe and our place in it, and I replied that yes, I do believe this, adding truthfully that Scripture itself is full of glorious fantasy. Yes, indeed, I take the Bible too seriously to take it all literally.

The story of Job is a wrestling with deep spiritual questions rather than dry factualism. And I love it when, in the beginning of this drama, the sons of God are gathered around, speaking to God, Satan was among them. Fallen angel or no, Satan was still God's son, and at that point was still speaking with his Creator. I wonder if he is still willing to do that, or if he has so separated himself from at-one-ment that he and his cohorts can no longer bear to be in the Presence?

And what about Ezekiel and those glorious wheels which some people think may have been U.F.O.s? There we have our first glimpse of the four horsemen of the Apocalypse. There we see the resurrection of those dry bones with living flesh, as we read the language of poetry which expands our understanding beyond its normal limitations.

The mythic interpretation is not a facile, shallow one, but an attempt to move into the deep and dazzling darkness of that truth which the fragile human mind cannot exhaustively comprehend, but can only glimpse with occasional flashes of glory. To live with an understanding that myth is a vehicle of truth is a far more difficult way to live than literally. The mythic world makes enormous demands of us, and that may be why it is so often shunned. The greater the good we are seeking, the greater the possibilities for perversion. But that does not make God's original good any less good; it simply heightens the challenge.

I am sometimes shocked by what I read in the Bible. There is much that I am still struggling to understand, such as the horrible story in Judges of the man who divided his raped and murdered wife into twelve pieces, sending one piece to each of the tribes of Israel. I still struggle with the story of the blighted fig tree. Does it mean that when Jesus asks us to do anything, he will give us the power to do it, whether we ourselves are able to do it or not? Some of the violence in both Testaments frightens me, caught up in this age of violence. But my response of shock may be a good thing, because it pushes open doors which I might otherwise be fearful of entering.

That limited literalism which demands that the Bible's poetry and story and drama and parable be taken as factual history is one of Satan's cleverest devices. If we allow ourselves to be limited to the known and the explainable, we have thereby closed ourselves off from God and mystery and revelation.

Once I remarked that I read the Bible in much the same way that I read fairy tales, and received a shocked response.

But fairy tales are not superficial stories. They spring from the depths of the human being. The world of the fairy tale is to some degree the world of the psyche. Like the heroes and heroines of fairy tales, we all start on our journey, our quest, sent out on it at our baptisms. We are, all of us, male and female, the younger brother, who succeeds in the quest because, unlike the elder brother, he knows he needs help, he cannot do it because he is strong and powerful. We are all, like it or not, the elder brother, arrogant and proud. We are all, male and female, the true princess who feels the pea of injustice under all those mattresses of indifference. And we all have to come to terms with the happy ending, and this may be the most difficult part of all. Never confuse fairy tale with untruth.

Alas, Lucifer, how plausible you can be, confusing us into thinking that to speak of the Bible as myth is blasphemy. One definition of *myth* in the dictionary is *parable*. Jesus taught by telling parables. Did Jesus lie? Blaspheme?

It is Satan who is the lie, who has chosen the lie, and turned his back on truth.

A study of the myths of various religions and cultures shows us not how different we human beings are, but how alike we are in our longing for God, for the Creator who gives meaning and dignity to our lives.

I am not sure how much of the great story of Abraham, Isaac, and Jacob is literally true, how much is history, how much the overlapping of several stories. Did *both* Abraham and Isaac pretend to Abimelech that their wives were their sisters, or have the two stories mingled over the ages? Does it really matter? The mythic truths we receive from these stories enlarge our perception of the human being, and that unique being's encounters with God. When the angel of God comes to wrestle with us we must pray to be able to grapple with the unexpected truth that may be revealed to us. Because Jacob, later in the story, had the courage to ask for God's blessing, we may too.

If we take the Bible over-literally we may miss the truth of the poetry, the stories, the myths. Literalism can all too easily become judgmentalism, and Jesus warned us not to judge, that we might not be judged.

How difficult it is! When I worry about those who castigate me for not agreeing with them, am I in my turn falling into judgmentalism? It's hard not to. But not all the way, I hope. I don't want to wipe out those who disagree with me, consigning them to hell for all eternity. We are still God's children, together. At One. Even if I am angry, upset, confused, I must still see Christ and Christ's love in those whose opinions are very different from mine, or I won't find it in those whose view fits more comfortably with mine.

Dear God. What am I looking for? Help me to look for Christ.

God can use unworthy material to accomplish magnificent purposes. Worthiness is not a criterion. One can be worthy and closed, like the Pharisees in all generations and all races, all religions, failing to understand that openness to God's revelation is first and foremost. One can be worthy and so wrapped in one's worthiness that one fails to recognize the three angels who came to Abraham, or the angel Isaac knew would pick the right wife for Jacob, or those angels ascending and descending the great ladder as Jacob lay with his head on the stone. Those three great patriarchs were unworthy, but they were open to change, change in themselves, change in their understanding of their Maker. All of them saw angels. Through them we, too, can learn to be open, not closed. We, too, can have eyes and ears open to the great challenges God offers us. This does not mean fluctuation with the winds of chance or whim, but recognizing the wind of the Holy Spirit, whose sign is always the sign of love.

Jacob at last was at one with the angel. So may we be, too.

Jacob wrestled all his life – with his brother, Esau: with his father-in-law, Laban. But it was God with whom he really had to struggle.

* * *

In the 1983 summer festival of children's literature at Simmon's College in Boston, the overall title for the week was, "Do I Dare Disturb the Universe?" The question is asked by T.S. Eliot's J. Alfred Prufrock, and it's a question we are not usually encouraged either to ask, or to attempt to answer, particularly in our various institutions. Especially not in the church. But it's a question we need to ask, with courage, as we look at what is going on around us in the world, with wars in the name of religion accelerating all over the planet, each group claiming to represent The Truth, and occasionally proclaiming it with acts of terrorism. Universe-disturbers can be destructive as well as creative.

If we disturb the universe, no matter how lovingly, we're likely to get hurt. Nobody ever promised that universe-disturbers would have an easy time of it. Universe-disturbers make waves, rock boats, upset establishments. Gandhi upset the great British Empire. Despite his nonviolence, he was unable to stop the shedding of blood, and he ended with a bullet through his heart. Anwar Sadat tried to work for peace in one of the most unpeaceful centuries in history, knowing that he might die for what he was doing, and he did.

Does it encourage our present-day universe-disturbers to know that Abraham, Isaac, and Jacob before them were universe-disturbers? Their vision of God, while undeniably masculine, was also the vision of a God who cared, who appeared to his human friends and talked with them. The patriarchs lived in a primitive, underpopulated world, and yet their vision of God as Creator of all, of God who cared, of God who was part of the story, was very new.

Jesus was a great universe-disturber, so upsetting to the establishment of his day that they put him on a cross, hoping to finish him off. Those of us who try to follow his Way have a choice, either to go with him as universe-disturbers (butterflies), or to play it safe. Playing it safe ultimately leads to personal diminishment and death. If we play it safe, we resist change.

Well. We all resist change, beginning as small children with our unvarying bedtime routine, continuing all through our lives.

The static condition may seem like security, But if we cannot move with change, willingly or reluctantly, we are closer to death and further from life.

If we want to play it safe, we have to settle for a comfortable religion, one which will not permit questions, because questions are universe-disturbers. (Children never hesitate to ask the disturbing questions: Who was God's mother? Do numbers ever come to an end? What is the meaning of life, the universe, and everything?) If we don't allow questions, we can fool ourselves into thinking that we are capable of defining God. Every new scientific discovery about the nature of the universe has shaken one religious group or another, and yet the new discoveries do nothing whatsoever to alter the nature of the universe: they simply force us to grow in our understanding and our love of the Creator of all.

And yet, somehow or other, we've managed to keep on believing that this planet, and we who inhabit it, are the chief focus of God's concern. The idea that we may be only a small part of el's concern is very threatening.

Can God, no matter how omnipotent, keep track of it all? There are quadrillions and quintillions of galaxies, with their uncountable solar systems. The world of the microcosm is as vast as that of the macrocosm. If we did nothing all our lives but count, we could come nowhere near to counting the galaxies, much less the stars. And as for the subatomic particles ... Can God possibly keep track of all galaxies and quarks and tachyons?

Yet in a small way even we human beings are capable of considerable multi-tracking, as Jean Houston calls it. It is said that Caesar could dictate seven letters simultaneously. During the tenure of one minister who irritated me profoundly, I found that I could listen most attentively to his sermons if, at the same time, I was memorizing the Psalms, thinking about the anthem, planning the meals, and sometimes thinking a poem. In a house full of children I was multi-tracking as my ears were open for each one of them, while I might be playing the piano, listening for the kettle to boil, and the timer to ring for the casserole in the oven. We all multitrack, even when we aren't aware of it. We've taught our computers to multitrack enormous quantities of information for us. Isn't God's ability to multitrack far greater than that of the most complex computer? God, showing Jacob the stars, needed no computer to call them all by name.

Somehow or other I must try to comprehend a God who not only can keep track of it all, but who is focused on all of it, who cares, who is aware, who is *there* for me when I call out for help, or cry a "Thank you!"

It doesn't work if I think of God as Out There. We've long known that God is not Out There, but we revert, and have to remind ourselves. I strain painfully to accept the obvious, because sometimes the obvious is not a gnat, but the whole universe.

Back when it was still possible to believe that this planet was the center of everything, that the sun and the moon and the stars were hung in the sky entirely for our benefit, it was quite possible to think of God as our Maker, Out There. God took nothing, and created a planet with water and land and fish and land animals, and proclaimed it good, looking at it all from a heavenly distance. We have too often thought of God as being *outside* the universe, creating us, and looking at what happens to us, concerned, but Out There. But as I contemplate the vastness of the night sky on a clear, cold night, God Out There does not work. Out There is *too* far out, God becomes too remote: I cannot hide under the shelter of el's protecting wings.

Scripturally, God is always in and part of Creation, walking and talking with Adam and Eve, taking Abraham out to see the stars, wrestling with Jacob.

And, in the most glorious possible demonstration of God *in* and *part* of Creation, God came to us in Jesus of Nazareth, fully participating in our human birth and life and death and offering us the glory of Easter.

If we shed our idea of God as being someone Out There, separate from all that has been made, and begin instead to think of God as within all Creation, every galaxy, every quantum, every human being, then we cannot hold ourselves "out there" either. We cannot set ourselves apart from anything that happens. Anywhere.

That's one reason some people shun fiction. Fiction draws us into participating in other lives, other countries, other ways of life or thinking. It is a way of helping us to be *in* and not *out* there.

To accept ourselves as part of everything is a big responsibility, and many would rather not face it. It is far too easy to take refuge in our own little group, rather than allowing the Creator to change us, as he changed Abraham and Isaac and Jacob.

If God created everything, if the Word called all things into being, all people are part of God's loving concern. The incarnation was not only for the Jews. Or the Christians. Christ did not come to save Christians, but to save sinners.

It's seductively pleasant to think that God loves Christians better than Buddhists or Hindhus; that, as one well-known evangelical preacher pronounced, God does not listen to the prayers of Jews. No? What about the beloved Twenty-Third Psalm? A psalm written by and for Jews, remember, with its glorious affirmation of faith: though I walk through the valley of the shadow of death, you (God) will be with me.

But what about bad prayers, ugly prayers? Damn my enemies, so that the dogs' tongues may be red with their blood.

What about the Iranian terrorists? Does God hear their prayers? Or the Irish Republican Army after it has bombed a store full of Christmas shoppers? Or the Christians who feel they can't be happy in heaven unless they're watching the tortures of the damned in hell? Does God hear these prayers? I am certain that el does, even as my own worst prayers are heard. But the answer to prayer is always the answer of love, and when we are hard of heart, our ears are closed to love.

Just as a human parent listens to the demands of the children, not excluding anyone, but trying to turn anger to love, greediness to generosity, willful disobedience to responsibility, so, I believe, God does with us, and it is the Holy Spirit, praying through us, who can turn our ugliest prayers toward forgiveness and reconciliation.

How do we pray for those whose hateful actions fill us with horror? How do we pray for the Russians who shot down a domestic plane full of unsuspecting people? For hijackers? for the Muslims who bombed our Marines in suicide missions? How do we pray for those in our own government who, I am told, did some experimenting with germ warfare in the New York subway system? or those who refuse to put anti-pollutant devices into their factories (because it is expensive enough to cut into their profits) and, wittingly, unnecessarily foul the air that even they have to breathe? Have we prayed enough? Not for revenge, but for the love that heals?

How do I keep from the pride of being judgmental? How do I open my heart in prayer? In love? The fact that I don't do it very well doesn't mean that I don't have to try. And then God can take my most fumbling, faltering prayers and make something lovely of them.

Jacob had to learn that prayer is not bargaining with God. He had to learn that the God he finally decided to accept as his own was not a God who could be tamed. When Jacob cried out for God's blessing, it was a cry to a great and extraordinary power.

Jacob learned, too, that he had to make peace with Esau, and to do so he had to be willing to open himself to change.

We, too, must open ourselves to change. It is only through prayer, be it no more than a cry of "Help!" that we are given the courage to let ourselves be changed, along with all the changes in the world around us, over which we have no control.

Like Jacob, we stand once again at the threshold of great change, not only the rapidly accelerating technological changes, but change in our understanding of God's revelation of the Divine Plan, as we are challenged to grow spiritually. Why has our spiritual development lagged so agonizingly far behind our intellectual development? We have accepted most of the outward changes – electricity, the telephone, the automobile, the plane, and the computer. But spiritually we are far behind. We know more with our minds than we do with our hearts, and this is breaking us.

Adam and Eve, eating of the fruit of the tree of the knowledge of good and evil, precipitated themselves into a masculine world, for knowledge, intellectual knowledge, is masculine. Wisdom, which we desperately need, is feminine, *sophia*, in Greek.

Better yet, *hagia sophia*, holy wisdom. We need holy wisdom to help balance our misuse of the fruits of the intellect.

We must not be afraid of becoming once again in tune with our whole selves, even when becoming whole disturbs the universe. We become whole never by being rigid or unloving or isolating ourselves from the rest of our fellow beings, but by opening ourselves to God's revelation of the unity of the universe.

What is our part in keeping this planet alive? Working toward stopping the folly and horror of atomic devastation? To say that nuclear warfare is inevitable is defeatism, not realism. As long as there is anybody to care, to pray, to turn to God, to be willing to be el's messenger even in unexpected ways, there is still hope.

How can we have a wide view of the unity of the universe and of God without lapsing into a vague pantheism? If God created *all* of Creation, if God is the author of Buddhists and Hindhus and Jains as well as those who have "accepted Jesus Christ as Lord," how can we avoid a wishy-washy permissiveness?

Not by retreating back into a closed system. Not by saying: Only those who believe exactly as I do can be saved. Not by insisting that only those whose god fits into the same box as my god will go to heaven. Not by returning to polytheism and proclaiming that our god is greater than the gods of other cultures.

Paradoxically, it comes back to us, to our acceptance of ourselves as created by God, and loved by God, no matter how far we have fallen from God's image in us. It is not a self-satisfied, self-indulgent acceptance, but a humble, holy, and wondrous one.

Look! Here I am, caught up in this fragment of chronology, in this bit of bone and flesh and water which makes up my mortal body, and yet I am also part of that which is not imprisoned in time or mortality. Partaker simultaneously of the finite and the infinite, I do not find the infinite by repudiating my finiteness, but by being fully in it, in this *me* who is more than I know. This *me*, like all of creation, lives in a glorious dance of communion with all the universe. In isolation we die, in interdependence we live.

If I affirm that the God of love does indeed love all of Creation, that the salvation of the entire universe is being worked out, what does that do to my own faith?

Two young women who run a Christian bookstore in the Midwest wrote me that they were concerned as to whether or not I accept Christ as my personal Savior. Even when I assured them that I do, they were not at all convinced that I was one of them. And perhaps the Christ I accept, by the grace of the Holy Spirit, is different from the Christ they want me to accept

But God made us all in our glorious complexity and differences, we are not meant to come off the assembly line alike, each Christian a plastic copy of every other Christian.

This insistence on sameness engenders divisions within the body of Christ, battering it still further. I have a friend who is a fine writer, openly a Christian writer, who teaches at a Christian college with a fine academic reputation. This friend has for many years been attracted to the Roman Catholic Church. I had heard new rumors about his imminent conversion, and a mutual friend of ours said to him, "Madeleine tells me that you are about to commit an absurdity."

And now that he has finally done what he considers to be going "all the way" as a Christian – he has become a Roman Catholic – I am not happy about his decision because it seems to me to emphasize the sad fact of a divided Christendom. I wish that his colleagues, instead of accepting his resignation, had gathered around him in love. I may feel that he has "committed an absurdity." But to say who is more and who is less Christian is not my privilege. No one comes to accept Christ because of personal virtue or impeccable morals, or even conviction. "No one comes to me except through the power of the Holy Spirit."

I accept Christ as my personal Savior only because of this loving, unmerited gift of the Spirit. Christ within me and within all of Creation is what makes the stars shine at night and the sun rise in the morning. Christ was in the birth of my children and grandchildren, is in the eyes of my friends, in the blooming of the daffodils in the spring and the turning of the leaves in the autumn.

In my heart I understand the Christ given me by the love of the Spirit.

But it is not up to me to tell the Spirit where this love is going to blow. When Nicodemus came to visit Jesus at night, Jesus made it very clear to him that "the wind blows where it wishes, and you hear the sound of it, but you cannot tell from where it comes or where it goes; so is every one who is born of the Spirit."

Through the power and love of this Spirit I accept Jesus as my Savior, the light of my life, and the light of the world. That is my affirmation and my joy.

In an interview in *Christianity Today* I was asked, "Are you a universalist?"

My reply is as true now as it was then. "No. I am not a universalist. I am a particular incarnationalist. I believe that we can understand cosmic questions only through particulars. I can understand God only through one specific particular, the Incarnation of Jesus of Nazareth. This is the ultimate particular, which gives me my understanding of the Creator and of the beauty of life. I believe that God loved us so much that he came to us as a human being to show us his love."

We live in an open, interacting, creative universe, and to try to close it into a safe little system is a danger to ourselves and a danger to everyone we touch. But if we are willing to be a small part of a great whole, then we know that no part in the dance is too small, too unimportant to make a difference. We are all like the butterfly in the amazing, unexpected magnitude of our effect. Even when we feel most helpless, when events we cannot control or prevent pile up, even in our most bitter brokenness, we do have our role in the working out of the great plan.

May God, through the Christ shown us by the Holy Spirit, open our hearts in love.

Alleluia.

6

Angel Unaware

THE WEDNESDAY OF THANKSGIVING WEEKEND, 1983, was cold in New York, and dark. But through the darkness came a sign of great hope.

One of the advantages of living largely on the crowded island of Manhattan is that people tend to come through the big city and so I see many friends, either en route to another destination, or sometimes simply here for a few days in New York. The day before Thanksgiving, 1983, was such a day of friends, a day that made me more than thankful to be in the city

At 12:15 on Wednesdays there is a communion service at the Cathedral of St. John. It is held in one of the small chapels behind the high altar, and that Wednesday I joyfully found myself sharing bread and wine and prayer and friendship with a diverse group, from Korea, Minnesota, Illinois. After the Eucharist six of us went across the street to our favorite Hungarian restaurant for lunch.

On the Sunday evening before, all of us, in our various parts of the world, had watched the television movie, *The Day After* about the horror of a nuclear war. In his homily the minister who had celebrated the Eucharist had talked about the Christian response to the possibilities and impossibilities the movie depicted.

Actually I had (as it were) seen the same movie thirty years earlier, in the fifties, in black and white TV. It took place in a suburb of New York, rather than Kansas, but the general story line was the same: the dropping of bombs on the city with total death and destruction, and then the horrors awaiting those in the suburbs who had survived – radiation sickness, starvation, looting, and the shooting of and by those trying to defend their homes and their dwindling food supplies. Desperate, untenable awfulness. In his homily the minister had talked of the severe serenity with which the believer should meet anything, even this, and of God's great and terrible gift of free will. How much does God interfere with our misuse of free will, we wondered? In that day's mail I had received a letter with the question," Is God going to allow us to blow ourselves up?"

Among the six of us was Mel Lorentzen, a teacher and writer from Wheaton. He told us a true story about his friend, the opera singer Jerome Hines. In 1961, Hines was in Russia singing Mussorgsky's great opera, *Boris Godounov*. Hugh and I saw a superb production of this opera in the Kirov theatre when we were in Leningrad. It was an opera I had always wanted to see, partly because of my mother's recounting of the first time she and father had heard it. When the great bells for the coronation music started, she said, they had stood up to see the orchestra, and the sound of bells was coming from two grand pianos, and their spines tingled. When Hugh and I stopped at Intourist in Leningrad and saw that *Boris* was playing that night, I let out an adolescent shriek of enthusiasm (something that evidently doesn't often happen in Intourist offices) and we were given the Royal Box – yes, it's still there! Although we shared it with several others.

So *Boris* has a special place in my heart.

Jerome Hines, who had learned the role in Russian, was to be the first non-Russian to sing the great opera in the original tongue.

At the close of the opera Boris has lost his crown and his throne, and the traditional ending is for Boris to roll from his throne in an anguish of defeat. Jerome Hines felt that Mussorgsky's music did not justify this interpretation, that the music is triumphant and therefore Boris's yielding of his power is part of that triumph, and he played it that way. The final performance in Moscow was to be televised, but at the last minute the singers were told that there would be no television cameras because Khrushchev was going to be in the audience.

Jerome Hines is a man of prayer, and while he was in Russia, prayer for Khrushchev had been foremost in his mind, not deliberately, but because the name *Khrushchev* kept being "given" to him. He sang superbly that night, and at the close of the opera, instead of the usual humiliating tumbling from the throne in defeat, he took off his crown and flung his arms heavenwards in triumph. The audience went wild with applause and cheers.

Khrushchev came backstage with an interpreter, to say how much he had enjoyed the performance, and as he was leaving, Hines said, in Russian, "God bless you, sir." Khrushchev turned, looked him in the eye without answering, and left.

There is a mighty time difference between Moscow and Washington. It couldn't have been too long after Khrushchev returned from the opera that night that President John F. Kennedy called Moscow. This was the time of the Cuban missile crisis, and Kennedy gave Khrushchev an ultimatum – Get out of Cuba.

And the Russians withdrew.

What might have happened if Khrushchev had not gone to see *Boris Godounov*? If Hines had not turned Boris's defeat into a triumph? If Hines had not said, from his heart, to the atheist head of an atheist country, "God bless you, sir"?

God, without interfering in human free will, was part of the story. The pattern was worked out through the music, through the singer, through the head of state, but without coercion. The opportunity was given, but it was not mandated.

This is for me a perfect example of how God calls us to write the story *with him*, lovingly, creatively, of our own free will.

God does not want us to blow ourselves up. He will not stop us if we insist on self-destruction, but every possible creative alternative will be offered us, and the Hines-Khrushchev story is only one example of disaster averted by love and prayer. It gives me great hope.

God sends angels in unexpected and mysterious ways. We children of the Highest are asked to be angels – messengers – whether we are aware of our role or not. We are called on to be angels not by God Out There, but by God In Here, *with us*, Emmanuel. May God continue to send angels. May we continue to hear, as Jerome Hines heard. And as Khrushchev, the God-denyer, surely heard.

Was Jacob, wrestling with the angel, a stranger person to be grappled with by God then Khrushchev?

Jerome Hines was a universe-disturber, a creative universe-disturber. Hines could have played the role of Boris the traditional way, safely. He could have refused the arduous task of learning the opera in Russian. He could have shunned the risk of calling for God's blessing on a man whom he knew denied God. He could have declined to pray for Khrushchev. But he took the risk.

If we refuse to take the risk of being vulnerable we are already half dead. If we are half dead we don't have to starve with the people of Ethiopia. We don't have to share the terrible living conditions of old people struggling to exist on dwindling social security payments in our overcrowded, hostile cities. We don't have to smell the stench of filth, and disease, and hunger in the favelas and barrios.

We are not all called to go to El Salvador, or Moscow or Calcutta, or even the slums of New York, but none of us will escape the moment when we have to decide whether to withdraw, to play it safe, or to act upon what we prayerfully believe to be right, knowing that with all our prayers we may be wrong, and knowing that we will probably be punished by those who do not want universe-disturbers to stand up and be counted.

Perhaps what we are called to do may not seem like much, but the butterfly is a small creature to affect galaxies thousands of light years away.

* * *

Not all universe-disturbers are creative, not all are listening to God's call. Many are destructively following the fallen angels, from Atilla the Hun, to Hitler, to Farrakan, to rapists, and terrorists.

Jerome Hines was one of God's angels. He did not go to Russia to be an angel. He went because he was an opera singer by training and vocation, and a man of prayer. God can use us wherever we are, in whatever we do. We do not have to do or be anything special in order to bring hope to the world. We may not even know when God has used one of us as an angel unaware, and that's just as well. Our part lies in being open, not to God Out There, but In Here, *with* us, *in* us.

When we visualize God as being only up in heaven, and heaven as being apart from earth, we lose the immediacy of God as part of the story part of our being, as intimate as was the angel who wrestled all night with Jacob and changed his story forever. God was not something apart from Creation, or apart from daily life, God was there, marvelously, terribly there.

* * *

If God is in and part of all creation, then any part can be a messenger, an angel. Sometimes our very questions are angelic. Questions allow us to grow and develop and change in our understanding of ourselves and of God, so that nothing that happens, and nothing that science discovers, is frightening, or disturbs our faith in God.

Some scientists in their arrogance have done terrible things.

But the great scientists are humble, and have imaginations as vivid as any poet's – "The butterfly effect," for instance. What a marvelous concept, and what a marvelous way of expressing it, and by a scientist, not an artist!

The quark, one of the smallest, if not *the* smallest, of our subatomic particles, is named from James Joyce's *Finnegans Wake*. The world of subatomic particles is so extraordinary that even to contemplate it implies an open imagination.

We have discovered the world of subatomic physics because we have split the atom. This has revealed many things which are horrible indeed. A considerable number of scientists have repented of the use made of their discoveries. True repentance opens our eyes to the God who heals and redeems.

As a nation we have yet to come to terms with our fire bombs which destroyed German cities and their civilian population during World War Two. We have yet to come to terms with having dropped not one, but two atom bombs, leaving the horror of death and radiation, maiming men, and women, and children who had nothing to do with battle lines. Part of our fascination with the atom bomb may be caused by our refusal, as a nation, to repent. We have yet to come to terms with Vietnam, and Lebanon, and El Salvador, because repentance is no longer part of our national vocabulary.

What would those who were responsible for the making of the automobile have done if some kind of prescience had shown them that the death toll from automobile accidents is already greater than the death toll of all of the world's wars put together? What would the scientists working on the splitting of the atom have done if they could have foreseen Hiroshima and Nagasaki? Many of the scientists who worked on early fusion and fission were appalled at the gigantic Pandora's box they had opened. A considerable number of those who had approached the work as humanistic atheists turned from their atheism to become deeply committed theists. A good many, not all, but a good many, looked at what they had unleashed and got down on their knees.

And the power of prayer is greater than the Pentagon. It is greater than the greed and corruption which can still conceive of a nuclear holocaust as survivable. It is greater than the bomb.

It can help bring wisdom to our knowledge, wisdom which is all that will keep us from destroying ourselves with our knowledge.

In an accidental and godless universe, where the human race on this particular planet in this particular galaxy appeared by happenstance, there would be very little hope. But in a purposeful universe created by a caring, loving God, there is great hope that ultimately el's purposes will be worked out in history.

My father was gassed in the trenches of the First World War because he would not let his men go where he had not gone first, and this concerned leadership spared the others from the gas. That war, which ended shortly before I was born, was closer to the old hand-to-hand warfare than the present impersonal ways of combat. Every year on Armistice Day, as it used to be called, the phone rang and kept on ringing, with one after another of Father's men calling him to thank him, and to see how he was. These calls continued year after year until his death. And that, to me is a sign of hope, as Jerome Hines is a sign of hope.

It is an example of community, of a community which lasted long after the physical proximity of those involved had been broken and they had scattered to many different parts of the world. But what had been the heart of that community still endured.

Quaker writer Parker Palmer says,

Most of us fear community because we think it will call us away from ourselves. We are afraid that in community our sense of self will be overpowered by the identity of the group. We pit individuality and community against one another, as if a choice had to be made, and increasingly we choose the former.

But what a curious conception of self we have! We have forgotten that the self is a moving intersection of many other selves. We are formed by the lives which intersect with ours.

The larger and richer our community the larger and richer is the content of self. There is no individuality without community.

That community of men calling my father, one after another, year after year on Armistice Day, told me a great deal about the individual person who was also my father.

The war in which my father served was followed by another war, and another, and it seems that war will never cease. We need – as a country, as individuals who cannot separate ourselves from either our country or the world – to face what we have done, and ask forgiveness. Forgiveness from God, from those we have hurt, and, what is harder, from ourselves. Then we may be able to regain a sense of wonder about our small planet and the fragile life it sustains, and once again become the good stewards God called us to be.

It is, as always, paradox. God will not force us, take away our free will, demand that we do the work of love like robots. We are free not to listen, to damn our enemies rather than pray for them. God will not intervene in our self-destruction unless we are willing. We will not hear God unless we listen. We can't just turn it all over to God; it is up to us, too. And yet, we can't do anything until we turn it all over to God. This turning it over is not a passive sitting back – an okay, you take care of it, Pop – but an active listening to the power of love, and a willingness to love our enemies as well as our friends. ("God bless you, sir," Jerome Hines said, and meant it.)

It was easier for Esau to forgive Jacob for his treachery than it was for Jacob to believe in or accept Esau's forgiveness.

When I walk my dog at night, the route on the way home takes me past a Buddhist temple with a terrace on which stands a huge statue of Saint Shinran Shunin, a Buddhist saint of the twelfth century. This particular statue was in Hiroshima when the bomb fell, and was sent by the Buddhists of that city to the Buddhists in New York as a symbol of forgiveness and hope. Each night as my dog and I walk by the great statue, the huge bulk of metal wearing a patina I have never seen on another statue, I say, "Good night, Saint Shinran. Forgive us, and help us," and for me, at that moment, Saint Shinran is one of God's angels. Am I worshiping a pagan saint? A lifeless hunk of metal? No! It is an attitude of heart, a part of turning to Christ.

I rejoiced to read in William Johnston's *The Inner Eye of Love* that Saint Shinran rebelled against legalism and proclaimed "the preeminence of faith and grace," and that "he has been frequently compared to Luther."

We don't have to drop nuclear bombs again. We don't have to blow ourselves up. We've had the capacity to destroy all life on this planet with germ warfare since World War One, and we haven't done it. But we need all the prayers we can possibly get, all the openness of love, no matter how much it costs. And we need to look for angels.

I wish that the made-for-television film, "The Day After," had added just a minute to its bleak and hopeless ending, that it had shown Lawrence, Kansas, in the spring, or harvest time, that it had ended with the wedding which was halted by the bombing. I wish it had ended with a message of hope: this is what we are working for – life, not death.

It is not good to send out only negative vibrations, to offer no alternative to disaster. We need positive energy too, which is something we can do something about, stopping ourselves when we are feeling negative, and looking for something positive. If sound waves stay in the ether for ever, then the voices of those men who never forgot to call my father are still there, too. The words of love are strong. We need to listen to them.

We have lived with the possibility of extinction since the planet was formed, extinction by natural calamity, by the shifting of the planet on its axis, by epidemic, by our own avariciousness. It should have taught us to live more fully – savoring each moment, using each day fully, seeing each sunrise and sunset and evening star, turning our hearts to those we love – but by and large we've gone on as usual, dragged down by ordinariness.

But even if we can expect to live out our full life span, nothing is ordinary. Life itself is extraordinary. *Little lamb, who made thee?* Blake asks. *Dost thou know who made thee?* He also asks: *Tyger, tyger, burning bright in the forests of the night, what immortal hand or eye framed thy fearful symmetry?*

❁ ❁ ❁

The sign of hope that Mel gave us in the story of Jerome Hines was with me as we gathered together for Thanksgiving dinner the next day, as we put on the banquet cloth, the best china and crystal and silver, lit candles, and held hands all around for grace.

Did Abraham ever gather all his various children and their mothers together for a meal of thanks and rejoicing? Did Isaac and Rebekah call Jacob and Esau to share a meal, thanking God for the fruits of the land and for Esau's mighty hunting? Did Jacob and his wives sit down with all their sons and their one daughter?

After Abraham's feast for three angels, and Lot's festive meal for two angels, it should be clear to us that there has always been a sacramental aspect to a shared meal. The guest at our table must be honored thereafter; you cannot break bread with someone and then stab that person. But if the meal has been desacralized, that obligation no longer holds.

As a twentieth-century society we have desacralized mealtimes as we have almost all aspects of our lives. At my alma mater the students still eat in the dining room of their house, at small tables, taking turns with the serving and washing up, but at most colleges and universities there is now something called Food Service, and meals are cafeteria style, catch as catch can (and usually make the institutional food I griped about seem marvelously gourmet food by comparison!).

Even at home families do not always eat together, because of conflicts in schedule, so the meal is further desacralized with plates in laps before the TV. and loses its link with the heavenly banquet.

How do we regain the meal as sacrament? As a foretaste of the at-one-ness to come? Does something as simple as a family meal make that much difference?

It does, oh, it does.

If there is a sense of sacrament about the meal, then it can spread out to all areas of life. No one with a vital sense of the sacred could go into a church or synagogue and commit acts of vandalism. And it took an overwhelming sense of the sacred for Jerome Hines to be an angel unaware when he sang *Boris* in Moscow.

Jerome Hines was granted the knowledge of the creative result of his prayer for Khrushchev, and he is a man so committed to God that he can accept the understanding without falling into pride, into taking personal credit for what he did. It is probably a blessing that most of us are not granted this knowledge. We do like to be patted on the back, to be told that what we did was terrific, or significant. And it sometimes is. But we never act alone. We simply participate in God's action. It may be action which is expressed through us, but the love is always God's and it is our joy to be allowed to share.

The butterfly does not understand that the beating of its wings can be felt in distant galaxies. The butterfly is simply, fully, and beautifully a butterfly.

So let us try to be simply fully, and beautifully human beings, bearing within us the image of God.

7

Bless the Bastard

JEROME HINES PRAYED FOR the atheist leader of an atheist country, and whether the atheists like it or not, theirs is a powerful religion. We, too, are called to pray for those whose religion differs from ours, those who condone acts of terrorism, who are zealots espousing destructive causes. We are also called to pray for those whose god is different from ours, and yet who live quiet, godly lives. How do we pray? Simply by offering to God our concern for all of Creation, not coercively or manipulatively, but lovingly, for it all belongs to the Creator. We separate ourselves from the stars and from God when we separate ourselves from any part of Creation.

But a wariness of "the others" seems always to have been part of human nature. The patriarchs were uneasy with peoples of other tribes and other gods, as we may be uneasy with Muslims and Parsees and Quiztanos. But today, with all the instant information from TV and radio, newspapers and magazines, we have less excuse for our lack of understanding.

As Abraham had not wanted Isaac to marry a foreigner, so Rebekah and Isaac did not want their sons (particularly Jacob) to marry any of the women from Heth, who worshiped different gods, who were "them," not "us," and so Isaac charged Jacob not to take a wife of the daughters of Canaan.

And God Almighty bless you, and make you fruitful, and multiply you, and give you the blessing of Abraham, that you may inherit the land where you are a stranger, the land which God gave to Abraham.

Paternalistic, nationalistic, and in terms of the late twentieth-century, distressing.

But Abraham and Sarah, Isaac and Rebekah, Jacob and Rachel, did not live in the late twentieth-century and we abuse all that we have learned in the intervening centuries if we try to rewrite history. Yet that is what we are unwittingly doing as we attempt to change language into what is called inclusive language, which ends up being more sexist than the language it is trying to replace.

Even by continuing to link Sarah with Abraham, Rebekah with Isaac, Rachel with Jacob, I'm slightly changing the emphasis, and I'd better be aware what I'm doing.

Abraham, Isaac, and Jacob were forefathers. Sarah and Rebekah and Rachel were interesting women, but they are seldom referred to as foremothers, though that is what they were. Sarah, Rebekah, and Rachel lived in a world of patriarchs, not matriarchs, and it is futile to try to see their culture as something it was not. We may hope to influence present and future history, but we must beware of altering the past unless we really and truly know what we are doing and have been called by an angel to do so.

T S. Eliot (in *Selected Prose*) says that it is not "preposterous that the past should be altered by the present, as much as the present is directed by the past. And the poet who is aware of this will be aware of great difficulties and responsibilities."

Such a poet is needed now; a casual or irresponsible altering of the past can be very dangerous.

The tents of Abraham, Isaac, and Jacob were not far from the tribes who worshiped the goddesses, the matriarchal religions which so upset the patriarchal Hebrew. But Jacob and Rachel did not live with Astarte, or Ashtaroth, or Ishtar, or any of the female goddesses, and there is no point in pretending that their world understood that the feminine is as important as the masculine. I suspect that our forefathers were afraid of the feminine, in the world, in themselves. That fear is still very much alive today, fear of the nurturing darkness of the womb, of the intuitive self which can give insights unavailable to the conscious will, of the tenderness of love with all its vulnerability. And that fear makes the feminine in Jacob all the more remarkable.

Our religion needs to change as our knowledge and understanding grow, but beware if we change it thoughtlessly. The new translations of the creed are a case in point. I love the new Episcopal prayer book, love it enough to feel free to criticize it where I feel it has fallen short of its best. We used to say that Jesus was *conceived by the Holy Spirit*. Now we say *He was conceived by the power of the Holy Spirit*. That's not the same thing at all. We are all (or should be) conceived by the power of the Holy Spirit. To say that Jesus was conceived *by* the Holy Spirit is far more exciting. The angel came to Mary and told her that "The Holy Ghost shall come upon you."

It's a shocking myth, but it's been our myth for a long time; we've held to it for two thousand years, even though it has kept some people from being Christian because they "cannot cope with the virgin birth." The virgin birth has never been a major stumbling block in my struggle with Christianity; it's far less mind-boggling than the Power of all Creation stooping so low as to become one of us. But I find myself disturbed at the changing, by some committee or other, of the myth which brought God and the human creature together in marvelous at-one-ment, as Jacob's ladder brought heaven and earth together. That's the wonder, that God can reach out and become one with that which has been created. This at-one-ment should not be broken thoughtlessly. Nor should we fall into that trap of rigid literalism. We don't have to know the *how* of parthogenesis. And even the word parthogenesis is a stumbling block, trying to use scientific jargon to express what is inexpressible mystery. All we need to know is God's terrible closeness, an intimacy which hallows our createdness.

A minister friend said, "It's very nice to know we're related to God on his mother's side."

The great mysteries of the creed are an affirmation which I find difficult to make in the new language which is watered down to make it easier, and which offends me because it tries to put the radically unbelievable glory by which I live into rational, palatable language, which I find so unpalatable that I gag on it. Not that I am against contemporary translations; I am strongly for them. But I want them to be in the very best "language of the people," not impoverished by unimaginative realism.

When our children were very young we started reading the King James translation of the Bible to them, and they weren't old enough for it, and were bored. So we switched to J.B.

Phillips' translation. One day our little boy was sent from the table for some misdemeanor and told to stay away for five minutes. At the end of five minutes he came rushing down the stairs crying, "What did I miss?" J.B. Phillips' translation worked beautifully for him. And Phillips still works for me, too, far better than some of the more recent translations which are tinged with condescension toward both the human creature and the Creator.

But don't let's stop trying. We need to do better in our new translations than we are presently doing. In trying to use inclusive language, we have blundered into inconclusive language.

What's wrong? Our language does indeed need changing as we come to accept the feminine as well as the masculine, the intuitive as well as the intellectual. But thus far our attempts are not working. I suspect that this is because the inadequacy of our language is a symptom of something far deeper, a brokenness between the human being and the Maker, and an equal brokenness within ourselves. We have lost the ability to see the marvelous ladder of angels uniting heaven and earth, and so we have become earthbound, separated from the stars and the music of the spheres.

Our lacks in language are a reflection of our brokenness. When we spend our energy futilely trying to fix pronouns, we can forget that we may be bleeding to death.

If we could stop focussing on symptoms, and allow God to heal us with creative love, the healing of language would follow.

Man, the image of God, male and female. Whole. Our Own image of God is unavoidably anthropomorphic. As human beings, we think in human terms; there is, for us, no other way. But the image of God within us is love. And God is a spirit.

We are reminded in the New Testament that we are the temple of the Holy Spirit. We honor our bodies because they are made to contain the Holy Spirit, the image of God, but they are not themselves what they contain. I have sometimes been most awesomely aware of the image of God in someone whose body is distorted; I saw the image in an old woman so crippled with arthritis that her body was nothing but knots; I saw the image in a young man born with terrible deformities; the image is there for us in the suffering servant of Isaiah, "his appearance was so marred, beyond human semblance ... "he had no form or comeliness that we should look at him, and no beauty that we should desire him. He was despised and rejected by men, a man of sorrows, and acquainted with grief; and as one from whom men hide their faces he was despised, and we esteemed him not."

If we bear the image of love in our own flawed, human bodies, it is this love which will ultimately renew language. And then perhaps we will be given a truly great writer, like Chaucer or Shakespeare, to transform language with genius.

Religion and language are like rivers, constantly flowing from the same source, as we respond to all that is happening in the world around us. Maybe one day we'll get the hang of it, the yin and the yang of it. Language changes most graciously through poets and storytellers, and most clumsily when it is being manipulated by reformers and committees.

I saw a small sign in one of the offices of Bethel Seminary in Minnesota. *God so loved the world that he did not send a committee.*

Not a committee, but the Word of love.

* * *

In Berdyaev's *Revelation and Truth*, which I continued to read during jury duty, he wrote that the age of the old Testament was the Age of the Father. The New Testament was the Age of the Son. And he referred to the time at which he was writing – several decades ago – as the Age of the Spirit.

We are now groping slowly toward the Age of the Trinity, of wholeness. The fact that we Christians are beginning to recognize our brokenness, our fragmentation, is a sign of this healing movement. We speak now of holistic medicine. We speak of certain people as being holy, which really means being whole. We are turning once again to the insights of myth, the lessons of story, as we seek to move beyond the limits of the intellect.

The Holy Trinity contains knowledge and wisdom and male and female and child and sage and artist and holy fool and philosopher and mathematician and musician and a few million other qualities. The glory of the stars at night is an image of wholeness, for the universe is a unity. The smallest subatomic particles have their share in this unity, in the perfecting of the pattern.

The human family, too, is an icon of the Trinity, but how we have defaced and cracked the icon. The sacredness of family is desacralized by the breakdown of family life and the so-called sexual revolution which promised freedom, but which has brought about alienation and terrible loneliness. When we focus on one aspect of the Trinity or of ourselves, at the expense of the whole, we blunder into disaster.

Maybe it was time for the sexual revolution, but it, like all revolutions, went further than the initial vision. Abortion is an ugly and unsolved problem, and while the theological answer may be clear, easy answers produce such unloving actions as the throwing of bombs. Herpes and AIDS have become epidemic, terrifying as the Black Plague. We may be more open about sex, but we have emphasized the purely physical at the expense of the fullness of love.

At first Jacob loved Rachel because she was beautiful. But then the love strengthened as they came to know each other in the truest, deepest ways.

No matter how objective I try to be when I read the story of Jacob, or any part of Scripture, I am reading into it, willy nilly, my own prejudices, hopes, culture. This is inevitable. I see past history from my place within present history. It is impossible to see it exactly as it was for even the most objective of historians. It is easiest to understand when it is in the form of story. Even so, I still read into it my own questions. My understanding of Isaac and Rebekah, Jacob and Rachel, is formed by my understanding of all my encounters with people. Did Rebekah love her son, Jacob, more than she loved her husband, Isaac? She was willing to deceive Isaac in order to get the blessing for the younger, favored son, Jacob. It was Rebekah, his mother who told Jacob what to do, who was the initiator of the plot to deceive blind old Isaac. And she deceived her son, Esau, too, the hairy one, who was loved of his father.

Isaac was old, and nearly blind, and he called Esau, his eldest son, and Esau said, "Behold, here am I."

And Isaac said, "Behold, now I am old, and I know not the day of my death. Therefore, I pray you, take your quiver and bow, and go out into the field, and take me some venison, and make me some savory meat, such as I love, and bring it to me, that I may eat, and that my soul may bless you before I die."

Rebekah heard this, so she went to Jacob and told him, and said, "Do what I command you. Go to the flock and fetch me two good kids of the goats, and I will make them savoury meat for your father, such as he loves, and you shall gring it to your father, that he may eat it, and bless you before his death."

And Jacob said to Rebekah his mother, "But Esau my brother is a hairy man, and I am a smooth man. Perhaps my father will feel me, and know that I am deceiving him, and will give me a curse instead of a blessing."

And his mother said, "Upon me be the curse, my son. Just obey me and go fetch the kids."

So Jacob obeyed his mother, and she made savory meat, such as Isaac loved. And she took Esau's best clothes, and put them on Jacob. And she put the skins of the kids and goats upon his hands, and upon the smooth of his neck. And she gave the savory meat and the bread, which she had prepared, to Jacob.

And Jacob went to his father, and said, "My father," and Isaac said, "Here I am. Who are you?"

And Jacob said to his father, "I am Esau, your first born. I have done what you have asked of me. So sit and eat my venison, that your soul may bless me."

Was old Isaac a little suspicious? He asked a penetrating question – how had his son found the venison so quickly?

And Jacob answered, "Because the Lord, your God, brought it to me."

The Lord, your God? Was God not yet Jacob's God? Did he have to wait for the night of wrestling with the angel to know God? Isaac, still seeming suspicious, told his son to come closer to him, to be felt

And Jacob went near his father, and Isaac felt him, and said, "The voice is Jacob's voice, but the hands are the hands of Esau."

And Isaac did not recognize Jacob because his hands were hairy, so he blessed him, and he asked, "Are you truly my son, Esau?"

And Jacob said, "I am."

And Isaac ate of the savory venison, and drank some wine, and then he said, "Come near me, and kiss me, my son."

And Jacob came near and kissed him, and Isaac smelled the smell of his clothes, and blessed him, and said, "See, the smell of my son is like the smell of a field which the Lord has blessed. May God give you dew from heaven and the richness of the earth, and plenty of corn and wine. Let people serve you, and nations bow down to you. Cursed be everyone who curses you, and blessed be everyone who blesses you."

And so Isaac gave to Jacob the blessing which should have gone to Esau.

And it came to pass as soon as Isaac had finished blessing Jacob, and Jacob had scarcely left the presence of Isaac, that Esau came in from hunting. And he also had made savory meat and brought it to his father, saying, "Let my father arise and eat of his son's venison, that your soul may bless me."

And Isaac his father said to him, "Who are you?"

And he said, "I am your son, your first born, Esau."

And Isaac trembled greatly and said, "Who? Where is he who took venison and brought it to me? I ate all of it before you came, and I blessed him. Yes, and he shall be blessed."

For a blessing, once given, cannot be retracted.

And when Esau heard the words of his father, he gave a great and bitter cry, and said to his father, "Bless me, even me also, O my father." And he wept.

But Isaac had given the blessing reserved for the first son. It had been given, and he could not take it back. He said,

"Far from the richness of the earth shall be your dwelling place, far from the dew that falls from heaven. You shall live by your sword, and you shall serve your brother. But when you win your freedom, you shall shake his yoke from your neck."

Esau's story is a tragic one, and all the more so because of his unloveliness, covered with red hair, smelling of the blood of the animals he had killed, over-easily duped by his brother. (And by his mother, though he may not have known that.) One can hardly blame him for deciding that after Isaac had died, and the mourning period was over, he would kill his brother.

He may have shouted this aloud in his outrage, for someone told Rebekah, and she called Jacob and urged him to leave quickly and go to her brother, Laban, in Haran, and stay there until Esau's anger had cooled.

So Jacob left, taking with him Isaac's blessing.

* * *

We take both blessing and cursing much too casually nowadays. When someone sneezes we say, "Bless you," hardly thinking. It used to be believed that when one sneezes one is very close to death, and therefore to say, "Bless you," truly meant something important. It does. We need to reawaken our sense of blessing.

Often I hear a casual "dammit," meaning nothing but momentary annoyance, but to damn someone is serious indeed, because even our casual irritations leave their imprint and cannot be erased.

How do we learn to bless, rather than damn, those with whom we disagree, those whom we fear, those who are different?

Cursing is more a matter of intent than of language. Listen to a group of construction workers, or stage hands, and you will hear the four-letter words fly, but more likely they are used with affection, rather than malice. The liberal use of such words is often no more than regional or vocational vocabulary.

Whereas someone can say, calmly, "I do want you to know that I understand why you did this, and that I forgive you," and more venom can drip from those words than from any amount of casual profanity. Most Christians object to swearing because it is specifically forbidden by Christ in the fifth chapter of Matthew's gospel. There is, of course, a difference between using God's name "in vain" and merely vulgar, gutter words.

But what offended Jesus was hardness of heart, not laxness of language, which often stems from paucity of vocabulary. I suspect that if we could have heard the speech of some of Jesus' followers we might be disturbed. It was those whose lives were whitewashed on the outside, but full of dead bones inside, who made Jesus angry.

Certainly I am not advocating coarse or careless language. Far from it. But I am concerned about the intent behind the words which may be more significant than the words themselves. When I read a novel I am concentrating on the characters' hearts, and if the heart is warm, and open to growth in love, I probably won't even notice a few racy words. After all, I've worked in the theater and heard the stage hands. I spend much of the year living on Manhattan's upper west side. I've learned that it is what's behind the words that truly counts.

Not long ago in Toronto, I was on a radio program with two Canadian writers. I was given some of their books to read, and was told that one of them, Kevin Major, "uses questionable language." That night I read his *Hold Fast*, a novel set in Newfoundland. I thought that it was a fine book, and that the language, according to the situation and place, was not at all inappropriate. And on page seven, Major himself expressed exactly what I feel. His protagonist says of his uncle, "The swear words, when he spitted them out of him, was almost enough to curl up my guts. Not the words, that was nothing. I was use to that. But the way he said them. People swear in different ways. Dad use to swear and he hardly had a clue he was swearing it. But the way the same words came out of Uncle Ted, it was like a set of teeth, tearing into her."

Those of us blessed with a good education have the responsibility to use vocabulary judiciously, not carelessly. And to bless, not curse. To affirm, not damn.

In this muddled world it is not always easy to bless, but that is our calling. To curse is not only to wound another, it is to put ourselves in bondage. To bless is to be made free to bear God's love.

* * *

A writer I admire horrified me by saying that perhaps we will see Jesus coming again on a mushroom cloud, that the sign of the Second Coming will be the rolling cloud of an exploded nuclear bomb. No! Everything in me rejects the conjunction of an act of destructive hate with God's act of Creative love. And yet I have come to realize with sadness mingled with horror that some Christians are beginning to equate the Second Coming with nuclear disaster.

That cannot be. Of one thing only am I certain: the Second Coming is an action of Love. The judgment of God is the judgment of love, not of power plays or vindication or hate. The

Second Coming is the redemption of the entire cosmos, not just one small planet.

St. Paul, writing to the people of Rome, reminds us that "The creation waits with eager longing for the revealing of the sons of God ... the creation itself will be set free from its bondage of decay and obtain the glorious liberty of the children of God."

All of Creation groans in travail. All will be redeemed in God's fullness of time, all, not just the small portion of the population who have been given the grace to know and accept Christ. All the strayed and stolen sheep. All the little lost ones.

To equate the Second Coming with nuclear holocaust is to expect God to curse Creation, not to bless; to look for hell, not heaven, which is a kind of blasphemy, for we are called to live in hope. A Second Coming on a sulphurous, radioactive death-dealing cloud would be a victory for Satan, not Christ.

It would seem that the majority of those who see nuclear warfare and the Second Coming together are those who see Christ's coming in glory as exclusively for them and their fellow brand of believers. They, and they only, will be raptured up to heaven, and everybody else will burn in hell. Heaven is somewhat like a restricted country club for a favored few and the Lord of Love, is quite willing to curse everybody else.

The Lord of Love?

There's a story of a good man who dies and goes to heaven, and who is welcomed at the pearly gates, which are thrown open for him to enter. He goes through them in a daze of bliss, because it is everything he has been taught, golden streets, milk and alabaster and honey and golden harps. He wanders the streets lost in happiness, until after a while he realizes that he is all alone, he hasn't seen anybody at all. He walks and walks, and he sees nobody.

So he goes back to the gates, and asks, "Peter?"

"Yes, my son?"

"This really is heaven?"

"Oh, yes, my son. Don't you like it?"

"Oh, it's just wonderful! But where is everybody? Where are the prophets? Where is the Holy Family? Where are the saints?"

Peter looks at him kindly "Oh, them? They're all down in hell, ministering to the damned. If you'd like to join them, I'll show you the way."

* * *

Jesus said "And many false prophets shall rise, and shall deceive many. And because iniquity shall abound, the love of many shall wax cold."

The prophets who are discovering and pointing out devil-worshipers, who sniff out pornography and dirty words, are also among those who equate the Second Coming with Judgment Day.

Cold. It is coldness of heart that prophesies falsely.

Jesus continues, "For there shall arise false Christs, and false prophets, who shall show great signs and wonders, so that, if it were possible, they shall deceive the very elect. But of the day and hour no one knows, no, not the angels of heaven, but my father only."

Throughout the centuries there have been countless false prophets proclaiming the end of the world. As the first millennium approached, a great many Christians thought that with the year One Thousand would come Judgment Day. Since then there have been many other predictions of the world's end, including a goodly number in our own century. Some of the prophets have backed their predictions with quotations from John's Revelation, but that great visionary book is not to be taken literally. It is a sign of pride to think we can predict the end which Jesus said was hidden even from the angels. We do not know when it is coming. We must prepare, lest the bridegrooms coming catch us unaware. But we do not know. Being prepared, and knowing when the bridegroom is coming are two very different things, Jesus was emphatic about that.

How do we tell the false prophet from the true prophet? The true prophet seldom predicts the future. The true prophet warns us of our present hardness of heart, our prideful presuming to know God's mind. And the final test of the true prophet is love. God came to us as Jesus because of love. All the ills of the Fall will be righted and redeemed in the Second Coming because of love.

We must be careful in our right and proper protests against the folly of nuclear stockpiling that we are protesting truly, that we are not being false prophets fearing only for our own selves, our own families, our own country. Our concern must be for everybody, for the Russians, the Chinese, the Iranians, for our entire fragile planet, and everybody on it. And for all of God's creation, because we cannot blow ourselves up in isolation. Indeed, we must protest with loving concern for the entire universe.

The Old Testament prophets were often reluctant. The false prophets took pride in their prophesying and told the people what they wanted to hear, and so were popular. Whereas the true prophets, warning the people of the consequences of their evil actions, were anything but popular. They risked their lives. A mark of the true prophet in any age is humility, self-emptying so there is room for God's Word. The true prophet receives the Word as Isaiah did: "Here I am, send me." Or Mary: "Be it unto me according to your word."

Terrible disasters may await us. The planet is already sundered by war, starvation, drought, famine, earthquake, flood, tornado. But we should not read too much into these signs. Those who study weather patterns tell us that until a decade ago we had approximately fifty years of extremely unusual weather, fairly temperate and predictable. Now we are back to ordinary weather patterns, violent, and unpredictable. "Why do we bother to listen to the forecast?" we say. "It's almost always wrong." So let us not read an easy eschatology into a return to the kind of weather patterns which have been the norm for our planet during most of recorded history.

Jesus said, remember, that even the angels in heaven do not know the time of his return. No one can prophesy that everything is going to be easy, that there won't be more tornados or hurricanes or volcanic explosions. But nuclear warfare is an ultimate cursing. And we are told to bless.

Zephaniah, after prophesying the terrible things which would result from hardness of heart, then proclaims, "Your God is mightily in your midst. He will exult with joy over you, he will renew you by his love, he will dance with shouts of joy for you as on a day of festival."

The love of God is a great mystery, so far does it transcend our own diminished capacity for love and blessing. The marvel is that God's love can transform and augment ours. As we turn our hearts to blessing, we share in Heaven's blessing.

How do we bless those who would damn? Those who would consign most of the world to eternal hell? How do we bless assassins and terrorists, or even the lawyers in the criminal courts who try to get verdicts of not guilty for people they well know to be guilty?

How do I bless the person who is no longer willing to be my friend because of a secret I never told? How do I bless the person who did pass on that secret?

One thing I have learned is that I do not have to do it graciously. A blessing given is a blessing given. I sat in my quiet corner one night after jury duty, the Bible open on my lap, and I knew that I still had hurt in my heart, and that I was still angry at whoever was permitting a great load of blame and shame to be laid on me. And I heard myself saying – and meaning – "Oh, God, bless the bastard."

What did I mean by that? Just what I said. I was not demanding justification, or vindication, or a change of heart on the other person's part. The blessing stood, just as it was.

We must bless without wanting to manipulate. Without insisting that everything be straightened out right now. Without insisting that our truth be known. This means simply turning whatever it is we need to bless over to God, knowing that God's powerful love will do what our own feeble love or lack of it won't. I have suggested that it is a good practice to believe in six impossible things every morning before breakfast, like the White Queen in *Through the Looking Glass*. It is also salutary to bless six people I don't much like every morning before breakfast.

If we all blessed Muammar Qaddafi, what do you suppose would happen?

If a blessing is irrevocable, what about a cursing? We human beings can, and do, hurt each other through cursing. Most of us are aware of the power of black magic and its hexes and spells and killing sticks, and are rightly afraid of and shun it. But the most powerful evil magic is weak before Christ, and shrivels in the light of Christ's love.

The light shines in the darkness, and the darkness cannot put it out.

Then what about all that primitive cursing of our enemies in the Bible? Here again we are pushed to move on beyond the spiritual place where some of the biblical narrators and singers of the psalms stood. God uses raggle taggle material, and there is hope that we will learn from experience. We do not have to invent the lever, the needle, the wheel over and over again. We are not expected to sit still in our understanding, but to add wisdom to knowledge, and to move on.

The vision of God in Genesis is varied, and contradictory. The God we read about in the stories seems often different from the God in the histories, or the laws. God was seen both as the Creator of the universe, and as the tribal God who helped his chosen people take over the neighbor's land. God was the Maker of all the stars, and God was the masculine warrior God. This jealous God commanded that all the foreigners be killed in case his own people became seduced by the neighboring gods and started worshiping them, him, her, or it – which often happened.

Even with the assertion that the other gods demanded literal blood sacrifice, the command to kill all the people seems forensically bloody. And of course, not all the people did get killed, because we read of many marriages between tribes. Despite the order for slaughter, the people of El Shaddai married the worshipers of other gods, and this angered their anthropomorphic god. It's all pretty primitive because they were, after all, a primitive people.

The contradictory views of God in the early book of Scripture can be confusing – the constant demands to destroy alien nations, the bloodiness of it all. But then there breaks through a shining, as when we read in the tenth chapter of Deuteronomy, "And now, Israel, what does the Lord your God require of you, but to fear the Lord your God, to walk in all his ways, and to love God, and to serve the Lord God with all your heart and with all your soul." And in contradiction to all the demands for bloodshedding, "Love you, therefore, the stranger, for you were strangers in the land of Egypt."

But Deuteronomy was written long after the saga of Jacob, after the giving of the commandments, the setting up of ceremonial laws, the moving into a more forensic way of life. Jacob was not bound by the details of hundreds of laws. He knew that he could not earn God's blessing, but he did not hesitate to demand it. He knew that he needed it. And this deep need and passion showed that his heart had a deeper understanding than his conniving head. If Jacob had had to earn God's love, he would not have gone far.

Nor would he have seen those angels and the wonder of at-one-ment, of knowing the place where he had slept to be a sacred place, the house of God. How often do we feel such wondrous awe? We have lost much of it in the effort to have God as a friend, or, not so much a friend as a pal. And that doesn't work, either. God is both transcendent and immanent, and often in the wondrous moments of sheltering under the eternal wings, we know ourselves and all the stars in all the galaxies as belonging to God. How can we not feel awe?

Oh, I am in awe of the maker of galaxies and geese, stars and starfish, mercury and men (male and female). Sometimes it is rapturous awe: sometimes it is the numinous dread Jacob felt. Sometimes it is the humble awe of knowing that ultimately I belong to God, to the Maker whose thumb print is on each one of us. And that is blessing.

⁂

Poor Esau. If he felt awe at the glory of the stars we are not told about it. He was more interested in satisfying his immediate hungers. He didn't get much love, either from his mother or his twin brother. But he did not hold grudges. Rebekah told Jacob to go away until Esau cooled off, and she knew her elder son well enough to know that he would indeed cool off. I like that in Esau, the unwillingness to hold on to anger, the lack of desire for revenge. Perhaps Jacob did not know his brother well enough to know that Esau had a generous personality. Despite Rebekah's rank favoritism of the handsome younger son, Esau had fine qualities, including the refusal to sulk and smoulder over past insults.

Even about marriage, Esau did not receive the loving parental advice lavished on Jacob. We read that, "Esau, seeing that the daughters of Canaan did not please Isaac his father," went to Ishmael, his uncle, and married Mahalath, one of Ishmael's daughters. That doesn't seem to have pleased his parents, either. Esau, from the moment of his birth, was given a hard time.

But he did not respond to the indignities heaped upon him with cursing.

Even if I do not feel "good" about it, I must learn to bless and not damn. During a period of discussion at one conference I emphasized this and mentioned, rather casually, that I had said of someone, "God, bless the bastard." Not only did this startle some of the people at the conference, it was also liberating. God loves us as we are, even at our most ungracious. And to bless, no matter how little we may feel like it, is to participate in love.

Cursing is a boomerang. If I will evil towards someone else, that evil becomes visible in me. It is an extreme way of being forensic, toward myself, as well as toward whatever outrages me. To avoid contaminating myself and everybody around me. I must work through the anger and the hurt feelings and the demands for absolute justice to a desire for healing. Healing for myself, and my anger, first, because until I am at least in the process of healing, I cannot heal: and then healing for those who have hurt or betrayed me, and those I have hurt and betrayed. I must hope for healing for those two arrogant men with their clever lawyers; healing for the clever lawyers, too, deliberately defending two men who had used knives with intent to hurt or kill, but who hadn't used them skillfully enough to hurt the old woman they attacked as badly as the assistant district attorney claimed.

Are they any less worthy of blessing than was tricky Jacob?

Or you? Or me?

Perhaps most difficult of all is learning to bless ourselves, just as we are. Before we can ask God to bless us, we must be able to accept ourselves as blessed – not perfect, not virtuous, not sinless – just blessed.

If we have to be perfect before we can know ourselves blessed, we will never ask for the transfiguring power of God's love, because of course we are unworthy. But we don't have to be worthy, we just have to acknowledge our need, to cry out, "Help me!" God will help us, even if it's in an unexpected and shocking way, by swooping down on us to wrestle with us. And in the midst of the wrestling we, too, will be able to cry out, "Bless me!"

I am certain that God will bless me, but I don't need to know how. When we think we know exactly how the one who made us is going to take care of us, we're apt to ignore the angel messengers sent us along the way.

There is a story of an old man who lived by a river. In the spring the rains were heavy and the river rose. The sheriff came by in his jeep, and said to the old man. "The river is going to flood, and I want to evacuate you."

The old man folded his arms confidently. "I have faith in God. God will take care of me."

The sheriff shook his head and drove off.

The river continued to rise. It lapped about the old man's house, rising up to the porch. The sheriff came by in a row boat, and said, "The river is continuing to rise. I really need to evacuate you."

The old man looked at the river which covered his steps and lapped across the porch. He folded his arms. "I have faith in God. God will take care of me."

The sheriff shook his head, and rowed away.

And the river inched higher. At last the old man was clinging to his rooftree. The sheriff came by in a helicopter and hovered above the old man. "I really must evacuate you. You'll drown if I don't."

But the old man repeated, "I have faith in God. God will take care of me."

Frustrated, the sheriff left.

And the river rose even higher. And the old man drowned.

In heaven, he was very upset. He went to God and said, "Why did you do this to me? Why did you let me drown? I kept telling the sheriff that I had faith in you, and that you would take care of me."

God said, "You ninny! I sent you a jeep, and a rowboat, and a helicopter!"

When we ask God for help, we can't insist that help come in the way that we have decided. If we are demanding specific blessings, we may miss the actual ones God has sent to us.

Bless the Lord, O my soul, and all that is within me, bless his holy Name.
Bless the Lord, O my soul, and forget not all his benefits.
He forgives your sins, and heals all your infirmities;
He redeems your life from the grave and crowns you with mercy and loving kindness.
The Lord is full of compassion and mercy, slow to anger and of great kindness.
For as the heavens are high upon the earth, so is his mercy great upon those who fear him.
Bless the Lord, you angels of his, you mighty ones who do his bidding, and hearken to the voice of his word.
Bless the Lord, all you his hosts, you ministers of his who do his will.
Bless the Lord, all you works of his, in all places of his dominion, bless the Lord, O my soul.

8

A Sense of Wonder

THERE WERE MANY TIMES in Jacob's life when he must have experienced intense loneliness. After he had stolen his father's blessing, with his mother's urging, he could not stay at home to enjoy it, but had to go away, to stay with his uncle Laban.

Is there anybody in the world who has not, at one time or another, experienced a deep loneliness, when all support systems fail, when there is nobody there – nobody? It is at such times that I reach out for God most longingly. Here, as God was present for Jacob, not God Out There, high in a distant heaven, but present, even in the loneliest depths of my heart. For if I cannot find God here, within, how can I find el anywhere else? Jacob's vision of glory came in the midst of his terror. We do not have to be at peace, or have perfect conditions, in order to glimpse glory. It was as possible for me to have a flash of heavenly understanding in that tiny box of a jury room as in church or out on the grandeur of the ocean.

The universe is immeasurably vast. God only Out There, looking on, does not help me. I seek and know a closer God. God not only within all that has been made, God not only within during the lifetime of Jesus of Nazareth, but God within, right now within me, in the salt of my tears, the beating of my heart.

Lancelot Andrewes wrote:

Be, O Lord, within me to strengthen me
Without me to guard me
Over me to shelter me,
Beneath me to stablish me
Before me to guide me
After me to forward me
Round about me to secure me.

Those lines were written four centuries ago. The idea of God everywhere is not new, but God has been pushed Out There, without, for so long, that we forget the within-ness, and the marvel that God can come and reveal wonder in the most ordinary things. One early summer day I came home from trying to clip back the weed alders which were blocking the view from the star-watching rock, and met a young friend, also returning to the house, carrying his shirt which was stained red with the miracle of tiny, luscious wild strawberries, and which remained pinkly patterned after numerous launderings. This uncovenanted bounty of the field was worth one shirt, and a reminder of the marvelousness of the ordinary loveliness on the hillside by Crosswicks.

Sometimes the loveliness of God's presence comes in the midst of pain.

I wasn't quite over a bad case of shingles when I went south to conduct a retreat. I felt miserable. The shingles blisters, which had managed to get even into my ear, had burst my eardrum.

The weather was not cooperating. Instead of being warm and sunny (I had hoped to be able to sit on the beach and bask in the sun and heal) it was cold, rainy, and raw.

When the rain finally stopped, I went for a silent walk on the beach with two caring friends. The ocean was smothered in fog, but occasionally the curtain lifted enough to reveal a fishing boat, and a glimpse of muted silver on sea. One of my companions found some lovely driftwood. The other picked up some tiny donax shells and put them in my palm. And there, in the silence, in the fog, in my pain, was a sensation of being surrounded by the almighty wings of God, right then, at that time, in that place, God with us.

As Lancelot Andrewes called on God to be.

When I think of Jacob alone, his head on his stone pillow, I can easily hear Lancelot Andrewes' words coming from him. The vision of angels which came to him when he fled from home, and had not yet reached Laban, changed Jacob's perception of God, and he vowed a vow, bargaining with his father's God, but finally affirming,

then shall the Lord be my God: and this stone, which I have placed for an altar, shall be God's house: and of all that God shall give me, I will surely give a tenth to God.

Jacob was in the habit of making bargains: You do this for me, God, and you can be my God. But he was beginning to learn wonder, and awe at the marvel of the vision he had been sent.

How often we are given visions, and walk right by them, or through them (like the old man by the river) because we have lost our sense of wonder, our belief in all that lies on the other side of reason.

On my desk I have a placard which my granddaughter, Charlotte, made for me as a Christmas present, copying out Shakespeare's words in large italic letters: "Oh, wonderful, wonderful, and most wonderful, and yet again wonderful, and after that out of all whooping."

This delightful gift was a result of a week Charlotte and her sister, Léna spent with us at Crosswicks. In the evening we would get into the big four-poster bed with mugs of cocoa, and read *As You Like It*, taking turns with the roles. Charlotte was reading Celia, one of Shakespeare's most delightful and liberated characters, when she hooted out this joy with a spontaneity and lack of inhibition which we often lose as we move from the childhood world of play and daydreams into the adult world where we have to worry about the price of fuel oil and the rising cost of living. How sad that so often we stifle our sense of joy and wonder.

A letter to me from an eleven-year-old girl posed the question, "How can I remain a child forever and not grow up?"

I wrote back, "I don't think you can, and I don't think it would be a good idea if you could. What you *can* do, and what I hope you *will* do, is remain a child forever, and grow up, too." That is what it means to be a whole human being, rather than an isolated fragment of our own chronology.

Charlotte, Léna, and I, reading *As You Like It*, aloud, were children, and they were also young adolescents, and I was also a grandmother, but we shared our wonder. We culled other quotable lines from the play, chortling as Rosalind says, "Why, know you not that I am a woman? When I think, I must speak!"

Perhaps that's one of the best of the feminine characteristics. When we think, we speak. Which means that we have the courage of our convictions. Sometimes we tell stories, or write stories. Children have not lost the notion, as many adults have, that to read is to speak, it is, in fact, a form of dialogue. That is probably the chief difference between reading a book and watching television. In viewing we do not engage in dialogue; we are acted upon, we do not, in any true creative sense, participate. But when we read, we are creators. If the reader cannot create the book along with the writer, then the book is stillborn. The reader is also an artist.

Léna and Charlotte and I were artists as we read aloud.

Rosalind and Celia were universe-disturbers in their own inimitable ways, Celia being willing for love of her cousin to go into exile. And because a sense of wonder was vivid in Celia, she was able to make a game of something that was supposed to be humiliating and shameful. And in the end the "wicked uncle," who had sent Rosalind and Celia into exile, repented. The wicked may "play games," but, paradoxically, they do not know how to play.

Abraham Joshua Heschel says that "indifference to the sublime wonder of living" lies behind all the evils which have befallen our sorry century. I remember Léna and Charlotte as little ones twirling with delight in a daisy-filled meadow, singing ring-around-a-rosy with me, until we all fell into the white and green field, breathless with laughter.

Heschel continues, "Modern man fell into the trap of believing that everything can be explained, that reality is a simple affair which only has to be organized in order to be mastered."

I cannot explain angels, nor do I need to. But I want to hear the lovely swish of their wings, to know that they are there, God's messengers of love and hope.

To lose our sense of wonder is to grow rigid, unable to accept change with grace. This has been a century of change, accelerating change, which gives every indication of continuing to accelerate. We tend to adjust to the technological changes fairly well. We're not like the old woman who announced, "If God had wanted us to fly, he wouldn't have created trains."

We're grateful for the advances of medicine. I love the electronic typewriter which is sensitive to my thoughts as they flow through my fingers. Technology's outer changes are very visible, and we've managed to keep up with them fairly well. But we haven't changed inwardly enough to keep up with the changes we've made outwardly, thus creating problems we're just beginning to recognize. Or to refuse to recognize. For if we recognize that our spiritual development lags woefully behind our intellectual development, and that we must do something to heal this brokenness before we are split completely asunder, then we must open ourselves to God. This is dangerous to our self-satisfaction or complacency. If we open ourselves to the untamed God, we may get hurt. We may make mistakes. We may find that our lives are being turned around. And that takes courage, a childlike courage.

We become whole by being all of ourselves, including the aspects of ourselves we like least as well as those of which we are able to approve. When we try to approve of ourselves (rather than to love ourselves) we tend to lose both our senses of humor and of wonder. Only if I retain the irradiating joy as I see the first trout lily in the spring, the first bright red of the partridge berries in the autumn, can I become a "grown-up."

Abraham, Isaac, and Jacob were "grown-ups" in the proper sense. They accepted themselves as they were, and they remained sensitive to the wonder of God. And they were willing to change, to move into new ways.

Not only did Abraham marry Keturah, after Sarah's death, and have children with her, he also (according to the custom of the day) had concubines, and more children by them as he lived out his one hundred threescore and fifteen years.

Did he really? Did the patriarchs live as long as Scripture tells us, or did they count age differently? I'm ready to grant the vast length of their years a willing suspension of disbelief. They lived on a planet as yet unpolluted. Air was clean and fresh to breathe. Rain water was pure and could be tasted with relish: acid rain was many centuries away. Food was simple and wholesome, rough and full of bulk. It is quite likely that people then lived longer than we do, whereas during the Dark and Middle Ages and for many centuries thereafter they had far shorter life-spans than we have – and by we, I mean those of us in the Western world, for the current life-span in the Third World is no longer than the life-span in Europe in the Middle Ages.

Ishmael – Abraham's first son, the little boy dying of thirst in the desert, to whom God gave a spring of water – Ishmael, too, lived to a ripe old age, "a hundred and thirty-seven years," when "he gave up the ghost and died."

A phrase much used in Scripture, to give up the ghost. What does it mean? Ghost = spirit = breath. In the liturgy we ask that our thoughts may be cleansed by the *inspiration* of the Holy Spirit, that the Spirit may breathe truth and renewal into us.

When we give up the spirit, we stop breathing, we give the ghost back to the Creator. When their time came, Abraham and the others of the day gave up the ghost and were gathered to their fathers."

That was enough. Life was full, and there was little questioning of what came after it. Such questions did not come until a more densely-populated world where the wicked flourished and the innocent suffered and the inequities of this life became more apparent.

"The world has enough for every man's need," said Gandhi, "but not for every man's greed." There are many who will hunger and thirst. But they are never beyond the saving grace of God's love, the tender shepherd who will lift the dying child into strong and gentle arms and say, "come, little lamb, into my Kingdom."

* * *

In that desert land wells were so important that they were given names. There was an honoring of the reality of water and stone, of tree and sand. Everything in the created order belonged to God, and what is God's is named. I have named many of my favorite pausing places as I walk across the fields and through the woods. I love the Grandfather Oak which somehow survived whatever disease killed off most of the oaks in our part of New England, and who now looks benevolently down on many grandchildren oaklings. There is one ancient maple tree which is known to me as the Icon Tree, and one mountain ash which we discovered one autumn, rising above the scrub cherry and alder, bearing a bright load of berries, and which is for me the Star Singer. One of the favorite anthems we sang in choir was to the melody of the Ash Grove, and we sang the song of the stars in their courses, and hence the name Star Singer for this slender ash tree. There is Cleft Rock (and the two largest clefts were noticeably wider after the earthquake and more difficult to leap across), and the Star Watching Rock and the Precipice.

I like houses to have names, not numbers, but I am told that when the present postmaster here in our village is retired we will no longer be able to use "Crosswicks" as our address, but will, instead, be limited to a number. A house may have a number, but a home has a name.

It is harder to name things in the city. Our apartment building has a number, and is also called the Clebourne, but the Clebourne means little to me; it is, maybe, the old lobby with its marble walls, reminders of a grander day, but it is not the rooms in which we live. Some of the rooms have names, though. The room with the big Morse portrait of my great-grandmother with her harp, and great-great-aunt with her flute, is, logically, the Portrait Room, in which I have my desk, and the Quiet Corner where I sit at night to write in my journal, to read Scripture, to pray.

The city is overcrowded, and Manhattan is an island whose boundaries cannot be widened. There is no way to make room for everybody except by moving up, in taller and more cramped buildings. This crowding is a precursor of violence. I used to have favorite trees and resting places in the Riverside Park, but now I no longer feel safe strolling and relaxing. I go to the park now to walk the dog, and I no longer linger, I walk the dog.

When we first moved back to the city, the dog was Oliver, a collie who appeared in the village, and then in our lives and who, of course, had to make the move to New York with us. After Oliver came Timothy, the Irish Setter. New York has a dog pickup law, (which maybe half of us dog-walkers observe) and when I put the leash on the dog, I also put a plastic bag in my pocket. Timothy like all Irish Setters, dropped large, redolent loads, and I picked his up with my hand in the plastic bag, so that my fingers touched nothing except the plastic, and walked along, holding his warm, cereal-scented b.m., and feeling absolutely fearless. Suppose someone came up to me? I'd simply hold out the odorous bag and say, "Yes?"

There came a day which I knew was Timothy's last. He was fifteen-and-a-half years old – extremely old for an Irish Setter – and I think he knew it was dying day. A friend helped me to get him to the animal hospital, driving me there through the city streets, with Timothy lying in my lap, his head against my breast like a trusting baby's. My friend carried him in for me, and while we waited for the vet, again he lay in my lap, not in pain, simply letting the life drain out of him. When we put him on the surgical table there was no question that his time had come. The doctor said to me, "Do you want to see him afterwards?" Not understanding, I replied, "Not particularly. I'll stay with him now."

"I wish you wouldn't," the doctor said. "People tend to get nervous, and that upsets the dog. I'm thinking only of what is best for the dog."

"Then you'll let me stay with him and hold him," I said. I was told later that this city veterinary doctor had had to deal with hysterical people who perhaps loved their dramatics more than their animals. Anyhow, he looked at me, looked at the dog, and let me stay. I held my old friend while the needle was inserted. I was not nervous, but there were tears slipping down my cheeks. I said to the doctor, "I do not think that anyone, animal or human, ought to die without being held."

Timothy was not the first animal I have held through death. Probably he won't be the last. When we take on an animal, we have to accept that a dog's life-span is considerably shorter than ours. Now I walk with Doc – Doctor Charlotte Tyler (named after my husband's role, Dr. Charles Tyler), a romping, loving, willful Golden Retriever.

Abraham's sons, Isaac and Ishmael, reconciled at their father's death bed, were with him, and I hope that they held the old man as life ebbed away, their own hands touching.

Ishmael, Scripture tells us, died in the presence of his brethren," Isaac, and the children of Keturah, and likely the children of Abraham's concubines. Perhaps Isaac held Ishmael, and Laughter eased Bitterness.

Isaac was forty years old when he married Rebekah, and his son, Esau "was forty years old when he took to wife, Judith, the daughter of Beeri the Hittite, and Bashemath, the daughter of Elon the Hittite, which were a grief of mind to Isaac and Rebekah." A grief of mind, not because the women made quite a harem for Esau – having several wives was customary – and also compassionate, since there were many more women than men, and a husbandless woman had a hard time surviving. What upset Isaac and Rebekah was that Judith and Bashemath worshiped alien gods. They would also give Esau more children, and, therefore, strength, if Esau wanted to pay back Jacob for all his trickery.

Esau and Jacob did not have the kind of intimacy often associated with twins. And certainly with their startling physical differences they were obviously fraternal rather than identical twins. Even when they made peace with each other, it may have seemed to Jacob an uneasy truce. It is often more difficult to accept forgiveness than to give it.

The long-gone world of the rival twins was not as different from the world of today as it might seem. We are still struggling with alien gods: we are still trying to learn what it means to forgive and be forgiven.

It is not just that the God of the Christian appears different from the God of the Muslim or the Buddhist, but that even within Christianity God wears so many contradictory aspects that Christianity seems appallingly inconsistent to many people. It is not surprising that Christians themselves (ourselves) have made many people not only mistrustful of Christianity, but anti-Christian.

A brilliant young professor, whose son had recently joined a rigid, orthodox Jewish sect in Jerusalem, where all questions were given final answers, all actions dictated, said bitterly, "Religion is divisive." I have to agree that yes, alas, it is. But we were together in saying that God is not. Religion is divisive when it becomes fanaticism – an insistence that we know all the answers, and that anybody whose answers differ from ours is damned.

The human being's attempt to understand the Creator can never be final, but dynamic, in motion, almost as though we were climbing that ladder of angels joining heaven and earth.

Do we get dizzy on the ladder? Refuse to climb? Turn over and tell the vision to go away?

One of J.B. Phillip's books is entitled, *Your God is too Small*.

Our God becomes too small when we make God in our own image, instead of heeding the image of God in us. In us, not outside us, but in us, waiting to be recognized.

Our call, no matter what our vocation, is to witness to the God within, the God who is One.

Cardinal Suhard writes, "To be a witness does not consist in engaging in propaganda, nor even in stirring people up, but in being a living mystery. It means to live in such a way that one's life would not make sense if God did not exist."

My faith in God, who is eternally loving and constant even as my understanding grows and changes, makes life not only worth living, but gives me the courage to dare to disturb the universe when that is what el calls me to do. Sometimes simply being open, refusing to settle for finite answers, disturbs the universe. Questions are disturbing, especially those which may threaten our traditions, our institutions, our security. But questions never threaten the living God, who is constantly calling us, and who affirms for us that love is stronger than hate, blessing stronger than cursing.

If our planet is frequently dark, it may be Lucifer's bitter breath blowing against the light – Lucifer, the prototypical anti-universe disturber, wanting the glory for himself, instead of rejoicing in being the most luminous of all the lightbearers.

It is easy to name myriad anti-universe disturbers. We have them in our own country. What confuses us is that people can simultaneously disturb the universe both creatively *and* destructively. Some of the greatest advances in medicine, which not only save human life, but improve its quality, have come about because of our blasting open the heart of the atom. The laser can be used to save lives and also as a terrible instrument of destruction. Almost everything the human being has made, from plastic to penicillin, can be an instrument of both good and evil.

We daily have to make choices between good and evil, and it is not always easy, or even possible, to tell the difference between the two. Whenever we make a choice of action, the first thing to ask ourselves is whether it is creative or destructive. Will it heal, or will it wound? Are we doing something to make ourselves look big and brave, or because it is truly needed? Do we know the answers to these questions? Not always, but we will never know unless we ask them. And we will never dare to ask them if we close ourselves off from wonder.

When I need a dose of wonder I wait for a clear night and go look for the stars. In the city I see only a few, but only a few are needed. In the country the great river of the Milky Way streams across the sky, and I know that our planet is a small part of that river of stars, and my pain of separation is healed.

Dis-aster makes me think of dis-grace. Often the wonder of the stars is enough to return me to God's loving grace.

9

Breaking the Taboo

THE STORY OF JACOB'S AND RACHEL'S LOVE reads like a fairy tale. Rebekah became Isaac's bride without trial or trouble. Not so with Jacob and Rachel. No prince in a fairy tale had more trouble in marrying his princess than did Jacob.

It started out, in the usual way by a desert well, where Rachel came with her father's sheep, to give them water.

Jacob saw Rachel, and went near and rolled the stone away from the well's mouth, and watered the flock of Laban, his mother's brother. And Jacob kissed Rachel, and lifted up his voice and wept. And Jacob told Rachel that he was her father's brother, and that he was Rebekah's son, and she ran and told her father.

Why did Jacob weep? With joy? Men wept freely before too much "civilization" taught them that tears are unmanly. But

Jacob was sure enough of his own manhood that he was free to do all kinds of things which would be frowned on today. It's a freedom we all need to regain, and surely men are as much in need of liberation as women. Their chains are perhaps less visible, but easily as crippling.

Jacob wept.

He was exhausted, fleeing for his life, leaving the known safety of home. And there at the well was a beautiful young woman, and he learned that she was Rachel, and he loved her, and wept.

So Jacob told Rachel who he was, and Rachel ran and told her father, and Laban ran to meet Jacob, and kissed him, and brought him to his house. And Jacob stayed with Laban for a month.

Then Laban said, "Surely you shall not serve me for nothing. Tell me, what shall your wages be?"

Now Laban had two daughters, and the elder daughter was Leah, and she was tender-eyed, while Rachel, the younger was beautiful, and well-favored. Jacob loved Rachel, and said to Laban, "I will serve you for seven years for Rachel, your younger daughter."

Laban agreed, and Jacob served him for seven years, which seemed to him just a few days, for the love he had for Rachel. Then Jacob said, "Give me my wife, for I have fulfilled my seven years. Give me my wife that I may go in unto her."

So Laban made a great wedding feast.

And that evening Laban took Leah to Jacob, instead of Rachel. The trickster was out-tricked in an extraordinary fashion. And here we must give the fairy tale an enormous suspension of disbelief. Even if Jacob had wined and dined extremely well at the wedding feast, it is hard to believe that he wouldn't have noticed that he was making love with Leah, and not with his believed Rachel. But, according to the story he did not notice the exchange until morning, and then he cried out to Laban, "What is this that you have done to me? Did I not serve with you for Rachel? Why have you tricked me?"

Laban said, "In our country we must not give the younger in marriage before the first born." So after marrying Leah, Jacob also married Rachel, and agreed to serve Laban another seven years for her.

It was Rachel Jacob loved, not Leah, and these things happen. We do not always choose those to whom we respond with love. From the moment he saw her at the well, Jacob loved Rachel, not Leah. However Leah was his number one wife according to the custom of the time, and he lived with her as his wife, and she conceived, and bore a son, and called his name Reuben, for she said, "Surely the Lord has looked upon my affliction; now, therefore, my husband will love me."

But it's never that easy. Nor was it any easier for Rachel, because she did not conceive. Jacob's love of her could not fill her empty womb. Meanwhile, Leah bore three more sons, Simeon, Levi, and Judah, and with each one she continued to hope that Jacob would come to love her. One wife had his children; one had his love.

Barren Rachel envied Leah, her older sister, saying to Jacob, "Give me children, or I will die." This made Jacob angry with Rachel and he said, "Am I in God's place, who has withheld from you the fruit of the womb?"

Then Rachel did what her grandmother-in-law, Sarah, had done before her; she gave her maid, Bilhah, to Jacob, saying, "She shall bear upon my knees, that I may also have children by her."

Bilhah conceived, twice, and bore two sons, Dan and Naphtali.

When Leah realized that she was through conceiving, she, in her turn, gave Zilpah, her maid, to Jacob, and Zilpah bore Gad and Asher. (How must the maids have felt, being offered to another woman's husband, like it or not, to bear children for their mistresses? It was customary, must it not also have been humiliating?)

We know more about Hagar, Ishmael's mother, than we do about Bilhah and Zilpah, but they each bore two sons who were among the twelve sons of Jacob who made up the twelve tribes of Israel.

Reuben, who must have been an adolescent by the time Gad and Asher were born, went out into the fields at the time of the wheat harvest, and found mandrakes, which he brought to his mother, Leah. The mandrake was supposed to have magic powers, and its root to resemble the human form. I think of Donne's lines,

Go and catch a falling star,
Get with child a mandrake root.

Rachel wanted her sister's mandrakes, and asked for them, and Leah, rather understandably, refused. "Isn't it enough for you that you have taken my husband from me? Would you also take away my son's mandrakes?"

Rachel said, "Then Jacob shall lie with you tonight for your son's mandrakes."

So when Jacob came in from the fields, Leah was the one who met him. And he lay with her that night, and she conceived, and bore fifth son, Issachar. And she conceived again, and had a sixth son, Zebulon. After that she had a daughter, Dinah.

And God "remembered Rachel," Scripture says, and she conceived, and bore a son, and said, "God has taken away my reproach," and she called her son Joseph.

After the birth of Joseph, Jacob went to Laban and said, "Send me away, that I may go to my own place, and to my own country. Give me my wives and my children, for whom I have served you all these years."

Laban did not want to let Jacob go, because under Jacob's care, Laban's flock had multiplied greatly. Finally he asked, "What shall I give you?"

Jacob answered, "You shall not give me anything. But I will go through your flock today, and remove all the speckled and spotted cattle, goats, and sheep."

Jacob would be allowed to keep the less desirable beasts as his reward for his years of service with his father-in-law, leaving for Laban the purer animals.

But Jacob was up to his tricks again, this time with an early example of genetic engineering, breeding the speckled and spotted animals for strength, so that they became more desirable than the others.

Laban was not pleased, and Jacob saw his father-in-law's displeasure in his countenance. So he quickly gathered together his wives and maids and children and set them on camels, and he stole away with all his goods and all his spotted cattle, fleeing once again because his trick had been found out.

Laban, unaware that Jacob and Rachel were running away from him, went to shear his sheep, when he discovered that his teraphim had been stolen. Household gods, as the Romans later called them.

When Laban discovered that Jacob and Rachel and Leah were gone, among with his images, he rushed after them.

Jacob had pitched his tent on Mount Gilead, and there Laban overtook him.

"What have you done!" Laban cried, "that you left without telling me, and carried away my daughters as though they were captives you had won in battle? ... Why have you stolen my gods?"

Jacob admitted to Laban that he had run away because he was afraid. His very willingness to acknowledge his fear was a sign of his courage. And cunning. But he denied taking Laban's teraphim, and suggested that his father-in-law search for these small images, swearing, rashly, that whoever had them should not live – a kind of cursing for which he would pay bitterly. For he was unaware that it was his believed Rachel who had taken the teraphim, perhaps for protection during their flight, perhaps because they were the familiar little gods she was accustomed to. Jacob, unknowing, called for the death of whoever had stolen the images. Was this curse irrevocable, as blessings are irrevocable? Did Jacob's rash words cause Rachel to die in giving birth to her second son, Benjamin?

Laban looked through Jacob's tent, and through Leah's tent, and then he went into Rachel's tent.

Now Rachel had taken the images, and put them in the camel's furniture and sat on them ... And Rachel said to her father, "Let it not displease my lord that I cannot stand to greet you, because the custom of women is upon me." And Laban searched, but he did not find the images.

The custom of women. The menstrual period. Blood.

Blood, the great taboo of the Old Testament. A woman during her menstrual period was thought to be unclean, because to shed blood is to shed life.

This attitude still prevails in some parts of the world today. I stood outside a Jain temple in Bombay and read the sign out front with its various prohibitions: *Do not enter with shoes on. Women in menstrual cycle not allowed.*

After walking on the filth of any city street, my own New York included, taking off one's shoes seems sensible indeed. But *blood*?

What is there about blood? I started reading an interesting and challenging article by an Islamic scholar. As I read, I was amazed at how completely I was able to accept all that he was saying, and I applauded internally when he affirmed that of course God is female as well as male – and of course women are just as important as men in the eyes of God – except during the menstrual period when women do not say the prayers.

At this point I closed the article. What kind of equality is this? What is there about this blood which is so terrifying to men?

I had cause to learn a good deal about blood this summer, and it has made a great difference in my response to this fluid which, to the ancient Hebrew, was taboo because it represented life itself.

* * *

It began in July when Hugh and I spent fifteen days on a fifty-foot boat with friends in the coastal waters of northwest Canada, near Prince Rupert Island and the Queen Charlotte Islands. There were six of us on the boat, and we were the crew. What there was to be done, the six of us did. We each took our turn on watch. Whoever was at the wheel needed someone else sitting right there on a stool, for drift watch, for in those far northern Canadian waters there are many drifting logs and "dead heads" difficult to see, which could do great damage to a small boat.

Hugh and I were not quite prepared for the vastness of the wilderness, and our almost total isolation. At night we would pull into an inlet, and anchor. Our only companions were seals, dolphins, loons. We saw bear tracks, though we never saw bears themselves. There was usually at least one great eagle perched watchfully high up on a tree in these climactic forests – forests which have grown as much as they can grow.

During those fifteen days and nights of the trip we never saw the moon or the stars; we were so far north that it was still daylight when we went to bed. We learned a lot of wilderness lore, and we ate almost entirely out of the sea. I never thought I'd take having a shrimp or crab cocktail every evening for granted. We caught more than we could eat. We had red snapper and rock fish, and we harvested abalone at low tide, and ate them thinly sliced in garlic butter. We ate the eggs of the sea cucumber. We learned that six people living together in a small amount of space with no privacy, no way to get away from each other, have to practice great forbearance, and maintain an acute sense of humor.

It was a good time, a special time. But there was an unsuspected serpent as there usually is in Eden. Our drinking water was put into the boat whenever we docked near a town, and in one batch of water was an organism known as *aeromonas*. It gets into the human intestine where it does very nasty things. Aeromonas is rare on the north American continent. It is usually found in Australia, almost entirely in the intestines of children where it is self-limiting and short lived. For an adult to be taken over by this little organism is unusual indeed, and in an adult the effects can be quite violent.

It didn't bother anybody else, but for some reason it got me. It invaded my intestines and wrought havoc. Not much is known about it in adults, except that it produces the symptoms of acute ulcerative colitis, and this means pain, severe cramping, and blood. Not unlike the dysentery which afflicted the English in India.

The people at the lab were absolutely delighted to have discovered their second aeromonas, the first having been in a child. My doctor had happened to read an article about aeromonas in *The Lancet*, the English medical journal, he also knew I had been in estuary waters, the only place aeromonas is found, and put two and two together.

It was a relief to have a name to put to my problem, but it didn't put an end to it. Basically, I lost August, spending it in bed. I was weak, tired, and in pain. At night when the pain kept me from sleeping, I listened to tapes, music, and then a series of tapes from a conference at Aqueduct Center in North Carolina, conducted by Drs. Paul and Margaret Brand. The Brands were both children of Baptist missionaries in India, and were missionaries themselves. They have given their lives to caring for lepers, first in India, and finally in Carville, Louisiana.

Dr. Margaret Brand is an opthalmologist, Dr. Paul Brand an orthopaedic surgeon. I listened to their tapes, at first rather reluctantly, because for this cradle Anglican there is something a little uncomfortable about some of the Baptist ways of speaking about God. But as I listened, night after night, I began to feel that I was in the presence of holy people. I was ready to listen when Paul Brand began to speak about the marvelousness of pain.

The most terrible thing to happen to the leper is the loss of pain. The hands and feet of the leper become useless stumps not because of leprosy, but because the leper feels no pain. If the leper loses fingers or toes, as so often happens, it is not because of the disease itself, but because the leper is not warned by pain that the fingers or toes are being hurt, and therefore damage or infection are not prevented. Pain is an angel to tell us that something is wrong. The body which cannot feel pain suffers terrible and often fatal injury.

My body knew pain, and I was doing something about it, taking antibiotics to kill the aeromonas virus, and finally heavy doses of steroids to mitigate the colitis symptoms. Had I had no pain it is quite possible that the little aeromonas could have finished me off. But I had pain, and this pain was alleviated and put in perspective as I listened to Paul Brand rhapsodizing about its wonderful function.

Other marvelous and unexpected insights were given me during those long nights. Blood. It is a scary thing to see the bowl bright with your own red blood. So I was ready and able to listen when, during the small hours of one night, Paul Brand talked about blood.

My husband left his southern Baptist background when he went away to college. We're both turned off by hymns about being washed in the blood of the Lamb. It sounds too graphic, too literal, to be for me a valid image.

Bleeding, blood, is seen as the source of life, especially for the Jew, for whom the eating of blood is the one real taboo. When God made the new covenant with Noah, after the flood waters subsided, and told him to repopulate the earth, Noah was given only one prohibition: "But flesh with the life thereof, which is the blood thereof, you shall not eat." This prohibition against the consumption of blood is repeated throughout the Bible, loudly, clearly, emphatically. Blood stands for life; that is why an animal must be completely drained of blood before it can be eaten.

Once my husband naively went into a kosher butchershop in our neighborhood in New York and asked for a leg of lamb, and the poor butcher nearly fainted. Jacob himself added a new taboo the night he wrestled with the angel. The angel smote him on the thigh, and Jacob limped thereafter, so that for Jews ever since, the thigh of the animal, with the sciatic nerve, is prohibited. But the chief taboo is blood.

So, when I was losing blood, I was very aware that I was also losing life. Paul Brand reiterated that the taboo against blood is the strongest taboo in the Bible.

We find mention of this ancient prohibition even in the Psalms. "But they that run after another god shall have great trouble. Their drink offerings of blood will I not offer."

So when Jesus said, in John's gospel,

"Truly, truly, I say to you, unless you eat of the flesh of the Son of man and drink his blood, you have no life in you, he who eats my flesh and drinks my blood has eternal life, and I will raise him up at the last day. For my flesh is food indeed, and my blood is drink indeed. He who eats my flesh and drinks my blood abides in me, and I in him. As the living Father sent me, and I live because of the Father, so he who eats me will live because of me. This is the bread which came down from heaven, not such as the fathers ate and died, he who eats this bread will live forever."

This he said in the synagogue, as he taught at Capernaum.

Many of his disciples, when they heard it, said, "This is a hard saying; who can listen to it?"

But Jesus, knowing in himself that his disciples murmured at it, said to them, "Do you take offense at this?" Then what if you were to see the Son of man ascending where he was before? It is the spirit that gives life, the flesh is of no avail; the words that I have spoken to you are spirit and life. But there are some of you that do not believe." For Jesus knew from the first who those were that did not believe, and who it was that should betray him. And he said, "This is why I told you that no one can come to me unless it is granted him by the Father."

After this many of his disciples drew back and no longer went about with him.

Drink my blood? Break the great taboo? What a shocker that is! For me it was a salutary shock, reminding me that Jesus almost never did what was expected of him, and that God, at all times, and in countless ways, is ready to shock and surprise us into seeing things in a new way. This new understanding about blood is very much with me at communion when I receive the cup. It is indeed a new commandment.

Was it because of the shock of this command of Jesus' that in the Roman Catholic Church until very recently the priest was the only one to drink from the cup, and the people received the bread only? Was it too strong, too shocking? Now, in many Roman Catholic churches, the cup is offered, too. But I don't want ever to take it for granted. I want to be reminded what an extraordinary thing I am doing.

Yet I still find it hard to think of being washed in the blood of the Lamb.

Jesus, little lamb, meek and mild. Jesus, tender shepherd. All right, these are images which have given comfort to countless suffering people. But there is also Jesus, the great Shocker.

Think of the story of the woman with the issue of blood. It has long been one of my favorite stories of the healing power of Jesus – the anguished, bleeding woman trying to reach for the hem of his garment, seeking for the help doctors had been unable to give her (and she had gone to many doctors). Without seeing her, Jesus knew that someone had touched him, because he felt that "virtue" had drained from him.

"Who touched me?" he asked.

The disciples, not understanding, wanted to know how he could ask such a question, with a mob pressing all around him. But the woman crawled forward and confessed that it was she who had touched him, and he told her, lovingly, that her faith had made her whole.

Again he had done something terribly shocking. He had broken the great taboo. The woman with the issue of blood was a woman whose menstrual bleeding had gone on and on without ceasing. She was unclean, and anybody who touched her, or was touched by her, was ritually unclean, and had to go through the prescribed purification procedures, according to the law, before touching anybody else.

So Jesus healed this unclean woman, and by her touch he became ritually unclean himself. He was on his way to the house of Jairus, whose daughter was mortally ill. But Jesus did not stop to follow the law, to purify himself. Ritually unclean, so that anybody who touched him was also unclean, he went to Jairus's house, and raised the little girl from the dead. Thereby he broke another taboo, going against the proscription against touching a dead body. He touched her. And she was alive, and he suggested that she be given food. Shocking behavior. Everybody he touched, after being touched by the woman with the issue of blood, was unclean. But he brought a dead child back to life, making himself doubly unclean, and the child, also. Ritually unclean, but alive! Jesus acted on the law of love, not legalism. As far as we know he never did anything about getting himself ritually cleansed. Because love, not law, is the great cleanser. In obeying this higher law he shocked everybody, including his closest friends, in his extraordinary and unacceptable ways of acting out love. Of being Love.

Jesus never broke the law simply to break the law, never as an act of rebellion, but always to obey the higher law of love.

That is the only valid reason for breaking the law. Does it violate the law of love? Truly? Then it may be broken, even if it shocks the establishment as Jesus shocked the establishment by healing on the Sabbath, by letting his disciples pluck grain, by reminding us that the Sabbath was made for man, not man for the Sabbath.

But his violation of the great blood taboo was the most shocking of all.

* * *

When Paul Brand was a child, he often went into tiny villages with his father who, although not a doctor himself, often had to lance people's ugly infections to drain them of pus and blood. The young Paul was put off by this. He did not want to become a doctor because he did not like blood.

God has ways of sending us strong messages, without tampering with our free will. In order to become a missionary, Paul Brand had to take a thorough course in first aid. There would be many times when he, like his father, would be in places where there was no doctor. He would have to learn something.

Part of the first aid course was a stint as an orderly in a large London hospital. One night, shortly after he had gone on duty, a young accident victim was brought in. She looked dead.

White, bloodless. There was great rushing around, and a blood transfusion was started. Paul Brand was asked to stay by the woman and to let the nurses know when the blood in the transfusion bag got low.

And so, he said, he watched a miracle. First a tiny flush of color came into the cheeks. Then the dead white lips were touched with pink. The girl's eyelids fluttered, and she opened her eyes. Blood was indeed life.

So Paul Brand became a doctor, with an entirely new concept of blood. Blood as life. Our life. Our life given to us in the blood and the body. And suddenly he saw all the exhortations to wash in the blood of the lamb not to be literal, as he first took them. Instead, he tells of it as an inner, not an outer washing, and likens it to the life-giving quality of a blood transfusion. He said that if people knew as much about the human body as we do today, they would not have said, "wash me in the blood of the Lamb," but "transfuse me with the blood of the Lamb."

So, when we receive Communion, we are transfused.

Sometimes it is spiritual pain which makes us aware that we need a transfusion. Just as physical pain is a marvel for the human body, an early warning system, so is spiritual pain. So is grief. Grief for the loss of someone we love, either by death, or by broken relationship, which can be more painful than death. Grief is a pain warning.

I grieved for the friendship broken when I was accused of breaking a confidence. And once I was able to grieve, rather than to be angry, and sorry for myself, and to want justice done, then healing became possible, healing which cannot occur without love.

If I was innocent in this case, surely there have been other times in my life when inadvertently I *have* broken confidences. We all say more than we ought to say, or more than we know we have said. Or we don't speak out when a word would make all the difference. Not one of us is totally innocent in either the words of our mouths or the meditations of our hearts. We are all part of this battered, bleeding bride, struggling to regain beauty and purity. And there is nothing, nothing but a transfusion of love which will make any difference at all.

But we need our pain warnings before we can turn to love.

If we watch television, read magazines, we come across a very different attitude toward pain. Avoid it. Deaden it. Take a pill, kill it, then you won't heed its warning. What do the media want us to believe in? Aspirin. Tylenol. Excedrin. Codeine. Or any of the other hard-selling painkillers. Anything but pain.

We don't want pain. We certainly don't go looking for it. But when it comes, we should heed its warning. I was not offered painkillers while I was struggling to get rid of the aeromonas. But listening to the music, and to the talking tapes was as effective as a narcotic would have been, and possibly even more so.

A young woman told me of a terrible eye injury for which she could be given no painkillers, because they would impede the healing of the eye. So, she said, she lay on the floor, writhing in pain, and asked her husband to play records, loud music, Beethoven and Brahms symphonies. And while she was being transfused by music, washed in the great orchestras, the pain subsided until she could lie still, listening. And slowly her eye healed.

There are times when it is appropriate to use painkillers, as I know through personal experience. Pain is not romantic, and I don't want to suggest sentimentally that it is never intolerable. James Herriot, the Yorkshire veterinarian, writes in one of his books about being called by a farmer to tend a sick animal. Nearby in her stall a cow lay bellowing in mortal pain. The farmer refused to let the vet touch the cow, saying she was going to die, anyhow, and he wasn't going to waste money on her.

Herriot could not stand the poor animal's agony, and when the farmer wasn't looking, he took a hypodermic needle and gave the cow a massive shot to assuage her pain so that at least she could die quietly. The next day when he returned to the farm to tend the other animal, he expected a dead cow, but there she was, peacefully munching hay. The painkiller had relaxed her anguish so that she was able to heal.

As usual, there are no valid generalities about pain. But I suspect we need medication less often than the media would have us believe. Sometimes healing and pain can work together to mend us. I don't envy those who have never known any pain, physical or spiritual, because I strongly suspect that the capacity for pain and the capacity for joy are equal. Only those who have suffered are able to rejoice.

It is only when we know ourselves wounded, know that we have lost blood, that we are aware that we need a transfusion. (Sometimes it is only the wise physician who recognizes pain that is intractable, as the Yorkshire vet recognized it, and knows that help is needed.) The transfusion is for someone who has experienced the warning wonder of pain, and the acceptance of the loss of blood, either physically or spiritually.

There are days when I go to the altar and I am less aware of my need for a transfusion than I am on other days. That is all right. But I am always aware that I am tapping into the source of a tremendous power of love. It is not a magic power. As far as I am concerned the experts can worry about words such as transubstantiation. When you need a blood transfusion you don't worry about things like that. The transfusion of love is not always a comfortable one, because such love may push me into letting go some cozy ideas, push me into a new way of looking at God, and therefore at myself.

What am I looking for? Sometimes God opens my eyes so that I see something totally unexpected, something which may cause pain and loss. And then I need to be transfused.

This is always a reminder that God loves us, just as we are. We don't have to perfect ourselves by adherence to the letter of the law. Jesus has broken the law, radically, with his violation of the taboo of blood, and in the breaking of the taboo has shown the healing power of love. We, too, violate the taboo, break the law. We must understand that when we take the bread and wine we are doing something shocking.

Jesus was not shocked by the woman who was ritually unclean, or the man who collected taxes for the Romans, or even the woman taken in adultery. But he was shocked and grieved by hardness of heart.

We are blessed indeed to be able to feel pain, our body's warning system that something is wrong, and that we need help.

Indeed, yes, I need to be washed in the blood of the Lamb, transfused with the blood of the Lamb, for that gives life, and life abundantly.

10

Let the Baboons Clap Their Hands

LABAN NEVER FOUND HIS HOUSEHOLD GODS; Rachel was too cunning for him. Had she learned this from her husband?

Jacob (feeling guilty about his genetic manipulation?) was immediately angry with the one he had tricked, and he said to Laban,

What is my trespass? What is my sin, that you have followed me so hotly? You have searched all my stuff, and what have you found that belongs to you? I've been with you for twenty years,

he continued, reminding Laban that his flocks and worldly goods had flourished under Jacob's care.

I served you for fourteen years for your two daughters, and six years for your cattle, and you have changed my wages ten times.

They quarreled elegantly in those days, and made up elegantly, too. Jacob and Laban made a covenant, and Jacob set up another stone for a pillar, and called the place by several names, including Mizpah, for, Laban said,

The Lord watch between me and thee, when we are absent from one another.

The word *Mizpah* has often been etched on pins and lockets, and given by lovers to each other. But it was said first by a father-in-law to his son-in-law after they had had a bitter quarrel. After that,

Jacob went his way, and the angels of God went with him.

Did the angels of God remind him that he had unfinished business with his brother, Esau? Jacob sent messengers to Esau, telling them,

Thus shall you speak to my lord Esau: his servant, Jacob, says, "I have stayed with Laban until now, and I have oxen, asses, flocks, menservants and womenservants, and I have sent to tell my lord Esau, that I may find grace in his sight."

And the messengers returned to Jacob, saying, "We came to your brother, Esau, and he is coming to meet you, with four hundred men."

This terrified Jacob, because he thought that Esau, after all these years, was coming out to kill him, and he divided his retinue, all the people and all the animals, into two camps, saying,

If Esau comes to one company and smites it, then the other will escape. (In his fear, he continued to punish himself for his own trickery.)

Then he turned to God and said, "O God of my father Abraham, and God of my father Isaac . . . Deliver me from the hand of my brother, for I fear him, lest he come and kill me, and the mothers and their children. And yet it was you, Lord, who said, I will surely do good for you, and make your seed as the sand on the seashore, which cannot be numbered."

Jacob stayed where he was that night, and prepared presents (bribes?) for Esau: two hundred she-goats, twenty he-goats, two hundred ewes, twenty rams, thirty milk camels and their colts, forty kine, and ten bulls, and twenty she-asses, and ten foals.

He did not know his brother very well, our too-clever Jacob. He took his own two wives, and the two womanservants, and his eleven sons, and sent them all over the brook with everything that he had, so that he was alone, completely alone.

And then came the angel to wrestle with him.

Long before, on his flight to Laban, Jacob had seen the ladder of angels, connecting heaven and earth; now he was wrestling with heaven in Person.

And Jacob was left alone; and a man wrestled with him until the breaking of the day. When the man saw that he did not prevail against Jacob, he touched the hollow of his thigh; and Jacob's thigh was put out of joint as he wrestled with him. Then he said, "Let me go, for the day is breaking."

But Jacob said, "I will not let you go, unless you bless me."

And he said to him, "What is your name?"

And he said, "Jacob."

Then he said, "Your name shall no longer be called Jacob, but Israel, for you have striven with God and with men, and have prevailed."

Then Jacob asked him, "Tell me, I pray your name."

But he said, "Why is it that you ask my name?" And there he blessed him, so Jacob called the name of the place Peniel, saying, "For I have seen God face to face, and yet my life is preserved." The sun rose upon him as he passed Peniel, limping because of his thigh. Therefore to this day the Israelites do not eat the sinew of the hip which is upon the hollow of the thigh, because he touched the hollow of Jacob's thigh on the sinew of the hip.

Jacob's angel wrestled with him all night. We don't always have the courage to keep it up as long as that, though night is often a time for the most intense spiritual struggle, and we don't always know who started it – we, with our unanswerable questions, or the angel, leaping on us unexpectedly.

Perhaps we need the angel to start grappling with us, to turn us aside from the questions which have easy answers to those which cause us to grow, no matter how painful that growth can be.

Luci Shaw condenses into this small poem some of the intense personal longing that was Jacob's, and is ours, in grappling with heaven:

With Jacob

inexorably I cry
as I wrestle
for the blessing,
thirsty, straining
for the joining
till my desert throat
runs dry.
I must risk
the shrunken sinew
and the laming
of his naming
till I find
my final quenching
in the hollow
of the thigh.

This was a critical point, a watershed in Jacob's life, when he came to grips with God – with the reality of heaven itself.

In the Bible, heaven is described metaphorically, not literally. We are given some hints and clues, but it remains for us a realm of mystery.

When my father died when I was seventeen, I pondered heaven and God's plan for el's complex and contradictory children, and it seemed to me evident that nobody I know, certainly including myself, was ready for heaven after this mortal life in which we are all, one way or another, bent and broken. There may be a handful of people who are prepared for the unveiled vision of God. But most of us are not, most of us still have a vast amount to learn. I don't know how God plans to teach me all that I need to know before I am ready for the

Glory, but my faith is based on the belief that I don't have to know. I have to know only that the Maker is not going to abandon me when I die, is not going to make creatures who are able to ask questions which simply cannot be answered in this life, and then drop them with the questions still unanswered.

"But the church says ..." I am sometimes reminded.

The church (of all denominations) has often said one thing, and then gone on to say something else again. The church pronounced that the earth is flat, that it is the center of creation and God's concern, with the sun and the moon and the stars revolving around us, all for our benefit. It is now generally acknowledged that the earth is part of a solar system on the outskirts of an ordinary spiral galaxy.

Within this century the church said that God is impassible and cannot suffer or grieve or feel pain. It is now generally acknowledged that God, rather than being aloof and impervious, is more like the suffering servant of Isaiah. God is in the desert with the starving children, is in the burning buildings, is present with the piles of bodies in the battletorn cities, a Maker who is part of all that happens and who suffers whenever the creature suffers.

As to who goes to heaven, there seems to be considerable division. Some churches are holding adamantly to a heaven for Christians only. Other churches are asking questions, wondering if this judgmental (if not forensic) attitude toward heaven is true to the love of God.

After Gandhi's death a friend of his was asked whether or not Gandhi was a Christian. The friend replied that the answer depended on what was meant by the question. If the question meant whether Gandhi belonged to one of the established institutions or not, then the answer was no. But if what was meant by the question was whether or not Gandhi believed in Jesus Christ, then the answer was yes.

Once when I was lecturing at a denominational college I was asked, during the question and answer period, whether or not I thought Gandhi was in heaven. "Yes," I said. "But," protested the young man who asked me, "Gandhi did not accept Jesus as his personal Savior." Didn't he? In any case, when Gandhi attempted to go to a Christian church, he was turned away because he was the wrong color. The Christian establishment was hardly offering him a Christ of universal love.

It became evident that this young man was far more interested in keeping Gandhi out of heaven than in getting him in. Finally I said, "For me, Gandhi is a Christ figure. I'll be perfectly happy to go wherever he goes. If you want to call that hell, that's your problem."

There is still room for change, change in us all. But we really haven't gone much further than the ancient Egyptians in thinking about the afterlife.

Hugh and I spent two intense weeks in Egypt last winter, with a small group – nine of us – and an excellent Egyptologist, traveling from Cairo and the pyramids and the Sphinx to Luxor, taking a small boat that followed a thousand miles, and penetrated back more thousands of years, on the still largely-unexplored Nile, and on to Aswan and Abu Simbel. We steeped ourselves in the world of ancient Egypt, a world we know about largely because of the Pharaonic faith in God – or the gods. We were filled with awe as we walked through the sacred spaces of the temples, through long, pillared halls to the altar and the holiest holy places.

My heart lifted with wonder at the searching soul of the human being, striving toward God, yearning for the Creator, for the power of love which made all the galaxies and all the solar systems, the Creator of all, for whom the life of our planet is no more than the flicker of an eye.

And it came to me as I stood on the desert sand, looking at the Great Pyramid, that what any civilization says about God tells us more about that civilization than it does about God. Nothing we say about the Creator can begin to be adequate. It is always small and fumbling and human and anthropomorphic – no matter how mighty our monuments.

What those ancient Egyptians were saying to me in their frescoes and carvings was that life would have meant nothing to them at all without their faith in God, even if their gods frequently came to them in both animal and human form.

Were they aware that human beings, marvelous as we are, are also fragile and fragmented? It would seem so, as we studied the complex patterns of their civilization, at least as aware as we are. It seems ironic that the people who refuse to admit any brokenness in themselves are often unhappy. Even if they announce that they are not broken, they still fail to live up to the model of perfection they have set for themselves, a dislocation which produces in them a deep unhappiness. We live most comfortably and lovingly with ourselves when we can look at our brokenness, physical or spiritual, know that God will help us, and that we are loved just as we are. God loves me with all my volatility, stubbornness, flaring temper, clumsiness, and that makes it possible for me to accept myself, loving myself in God's love of me. It also makes it more possible for me to love other people as they are, and not set impossible standards which they cannot meet.

Jesus had visibly imperfect people as friends – a tax collector, a woman who had been possessed of seven demons, a Pharisee who dared speak with him only in the cover of darkness. Where Jesus leads, it is easier for us to follow.

Christ, the second person of the Trinity, was revealed to us in Jesus of Nazareth in an incredible act of love. But Christ can speak to me in other ways, too, ways which do not diminish my love of Jesus as Lord. Christ spoke to me through the ancient culture of the pharaohs, although I am not tempted to worship their pantheon of gods. Christ can speak to me through Saint Shinran Shunin as I walk my dog to and from the park. Obviously I do not see Saint Shinran as a Buddhist would see him. I see him from my point of view as a Christian torn by the horror of man's inhumanity to man. I see him as Christ would have me see him, and with a hope that with Christ's love our swords can be beaten into ploughshares, our bombs defused as we seek food for our overcrowded and hungry planet.

Christ can speak to me through the white china Buddha who sits on my desk at Crosswicks and smiles at me tolerantly when I fly into a torrent of outrage or self-pity. That forbearing smile helps restore my sense of proportion, and rids me of that self-will which keeps me caught up in myself so that I am isolating myself from Christ. Of course I am no more likely to become a Buddhist than my parents were likely to turn to Islam when they framed those lovely verses from the Koran.

There is no limit to the ways in which Christ can speak to us, though for the Christian he speaks first and most clearly through Jesus of Nazareth. Indeed, my icons would be idols if they did not lead me to follow more closely in Jesus' steps.

And Christ spoke to me as I walked through a great column of stone lions leading into the temple at Karnak. We were there at dawn, to avoid flies, tourists, the heat of the sun, and those great soaring columns provoked in us a cathedral sense of awe.

"Why are there so many rams, in the carvings and the frescoes?" someone asked our guide.

To my delight she told us that the ram in the Egyptian temples is Abraham's ram. I remembered that Abraham had indeed been to Egypt, and so had Isaac, and so had Jacob. The desert we were seeing was very much like the desert they had crossed. Because the pharaohs of Abraham's day knew the story of the near-sacrifice of Isaac, and the last-minute substitution of the ram, the Egyptians adopted the ram into their pantheon of gods as a symbol of life.

Possibly Abraham had stood where we were standing; possibly he had even seen the reproductions of the ram, his ram, who had saved Isaac, and thereby Jacob as well.

"Why are there so many cobras?" we asked, "so many vultures and crocodiles?"

"In those days they worshiped what they feared" our guide told us. Placating the gods, it has been called, and it's still something we tend to do if we're not careful. If we view God as a vengeful judge, and turn to Jesus to save us from the furious father, aren't we worshiping what we fear?

Those old Egyptians also worshiped the baboon because every morning when the sun rose, the baboons all clapped their hands for joy, applauding the reappearance of the sun. What a lovely picture, the baboons all clapping their hands and shouting for joy as the sun rose! So it seemed to the Egyptians that the baboons must have had something to do with the rising of the sun, and that their applause helped to bring the sun back up into the sky.

The scarab beetle, too, was an object of worship, because it disappeared down into the desert sands at sundown, and then came up again in the morning as the sun rose, and was, therefore, a symbol of the resurrection for them.

What? The resurrection? Yes, our guide told us, that is what it was called, their firm belief in the resurrection of their bodies, not immediately after their death, but at some unknown future date, which was why so much elaborate preparation went into embalming. I'm not sure how much essential difference there is between the tombs with food and jewels in them, and our own recently abandoned belief that our bones will rise up out of our graves at the Second Coming. Cremation is impermissible because God can't do anything with ashes: if someone dies in a shipwreck and the body is lost at sea and eaten by fish, that's just too bad. Or, if someone is trapped in a burning building and incinerated by fire, that, too, is just too bad. If there is no actual body to be raised, there can be no resurrection. What kind of powerless God is being worshiped? God, who made our bodies, can raise them again from nothing, if need be.

All I know is that neither death, nor life, nor angels, nor principalities, nor powers, nor things present, nor things to come, nor height, nor depth, nor any other creature, shall be able to separate us from the love of God.

And if that is what the ancient Egyptian believed, then we are, at least, cousins

Hugh and I were in Egypt at the time of the sugar cane cutting. It is harvested today as it was thousands of years ago, cut by hand, with the great sheaves of green loaded onto donkeys' and camels' backs. Time intersected for us as we watched the people working, saw the lush green of land near the Nile, with the Sahara encroaching. Where there was no water, no irrigation, there was sand.

We saw the statue of Rameses II, made famous in Shelley's poem, "Ozymandias." The enormous statue lay in pieces on the sand, and we recited Shelley's lines: *My name is Ozymandias, king of kings. / Look on my works, ye mighty, and despair.*

Our guide was of Islam, and her loving religion was impressive and, rather than making me feel estranged from her, made me feel very close. She was on fire with love of her country and its history, and surely she gave us the equivalent of an advanced college seminar as we moved from temple to temple, archaeological site to archaeological site. It was hard not to let our minds become a jumble of gods and pharaohs and warriors and priests and animals and the crowns of upper and lower Egypt.

What we saw told us more about ancient Egypt than it did about the eternal God, as all civilizations reveal more of themselves in their religious practices than they reveal of God. And I began to wonder what we reveal of ourselves as we struggle toward love and understanding of our Maker. What will be said of us in a thousand years if historians study our troubled civilization? What will they write about our forms of worship as they collect artifacts from our churches and cathedrals and temples? Will they understand that for us God is a God of love?

If the ancient Egyptians worshiped what they feared (as well as the celebrating baboons clapping their hands), we worship the God we love and trust. Or do we? Do we show that in our lives? In our care for and concern of each other? If we assume that anybody is outside the Maker's loving concern, aren't we revealing more about ourselves than about God?

There is probably much that we do not understand, or that we misinterpret, as we think of the Egyptians with their rams and scarabs and crocodiles. A friend of mine in the Middle East heard someone say in horror "Oh, the Christians are the people who drink blood." What a terrible misunderstanding. Perhaps many times we equally fail to understand other peoples and their beliefs.

For the ancient Egyptian there was love and trust in their faith as well as fear. The pharaohs were often referred to as "shepherds," and the god, Osiris, was said to be the shepherd of the underworld. A pyramid text reads, "Thou hast taken them up in thine arms as a shepherd his flock."

The shepherd imagery was particularly vivid to us because we were in Egypt at the time of the new lambs, the baby kids, the foals, the colts. The land was radiant with spring. We saw ancient water wheels being turned by water buffaloes, heads heavy with their curving horns. We saw the people working the land wearing their galabiyehs, those loose-flowing and practical garments which have been worn by working Egyptians for centuries. They are loose and comfortable in the heat, they give protection against flies, and against the sun.

"Thou hast taken them up in thine arms as a shepherd his flock." Did that lovely image pre- or post-date the 23rd Psalm? Was it not a prefiguring of our own Good Shepherd? For me it was beyond contradiction because Christ was, before anything began, always is, and always will be.

I saw a young woman wearing a red sweat shirt patterned with dozens of small white sheep, and *one* black sheep, and I thought of Jesus, the good shepherd, leaving the ninety-nine white sheep and going after the one strayed black sheep, searching until he found the black sheep and put it across his shoulders and carried it home. And he said that there will be more rejoicing over the one repentant sinner than over all the virtuous people who have not strayed. I pray that I, too, will rejoice in the return of the black sheep, and not be like the elder brother in the parable of the Prodigal Son, who really didn't want the father to forgive the repentant black sheep, much less give a party for him.

It is a human tendency to get caught in the self-righteousness of the elder brother, so that we don't want the shepherd to go after the strayed sheep, but to stay in the pen with the virtuous flock. And that is just not scriptural. It is, of course, the forensic stumbling block. If we are forensic, do we then become black sheep ourselves?

In the ancient temples, we saw faces and legs of Egyptian gods scratched out by the early Christians as they took refuge there. Despite their acceptance of Christ as their Lord, we were told, they still believed in the old magic, and the face and feet were supposed to have the most power, so these early Christians took sharp stones and mutilated the paintings and carvings.

Later, in the Coptic museum in Cairo, we saw stone carvings made by the early Christians which had been similarly mutilated by the Muslims.

What are we human beings telling the future about ourselves in what we proclaim about God? Are we saying something loving and creative, or are we being arrogant and spreading fear and suspicion? Are we furthering the coming of the Kingdom, or are we setting up barriers and road blocks?

As I read the papers, listen to the news, I am concerned about what we are telling the future about ourselves, as Christians fight Muslims in Lebanon, as Protestants fight Catholics in Ireland, as acts of terrorism are performed in the name of religion. What are the Right-to-Lifers telling about themselves as they heave bombs into abortion clinics? What are women telling as they proclaim absolute rights to their own bodies?

The Quakers have a way of meeting, without contempt, those with whom they disagree, or those who threaten them. There's a story of a Quaker who heard noises in his house one night, and went downstairs to find a burglar busily stashing things into a pillow case. The Quaker said, "Friend, I would do thee no harm for the world and all that is in it, but thou standest where I am about to shoot." The burglar left.

And yet, there are Protestant and Catholic women who cross battle lines in Ireland to pray with each other. I wonder if that will happen in Lebanon – Christian and Muslim women praying together for peace. White and black women praying together in South Africa? It's not impossible. To cross battle lines to pray is a dimension of the cross which women have long understood. And perhaps it is a special symbol of the cross to cross battle lines?

For the human being the cross is an ancient symbol, used thousands of years before Jesus of Nazareth was crucified. The Bushmen of South Africa painted small red crosses in their caves, and it is thought that these small, apricot-skinned people originally came to South Africa from Egypt. They listened for guidance from God in the tapping of the stars. Sometimes on a cold, clear night I think I can hear their tapping, too. The Bushmen were not separated from the stars, or the coinherence of all of creation. Other peoples have tried to exterminate these tiny, untamed people. Surely their loss is felt in great waves throughout the galaxies, an agonizing butterfly effect.

Jesus of Nazareth could not be tamed, either, and so he, too, had to be wiped out, hung on a cross in the dust and the heat and the flies. Those who cannot be tamed are disturbers of the universe, and without them we would be infinitely poorer. But because they are a threat to the control of local governments they must be put down, ruthlessly.

The true universe disturber has no arrogance. The arrogance and vanity of the terrorist is chilling. It takes humility and faith in God's loving concern to cross battle lines, be they geographical or ideological.

I was given a small Mexican cross, a copy of an ancient one, many thousands of years old, and it, like the cross of the African Bushman, gives me a feeling of continuity and hope. The second person of the Trinity was with us "before the worlds began to be. He is alpha and omega, he the source, the ending," as the ancient hymn says. All of God has always been part of creation, part of the story, taking us in the everlasting arms as the shepherd clasps the lost lamb.

I don't want a closed-in religion of smug sheep, a religion in which all the answers are given and honest questions are discouraged. I don't want a religion which allows me to feel superior, or which gives me the truth denied to others.

So what am I looking for? What is my hope? First, I must accept that I am broken, as all we human beings are broken, but that my creative urge toward healing and health is strong, and that I can be healed with the blood of the Lamb (how lovely that Christ is both shepherd and lamb!). I want to be willing to do God's will, but not to superimpose my will on el's. The distinction is not always easy. I want to help the battered bride to become beautiful. I want to be ready to meet the bridegroom, and so be part of the heavenly kingdom and the redemption of all things.

Sometimes something small and unexpected will turn on a brilliant light for me. Every other summer for the past several years I have taught a writers' workshop at Mundelein College. Many of the people who are taking this two-week course for credit are teachers, going on for their Masters degrees, or their Ph.D.s. One afternoon in the large room overlooking Lake Michigan, where we sat in a circle, we spent an hour sharing stories which meant something to us. One of these stories was that of the old man by the river who did not recognize what God sent him. A few of the stories brought healing tears. And one, for me, brought glory.

A teacher of small children told us of a child who said to her, "Jesus is God's show and tell."

How simple and how wonderful! Jesus is God's show and tell. That's the best theology of incarnation I've ever heard. Jesus said, if you do not understand me as a little child, you will not be able to enter the kingdom of heaven.

That child's insight works more powerfully for me than dogma. When I am informed that Jesus of Nazareth was exactly like us except sinless, I block. If he was sinless he wasn't exactly like us. That makes no sense. Jesus was like us because he was born like any human child, grew up like the rest of us, asked questions in the temple when he was twelve, lost his temper in righteous indignation at the money lenders in the temple, grieved when at the end his disciples abandoned him. I want Jesus to be like us because he is God's show and tell, and too much dogma obscures rather than reveals the likeness.

If Jesus is God's show and tell, the wonder, the marvel is that Jesus and the Father are one. Not I, says Jesus over and over, but the Father in me, the Father who is such love that he is willing to be in the story with us.

Alleluia.

But God's show and tell includes the cross. For us all.

Many years ago when our children were small, I encountered my first Episcopal monk, a priest of the Order of the Holy Cross. Although I am what is called "a cradle Episcopalian," I hadn't known that there were Episcopal monks or nuns. This was a gentle young man who had just come back to this country after several years in Liberia, and who had been brought to Crosswicks for tea by a mutual friend. He said, "Don't be afraid to make the sign of the cross. All it means is: God be in my thoughts, and in my heart, and in my left hand, and in my right hand, all through this day and night." That was another illumination for me. It helps me to ask God to be in me, to be in my head and my heart and my left hand and my right hand. That may tell more about me than about God, but I am not ashamed to admit that I need God in me, in all of me, in my down-sitting and in my up-rising.

While I was in bed last summer, bleeding, hurting, a friend sent me a tape of a record of Hildegarde of Bingen, *A Feather on the Breath of God*. Hildegarde, a medieval abbess, was on fire with her passionate love of God, and she was not afraid to use passionate language to express her love. Listening to the singing on the tape was another part of my healing. Hildegarde's love of the Creator and of creation reminded me of Ikhnaton, the only pharaoh we know about who worshiped one God with adoring love, Aton, the sun, the giver of life. Ikhnaton's hymns to Aton would have been understood by Hildegarde. Perhaps they sometimes sing together now.

The sun is feared as well as revered in desert countries, where the fierce rays of the heat of the day burn and parch, and only the annual flooding of the Nile keeps Egypt's shores green. Ikhnaton wrote love poems to his one God which, as our guide recited them, reminded me of John of the Cross as well as Hildegarde of Bingen. During this young pharaoh's brief reign he rejected polytheism, forbidding the worship of many gods, and turned all the passion of his adoration to Aton. This inevitably shook the domain of the powerful priests and they had to get rid of him. They murdered him.

He had some kind of glandular imbalance which deformed his lower body, swelling his abdomen so that he was pear-shaped. But unlike other pharaohs he allowed sculptures to be made of himself as he actually was, rather than demanding the usual glorified image – what the pharaohs wanted people to think they were like.

I was awed by Ikhnaton's bravery in overriding the extremely powerful and ruthless priests of the old gods, and proclaiming the one God. I was awed also by his acceptance of himself exactly as he was, without one plea. Our guide, too, felt drawn to him, saying that he was somewhat like Sadat, defying danger in order to remain true to what he believed – and that was the greatest compliment she could have given him.

I knew, as I stood looking at the statue of Ikhnaton, at his sensitive, intelligent face, that there is nothing he could say, nothing Hildegarde of Bingen, or John of the Cross, or Lancelot Andrewes, or any single one of us can say about God which is adequate. What we say about God may explain us, our warm or coldheartedness, our humility or our vanity, our loving forgiveness or our resentful demands for vindication. But it cannot explain God.

Probably the Egyptian priests thought they were correct in killing Ikhnaton, just as the high priest thought he was doing the right thing in condemning Jesus to crucifixion. To wipe out anyone from God's love is a form of murder, even if it is not literally acted out. One way or another, most of us commit some form of murder every day and we need to repent, and ask for forgiveness, so that we may turn to love in a world which is anything but fair.

Then I thought of the parable of the workers in the vineyard, and how we really don't think it's fair for the owner of the vineyard to give the man who worked only the last hour the same wages as those who worked all through the heat of the day. After all, it's not fair! But when we insist on that kind of fairness, aren't we thinking forensically? This kind of thinking inevitably leads to a forensic view of Jesus and the cross – a view which may be long on justice, but is short on love.

If we receive nothing but justice, untempered by mercy, not one of us will be invited to the heavenly banquet, not even those who teach that the banquet is prepared only for the selected few.

It won't do. What about all those ancient Egyptians with their longing for resurrection? What about Ikhnaton and his love of the one God? Can there never be a party for them? Will not God bring out the silken robes and order the fatted calf to be prepared? What about those who worshiped what they feared – the vulture, the cobra, the crocodile? And the baboons, clapping their hands for joy at the rising of the sun?

Will all those born before Christ be excluded from the party? Didn't God make them, too? I don't have any answers here, just a lot of questions and hopes, about a God of love who prefers parties to punishments.

I don't understand why the idea of emptying hell upsets some people so. To be upset about it is to think forensically, and while we all suffer from a touch of this, we can surely recognize our own lack of generosity. If we don't, how can we enjoy the party any more than did the prodigal son's elder brother? Do we, too, want to go out and sulk? I don't need to know how God is going to make it all come out all right in the end, but it is God, not us creatures, who will see to the coming of the Kingdom, and el is not going to fail with Creation, not with me, not with any of us.

God be in my thoughts, and in my heart. In my left hand and in my right hand. Atone me. At-one me with you and your love. Help me to pray for those I fear as well as those I love, knowing that you can take my most ungracious prayers and give them grace. Whenever we pray, we are tapping the power of creation, and that's a mighty power. There are a lot of battle lines to cross in order for us to pray with each other, and with the rest of the world, with those who do not agree with us, with those who worship God in ways we do not understand. But that is all right. We do not have to understand. We do have to try to turn to love, to know that the Lord who created all, also loves all that which was made.

It is easy for me to pray for the Egyptologist who taught me so much. She loves God, and so we have that in common.

That is enough.

It is far less easy for me to pray for the terrorists, or even for those two men who sat in the courtroom last January and wished the jurors no good. It is not easy for me to pray for the forces of evil in this world expressing themselves through their lust for power, their greed, their corruption in high places. But if I take the cross seriously, that is part of the demand. These are people for whom Jesus died.

At this point I'm not sure I want those two men who stared so malevolently at us poor jurors to come to the party, but it won't be complete until they are there, come to themselves, turned, returned to love, part of the at-one-ment.

Somehow I am helped when I remember the baboons clapping their hands and calling for joy that the sun is coming up again over the horizon, that night is over, and the Light of the world is bright.

11

Redeeming the Symbols

DURING THE YEARS WHEN WE WERE raising our children and living in Crosswicks year round, being part of the community of the Congregational Church in the center of the village, there were no symbols of any kind in the church. Today there is a plain wooden cross. A quarter of a century ago that was taboo. When the minister said, "let us pray" we did no more than slightly bow our heads: any more would have been capitulating to Rome. When I directed the choir in a Latin anthem, we half expected the roof to collapse on our heads. Following the calendar of the church year was unheard of. The word *liturgy* was not in our vocabulary.

I knew true Christian community in that church, but I missed symbols. As a storyteller I live by symbol. It fills and feeds me so that in a symbol-less church I feel undernourished. It is true that any symbol can be made into an idol. Any symbol can be elevated or distorted into something it was not meant to be. But that does not destroy the truth of the original symbol. Was God not showing Jacob a marvelous symbol in the glorious ladder of angels?

A few Christmases ago my son and daughter-in-law gave me a pretty pair of silver earrings. Each earring was in the shape of a crescent moon, containing a scattering of stars. I don't think any of us realized that this was the Proctor and Gamble logo until the recent brouhaha in which it was alleged that this logo was an ancient trade mark of the devil. So much noise has been made about this that sales have fallen, and I understand that this logo is to be phased out, and no longer used on Proctor and Gamble products.

What!?! The crescent moon and the stars Satan's symbol? How can that possibly be? Who *made* the moon and the stars? Genesis makes it very clear that the heavens are the Lord's, and that el is the loving Creator of the universe. How can we be so stupid as to call the loveliness of the night sky a sign of Satan? I am totally baffled.

And horrified. I am not about to give over the beauty of moon and stars to Satan or to Satan worshipers. God took Abraham out at night to see the stars, the stars made in the mighty acts of creation. The Maker's stars. The Maker's moon.

In some early civilizations the crescent moon was a symbol of worship of the goddess, Ishtar or Ashtaroth, and other female deities, like Diana, whose symbol was the moon. These goddesses were said to be beneficent when the moon was waxing, and maleficent when it was waning. In countries where the crops followed the phases of the moon, where earth was mother, the worship of the moon goddess was natural. In the western world of Protestantism we have swung to the opposite extreme, criticizing the Roman Catholics for their reverence of Mary, the most holy birth-giver (as the orthodox call her), and have emphasized a masculine, patriarchal God who sometimes seems to have more of the attributes of Zeus with his bolts of lightning, than the loving Abba of Jesus.

Perhaps the fear of the symbol of the crescent moon and the stars is a masculine fear of the feminine. But we need to regain the feminine, the intuitive, the nurturing element in ourselves, and in our understanding of the Godhead, our Maker, who is all in all, mother, father, brother, sister, lover, friend, companion. The great mystics of the church, such as Hildegarde of Bingen, Meister Eckhardt, Lady Julian of Norwich, were casual about the gender of God, using the male or female pronoun as the need arose. Let us not be bullied into fearing the feminine symbol of the crescent moon. We see our tides swing to the rhythm of the moon. Our bodies follow the moon's phases. Our words *month* and *Monday* come from the same source. Our dependence on the rhythm of the moon is part of the interdependence of all nature, all life, all Creation.

Christ's cross has been a vital symbol throughout the ages: it does not belong exclusively to the Christian era. The butterfly (like the ram) has long been a symbol of metamorphosis and resurrection, adding new meaning to the "butterfly effect." The extraordinary world of particle physics is providing new symbols for me, and new understanding of old symbols. My response to my discovery of Einstein's theories of relativity and Planck's quantum theory was to write *A Wrinkle in Time*, as I struggled to understand the wonders of the Creator and creation.

Was it a coincidence that I picked up Berdyaev's book warning against a forensic view of God just as I started jury duty and especially just as I needed to pay heed to this message? Or that I began to read about particle physics with its theory of the total interdependence of all creation just when the church and the world seemed to be shattering into inimical, isolated fragments? Is there such a thing as coincidence? (A priest friend told me that "a coincidence is a small miracle in which God prefers to remain anonymous.")

So it did not surprise me when I settled myself in my seat for a plane journey that I opened the New York Times science section to an article on particle physics; nor that the two books I carried in my bag were Robert Alter's *The Art of Biblical Narrative*, and John Boslough's *Stephen Hawking's Universe*, and that all three were mutually nourishing, each reinforcing the others.

The world of particle physics is a new world in my generation, and has revealed a universe of such complexity that even the greatest physicists do not fully comprehend it.

My parents, growing to adulthood in those strangely placid years before World War I, lived in a far simpler world. Their understanding of the nature of the universe was closer to that of Jacob's day than of ours, so rapidly has our knowledge grown. For them, despite the fact that it was acknowledged that stars are suns, and our planet part of an ordinary solar system, creation was infinitely smaller and easier to comprehend than it is today. Ants and gnats and the no-seeum-bugs that came out in the spring were as small as anyone needed to comprehend. There were smaller things, such as germs and viruses, which could be seen only through microscopes, but, still, they could be *seen*.

And then the heart of the atom was opened. Scientists, struggling to make a bomb to end all bombs, were given more money for their research than ever they would have been given in time of peace. How did they dare set off that first atom bomb, when they were not at all sure that it would not start a chain reaction that would blow up the entire planet?

And yet, knowing of this possibility they went ahead. Was it bravery or folly?

Whichever it was it has opened up a new understanding of the universe, and it is up to us to try to understand it creatively, as a further revelation of the wonders of the mind of the Maker.

I turn to the study of astrophysics and particle physics because these disciplines are about the nature of being, and so may be for us revelations of what God is like, and how Christ's love works to enflame our own.

So I sat on the plane, fastened my seat belt, and started the Times article, by Walter Sullivan, and read that not only do quanta (subatomic particles) have the ability to communicate instantaneously, but according to French theorist Bernard d'Espagnat, such instantaneous signals exceed the speed of light.

What does that mean, I wondered? And then I remembered that we have instances of inexplicable, instantaneous communication in our own lives. There are stories, many authenticated, of people calling each other, instantaneously, across vast distances. A mother will sit up in bed, abruptly wakened from sleep, and rush, unthinking to make a phone call. Her moment of waking comes just as the grandbaby begins to choke, and the call alerts the parents and the baby is reached just in time.

My grandfather had passage on the Titanic, his bags had already gone onto the ship, when a voice told him to leave the gang plank, not to sail. The warning was so clear that he heeded it.

We don't understand such phenomena any more than physicists understand the behavior of some subatomic particles. But this is no reason to say that such things do not happen. It is no reason to say they are works of the Devil, rather than of Christ. There are many occurrences that we must admit we do not understand. As long as this world belongs to the Word who made all that was made, that is all we need to know. Maybe one day, as we develop spiritually, we will understand more than we do now. When we are in heaven, in the Presence, we will "know as we are known."

Quantum mechanics, according to the Times article, "indicates that properties usually attributed to matter have no real existence until measured."

This parallels Parker Palmers affirmation that the self becomes real only when reacting with other selves. We do not become real in isolation, but in response to the others we encounter along the way, and who call us into being, as the observing scientist calls quanta into being.

And how do we, ourselves, become real? Hugh married an introverted, shy, undefined young woman. I became real as I responded to him, to our children, to our friends, who quite literally *brought me out* of the shell in which I had hidden myself.

Destructive criticism is devastating because it does not make *real*; instead, it negates and destroys. Constructive criticism builds, bringing out the hidden reality.

In the world of particle physics, I am encountering a new reality, which enlarges and enhances my own.

The indeterminacy of quantum mechanics seems to upset scientists as much as it does theologians. But why is this "probability" aspect of quantum mechanics more perplexing than the "probability" aspect of sperm?

Of all the thousands of the male sperm ejected during coitus, only one will meet and unite with the female ovum. Which one? Who can guess? Is it complete indeterminacy? Had another sperm met and united with my egg, I would have a very different child from the one who came from the particular sperm and ovum which succeeded in bonding.

Yet this randomness in the mechanism of human reproduction doesn't seem to upset anybody, and it has been known, at least since biblical times, that the male sperm, as well as the female egg, is needed for conception.

Just after I wrote these thoughts in my journal, I picked up Alter's book and read about "the vigorous movement of biblical writing away from the stable closure of the mythological world, and toward the *interdeterminacy*, the shifting causal concatenations, the ambiguity of a fiction made to resemble the uncertainties of life in history." Fascinating to come across the word *interdeterminacy* in two such different contexts, though I don't agree with Alter's definition of "the mythological world" as offering "stable closure." It's the old misuse of the word mythological, and I might rather substitute the word, "cultic." The important thing is that both the world of Scripture and the world of quantum mechanics are worlds of indeterminacy. That is a freeing thought, because a world of determinacy is a world where everything is preordained beforehand, where there is no free will.

I shudder at the once widely-accepted theory that God preordained us all before we were born for either heaven or hell, and nothing we did would change this predestination. What kind of god would predetermine part of his creation to eternal damnation? This is surely not consistent with God's creation in the early chapters of Genesis, when Elohim looked at all that had been made and called it good, very good. And yet this brutal theology used to be widely accepted and taught, a kind of spiritual terrorism.

One time when I was visiting my family in Lincoln, England, I was given a tour of the cathedral. Two things remain with me. We went into the cathedral through one of the side doors, and a wooden inset in the stone each above the door was pointed out. This had been put into the arch to hold a canopy so that a king could walk under it, protected from the elements. Since that time, nobody had bothered to take down the inset. The king was Richard the Second.

Suddenly I realized how very old England is. Crosswicks, well over two hundred years old, seems ancient in North America, but many places in England and on the European continent are so much older that our oldest buildings seem new in comparison.

The other thing that has stayed firmly in my mind is a story. After we had been through the cathedral, we went to the library, one of the most beautiful buildings I have ever seen, with an unusually fine collection of books. The dean who went into exile at the time of Cromwell spent his years away from England in Holland, which was then the center of the book world. He returned with a superb collection of books.

On one of the walls of his library hangs the portrait of a woman with a pleasant face, and a ruff around her neck. This was the dean's mother. Long before he was born, this woman, then a young girl, was convinced that she was one of those predestined to be damned. This was her firm conviction, and it did not make her very merry. One evening she was having dinner with some friends, and they tried to assure her that she could not be certain that she was damned. But, she told them, she was certain, absolutely certain. "I am as certain that I am damned as that this wine glass will shatter when I fling it to the stone floor." She flung down the fragile glass. It did not shatter.

So she cheered up, married, and ultimately became the mother of the dean.

Thank God for indeterminacy!

There are people, however, who seem so plagued by terrible things that it would indeed seem that they have been damned. In their lives one tragedy follows another. It is a terrible mystery. But do not come to me when something terrible has happened saying, "It's God's will." No! Death, disease, murder, may be from man's error, but never God's will. In the face of suffering and tragedy, we can only have faith that somehow, ultimately, in God's time all wounds will be healed.

For God is the God of love, and love will not rest while there is any suffering left, any rebellion, any anguish. The song of the stars in their courses will not return to the full beauty of the ancient harmonies until the coming again in glory of the Lord of Love.

* * *

The great British biophysicist, J.B.S. Haldane, said that "The universe is not only stranger than we imagine, it's stranger than anything we can imagine."

More recently, Douglas Adams, in introducing Chapter One of *The Restaurant at the End of the Universe*, wrote, "There is a theory which states that if ever anyone discovers exactly what the Universe is for, and why it is here, it will instantly disappear and be replaced by something even more bizarre and inexplicable. There is another which states that this has already happened."

I laugh, and yet I marvel, too. If the universe is in a state of flux (one theory), expanding out from a mass denser and smaller than a subatomic particle, to form all the galaxies, moving out into the darkness of space, even further away and further apart, until the procedure reverses itself and pulls back in until once again it is the infinitely small primal unity, who is to say that God's design is going to be the same every time? And what about the theories of alternate universes, or multiple universes? These concepts are frightening only if we forget that whatever it is, and however it is, it is God's. And as long as the Maker knows what it is all about, and as long as we test our speculations against the love of God, as well as the laboratory, all shall be well.

Haldane's description of the universe as "stranger than anything we can imagine," is an exciting one for me, because nothing is strange for the Creator of it all. And in the fullness of time, *kairos*, God's time, we, too, shall see the full glory as it really is.

Alter, in *The Art of Biblical Narrative*, refers to the "double dialectic between design and disorder, providence and freedom. The various biblical narratives . . . [form] a spectrum between the opposing extremes of disorder and design." He is talking about the Bible, but he could just as well be talking about particle physics. Or about our own lives, which often seem an incomprehensible mixture of accident and pattern. We are created by God, who has given us free will. Therefore we can work either for or against God's design. It is a splendid paradox.

And, as always with paradox, it can be expressed best in symbols.

I am more at home with the symbols which come from astro- and particle physics than I am with those which are coming from the computer. The computer, it has been suggested, is going to change the way we think, and I hope that we will use enough free will so that this change will be constructive, not disastrous. But great care must be taken.

The computer has proved itself to be anything but infallible. It can make horrendous mistakes, including the near precipitation of nuclear war. Daily it makes minor mistakes, and not long ago I was the victim of one of them.

I had been on an intense and overscheduled lecture tour in the Pacific Northwest. On the last day, when I was in Spokane, Washington, at a Young Writers Conference, I phoned to reconfirm my flight home to New York the next day. I was told that everything was fine, I was in the computer, but my flight would leave at 11:25 A.M., rather than 11:35, as my ticket said. Fine. No problem.

The next day I went to the airport bright and early, ready to relax and sleep on the long flight home. I handed over my ticket, and the man behind the counter looked at it and told me, "That flight was cancelled three weeks ago."

"But I reconfirmed it yesterday!"

He played for a long time with his computer. Finally he looked up, saying, "I think the computer thought you were leaving from Portland, Oregon."

"As you can see," I replied icily, "I am in Spokane, Washington. What are you going to do?"

Again he played with his computer, and at last offered to send me to Chicago's O'Hare Airport where I could change planes and ...

"No," I said flatly. "Not O'Hare. I am too exhausted for O'Hare."

Finally he sent me to Seattle, where I had to go from one arm of the satellite to another as far away as possible, changing planes and airlines, and accept the fact that I would get to New York several hours later than I had expected, and at the airport furthest from Manhattan.

I capsized into my seat, telling the sympathetic hostess what had happened. "To err is human," she said. "To foul it up completely takes a computer."

I was so exhausted that I reached for the airline magazine and began leafing through it. Almost immediately I came across an article describing in glowing terms the world of the microchip which we are inheriting. And I read, appalled; "What the automobile has done for the legs, what television has done for the eyes, the computer will do for the mind."

No!

I don't like what the automobile has done for our legs, or what television has done for our eyes, and I certainly do not want the computer to manipulate our minds.

The computer, unlike subatomic particles, or biblical stories, is deterministic. It does not ask questions. It gives answers, sometimes useful ones, sometimes not, as when it "thought" I was leaving from Portland, Oregon.

The computer is either/or. Yes/No. There is no room for *perhaps*, or *on the other hand*. There is no room for complexity which draws us into contradiction and paradox.

The computer is here to stay. I can't afford to put my head in the sand, like the ostrich, and hope it will go away. Ultimately, when word processors become a lot more portable than they are at present, and suit my needs better, I'll likely write with one. I already have a six pound little electronic typestar, which is even more sensitive to my fingers and my mind than the heavy old electric typewriter. But I don't want the computer to change my way of thinking without so much as a by-your-leave.

The indeterminacy of both Bible and physics is symbolically far more creative than the determinacy of high technocracy.

Fritjov Capra, in *The Tao of Physics*, quotes atomic physicist Robert Oppenheimer: "If we ask, for instance, whether the position of the electron remains the same, we must say 'no,' if we ask whether the electron's position changes with time, we must say 'no;' if we ask whether the electron is at rest, we must say 'no;' if we ask whether the electron is in motion, we must say 'no.' "

He also quotes from the Upanishads.

It moves, it moves not.
It is far, it is near.
It is within all this.
And outside all this.

There appears to be a tacit assumption that the world of particle physics and the world of eastern mysticism (Hinduism, Buddhism) are compatible, but not the worlds of particle physics and Christianity. This is not only blindness on the part of those who claim this, it is a misunderstanding of Christianity. Christianity *is* an Eastern religion. It is to our shame that we have westernized it, imposed on it our forensic thinking. But if we go back to the Gospels and the good news Jesus brought us, the contradictory, paradoxical elements of the new physics fit most compatibly with those of Scripture.

"Before Abraham was, I am," Jesus proclaimed. He spoke with Moses and Abraham on the mountain, overriding chronological time. When Moses asked God, "What is your name?" God replied, "I will be what I will be."

The Athanasian creed surely cannot be understood in terms of Western logic: God the Father incomprehensible. God the Son incomprehensible. God the Holy Spirit incomprehensible ...

That is surely oriental, rather than occidental thinking, or rather, it is truly cosmic thinking.

Listen to the Lord speaking in Isaiah 55:

For my thoughts are not your thoughts,
neither are your ways my ways, says the Lord.
For as the heavens are higher than the earth,
so are my ways higher than your ways and
my thoughts than your thoughts.

For as the rain and the snow come down from heaven
and return not thither but water the earth,
making it bring forth and sprout,
giving seed to the sower and bread to the eater,
so shall my word be that goes forth from my mouth;
it shall not return to me empty,
but it shall accomplish that which I purpose,
and prosper in the thing for which I sent it.

Then there is Hildegarde of Bingen likening herself to a feather on the breath of God, and Julian of Norwich seeing the entire universe in "the quantity of a hazelnut." Henry Vaughan "saw eternity the other night like a great ring of pure and endless light."

In an equally "eastern" mode of thinking, the anonymous author of *The Cloud of Unknowing* wrote thus: "Heaven ghostly, as high down as up, and as up as down, behind as before, on one side as another. Insomuch, that whoso had a true desire for to be at heaven, then that same time he were in heaven ghostly. For the high and the next way thither is run by desires and not by paces of feet."

Beyond cold rationalism, such a way of viewing heaven's reality reminds me of the words of St. Paul as he spoke to the people at Corinth:

The foolishness of God is wiser than men ... God has chosen things that are not, to bring to nothing things that are ... For we impart a secret and hidden wisdom of God ... What no eye has seen, no ear heard, nor the heart of man conceived, God has prepared for those who love him.

This is for me a happy and comprehensible understanding of heaven. It is by accepting all the "contra-dictions," these indeterminate non-answers, that we are given an intuition of heaven. If we do not recognize it now, by "a true desire," it will be all the more difficult later. Heaven is nothing we can seek through our own virtue; it cannot be earned, it is a gift of the God of love. When we are self-emptied enough to make room for this love, it is not as a result of our own moral rectitude or willpower. But it is sometimes given to us, this lovely emptiness, and then the Holy Spirit can fill it, with prayer, or music, or a poem, or a story or, sometimes, it goes beyond all these to the greatest gift of all, being filled with that which is beyond all symbols, with God's Presence.

And then we *are*, far more than when we are filled with self-probing, self-centeredness, or self-righteousness.

Gregory of Nyssa expresses this in language which is just as difficult as the language of particle physics, but which is rich indeed:

Abraham passed through all the reasoning that is possible to human nature about the divine attributes, and after he had purified his mind of all such concepts, he took hold of a faith that was unmixed and pure of any concept, and he fashioned for himself this ikon of knowledge of God that is completely free from error, namely the belief that God completely transcends any knowable symbol.

We are closest to contemplation when we move into, through, and beyond symbol, but during most of our lives we need symbols, such as this of Saint Bonaventura: "God is a circle whose center is everywhere, and whose circumference nowhere."

Numbers are symbols, powerful symbols. Combined with letters of the alphabet, as equations, they can change our way of looking at the universe.

Einstein's most famous equation is $E = MC^2$: Energy equals mass plus the speed of light squared – a symbol so potent that the depths of its implications have not yet been plumbed. And, like all symbols, it can draw us closer to God to whom all numbers belong, or it can be a barrier between us and the Creator.

I had a letter from a young woman who asked me seriously whether or not the number 6 belongs to the Devil. I replied that if everything belongs to the Creator, then so do numbers, and the Devil can't take over a number unless we are willing to give it to him. Where did she get the idea that number 6 belongs to the Devil? From 666?

According to Revelation 13:18, 666 is the number of the beast: "If anyone has insight let him calculate the number of the beast, for it is man's number. His number is 666." The beast is often assumed to be Satan (the sum of the letters in Nero Caesar in Hebrew adds up to 666). But even numbers, when abused, can be redeemed, and ultimately 666 will return to God.

Slowly I have learned the beauty of numbers, particularly as I studied harmony and counterpoint on the piano and learned the intricacies of the fugue. Through music I have come to see numbers as a way of giving glory to God, and I would rather dwell on the bright side, not the dark side, of a symbol.

In Jacob's day, numbers were for counting your camels, your sheep. And the stars were a symbol of numbers beyond the human capacity to count.

Jacob came from a small, insignificant tribe on a sparsely populated planet. Yet he, like his father and grandfather, was told that his descendants would be as the stars of the sky, as the grains of sand. In God's eyes, insignificance doesn't even exist. If something *is*, then it is significant.

Particle physics has a similar sense of the absolute significance of the very small, the so incredibly small we can't even imagine such smallness.

In *Particles*, Michael Chester writes, "Not only does [the neutrino] have zero charge, it has zero mass. The neutrino is a spinning little bit of nothingness that travels at the speed of light." I love that! A spinning little bit of nothingness! It so delights me that I wrote a Christmas song about it.

The neutrino and the unicorn
Danced the night that Christ was born.
The spinning little bit of nothingness
that travels at the speed of light
an unseen spark of somethingness
is all that can hold back the night.
The tiny neutron splits in two,
an electron and a proton form.
Where is the energy that is lost?
Who can hold back the impending storm?
cosmic collapse would be the cost.
A spinning nothing, pure and new,
The neutrino and the unicorn
danced the night that Christ was born.
The sun is dim, the stars are few,
The earthquake comes to split and shake.
All purity of heart is lost,
In the black density of night
stars fall. O will the heavens break?
Then through the tingling of black frost
the unicorn in silver dress
crossed the desert, horn alight.
Earth's plates relax their grinding stress.
The unicorn comes dancing to

make pure again, redeem and bless,
The neutrino and the unicorn
danced the night that Christ was born.

Pauli postulated the existence of the neutrino to account for the tiny amount of energy lost when a neutron breaks into a proton and an electron. Energy can*not* be lost – and the neutrino, thus far, is the best explanation: a spinning little bit of nothingness that travels at the speed of light.

We human beings do like explanations, and we'd really prefer them to be simple, if not simplistic. But the postulation of the neutrino is as wildly imaginative as those angels ascending and descending the ladder joining heaven and earth. And each postulation that seems to be a workable one leads on to even wilder uses of the imagination – not the imagination gone insane (though we must accept that possibility), but the imagination exploring all probabilities and possibilities.

If the neutrino is, it is God's, and it is as valued by el as Jacob. Or you. Or me.

The concept of subatomic particles plays havoc with ordinary concepts of time. Chester writes:

Actually, one millionth of a second is not so brief on a subatomic time scale. Both the pion with its lifetime of one-hundred millionth of a second and the muon with one millionth of a second are extremely long-lasting. Compare these times with the time that it takes a pion to interact with a nucleon, and they are enormous time-spans. Comparing the pion-nucleon interaction to the pion lifetime is like comparing one second to 100 *million years. Comparing the pion-nucleon interaction to the muon lifetime is like comparing one second to ten billion years.*

Is that any more formidable to think about than comparing the lifetime of a human being to the lifetime of a sun, or to the lifetime of a galaxy?

It makes sense only if we think of it all as part of our rootedness in cosmos, our *enkosmismene*. And it knocks our ordinary concepts of chronological time into a cocked hat. Time, as chronology, makes me dizzy with both lack of meaning and unreachable meaning. We need ordinary, chronological time so that we can, for instance, get to the airport or to the office on time, but here time is only an agreed upon fiction so that we will be enabled to get through the day's work with as little confusion as possible. And even in flying across the continent, our bodies are agonizingly jolted with time change and jet lag, so that we become aware that our bodies do function in ordinary time.

Yet, when I think of the pion and the muon, of the great spiral galaxies, and of our own little lives in terms of *kairos* – of rootedness in cosmos, in God's time itself – it opens vast vistas which can be awesome, even terrifying ("What a dreadful place is this!" Jacob cries), but less terrifying than it is wondrous, because God's time is far more real than ordinary *chronos*, and we are part of both.

During our mortal lives, however, *chronos* is not merely illusion. My body is aging according to human chronology, not nucleon or galactic chronology. My knees creak. My vision is variable. My energy span is shorter than I think it ought to be. There is nothing I can do to stop the passage of this kind of time in which we human beings are set. I can work with it rather than against it, but I cannot stop it. I do not like what it is doing to my body. If I live as long as many of my forbears, these outward diminishments will get worse, not better. But these are the outward signs of chronology, and there is another Madeleine who is untouched by them, the part of me that lives forever in *kairos* and bears God's image.

(My mother said, "I may be an old woman in my eighties, but inside me I am still a dancing girl.")

In particle physics there is a theory posited by Feynman, that positrons are electrons traveling backwards in time. The positron, unlike the human creature, is not bound by one-way linear time – the past-to-future track – but can move backwards in time as well as forwards. That's fine for the positron, but not for the human being. Who wants second childhood in an old body?

To move backwards as well as forwards is still linear. *Kairos* is not bound by time at all. And that marvel which makes us unique as well as interdependent is free in *kairos*.

As I type these words I am in Crosswicks, where Hugh and I are house- and animal-sitting while Bion and Laurie are away. The mercury is subzero, and the antifreeze in one of the pipes leading to the tower – my over-the-garage study – has frozen, and the tower is a deep freeze, and unusable until the mercury climbs to thirty, and the antifreeze thaws, and we find where the problem is.

Antifreeze shouldn't freeze! I am sitting in the corner of the kitchen-dining room where my son has his desk, and through the windows I look past the three tall spruce trees to the sun slanting against the bare branches of a maple and outlining them in gold. The ground is white, and the hills beyond the fields are mauve. These hills are old, many thousands of years old, worn down through the years by wind and rain. The spruce trees, now more than thirty feet high, were given me as a mother's day present more than three decades ago: the dark smudges of the brussels sprouts plants, the only vegetables left in the garden, were planted last June: the snow fell only a few days ago. In that one glance I have seen a considerable spread of chronology. This is something I might not have noticed before my fascination with particle physics. I read Michael Chester's book this past summer, often while in the waiting room at the hospital lab between various tests while we were trying to get rid of the aeromonas.

Particle physicists talk about "strange particles," seemingly less afraid of that which is strange than are many people looking for a safe religion. Was it because Isaac's God was strange and anything but "safe" that Jacob was so slow in taking El Shaddai as his God?

Chester says, "There was a serious problem concerning these new particles. They were all [kaons] created in strong interactions, but decayed slowly to weak interactions. This was very unexpected. Physicists were used to the idea that particle events are essentially reversible. A particle born in the instant of operation of the strong force should not fade away over the vast ages of time (such as one billionth of a second or even one millionth of a second) required by a weak force. Because of this peculiar imbalance, these new particles were given the name of *strange particles*." (scientists can be as upset by the unexpected in the universe as theologians.)

Chester goes on to say, "Certainly the physical universe is much more dreamlike and much less mechanical than we generally realize."

The physicist can and sometimes does say that the physical universe exists only in the mind.

Whose mind? The mind of the physicist with an imagination as wild as that of the teller of fairy tales? Haldane says we cannot imagine it. Whose mind, then? The mind of God?

With our capacity to misuse, abuse, or even annihilate our planet with all we have learned about the physical universe, what are we doing to the glorious designs of the mind of God? It is one of the problems and responsibilities of free will, and, unless we believe in predestination, in a deterministic universe, we can't let ourselves off the hook of personal responsibility. Though the butterfly may not be aware that it affects galaxies thousands of light years away, we humans are given at least an inkling of the results of our most casual actions.

A small example is cigarette smoking. If I am in a room where someone is smoking, not only does it irritate my eyes, but I am being made a passive smoker like it or not, and receiving all the detrimental effects of the cigarette as much as if I were smoking it. We can do nothing in isolation, no matter how much we try to separate ourselves from our cosmic community.

* * *

A true symbol is an open window, never leading to a closed, deterministic world, but to an open, indeterministic one. Symbols are mind, heart, and soul stretchers.

Recently I was shown a color photograph of an icon – from Armenia, I think – which absolutely delights me. It is a picture of King David, sitting and holding his harp with one hand. With the other he holds a child who is sitting on his knee, and the caption under the picture reads: *King David with Christ on his lap.*

What a glorious reminder that Christ always was! Jesus of Nazareth lived for a brief life span, but Christ always was, is, and will be, and the picture of King David with Christ on his lap is my treasure for this year, a treasure largely in my mind's eye, because I do not have a copy of the picture of this icon.

So, like King David, we may hold Christ on our laps, and we will be taught to live lovingly with paradox and contradiction, with yes and with no, light and dark, in and out, up and down.

Jacob, wrestling with the angel, was in his own way holding on to Christ. And the angel blessed him.

After that glory he went on and tried to bribe Esau to forgive him, typical Jacob-fashion. And Esau "ran to meet him, and embraced him, and fell on his neck, and kissed him, and they wept."

Esau wept with joy to see his brother again. And Jacob? Were they tears of relief that Esau wasn't still angry?

Esau did not want all the gifts Jacob had brought in order to placate him. He said, "I have enough, my brother. Keep what is yours."

But Jacob urged him, "Take, I pray you, my blessing that is brought to you, because God has dealt graciously with me." And he urged him, and he took it.

The King James translation uses the word blessing. Jacob has just been blessed by the angel who wrestled with him all night and smote him on the thigh. He also has his father, Isaac's, blessing, stolen from Esau. Surely it is time for him to give a blessing to his brother.

The Jerusalem Bible uses the word *gift*, rather than *blessing* but for me the symbol of blessing is deeper and richer.

Alter says that he feels that the King James translation of Hebrew Scripture is truer to the intent of the original than any other. Other translations, in trying to avoid the frequent repetitions of the Hebrew, for instance, miss the point that these repetitions are a conscious artistic device, building in power. I read from many different translations, but I return again and again to the King James.

And I like it that Jacob is at last willing to give Esau a blessing.

Jacob and Esau were not either/or people. They had the full complexity of the both/and human being. Open at one moment, closed at another. Brave, cowardly. Loving, lying. Jacob never hesitated to cheat, and yet God called him Israel. How are we to understand?

We are at a demanding threshold of understanding right now, as we move from deterministic, forensic thinking, to more indeterministic, vulnerable thinking. We are unique, incomparable creatures, but was creating us God's chief achievement or ultimate aim? We can no longer separate ourselves from the rest of creation, nor think of ourselves as more important in God's eyes than stars or butterflies or baboons. We are part of a whole which is so intricately balanced that the smallest action (watch that butterfly) can have cosmic consequences.

We need to step out of the limelight as being the pinnacle of God's work. I suspect that those first human creatures who walked upright on their hind legs and so freed their hands to make and use tools, most likely thought of themselves as the pinnacle of creation. Look at us! We are man who uses tools! God has done it at last!

Perhaps we have just as far to go in the long journey toward being truly human.

It is not easy to accept the both/and-ness of the people we love. Or ourselves. I am highly intelligent; I am also frequently extremely stupid. When somebody I love and admire does something which seems to me to be totally unworthy I am devastated, and it takes a while before I find balance and allow that person to be as both/and – or even more so – than I am. Sometimes it seems that the greater the human being, the deeper the potential for stupidity or sin.

I was brooding about this when a young friend of mine came to tell me that ultimately the computer will no longer be binary, but trinary (A trinary [trinitarian] computer would not have "thought" I was leaving from Portland, Oregon.) Right now the computer works on the binary system: one/zero. Either/or Yes/no. Lewis Carroll could have been forecasting our present computers when he had the Red Queen ask Alice "What's one and one and one and one ..."

When Alice says she doesn't have the faintest idea, the Red Queen says scornfully, "She can't do sums at all." One and one and one and one ... that's the way the computer counts, incredibly swiftly. But ultimately, even this is not going to be adequate. We are going to have to move to a computer which is trinary.

In technical language, my friend told me, the trinary computer will have positive polarity, negative polarity, and neutral polarity. Or: *yes/no/mu*. *Mu* means that neither yes nor no is a workable answer.

He illustrated this by a Zen koan. The Zen master asked his student to go to the nearby mountain and bring him the top mile. The student went to the master's study and brought him his pipe.

"What," my friend asked me, "is a *mu* answer to, 'Are you still beating your wife?' "

"I'm cooking chicken for dinner," I said.

And I thought that there are times in any marriage when, if one partner asks the other, "Do you love me?" Neither yes nor no is a true reply. There are times when I don't love my husband. On the other hand, I don't *not* love him.

And there are times when that question should not be asked!

Jesus gave *mu* answers. When he was asked whether or not it was proper to pay tribute to Caesar, he said, "Bring me a coin." A scribe said to Jesus, "Master, I will follow you whenever you go." A binary answer would have been, "Come with me," or "Go home." Jesus' trinary answer was, "The foxes have holes and the birds of the air have nests, but the son of man has no place to lay his head."

Occasionally other people responded to Jesus with trinary answers. He was brought a child who was possessed of an unclean spirit, and when the father begged for help, Jesus said, "If you can believe, all things are possible if you believe." And the child's father answered, "Lord, I believe. Help thou my unbelief."

When the disciples quarreled over who was greatest among them, Jesus reached out and pulled a small child onto his lap .

When Nicodemus asked him, "Who is my neighbor?" Jesus told the story of the man set upon by thieves.

A man said to Jesus, "Master, speak to my brother and make him divide our inheritance with me." And Jesus said, "Man, who made me a judge or divider over you?"

When the scribes and elders asked Jesus by whose authority he was preaching, he answered with another question, "The baptism of John, was it from heaven, or of men?"

(Oriental or occidental?)

Mu responses.

Often he replied with a story and a story is usually *mu.* This is not an either/or, a yes/no. It is both/and/maybe.

Surely when Jacob fled from Esau's anger, and was given a vision of angels, that was not the yes or no that we human beings tend to expect. Angels, too, are *mu.*

A *mu* answer is redemptive, never destructive. It opens our eyes and ears. It helps us to be willing to move out of our comfortable rut, and to go out into the wilderness of questions which have no easy answers. How we long for easy answers and blanket statements. If we can label all problems, premarital sex, divorce, abortion, then we can safely refrain from thinking about the people who are suffering from these problems. Jesus made no blanket statements about social or political issues. Each person he met was given his focussed attention – the *person*, rather than the problem.

If you can label things, make blanket statements to cover all contingencies, you don't need symbols. Story is an alternative to labelling. Story is symbol.

Perhaps we human beings with our desire to label are very strange particles indeed. We live in a new world of radical change which is, nevertheless, as primitive in its own way as the world where Jacob poured oil on the stone he had used for a pillow, and proclaimed it to be the house of God.

Sometimes a new awareness of symbols is given along with small, unspectacular events. I spent a day with a group of men and women who had been through seminary and were ready to be ordained. One man, in his thirties, had read the *Time Trilogy* the week before, and wanted to know why I had used so many occult references.

Occult references? I was baffled and a little shocked. I asked him to explain.

He mentioned the three Mrs W, Mrs Whatsit, Mrs Who, and Mrs Which. Especially Mrs Which. But – I thought the text made it quite clear that she (like the other two) is a guardian angel, and the name is a pun on which and witch, a play on words, and a deeper understanding of the godly possibility of the word. It has nothing to do with black magic or witchcraft. As Mrs Which herself remarks, when things are desperate we need to keep a sense of humor.

The young man thought the way I described Progo, the cherubim, as quirky and sometimes irritable might disturb people. But Progo is a very scriptural cherubim as I describe him, and it wouldn't surprise me a bit if those cherubim guarding the gates of Eden didn't get irritable on occasion. Was this young man thinking of renaissance cherubs, little baby heads with small, ineffectual wings? Hadn't he read (for instance) Ezekiel lately?

Then he asked me why I had used the dog, Ananda, as a familiar. Again, I was shocked. A familiar is an animal companion to a witch or warlock, frequently a black cat which talks, and gives the owner Satanic information. Ananda a familiar? Horrors! Ananda, who is joy, God's joy, could never be a familiar in the sense that the young man was using the word. That it was even possible for him to so misinterpret the story that he could think of a Satanic familiar in connection with this loving dog was appalling to me.

We do have a loving, kything relation with dogs; Ananda is not unlike one of our family dogs, Tyrrell, half Golden Retriever, half Shepherd, who had an unerring understanding of people. She was gentle, loving, affectionate. Like most Golden Retrievers she had a dolphin's smile. But she could smell wrongness. One time in the Cathedral Library I was introduced to a personable young man who was going to be working in the mail room. As he approached me, Tyrrell's hair bristled, and I heard a low, warning growl. Within the week the young man had stolen all the Cathedral keys and a large sum of money. I said, "Whenever Tyrrell is suspicious of someone, take the dog seriously." Tyrrell was a dog, a friend of human beings, guarding her people as best she could. She was not a "familiar."

Doc, my present Golden retriever companion, has Tyrrell's nose for the psychotic. A Cathedral attracts people with problems and if Doc does not want someone to come into the library, she stays pressed close against me, I know that whoever it is has problems beyond my competence to handle. Often a listening ear is enough. Doc lets me know when more professional help is needed. Doc is a hurtling, golden rocket of love. She is not a "familiar."

Within the past year I have seen several articles on the need for many people to have pets, and that when someone with high blood pressure strokes a dog or a cat, the blood pressure is lowered. When the young man saw occult meanings in the *Time Trilogy* what was he looking for?

Someone else in the group remarked that "occult" is not necessarily a bad word. It simply means "hidden."

It would certainly be possible to call the *Revelation* of Saint John the Divine "occult," for there is much in that extraordinary last book of the Bible that is hidden, and we show no evidence that we have come near to plumbing its depths.

I said that perhaps what I was inadvertently doing was hoping to redeem the symbols. The powers of darkness have no need to come where evil already is, but try to pervert the good. So I pray that my symbols were referring to the original good.

That is what we need to look for, the good in what God has created.

There is much that is hidden, and much of it is good and lovely and true. There is much in the life of Jesus that is hidden. We know almost nothing about him from the time when he spoke with the elders in the temple at the age of twelve, to the time when he began his adult ministry. There is much in our own selves, our own spirits, which is hidden, which only God knows. And there is much that we can understand only symbolically.

The new symbols created by the new physics are helpful to me in keeping my doors open. The butterfly effect, strange particles, or even particles that have a tendency to life (how alive are we?) and that are called virtual particles. And I do not want to forget the particles with the unusually long lifespan of one millionth of a second.

The new symbols do not replace the old, but give them renewed vitality, so that they continue to inform my faith. Christ, small as a child, sitting on King David's lap. The small cross of the African bushman. The cup of salvation. Once again *chronos* and *karos* intersect in the cross.

And yet, what about the cross? More and more crosses are being found today in churches where they would not have been tolerated a few decades ago. At the same time, the symbol has been weakened. The sign of the cross used to make the Devil take flight. A church was a sacred place of sanctuary. A thief who would rob a great house without compunction would not go into a church and touch the sacred vessels. Not so any more. At "my" Cathedral in New York, all the valuable crosses and candle sticks have had to be replaced with wood or ceramic ones, to prevent continuing theft. Great tapestries have been ripped from the high walls. Stones have been thrown through windows.

How do we reawaken a sense of the sacred?

First of all, we must look for it. Jacob fled Esau, and was given a vision of God. He was realistic about people, including himself, but he did not look for evil. So he was given the greatest good.

What are we looking for? For God and love and hope? Or for wrongness and evil and sin?

If the totally interdependent, interconnected world of physics is true, then this oneness affects the way we look at everything – books, people, symbols. It radically affects the way we look at the cross. Jesus on the cross was at-one with God, and with the infinite mind, in which Creation is held. The anguish on the cross has to do with this at-one-ment in a way which a forensic definition of atonement cannot even begin to comprehend.

For Jesus, at-one-ment was not being at-one only with the glory of the stars, or the first daffodil in the spring, or a baby's laugh. He was also at-one with all the pain and suffering that ever was, is, or will be. On the cross Jesus was at-one with the young boy with cancer, the young mother hemorrhaging, the raped girl. And perhaps the most terrible anguish came from being at-one with the people of Sodom and Gomorrah, the death chambers at Belsen, the horrors of radiation in the destruction of Hiroshima and Nagasaki. It came from being at-one with the megalomania of the terrorist, the coldness of heart of "good" people, or even the callous arrogance of the two men in criminal court.

We can withdraw even in our prayers, from the intensity of suffering. Jesus, on the cross, experienced it all. When I touch the small cross I wear, that, then, is the meaning of the symbol.

May the Holy Spirit come and help all our symbols to be redeemed.

12

Echthroi and Angels

ON THE CROSS JESUS WAS AT ONE WITH GOD and the holy angels and rainbows and butterflies. And he was also, to his anguish, at one with Satan and all the fallen angels, with those who would viciously destroy what God has made with love and joy, with those whose pride is even greater than that of the terrorist. Because Jesus took into himself on the cross every evil and every sin and every brokenness to come upon this planet, there is the fragile but living hope that one day even Satan may once again join the sons of God when they gather round their Maker, and that he will beg to be allowed once again to carry the light. For, as Saint Paul wrote to the people of Philippi, "Every knee shall bow in heaven and on earth and under the earth, and every tongue confess that Jesus Christ is Lord, to the glory of the Father."

We know that the redemption of the cosmos is no easy matter. The actions of the dark angels are visible throughout Scripture, and even the protagonists of the stories bear the taint.

They lied; they cheated. They made great, inordinate demands of God, and in turn accepted the great and inordinate demands God threw at them. They looked at the stars and were given great promises, and their response may have been incredulity, but never indifference or smugness. They did wonderful things, and they did terrible things.

One of the stories related to that of Jacob which we seldom hear is the story of his daughter, Dinah. It is not a pleasant story, and we would rather forget it. But there it is.

Dinah, the daughter of Leah, the tender-eyed, "went out to meet the daughters of the land ... in Shalem, a city of Shechem, which is in the land of Canaan ... where Jacob, her father, had pitched his tent."

According to some translations, she was raped by Shechem, the son of Hamor the Hivite, prince of the country. However, the King James translation says that when Shechem saw her, "he took her, and lay with her, and defiled her. And his soul clave unto Dinah, the daughter of Jacob, and he loved the damsel."

That does not sound like rape. Shechem wanted to marry Dinah, because he loved her so much, and it would appear that Dinah wanted to marry him. However, no matter how it happened, he had defiled Dinah by lying with her before they were married, and her brothers were angry.

But Shechem told his father, the prince of the country, that he loved Dinah, and wanted her for his wife, and Hamor went to the sons of Jacob, saying, "The soul of my son Shechem longs for your daughter. I pray you, give her to him as wife, and all of you make marriages with us, and give your daughters to us, and take our daughters for yourselves. And you shall dwell with us, and our land shall be yours."

And Shechem said to Dinah's father, Jacob, and to her brothers, "Ask me for anything you want, and I will give you whatever it is you ask, only give me Dinah for my wife."

The sons of Jacob were still outraged because Shechem had defiled their sister, and they answered him deceitfully, telling him that they would give Dinah to him only if the Hivites would become as the Hebrews, and would circumcise every one of the males of their tribe.

The Jerusalem Bible says that Shechem "was the most important person in his father's household," and that he agreed to the circumcision. The King James translation reads "And the young man deferred not to do this thing, because he had delight in Jacob's daughter, and he was more honorable than all the house of his father." I like to think that Shechem, despite his rash act, was a man of honor.

At any rate, all the male Hivites were circumcised, and on the third day, when they were still sore and in pain, Simeon and Levi, two of Leah's sons (and therefore Dinah's full brothers) took their swords and slew all the male Hivites. They killed Hamor and Shechem, and took Dinah out of Shechem's house. Then all the sons of Jacob pillaged the town and took everything – flocks, cattle, donkeys, children, wives (in that order).

Jacob was very upset by all of this, not so much the massacre, as the effect it would have on his reputation. He said to Simeon and Levi,

You have done me harm, making me stink among the people of this land. There are many of them, and I have few in number, and they will gather themselves together against me, and slay me, and I shall be destroyed, and my house.

And Dinah's brother said, "Should he deal with our sister as a harlot?"

And God said to Jacob, "Get up. Go to Beth-el [where Jacob had seen the ladder of angels uniting heaven and earth] and dwell there, and make there an altar [another altar!] unto God, who appeared to you when you were fleeing from your brother Esau."

And Jacob told his household, "Get rid of all the strange gods you have with you, and wash, and change your clothes, and we will go to Beth-el."

And they gave Jacob all their strange gods. And all their ear-rings.

It would still be a long time before El Shaddai would truly be understood as the God Who is One, the God Who is All.

It will still be a long time before we who call ourselves Christians will understand that God is One, that God is All, because we still worship many strange gods. When we set ourselves up as being the only people in Creation who have the truth and who will inherit the kingdom, we are worshiping the little god of our own pride.

When we greedily and proudly count the money we have taken in on a Sunday at church, or pride ourselves on the funds that we have sent into the mission field, we are in danger of worshiping the little gods of money and our own superiority.

When we divide ourselves into *us* and *them*, we court disaster.

I may be horrified and outraged when an assassination is committed in the name of religion, and when I discover a way of looking at God which is not mine, but I still may not separate myself from this horror with any sense of my own virtue. The butterfly's wings quiver with pain, and distant galaxies are shaken.

Is the killing of Gandhi, Martin Luther King, John or Robert Kennedy so different in essence from the killing of Hamor or Shechem?

There it is, the story of Dinah and her brothers, those brothers who would head the tribes of Israel. I don't know what to make of it, but I have to accept that it is part of the story – and that there is much to be learned from it.

This is all we know about Dinah. We are given no hint as to how *she* felt. Was she in love with Shechem? Between the lines, I sense that she was. But she, along with Shechem, had broken the taboo, and retribution followed.

Later on in history, when Moses the lawgiver came into the story, a woman who had committed adultery was to be stoned, stoned to death. The fault, according to the law, seemed to lie more with the woman than with the man. At least Dinah was spared stoning.

When Joseph first learned that Mary was pregnant, he should have given her over to be stoned to death, according to the law. What an extraordinary man he was! He was willing to bypass the law by putting Mary away quietly. And then, even more remarkable, he was able to accept the words of the angel, that the child – the holy seed – in Mary's womb had been sown there by the Holy Spirit.

What was Joseph looking for? Not anger, not retribution, not even justice, but love.

"What are you looking for?" Jesus asked the people.

There are, praise the Lord, only a few Christians who are hoping to find those who are less Christian than they are, in order to feel superior by contrast. There are only a few people who are reading books looking for pornography, or counting the number of dirty words rather than reading the story. There are far many more people who are truly looking for God, however and wherever the Creator may choose to reveal the divine nature. There are many more people who are looking for the revelation of infinite compassion in Christ.

We do find what we look for. Or do we? In a way, yes. But it's not quite that easy. Pilgrim struggled a long way from the wicket gate to the Celestial City. If we are looking for love, that is what we will find. But love never promised there would be no suffering. Love never promised to stop all the attacks of the echthroi. Love led Jesus to the cross, rather than sparing him.

Echthroi is a word which I first used in the *Time Trilogy.* It is a Greek word, meaning *the enemy.* It is an enemy-sounding word. *Echthroi* is the plural noun: *echthros* is the singular. The echthroi are those who would separate us from the stars and each other, un-Name, annihilate. The fallen angels are echthroi, and so are disease and famine and hate and vanity and a host of other little nasty things. The echthroi would teach us despair, indifference, would have us believe that unmerited suffering is deliberately inflicted on the creature by an angry Creator. The echthroi are forensic. They are powerful. But love is greater.

I spent nearly a week at Holy Cross monastery to teach a writers' workshop, followed by a weekend retreat. At the end of a hard day's work, my old bones need to soak in a hot tub. Because the only room in the monastery with a tub, not a shower, is in the monastic enclosure, I was allowed to sleep there. Was I the first female to sleep in this all male bastion? The cell I was in has been slept in by bishops, missionaries, preachers, from all over the world. It is likely that many spiritual battles have been fought within its white walls.

I was struggling with something minor, a nasty cold which had been hanging on for weeks, giving me a bronchial cough and fever, and I was finally on antibiotics to help me through the workshop and the retreat. Kind people gave me cough drops and vitamin C, and one of the monks loaned me a heavy cape in which to wrap myself, and another gave me his bottle of cough medicine.

The third night I was there I had a dream in the early hours of the morning. It was very cold, and the cold had wakened me, and I lay there, trying to warm up and go back to sleep, saying the Jesus Prayer: "Lord Jesus Christ, have mercy on me." Then there was a sense of pressure by me, of someone, something on the bed, and then there was a feeling of terrible evils battling, and I clung frantically to the Jesus Prayer, calling it out, over and over: "Lord Jesus Christ, have mercy on me." Then it seemed to me that although I was caught in the great winds of horrible evil, I was not the target, I was simply in the path of the storm, and I kept calling out the prayer, until the storm was over. In my dream a monk came in, which seemed quite natural, and pointed out the evidence of the storm. The wallpaper had been stripped from the far wall, and the plaster beneath was violently pockmarked.

What I told the monk was that this horrible episode proved to me that my faith in Jesus Christ was really real, and that had I not been holding on to the name of Jesus, the storm of evil would have killed me, and Christ truly was, is, salvation.

This was Epiphany Eve – when Christians celebrate God's revelation of love to all humankind. What a marvelous showing forth!

The transition from sleeplessness to the dream was seamless, and so was the transition from the dream to being awake, alone in an untouched room. So real had it been that it took a while for me to realize that it had been a dream. I looked at the far wall, and there was no wallpaper, only smooth, unpocked plaster.

The amazing thing is that as I looked back at the dream it was not a "bad" dream, or a nightmare; it was a glorious affirmation of the power of Christ. The storm of evil had not only not put out the light, it was proof that the light was there and the light could not be extinguished.

The echthroi, quite logically, attack the Good. Saint Anthony in the desert (the same desert on which Jacob pitched his tent) was attacked by all kinds of venomous demons. In the past year or so the attacks seem to have become more frequent and more vicious all over the world. Drawing back in fear is more dangerous than staying in the vanguard, but that does not make the echthroid attacks any less terrible.

In the past few months I have had more calls than I want to count asking for prayers – prayers for good people who have been stricken with cancer, multiple sclerosis, terrible accidents. Why?

Why, if we find what we look for, why do terrible things happen to people who are looking for good, and who serve the good?

That question has never been answered. It is asked, one way or another, all through the Old Testament. The entire book of Job grapples with it, but gives no definitive answer. Yet, underlying the lack of an answer is an unspoken affirmation that ultimately all shall be well.

God is still the author of the story, and even if the echthroi tear and crumple the pages, or smudge the ink, it is still God's story, and the Author will correct, revise, retype, redeem, as necessary. Meanwhile, we are part of the story, and we may not know what the lines we are given mean, why we suffer, bleed, die. Perhaps what we see as death is really necessary for rebirth.

Recently I was negotiating a contract for a movie of one of my books, *The Arm of the Starfish*. The problem with the standard Hollywood contract is that it has a clause giving the producer freedom to change character and theme. Not only can I not sign that clause, the contract must reverse it. I became aware of the absurdity of the Hollywood legal mind when, in the contract for *A Wrinkle in Time* (where that nasty clause had been reversed), I was to grant rights to the work in perpetuity throughout the universe! I took a red pen, made a *, and wrote, "with the exception of Sagittarius and the Andromeda galaxy." They actually accepted it. And I was told later that there was considerable discussion about this. Could I possibly know something about Sagittarius and the Andromeda galaxy that they didn't know?

Will *Wrinkle* be made into a movie? Supposedly. But there are times when I think it is more likely to happen on Andromeda galaxy than here. We'll see.

Meanwhile, in discussions with the potential producers of *Starfish*, we had to make clear what I would and what I would not allow to be changed. We all agreed that it needs updating.

The world of the eighties is very different from the world of the sixties, when the book was written.

It was suggested that Adam, the young protagonist, would not be apt to carry secret papers: it would more likely be some kind of microchip. All right.

"What about Adam and Kali?" I was asked. "Wouldn't their relationship go a little further?"

I had to agree that now, twenty years later, it probably would.

The word *relationship* wasn't even in our vocabulary twenty years ago. We used to have friendship, and love.

"Does Joshua have to die?" I was then asked.

"Yes."

"Why?"

"Because that's what happened," I said firmly.

"But Joshua was *good*."

"Yes," I agreed.

"But doesn't *good* imply *protection*?"

"No," I said. No. And then it came to me that the only one who has ever offered protection is Satan. That was one of the temptations given to Jesus on the mountain after his baptism. Worship me, Satan urged him, and you can have it all free, no being deserted by the disciples you had counted on to stay with you, no cross, no pain, no suffering. I will protect you.

But does the God of love not offer that kind of protection?

Again I am caught in paradox and contradiction.

I have on occasion been blessed by extraordinary miracles of healing. At other times, not. Why does God miraculously cure one person, and allow another to die in agony? Why does one child appear to be under the protection, while another is struck by a drunken driver?

Why? There are no easy answers. The easy answers, such as a predetermined universe, do not seem compatible with a God of love.

And yet –

I have been offered prayers of protection, and I believe in them. But they are not magic. Magic is manipulation. Prayers for protection are not.

It helps a little if I think of myself as a human parent. My deepest desire is to protect my children. My lioness instinct toward my cubs is great. But I cannot offer my children complete protection. We may want to make everything all right for our children, but we cannot. All we can do is love them, and help them grow up. We have to let the baby struggle to its feet and fall, and stand again, and fall again, as it learns to walk. All during our children's lives we have to let them learn to walk alone, to let go the hand. The overprotected child becomes incapable of growing into a mature human being. We must allow our children to be themselves, not manipulated appendages of their parents. We can try to give them standards, to teach by example, and we hope they will use the standards in resisting the many temptations they will be offered, but we can't resist the temptations for them, they have to resist for themselves. God did not resist the temptations for Jesus; Jesus had to confront Satan alone.

Satan, Lord of the echthroi. The enemy of Christ. The enemy of each one of us. Of the cosmos

But Satan did not come from outside the cosmos. He was one of the sons who met with God at the beginning of the book of Job. He was the beautiful angel Lucifer – the light bearer – who thought he could do it all better than God. Just look at life here on this planet, what a mess it is! Christians killing in the name of Christ, hardness of heart, famine, drought, greed, filth, inequity, imbalance. Don't we all think we could have done a better job of it? Satan certainly thought he could. And he is tempting us, assuring us, "You are better than the others, better than *them*," and we fall for it all too often.

"It must have been so hard on Michael," my friend Sister Mary Michael said, "when he had to fight Lucifer, because they were best friends."

Is it possible for them to be best friends again, at the end of time, when Satan no longer wants to do it all himself, and is willing to return to the joy of interdependence? That is what I hope for and desire. I equally hope for reconciliation for many estranged friends, parents and children, brothers and sisters, for churches split apart by discord over trivialities, for races isolated from each other because of a sense of superiority. And there is hope. Listen to St. Paul again, in Colossians 1:

For in Christ all the fullness of God was pleased to dwell, and through him to reconcile to himself all things, whether on earth, or in heaven, making peace by the blood of his cross. And you, who once were estranged and hostile in mind, doing evil deeds, he has now reconciled in his body of flesh by his death ...

Sometimes when I am working my way through a Bach fugue I hear strange dissonances before ultimately the theme emerges, triumphant. The dissonances, rather than spoiling the fugue, make the working out of the theme more beautiful. Bach was criticized for some of the strange discordancies in his music, but the ending always resolved all discord into harmony.

If it is difficult to understand that sin and evil come from within Creation, rather than from without, a look at our own bodies, our own inner selves, can be helpful. Few of us have bodies of flawless perfection, yet we would not throw away the body because of nearsighted eyes, weak ankles. When I have a fever or hurt myself, I pray for my body's healing. Our thoughts are not always pure and loving, but when I feel resentful or self-pitying, these unhappy qualities come from within me, not without me. And I pray that my ill-feelings will be turned to healthy, loving ones. At the Second Coming, when all things are redeemed, then we, like all of creation, will know wholeness and holiness through Christ, "who will change our lowly body to be like his glorious body in the power which enables him even to subject all things to himself" – Paul's radical affirmation.

Meanwhile we pray that we will be given our own parts to play in healing the fragments which separate us dis-astrously. In anguish we pray for the healing of the universe, for as long as any part of Creation is in rebellion, all of it cries in pain. "If one member suffers, all suffer together; if one member is honored, all rejoice together." And then Paul moves into "a still more excellent way," the way of Love in his first letter to the people of Corinth. It is not easy to understand that love is the most powerful of all weapons, love in its very weakness.

How do we bless the echthroi? When they attack (and surely they have been attacking) I call on the angels.

When Jacob wrestled with the angel he understood that the angel was not only a messenger of God, but an aspect of God. When I call on the angels, I feel that I am calling on Christ, in whose service the angels perform their works.

Jesus taught us that God is love; so what am I calling the angels to do when the enemy attacks, leaving pain and grief and bitter tears?

I have had to move from thinking that the echthroi have to be killed by God's avenging angels, to wondering whether they, like the rest of creation, may be redeemed and blessed. Turned from despair to hope. Changed even more radically than Paul was changed, so that they may no longer be destroying angels, but angels of light. The symbol of the avenging angel itself has to be transformed. The two-edged sword is no longer a weapon of death, but of healing.

Big words. Yes. And I mean these big words. But how? It would be obscene to get sentimental about the "poor" echthroi, poor though they may be.

It is not difficult for me to want those two defendants, whom I observed while I was on jury duty, to be healed and redeemed from their own evil. After all, they didn't hurt me. This hope for a blessing might not even be too difficult for the feisty old woman they'd attacked; after all, they had succeeded only in nicking her with their knives.

But what about the parents whose only daughter has been raped and then stabbed to death? Granted, the "Christian duty" is for them to pray for the murderer's redemption. But this kind of holiness doesn't come without terrible anger to be gone through, without terrible pain. "Though we went through fire and water," the psalmist sings to the Lord, "we have not forgotten you." Was such anger and pain the fire and water to which the psalmist referred?

Esau has something to teach us here. "Bless me, too, oh, my father, bless me, too." And he walked through fire and water and forgave Jacob.

What greater grief could any woman have than Eve? Her younger son, Abel, was dead. Her elder son, Cain, had killed him. With all the empathy of which I am capable, I cannot imagine the intensity of such anguish.

And yet God came into this world as one of us, not to destroy, but to heal. To redeem. To bless.

A friend of mine in the Midwest showed me an article on a possible new and very different way of treating cancer. Instead of trying to kill the cancer cells, the new hope of cure is to turn the malignant cells back into normal, benign cells, to change them from being destroyers into cells which once again play their own essential interdependent part in the functioning of the body. If Paul Brand is right in saying that cancer cells are the only cells in the body which insist on being autonomous, with no concern for the other cells they destroy, then our hope is that it will ultimately be possible for them to be transformed, and returned to the creative interdependence of normal cells.

So we must seek to change the echthroi from being destroyers, as cancer cells are destroyers; we must hope to see them changed into holy angels once again, each with a unique but interdependent role in the working out of the fulfillment of the cosmos.

How do we very human creatures help change the fallen angels into the radiance of love again? Of course, it is nothing we can do of ourselves at all, but the more we open ourselves to the holy angels, the less room there is for the fallen ones.

If I remain stuck in a groove of self-pity, if I insist on vindication, I am opening myself to the echthroi. We all want justice, but if we demand it at the price of love it will be dark justice indeed. I pray, fumblingly, for those who have hurt me, for those I have hurt, for those who have been attacked by the echthroi. Not a demanding prayer, just an offering of a timid hope of love. Neither coercion nor manipulation are effective in turning anyone toward Christ. Coercion and manipulation only *add* to the pain of the cross. My prayer is simply a holding out of whoever it is, friend or foe, to the love of God. That implies that I am willing, reluctantly or no, to accept some of the cross. If I hold out in prayer a teenage boy dying of leukemia, I cannot do it without accepting some of the anguish of the parents, the confusion of the siblings, the thrust toward life and then the letting go of the boy himself.

If I try to hold up in prayer the friend whose life is radically changed because of a love shattered and killed, I cannot do it without being part of the wounds and the anger. To hold someone lovingly in my hands, my hands held out to God, is to share, even in an infinitesimally tiny way, some of the agony of the cross. Blessing is not easy, and it cannot be reversed.

The promise is that not only can we bear the dark night, but that dawn will come.

For, as Paul said to the people of Rome, "... the creation itself will be set free from its bondage to decay and obtain the glorious liberty of the children of God ... We know that the whole creation has been groaning in travail together until now, and not only the creation, but we ourselves ... But if we hope for what we do not see, we wait for it with patience."

And then it is time to move from those close to me, or known to me personally, to the powers of darkness themselves.

Bless the bastard.

Bless the echthroi ...

How? By holding them out to the love of God.

Make no mistake. This is no permissive, wishy-washy cozy love. The best of us will be burned by it. Malachi warned that this love "is like a refiner's fire, and like fullers' soap; and ... shall ... purge them as gold and silver, that they may offer unto the Lord an offering in righteousness." It may take eons before self-will is diminished enough so that we want this terrible purging. And for the echthroi, the fallen angels, it will be terrible indeed.

But that is God's part in it. What is ours?

Simply to bless, no matter how ungraciously. To begin with blessing the easily identified echthroi: disease, terrorists, rapists, powermongers. Then keep coming in closer. Hold out to the love of God those who have hurt us. Those who have let us down. Who, for one reason or another, slap out at us, put us down, reject us. Those whose forgiveness we must accept when we have done any of these things ourselves.

Those we encounter in our daily lives, family, friends, people we pass on the street. And I had to think about those two defendants on the jury duty case whose clever lawyers managed to dance legalistic circles around the more straightforward assistant district attorney. Those two men were guilty, but they were charged with more injury than they actually inflicted. The intent to injure or kill was there but the result was not. Therefore, according to the law, and according to the charge, the assistant district attorney did not prove them guilty beyond a reasonable doubt.

We jurors spent at least an hour during our deliberation trying to find a loophole in the defending lawyers' cleverness, to find a way where we could legitimately avoid saying Not Guilty but, according to the law we could not. The judge had told us that in England a jury can bring in a verdict of "Not proven guilty," and that is what we would like to have done. But we had to say "Not Guilty" because this is the American way, and we felt heavy about it, but not nearly as heavy as we would have felt in a judicial system where guilt is assumed, rather than having to be proved.

Bless the brutes. With the blessing, help them to see that their brutality hurts them as much as the old woman they attacked. Bless them so that they may turn from the echthroi, turn their anger and violence and resentment to the light of love for healing.

"God bless you, sir," Jerome Hines said to Khrushchev.

Oh, God will indeed bless, but we must play our own part in the blessing.

Pope John Paul II played his part when he was willing to talk, lovingly, with his would-be assassin.

St. Stephen played his part when he asked that his murderers' action not be held against them.

Mozart, composing the grief-filled and yet joyous Requiem Mass, was playing his part.

* * *

Then it's time to move in even closer. To call on God to bless and transform the enemy within ourselves. (Remembering that a blessing once given can never be retracted.)

Only if I am able to bless the parts of myself which are furthest from God's image, are these objectionable parts redeemable. How do I go about this blessing? It is not easy, I am often too hurt or too angry to have the least desire to bless. Yet, ultimately, I know that the blessing must be given in a context of love, not my own love, but that of other people, my husband, my family, my friends, who allow me to be complex and contradictory. Who thereby bless me. I cannot do it myself! I can only pray that it will be done.

* * *

Are there people who have been so damaged by lack of having been given love, or having been so manipulated or corrupted by the self-serving sham that masquerades as love, that they are beyond the possibility of blessing, or knowing themselves blessed?

I'm not sure. At least, there are those who, in this life, are wounded spiritually beyond relief. But God will not give up.

Nor need we, though we must bless with a full awareness that we may not succeed. In the view of the world, Jesus did not succeed. But the world, and often the church, puts expectations of success on us which are such burdens that they can become a form of cursing. It should be only the echthroi who tempt us by making us believe that our love, in human terms, ought not to fail. But it does – often it does. Yet that need not stop love from growing.

Those echthroi within us: can I always tell what they are? Sometimes it's easy. Self-pity, jealousy, resentment, are echthroid. But often it is not possible to tell whether something is good or bad, virtue or vice. We cannot take a pad and draw a line down the middle, and then list our good qualities on one side, our bad on the other. What is good in one situation may not be good at all in another. And vice versa. I am very stubborn, nay, pigheaded, which can be very hard on those I love. On the other hand, during those long years of rejection slips for writing that I believed in, it was that very pigheadedness which kept me going. It has helped me "hang in there" in other times of crisis, too. So the very flaw of stubbornness can be a blessing. And ultimately, all shall be blessed, all the wounds and cracks in the universe.

There is an enormous difference between wallowing in our own brokenness and sense of sin, and in accepting it, and then turning to the Lamb for a transfusion. There is an enormous difference between seeing ourselves as virtuous and morally correct, so that therefore anything we do is permissible and innocent, and recognizing ourselves as God's children, loved simply because we *are*.

I suspect that those who would look for Satan-worshipers instead of fellow companions journeying to Christ, that the terrorists with their holy fanaticism, that those who would curse, wipe out, unName, do other than bless, are all caught in *chronos*, bound by time. When Lucifer and the fallen angels refused to bear the light, they also refused God's time, *kairos*. The prince of this world and his cohorts reign in time, limited time. They are fearful, for the winds of the Holy Spirit are blowing, and so the attack is accelerating. As we look around our wartorn planet, our own disturbed and dissatisfied country, the echthroi appear to be making more progress than the angels.

But they are not. They are not.

They have been around the planet ever since the serpent offered Eve the apple. But their victories are hollow.

Terrible things happen, as in the story of Dinah and her brothers, in which the echthroi surely had their part, but God's blessing is more powerful than the echthroi's cursing.

This is something we cannot truly know until it has been tested.

Did I really mean it when I told the movie producer that being good implies no protection? Yes. Accepting Christ as

Lord implies no protection, not in mortal terms. Nothing is guaranteed. No one is immune.

I was told a horrible story about a good Christian family. One afternoon the mother is giving the baby a bath. The doorbell downstairs rings, shrilly, urgently. She rushes to answer it. Her older child follows her, trips, falls down the stairs and breaks his neck. She opens the door to be told that her husband has just been killed in an accident at work. Upstairs the baby drowns in the tub.

How can we react to such horrors except "curse God and die"? Why don't we?

I have been praying during these past months for several people with multiple tragedies. Ma Katzenjammer in the old comics used to say, "Too much is enough." It seems not to be so.

In my own small way – and it is *very* small, merely inconvenient, not tragic – I am witness to the fact that we cannot say when enough becomes too much. 1984 was not a good year for my body. In January, I came down with shingles. One does not wish shingles on one's worst enemy. This was followed by a crashing fall on Broadway, when I tripped over a puppy who was terrified of city noises and ran between my legs. As my face hit the sidewalk, my dark glasses frame hit my cheekbone, and I had a hematoma which would make Lon Chaney in one of his worst roles look pretty. Hugh said, "If this was TV they'd send you to makeup to take some off."

Then there was a weird virus which manifested itself with stabbing pains in the head, and finally, after giving me a couple of weeks of acute discomfort, faded away. Then there was the aeromonas with its painful cramping and bleeding. And then, when my body's resistance was low because I was just off steroids for the aeromonas, I came down with the current bronchial cold which continued all through December and into

January. But it was *last* year's cold. I couldn't blame it on the new year, 1985, which I superstitiously counted on to do better by me.

On the second Sunday of January, I went for a walk in the woods around Crosswicks with three young friends. I knew that there was ice under the snow, so I wore my stoutest boots, took a stick, and my friends confirmed the fact that I was being very careful indeed. Careful or no, all of a sudden my feet went out from under me, and I crashed down on a rock.

One young friend said, later, "When you just lay there and didn't move, I knew something bad had happened."

It had. I'd broken my right shoulder. We were quite a distance from home, and I said, "Don't touch me, please. Don't touch my arm. Just let it hang." That, it happened, was the best thing I could have done, because the weight of the arm provided its own traction, and by the time it was x-rayed in the hospital, the bones were in place. It also happened that the orthopedist I wanted was on call that Sunday.

In the emergency room I said to him, "In just over a week I have to be in Chapel Hill, North Carolina." He looked at me and raised his eyebrows. Then he proceeded to truss me up in a shoulder-immobilizer.

Shoulder-immobilizers were designed by a man, for people with flat chests. If anybody wants to get rich and retire early, I suggest designing a female shoulder-immobilizer for people like me, who do *not* have flat chests.

I went home, helpless and hurting. And angry. I had not been careless. I had not caused myself to fall. I called my friend, Tallis, and told him that I had been pushed by an echthros, and no, I was not trying to be funny.

Nevertheless, is there anything to do except laugh? Such an accumulation inevitably becomes comic. I, however, did not find it humorous in the least. For the first few days the pain was excruciating (people who have had shingles get the idea when I tell them that it hurt worse than shingles).

I wept.

Who was I to think that a year of bodily vicissitudes was enough? Very clever, echthroi, tempting me into this kind of superstition. Very funny, tripping me up like that.

No, I don't think God willed my broken shoulder. God does not want pain for his creatures. But whatever happens, God will come into it and use it for good. I cried a lot the first couple of days. I hurt a lot. But it wasn't long before I began to see God's blessing in the midst of the pain of the shoulder and the discomfort of the masculine shoulder-immobilizer, which still makes me growl.

To keep myself sane, I struggled to type with my left hand. Holding a pen or pencil was impossible. But, even the day after the accident, I could sit at the typewriter for short periods of time, the electronic typewriter so sensitive to touch that it calls for almost no muscle expenditure. Of course I made all kinds of typographical errors with my clumsy left hand, but at least I could do a little work, and that was a needed affirmation. The echthroi hadn't completely conquered me: I was still human.

When I wasn't attempting to type with the left hand, I lay in bed, propped high on pillows, so that gravity could continue to provide traction for the broken humerus and shoulder. Usually I sleep flat, but I had to learn to sleep sitting up.

Now that we live in New York for much of the year, we can no longer take an active part in village life. I go to the church where once I directed the choir. But I am not there regularly enough even to sing in the choir. We left our tight-knit little community twenty-five years ago when we moved from the village back to New York.

But the day after I broke my shoulder I discovered that the old support system was still there, and still working. Somehow or other, as happens in a village, news of my fall got around. The phone rang. It was Eunice. "I'm sending dinner over tonight. Bernie will bring your dinner tomorrow." Martha, recovering from a serious operation, called to see how I was.

After twenty-five years!

And once again I was part of the church at work.

And the bride was beautiful.

After all, I did go to Chapel Hill, to Aqueduct Conference Center, started by the evangelist, Tommy Tyson, who quickly became a healing friend. Tommy has a strong healing ministry, and the first evening he anointed me with oil, put his hands on me, and prayed for healing. I think he was a little disappointed the next morning that there was no dramatic and visible result. But I told him, truthfully, that indeed I could feel healing.

And the truth of this was borne out six months later. I had been warned by my doctor that the break was so severe that I would not regain the full mobility and strength of the right arm. At the final visit he had me raising both arms, reaching behind my back, moving in every direction, and at last he said, "Which shoulder was it?" And then, "I wouldn't have believed it!"

Progress came in steps: the first joy was when I could hold a pen in my hand and write. The second was when I began to play the piano for therapy, at first miserably but then with more and more freedom. And a great day came when I could fasten my bra in back again!

Granted, I worked very hard at rehabilitation, but I did it at home. I did not have physiotherapy because the doctor said that I was doing the exercises myself. I met two women who had broken their shoulders and had not regained their mobility and were unable to carry anything heavy, and I was determined

I was not going to have a crippled arm. But all the determination in the world cannot do everything. I had Tommy's prayers, and I had the prayers of other loving friends. And I am grateful. Thank you, Tommy. Thank you, Spirit of Love.

Hugh was free to go to North Carolina with me, otherwise I could not have made it. I was, indeed, physically helpless. I could talk, which was the main thing expected of me at Aqueduct, but that's about all. Believe me, a broken shoulder doesn't immobilize only the shoulder. It was painfully difficult for me to get on and particularly *off* the toilet, so the doctor suggested a toilet seat extender, a large plastic insert which raises the seat six or so inches, and which made an incredible amount of difference. I told Hugh, wistfully, that I would really need this plastic extender in North Carolina, so he went back to the store where he had bought it, and asked for a cardboard box. The only available box was marked in large black letters: ADULT INCONTINENT PADS. So off we went to the airport with a suitcase, and a large cardboard box packed with the toilet seat extender, books, and clothes.

Ever since Hugh retired from his TV show I had been trying unsuccessfully to get him to do readings with me. I think he realized that being nothing but a nursemaid at Aqueduct wouldn't be a good idea, so he agreed to do the readings, and we started each session with dramatic readings from one or another of my books, and he was a tremendous success. Everybody thought he was marvelous – as indeed he was.

We were together on our 39th anniversary on January 26th, 1985, only because he was with me at the conference. In the morning he was washing me, since I still couldn't do even that much for myself, and he remarked "Who would have thought, thirty-nine years ago, that this is what we'd be doing today!"

One morning Carolyn, the hostess at the conference center, brought me in a cup of coffee. Hugh was sacrificing himself by eating in the dining hall with all the women, and Hugh is not chatty in the morning, and the acoustics emphasized his deafness. But he went, and he was gracious, and loved. And I said, "Carolyn, all kinds of blessings have come about because Hugh is at this conference with me, but did God need to break my shoulder to do this?"

Carolyn simply smiled and said, "Madeleine, God didn't break your shoulder. He's just using it."

Of course. But at that moment I needed blessed Carolyn to articulate it for me. God does not cause any of the bad things that happen, but God can take anything and redeem it. We still ask why terrible things happen to good people, why a loving God can allow war and illness and accident and death. We still grapple with the thorny problem of a loving God who has given his people the terrible gift of free will. Over and over again we abuse that gift, but God can come into whatever it is, and make it new.

God didn't cause me to fall and break my shoulder. I didn't cause it, either. It was an accident. It happened. And God came into it and used it for good.

Not long after the week in North Carolina, the United States Information Agency had made plans to send me, as a cultural representative, across Egypt and Austria. By then I was able to do a little bit more for myself, but not much, and I certainly couldn't have traveled alone, so Hugh went with me, and again, we did readings, to all kinds of groups, in Cairo and Heliopolis and Alexandria, in Vienna and Klagenfurt and Salzburg, a fascinating experience for both of us. What we were aiming for with our readings and our conversations was to make connections, to affirm that the things which unite human beings are more central than the things which separate us, and we did indeed make connections, and find at-one-ness, and we made friends – friends to be treasured all our lives. And we have continued to give readings together.

Someone said to me, "It was worth breaking your shoulder, wasn't it?"

And I replied, "Well, I can't quite go *that* far." But many blessings came out of the pain and the helplessness. And a new understanding of God's loving concern for us, the children.

This loving concern did not spare Jesus from the temptations. God did not stop the disciples from betraying him, or the Romans from crucifying him. But God offered Jesus, and offers us, the one protection that Satan does not give: *God is in it with us*. The God of love, unlike Satan, does not stand aside and look on suffering, unmoved. God is part of it, and because of that, we are given strength to bear things we did not think we could possibly bear. And because God is in it with us, our souls are helped to grow strong and to mature.

God does not want, or cause, the bad things to happen. But with God's patient and unfaltering love, they can be redeemed.

* * *

So did I really mean it when I said in the discussion of a movie of *The Arm of the Starfish* that there is, in mortal terms, no protection?

Yes. Only Satan can give us mortal protection, but what kind of protection is that? Satan can offer great length of years, but only in these mortal bodies. He cannot offer us the real body, the pre-Fall body, the resurrection body. Satan can probably find us parking places, keep us from getting colds, even protect us from bullets, and bombs, and cancer. But the only protection worth having is something Satan cannot give: oneness with God.

Satan fractured the original oneness when he took himself and his fellow echthroi and rebelled against Love. Even when, on the surface, Satan protects, his chief mission is to continue to break, fragment, separate. Satan never offers himself, except as an object for abject worship.

If our worship of God means anything at all, it must be voluntary not coerced. Satan will bargain with us. God (as Jacob discovered) will not. What God does offer is the Presence itself. Whatever it is, God is part of it, working to heal that which is broken, put together all the shards and fragments. God is with us in all our pain and grief and confusion, sharing, being, redeeming. This love does not stop with our deaths. That is the Christian affirmation. We do not ever stop being part of God's plan, part of the Unity, part of the work of the coming of the Kingdom, when all shall be made new.

I need to reiterate here what is a basic affirmation for me. When the world was created, as the story is told in the beginning of Genesis, God did not say, "It is finished." That did not come until the Cross. What God said after making the world was, "It is Good. It is very Good."

In March I saw my newborn grandson, a gorgeous, beautiful baby. Complete. Perfect. But finished? No! Anything but finished!

As this baby's parents are going to have the joy of watching him grow and develop and mature, so it is God's joy still to be part of Creation. And it is our calling to share in that loving creativity, to be willing to be open to change, to new revelation, new growth, as we are offered opportunities to go on with the work of that Creation which is called very good. I do not know why these opportunities are so often given us through the things which hurt us, or even kill us, but God knows, and that is all that is necessary.

When I receive Communion, when I am given the strengthening bread, the transfusion of the wine, this is the great symbol of God's oneness with Creation, the ultimate protection, God in us, we in God.

It is enough.

* * *

Immediately after his sons' horrible slaughter of Shechem and the Hivites, Jacob left that place, and went to "Luz, which is in the land of Canaan, that is, Beth-el (where he had seen the glorious ladder), he and all the people that were with him. And he built there an altar, and called the place El-Beth-el, because there God appeared unto him."

Deborah, Rebekah's nurse, died (she must have been very old), and was buried there under an oak tree.

And God appeared unto Jacob again, and blessed him. "And God said to him, your name is Jacob; you shall not be called Jacob any more, but Israel shall be your name."

So they moved from Beth-el toward Ephrath, and were nearly there, nearly to the place which would later be identified with Bethlehem, "and Rachel travailed, and she had hard labor." In giving birth to Benjamin, Rachel died, and was buried on the way to Ephrath, which is Bethlehem.

"And Jacob set a pillar upon her grave, and that is the pillar of Rachel's grave to this day."

Next we come to another difficult part of the story. Reuben, Jacob's eldest son, "went and lay with Bilhah, his father's concubine." Bilhah was one of the maids who had given sons to Jacob – Bilhah, Rachel's maid. Jacob heard what Reuben, his son, had done. It was the breaking of a taboo, and Reuben was to suffer for it. Yet it was Reuben who prevented the rest of the brothers from killing their braggart younger brother, Joseph. Reuben, like all scriptural heroes, was complex. But he had compassion, and for that I like him.

Jacob returned at last to Isaac, his father.

And chronology shudders.

When Jacob stole Esau's blessing from his father, the old man seemed to have been on his death bed, his eyesight gone with age, urging his son to come to him with a savory stew to give him strength that he might give his blessing before he died. And here it was, more than twenty years later. Either the biblical narrator is playing very free and easy with chronology, or Isaac had the longest deathbed scene in history. But biblical time is not linear, like our chronology in the Western world. If King David could hold Christ on his lap (and of course he could) why shouldn't Isaac be alive when the narrator needs him?

"Isaac was one hundred and four score years, and he gave up the ghost, and was gathered unto his people, being full of days, and his sons Esau and Jacob buried him." And though Jacob and Esau were thoroughly reconciled, they had both acquired so many flocks and herds that the land could not support them both, so they parted their ways.

Jacob, through tears and laughter, had learned something of God's promise. He had demanded a blessing; he had demanded protection. And God had blessed him, but had not given him the protection Jacob had tried to bargain for. God blessed Jacob and made him vulnerable. His beloved Rachel died in childbirth. His elder son betrayed him with Rachel's maid, Bilhah, who had given him children. He was to think for many years that his favorite son, Joseph, was dead.

Still he loved God, although he never understood the nature of El Shaddai, but that didn't seem to matter very much.

He learned not only that God gives us the gift of vulnerability, but also the gift of pain, instead of the affliction of the absence of pain.

How do we tell the echthroi from the true angel (like the great one who wrestled with Jacob all night)? How do we join with God's holy angels in loving the fallen ones so that they may become light-bearers again? How do we continue the blessing of Jacob through our own lives?

Jesus came into the world to save sinners, to look for the lost sheep, to heal the blind, and deaf, and dumb, and leprous, and those possessed by demons, to give hope to the wounded and bleeding and broken. And Jesus came to fulfill the prophecy and go to the Cross and break the barriers of time and space in the mighty act of at-one-ment with all of Creation.

God does not promise us protection any more than he promised it to Jesus. Or Jacob. We are not given protection. We are given vulnerability.

We are promised not the absence of pain, but the blessed warning of pain.

We are promised not that we won't be wounded, that we won't bleed, but that we will be transfused.

We are promised not that we won't die, but that we shall live.

* * *

What must Jacob have felt, after Rachel's death, when he held baby Benjamin in his arms, the baby whose birthing had caused his beloved wife's death? Opposing waves of anguish and love must have rolled over him. But he did not deny God because there was no justice in a woman's death in childbirth. He did not try to make things right by his own actions; he knew that he could not.

To know that we need to be transfused with the blood of the Lamb is not to succumb to illness, but to move toward health. Along with the revivifying transfusion is given an understanding that we are all part of the butterfly effect. As long as there is any pain in the universe, the Creator is part of that pain, and we bear our own small part in carrying it. It is bearable as long as the burden is shared.

And if in the fullness of God's time, Lucifer and Michael are again friends, there will be no more echthroi.

No echthroi. I think of those two men in criminal court, and pray for their healing. For my own letting go of residual anger and hurt, and my acceptance that I have often been betrayer rather than betrayed. Perfection of virtue is not required of me. Perfection of love is, and that is a very different thing.

Jesus said, "What I want is mercy, not sacrifice." How wonderful! Christ did not come into the world to save the virtuous, but to save you, and me, and Jacob (lying with his head pillowed on a stone), and Ikhnaton, with his psalms of praise for the One God, and all of us who turn to the Source of all love, knowing that we need to be transfused.

Jacob was weak and he knew that he was weak: nevertheless he would not leave off wrestling until the angel blessed him with the wound of love.

God's angel wrestles with us, and we cry out, "Bless me!" And God will bless us and we, like the baboons, will clap our hands and cry out our joy as we join in the glorious music of the spheres. In this harmony we will no longer be separated from the stars, and we will be at-one, too, with the infinitely small things of creation. In this communion we will be blessed indeed.

A jury room in Manhattan's criminal court, January, 1984
Wheaton, Illinois, October, 1985

SOLD INTO EGYPT

1
Reuben

thou art my firstborn, my might, and the beginning (first fruits) of my strength, the excellency of dignity, and the excellency of power:

Unstable as water, thou shalt not excel; because thou wentest up to thy father's bed; then defiledst thou it: he went up to my couch.

Genesis 49:3–4

HE WAS A SPOILED BRAT, Joseph, the eleventh brother. Indulged, self-indulgent, selfish. He clung to his father and the women. Whined. Got his own way. If one of the wives said no, another would surely say yes. When he was crossed he wailed that he had no mother. His older brothers took off in the other direction whenever he came around.

In his adolescence he became arrogant. He knew that he was the favored one of the twelve brothers, but he was not yet old enough to know that a father does a son no favor in singling him out, giving him a beautiful coat, lavishing him with love.

He dreamed big dreams, and he was not wise enough to keep them to himself.

Pouring fuel on the fire of his brothers' resentment one day, he said, "Listen to this dream I have dreamed! We were binding sheaves in the field, and my sheaf rose and stood upright. And all your sheaves stood round about, and bowed down to my sheaf."

Not surprisingly, his brothers were angry. "Will you reign over us indeed? Will you have dominion over us?" And they hated him all the more because of his dreams and his bragging.

Joseph could not keep his dreams quietly in his heart, but went on boasting. "Listen. I have dreamed another dream! In this dream the sun and the moon and the eleven stars bowed to me."

This time even his father Jacob scolded him, saying, "What is this dream that you have dreamed? Shall your mother and your brothers indeed come to bow down before you?"

Which mother was Jacob referring to? Rachel was dead – Rachel who had borne Joseph, and then died, giving birth to little Benjamin. Was Jacob thinking of Leah, Rachel's elder sister, who had given him six sons and a daughter? Or Bilhah or Zilpah, the maids, who had each given him two sons? Or was he, deep in his heart, still thinking of Rachel, the one he most loved? Could it be, that after all these years, more than ten, Jacob still did not, deep in his heart, believe in Rachel's death?

There is something in all of us that shares this disbelief, especially after we have lost those dearest to us. I still want to turn to my mother, saying, "Mother, you're the only one who knows about this –" It is a reflex that will never completely vanish. The mortal fact of my husband Hugh's death is still, sometimes, a matter for total disbelief.

Many African tribes do not believe in the deaths of their members, but hold that they are still available, can be talked to, conferred with, asked for advice. Across the world and across time in the Episcopal Church (and in other liturgical churches) we celebrate All Saints' Day and talk about that great cloud of witnesses with which we are surrounded – all those, known and unknown, who have gone before us. We talk of the communion of saints, and by saints we mean not only those especially endowed with holiness, but the saints as all of God's people. This communion is the gift to us of the Resurrection. So, although the death of this mortal body is undeniable, in a very deep way we do not believe in death. I believe that it was Rachel in Jacob's heart when he referred to "your mother." Joseph's mother in fact. Jacob's beloved always.

Joseph's brothers were poisoned by envy. But his father observed and thought about what Joseph had told about his dreams. Perhaps the old man was secretly proud that his favored son was going to be a great man. He was rich, old Jacob, having settled in the land of Canaan, but keeping himself apart from the natives who worshiped alien gods. These natives were, in fact, distant cousins, being descended from Noah's son, Ham. But they worshiped the storm god Baal, giver of rain, which was desperately needed in this desert land; and they worshiped Mot, a god who could strike those he disliked with sterility and death. Goddesses were part of the Canaanite pantheon, too, fertility goddesses who ruled over the crops and animals.

Jacob held to the one god he had chosen, the God of his father, Isaac, and his grandfather, Abraham. And he prospered; his flocks increased in number so much that his sons had to take the beasts further and further afield to find pasture.

Joseph, the braggart, like the baby brother, Benjamin, was not given his full share of the work, and this, too, was resented.

Joseph was fourteen, more than old enough to pull his own weight. In those days so many thousands of years ago, a lad was a man at fourteen, and most girls were married, and had borne children.

Being the favored one is lonely. Benjamin, the baby, was pampered in a different way, adored by Dinah, the one sister, worshiped by the two concubines. He was happy, easily pleased, demanded little. He did not remember his mother and accepted, without question, the mothering of the other women. He was not a question-asker.

But Joseph was inquisitive, wanting to know everything.

"Why does the moon get bigger and then smaller and then bigger?" He was not satisfied when Bilhah, who had been Rachel's maid, told him that the goddess ruled the moon. "What is the goddess like? Is she beautiful? Why don't we have a goddess? Does a goddess look like my mother?"

Bilhah put her finger to her lips. "Hush."

"Why?"

"Your father doesn't approve of goddesses."

He turned to Zilpah, Leah's maid. "Why is the sun so hot that it withers the crops? Why did El put the stars in the sky since they're not bright enough to see by? Why?"

When he was given answers, they were simple, because the world then was a smaller and simpler world than ours. The sun and the moon and the stars were put in the sky by the Creator for the benefit of human beings. Crops, calving, lambing, all were determined by the rhythm of the heavenly bodies which in turn determined the essential rain, and the cycles of the females of all species. The cosmology of creation was accepted, rather than understood. It was a knowledge which had been passed down from Abraham to Isaac, from Isaac to Jacob, and which Jacob was now passing on to his twelve sons.

Twelve sons. Four mothers. Polygamy was customary. There were more women than men. The planet was sparsely populated and sons were important. *"As arrows are in the hand of a mighty man, so are the children of the youth. Happy the man that hath his quiver full of them; they shall not be ashamed, but they shall speak with the enemies in the gate."* Thus spoke the psalmist centuries later.

For a man to have a quiver full of sons, he needed more than one wife and, in addition, concubines. As far as we know, it was not the custom for a woman to have more than one husband. Because men were killed in skirmishes with other tribes, or by wild animals when they were out hunting, there were extra women, and surely it seemed the kindest thing to take these otherwise superfluous women into the family circle as wives. Customs tend to reflect the realities of a time and culture. We, of the late twentieth century, have tended to impose our own mores on others, without trying to find out why certain customs have arisen. Because we have failed to listen to each other's stories, we are becoming a fragmented human race.

I try to listen to the story of Joseph and his brothers, and of his father, Jacob, because it is a story of human beings becoming more human through their adventures and misadventures. The story of Joseph is the journey of a spoiled and selfish young man finally becoming, through betrayal, anger, abandonment, unfairness, and pain, a full and complex human being. I have much to learn from his story.

Jacob and his sons lived in a masculine world, with a masculine God, surrounded by alien deities, many of them feminine, who directed the planting of the crops. It was a polytheistic world full of rivalry, each tribe convinced of the superiority of its own particular deity. The One God of the Hebrew, the God who is One, the God who is All, was still remote. A pantheon of gods was accepted by our forbears, as the psalmist makes quite clear: *"Whose god is like unto our god?"* Or, *"Among the gods there is none like unto thee, O Lord; there is not one that can do what you do."* It was normal to assume that one's own particular god was more potent than other peoples' gods.

And yet for Joseph and his family there was also the paradoxical and contradictory belief that God, the Creator, had made everything, the earth with its seas and land masses and all the various species of fish and birds and animals and finally, as the culmination, the triumph of creation, man – male and female. Homo sapiens, the creature who knows. We know that we know and consequently we ask unanswerable questions.

Joseph's questions were simpler than ours, but still questions.

When Joseph's mother, Rachel, left the home of her father, Laban, the home where she had grown up, where she had married Jacob, where she had finally given birth to Joseph, she took with her – stole – her father's household gods, her teraphim, the little clay creatures who might make the rain fall, the sun burn less harshly, the journey safe. But they had not kept Rachel from death, those little teraphim. They were idols, man-made things. What kind of power did they have? Why did Rachel treasure them enough to steal them from her father? To lie, in order to keep them? Why?

And where were her teraphim now that she was dead and the rest of the family was settled in Canaan? Had Jacob given them back to his father-in-law, Laban? Joseph – the questioner, the dreamer – had overheard the concubines talking about the lost teraphim and, secretly, had searched for them, but found no trace of the little figures.

The other brothers did not have the time or inclination for questions, or even to remember their dreams. Life was rugged.

They had to tend the animals, take them to pasture, make sure the women brought enough water from the well for human and animal needs, keep the cook fires going, peg down the nomad tents in case of sudden wind. The more successful Jacob, the patriarch, became, the more work there was for his sons.

It was good for Jacob to keep busy. It helped to assuage his unremitting grief over the death of Rachel, the one woman he truly loved. The other women? Oh, they gave him sons, and sons were valuable, but it was Rachel who was loved, Rachel who died giving birth to Benjamin, Rachel for whom he grieved.

How hard it must have been for Leah, his first wife. The Book of Genesis suggests that Leah was cross-eyed. Certainly she was not beautiful, like Rachel. But she bore him six sons, and his undying grief for her sister may well have seemed to her yet another rejection.

But we do not choose who we love, and Jacob loved Rachel.

In these late years of the twentieth century it seems to be more usual for a woman to outlive her husband than vice versa. In the early Genesis days the patriarchs buried their wives, dead in childbirth, or worn out from childbearing. The patriarchs grieved, went on living, sometimes remarrying and having children in their old age like Abraham. Old age was treasured, revered, not hidden away because then, as now, it was a reminder that we all grow old and die. In Deuteronomy 34:7 we read, *And Moses was an hundred and twenty years old when he died: his eye was not dim, nor his natural force abated.* What a triumph that Moses, dying at a venerable age, still had "his juices"!

Not long after I started working on this book my husband became ill, and I lived with the story of Joseph during his dying and his death. I grieve for my husband, and as time goes by the grief does not lessen. Rather, as the shock wears off, it deepens, and through my own grief I have at least a flicker of understanding of Jacob's continuing grief for Rachel. Hugh and I were married for forty years. How long were Jacob and Rachel married? Not quite that long, but long enough. Dinah, the one daughter, Leah's last child, born before Joseph and Benjamin were born to Rachel, was old enough to be married before Benjamin was born.

And love cannot be timed, judged chronologically. Love transcends time. And the love of one human being for another transcends animal sex (which is sheerly for the purpose of procreation). The human being, it would seem, is the only being whose love-making is not limited to the reproduction of the species, who makes love for the sheer joy of loving. It is the depth and width of love that makes us human.

Human. How do we become human? What does it mean to be human? We human creatures seem to become less and less human as this sorry century staggers to a close. We have been made dependent on Social Security numbers, on plastic credit cards; we are overwhelmed by paper forms in duplicate and triplicate and quadruplicate. The amount of legal/financial paperwork following Hugh's death was staggering, not to mention the personal correspondence.

Jacob, after Rachel's death, had no such problems with banks, Social Security, insurance. I've had to produce papers to prove that I was born ("Since I'm standing here, talking to you, it seems quite evident that I was born." Still I was told, "You must produce your birth certificate."), or that I was married; sign affidavits that I was still married to Hugh at the time of his death, that we were not divorced or living separately. Our joint bank account was frozen, and I was made very aware that this is still a male-dominated and male-chauvinist society, less paternalistic, perhaps, than in Jacob's day, but equally male-oriented. Hugh and I had had that account for over twenty-five years, and yet I had to prove that I, Madeleine, the ux, the wife, in this case, was capable of having a bank account. (Occasionally, even today, in financial or legal documents, the wife is still referred to with the Latin *ux*, for *uxor* – woman.) Fortunately I also had my own personal bank account in another bank, or I would have been hard-pressed to pay my bills during the quarter of a year it took me to get that bank account activated. One reason I had always had my own bank account was that a friend, after her husband's sudden death, had to live on the charity of friends until the bank where she had a joint account deemed that she had a right to have her own account there.

Someone said that all this paperwork gives the bereaved something to do. But I don't think that's it at all. The paperwork protects everybody who encounters the bereaved person from her – or his – grief. If there is a lot of paperwork to be done we can forget that we, too, may lose the one dearest to us. We can put out of our minds the fact that we, too, one day will die. The impersonality of paperwork emphasizes our inhumanity, whereas grief is one of the most human of all emotions.

Rachel died, and Jacob grieved. It wouldn't surprise me if he had gone out into the desert and howled his anguish, away from the tents and the campfires, alone, on the strange journey to Canaan. The ancient people of Genesis were human. Imperfect, like us; but human.

Why are we so afraid to be human, depending on legalism and moralism and dogmatism instead? Jesus came to us as a truly human being, to show us how to be human, and we were so afraid of this humanness that we crucified it, thinking it could be killed. And today we are still afraid to be human, struggling instead with a perfectionism which is crippling, or which in some cases can lead to a complete moral breakdown. We are not perfect. Only God is perfect. And God does not ask us to be perfect; God asks us to be human. This means to know at all times that we are God's children, never to lose our connection with our Creator. Jesus was sinless not because he didn't do wrong things: he broke the law, picking corn, for instance, on the Sabbath. He was sinless because he was never for a moment separated from the Source.

We are called to be God's holy and human people. What has happened? This falling away from our calling is nothing new. Jeremiah called the people of his day – the people of God – a horror and a hissing and an everlasting reproach. Jeremiah, once he had accepted his calling, did not hesitate to say what needed to be said, and nobody likes being called a horror and a hissing and an everlasting reproach.

What would that bank official, with his cigar, and his assumption that because I was a woman I wasn't capable of having my own bank account, what would he have done if I had called him a horror and a hissing and an everlasting reproach? It would certainly have slowed things down even further, so I held my peace.

Those who are a horror and a hissing and an everlasting reproach have failed to be human. When we are totally centered on legalism, or when we are totally centered on self (as the adolescent Joseph was totally centered on himself and his vainglory), we are unable to be human. When we, like Joseph, are centered on our own power we have alienated ourselves not only from our brethren (or sistren or friends or bank clients or patients) but from God, and from the possibility of being truly human.

Odd contradiction here: this has been called the "me" generation; the emphasis on self-gratification is epidemic. Yet we are also a generation alienated by our legalism, I.D. cards, numbering, all the impersonalism that dehumanizes us. Perhaps the two go together: overemphasis on self results in loss of self.

Joseph, in his pride, alienated himself (it is interesting that psychiatrists used to be called alienists). But Joseph's alienation was a result of his father's favoritism, which turned a potentially nice child into a nasty brat. If Jacob had understood himself better he might have been a more understanding parent. But Jacob was a complicated man, unable to say "I'm sorry" for any of his trickery and cheating, and therefore unable to accept forgiveness. He was never able to acknowledge that his behavior towards his brother Esau was selfish and unscrupulous, and so he was not able to accept himself.

Of course the assumption throughout the centuries (and, it would seem, especially today) has been that unscrupulosity is fine as long as you don't get caught. It's all right to cheat on an exam as long as nobody sees you doing it. It's all right to fudge on income tax as long as you can get away with it. Shady business deals are simply the nature of the world.

Jacob's cheating of Esau was in keeping with this philosophy of instant gratification at any cost – especially if the cost was to someone else. Some people seem to manage to cheat and lie and wheel-and-deal with no pangs of conscience – at least no conscious ones. But I suspect there is an inward gnawing, as there was with Jacob.

It is an amazing thing that Jacob wrestled with an angel and yet seldom wrestled with himself. And he bequeathed his complexity to his family as, indeed, in one way or another, do we all. The story of Jacob and his twelve sons and one daughter is a family story, and all interesting families are complicated, as I know from experience.

The psalmist sings, in Coverdale's translation, *"Behold, how good and joyful a thing it is, for brothers to dwell together in unity."* It is a cry of wistfulness rather than of triumph, because throughout Scripture, as through life, brothers seldom dwell together in perfect unity. Many of the psalms are attributed to David, and certainly David's children were not able to dwell together in unity. There was infidelity and lust. There was incest. There was Absalom turning against his father and battling him for the kingdom. There was quarreling and bickering and jostling for power.

And so, it seems, it has always been with the human race, beginning with the family of Adam and Eve.

The first lines of Tolstoi's *Anna Karenina* are, "Happy families are all alike. Every unhappy family is unhappy in its own way."

What is a happy family – a perfectly happy family? I'm not sure. I suspect it doesn't exist, the family that lives in constant concord, with no lost tempers, no raised voices, where everybody smiles and is unfailingly courteous. No. Wait. As a matter of fact I have encountered one family where everybody smiled and was unfailingly courteous, and underneath the surface perfection I sensed barely banked rage and terrible unhappiness.

Joseph and his brothers did not dwell together in unity. And yet as the story unfolds we see that they were family, in the deepest sense of the word. Happiness is not a criterion for the truest kind of family loving, any more than instant gratification is a criterion for joy. There seems to be an illusion in some of Christendom today that Christians are always happy. No matter what tragedies happen, Christians are supposed to be happy if they truly have faith. It's only an illusion and can cause enormous trouble. Jesus was not always happy. He was, indeed, the *suffering servant* Isaiah talks about. Happiness, blind, unquestioning happiness, is not the sign of the Christian. Even the Holy Family was not, in the superficial sense of the word, happy. Simeon warned Mary that a sword of anguish would penetrate her own heart. And, indeed, it did.

Usually in Scripture when it is predicted that a sword is going to pierce the heart, it is the heart of the enemy, the marauder, the violent man, as in Psalm 37: *"The ungodly have drawn out the sword, and have bent their bow, to cast down the poor and needy, and to slay such as be upright in their ways. Their sword shall go through their own heart, and their bow shall be broken."*

But Simeon makes this prediction to Mary, the mother of Jesus. *When Mary's days of purification according to the laws of Moses were accomplished, they brought [the baby] to Jerusalem to present him to the Lord. And there was in the temple an old man who had been told by the Holy Spirit that he would not die before he had seen the Messiah. He recognized the baby as the Lord's Christ, and took him up in his arms, saying, "Now, Lord, let your servant depart in peace."* These words, the "Nunc dimittis" from Luke, are sung or said daily in the evening office in the Episcopal Church. During the long days of my husband's dying they came to have new and poignant meaning for me.

After these familiar words Simeon goes on to say to Mary, " *A sword is going to pierce through your own soul."*

Surely this happened more than once. What anguish Mary felt when Jesus was a boy of twelve and disappeared, and his parents searched for him frantically. I remember my own sense of panic when my little boy vanished in a crowded department store, and the surge of relief when I found him. I expect most mothers have gone through a similar experience.

A sword must have pierced Mary's heart again when she sought Jesus and he said, *"Who is my Mother?"* seemingly disowning her. She watched him moving further and further away from his family as his earthly ministry proceeded. And she watched him die, like a common criminal, on a cross, between two thieves.

And yet Jesus' family was a holy family. As all families are called on to be holy; with all our differences, opinionatedness, selfishness, we are redeemed by a love which is deeper than all our brokenness, a love given to us when the Maker of the Universe came to Mary's womb, to show incredible love for us all by becoming one of us. And so the holiness of all families was affirmed.

By the time that Jesus was born in Nazareth it had become the norm in his part of the world for a family to consist of one husband and one wife. But at the time of the story of Joseph and his brothers this was not so. Family and sexual mores had a pattern different from ours. It was a permissible (though not laudable) part of the moral code for both Abraham and Isaac to pass their wives off as their sisters to King Abimelech and his son, because the code permitted the Philistines to sleep with a man's sister, but not his wife. Odd indeed that seems to us. But it was a different world, the world of the patriarchs, indeed a patriarchal world, and we will not even begin to understand it if we try to apply twentieth-century standards to it.

Jacob's family, his two wives, their maids, and twelve sons and one daughter, was the family which began the twelve tribes of Israel. And how different Jacob's children must have been, with four different mothers.

LEAH	**BILHAH**	**ZILPAH**	**RACHEL**
REUBEN			
SIMEON			
LEVI			
JUDAH			
	DAN		
	NAPHTALI		
		GAD	
		ASHER	
ISSACHAR			
ZEBULUN			
DINAH			
			JOSEPH
			BENJAMIN

Jacob had been tricked into marrying Leah before he married his beloved Rachel, and Leah bore him Reuben, his first son. And then came Simeon, Levi, and Judah.

To Rachel's sorrow she seemed unable to bear children. Sorrow and humiliation it was, for in those days if a woman was barren it was considered to be her fault. So, according to the custom of the time she sent her maid servant, Bilhah, to Jacob to have children for her, and Bilhah bore Dan and Naphtali. Then Leah, thinking that she was through childbearing, sent her maid servant, Zilpah, in to Jacob, and she bore Gad and Asher. Then Leah conceived again, and bore Issachar and Zebulun, and then her only daughter, Dinah. And then, at last, Rachel conceived, and gave birth to Joseph. And, in the end, to Benjamin. Reuben, Simeon, Levi, Judah, Dan, Naphtali, Gad, Asher, Issachar, Zebulun, (Dinah), Joseph, and Benjamin. And of all the brothers it is Joseph, the penultimate son, whose story we know best.

Joseph's story starts with dissension. He brags of his dreams and infuriates his brothers. Then, when he is seventeen, he is out feeding his father's flocks, as David was to do many generations later. Joseph was with his brothers, Dan and Naphtali, who were Bilhah's sons, and with Gad and Asher, who were Zilpah's sons. Bilhah was Rachel's maid, and Zilpah was Leah's maid, and the sons of the two maids may have been made to feel inferior to the sons of the wives.

Joseph left the sons of the maids, and went to his father with *an evil report*. In the southern United States this would be called "bad-mouthing," and in checking several Bible translations I have not found out exactly who was bad-mouthing whom, or what the evil report was. But someone was the teller of ill tales, and this never brings good.

But Joseph, the favored one, went tattling to his father, for Jacob *loved Joseph more than all his children, because he was the son of his old age, and he made him a coat of many colors*.

What about little Benjamin? Was he too poignant a reminder of Rachel's death?

A family of twelve or thirteen children used to be commonplace. It is not, nowadays (though there have been times when I have felt that there are at least that many in our family). A family that size is a community in itself. Almost all human needs can be met within the family group.

The people who built Crosswicks, the old house my husband and I loved and lived in for so many years, and where we raised our children, could live off the less-than-one-hundred acres that made up their dairy farm. Two hundred plus years ago they grew all their own food, eating from the garden and from the herd. They made their own soap and candles, wove their own cloth. In the close-knit community of the village of Goshen, what one family did not produce, a neighbor did. In a much smaller and more trivial way, Hugh never planted zucchini or squash, knowing that we would get the overflow from our neighbors.

Today, with farms being broken up, many being sold for housing developments or condos, with more and more people working, if not living, in cities, the family is now what is called "nuclear." The larger family of uncles and aunts and cousins is often a continent away, and so the grouping of community is necessarily different. Sometimes it is the people on the block. Or in the development. In a small village it is the nearest neighbors and the community of the church.

My mother, growing up in a southern town, was surrounded by uncles and aunts and cousins. At the four corners of St. John's Episcopal Church lived four great-uncles. Almost all my mother's friends were cousins.

My mother-in-law lived in a southwestern city – a new city in a new state – where the people in the neighborhood were divided into the Baptist families, the Methodist families, the Presbyterian families. At a further remove were the Episcopalian families. Further out yet, the Roman Catholic families. And, almost on another planet, the Jewish families.

This artificial barrier of culture and religion and race was at least lowered when a Jewish woman came to spend the High Holy Days at my Baptist parents-in-law's house, since she had to be able to walk to the synagogue and could not take public transportation or drive during those special days. This became a yearly occurrence, and though the requirement seemed outlandish to my Baptist mother-in-law, the two women became, in their own way, friends, able to share stories of children and child-raising, to swap recipes. There was at least as much to bring them together as to separate them, which seems to have been a salutary surprise to them both.

And whose God was more real? Did they not both worship the "God of Abraham, Isaac, and Jacob?" How essentially different were their Gods? This is a question I do not presume to answer. In Psalm 50, we are warned not to think that God is like us: "*You thought wickedly, that I am like you, but I will reprove you.*"

God reproves us whenever we decide that El is like us, or like our own particular group. There is only one criterion to use in deciding whether or not the image of God we are finding within us is really God's image, or a projection of ourselves. The one thing we know about God for certain is that *God is love.* Where there is not love, even if there is righteousness, or justice, it is not God.

This is perhaps the most difficult lesson of all to learn. If we love God, then we must also love each other. Indeed it would be a good and joyful thing if all God's children could learn to dwell together in unity.

Can the heavenly kingdom come until this happens? Joseph's relationships with his brothers are an example of disunity, and there would be no rest in Joseph's heart until at last there was reconciliation.

Reuben was the eldest of the twelve sons, and the one most interested in reconciliation. But he was not favored.

* * *

REUBEN

I was never anybody's favorite. Elder sons tend not to fare well in my genealogy, despite the emphasis on primogeniture. Cain killed his younger brother and is not likely to be forgotten for it. Ishmael was sent into exile, leaving the favored younger brother, Isaac, at home. Of my Grandfather Isaac's two sons, my father, Jacob, the younger son, got all the plums. And there's an old story of a younger son who took all his share of his father's money and squandered it on women and riotous living, and yet, when he hit the bottom, and came home, his father gave a big party, and the elder brother went out and sulked. It is not an advantage to be the firstborn.

And I was a disappointment to my mother, Leah, who had hoped that when she gave my father a son he would come to love her. But he had eyes only for the younger sister (the younger, again!) Rachel, the beauty, and the clever one. My mother was loving, and tender-eyed, and wouldn't have been considered bad-looking if she hadn't always been compared to Rachel.

It wasn't that my father disliked me. He was pleased to have a son. But my mother was Leah, not his adored Rachel, and my birth didn't turn his – well, fondness is the best I can call it – for Leah into love. I was a disappointment all round.

So were my mother's next three sons, though her fourth-born, Judah, ended up doing pretty well for himself. We four were fairly close in age, and we played together a lot, quarreled, hit each other in anger, and stood up for each other whenever anybody criticized us.

But none of us made our mother truly happy because our births didn't change anything between her and our father. On the other hand, our Aunt Rachel was jealous because our mother, Leah, had babies, and she was barren. She was beautiful, oh, was our Aunt Rachel ever beautiful, and when I was little I would have liked to sit on her lap. But when I tried to climb up on her she pushed me away and burst into tears.

Our mother didn't conceive again immediately after her fourth son, Judah, was born, and she was still trying to get our father to love her. It was a long time before I understood that a man could go to a woman's tent, and do all the things done to a woman who is loved, without love being there. Our father tolerated our mother. Yes, he was even fond of her. But he did not love her. He loved Aunt Rachel.

And still Aunt Rachel did not conceive. So she sent her maid, Bilhah, in to our father, and Bilhah, too, gave him two sons, and still he was not satisfied.

So my mother, Leah, sent her maid, Zilpah, in to our father, to give him more sons. Zilpah, in her own foreign way, was beautiful, so our father had no objection, and she gave him two more sons. What a passion he had for sons!

I was quite a big boy when one day I came across some mandrakes. Mandrakes are a plant shaped like a human man's body, and have magical powers, so I brought them to my mother, thinking to please her. If she wanted our father, Jacob, to love her, I wanted her to love me. Neither of us was very successful.

But she was pleased with the mandrakes, if not with me, but then Aunt Rachel saw the mandrakes and wanted them, and my mother and my aunt had one of their quarrels. But my mother kept the mandrakes, and my father came in to her that night, and she conceived and had another son, and then yet another, and then our little sister, Dinah, who was beautiful and loving. I was her big brother, her biggest brother, and at last somebody loved me, really loved me. I would carry her about on my shoulders, as soon as she was big enough, and throw her into the air and catch her, and she would shriek with terror and joy and cry, "Again! Again!"

Not that there was much time to play. We all worked hard, tending the land, the flocks of camels and sheep and goats. We lived with our Grandfather Laban, our mother's and Aunt Rachel's father. Laban's land was our home. We were all born there, and I think he regarded us as his sons.

One day we saw Aunt Rachel looking as though she'd walked out of the sunrise. At last she was pregnant, and had a son, Joseph. You should have seen our father. Lambs were roasted.

Wine skins were emptied. You'd have thought he'd never had a son before. You'd have thought the ten of us meant nothing to him at all.

I tried to talk to my mother, but she sent me off to take care of my two youngest brothers – not precious Joseph, of course, but my mother's two youngest.

But Zilpah was taking care of them. It was her job, not mine, anyhow. Bilhah saw me and asked what was the matter.

I told her.

Bilhah was always kind to me, kinder than any of the other women. She took my face in her hands and looked at me with her gentle, deep eyes, blue as dawn. "You're nearly a man now, Reuben," she said. "If your father is to love you, he will love you for what you do as a man. Let him have pleasure in this new baby. Now he has eleven sons and a daughter and I hope he is satisfied." She dropped her hands from my face. "You're a handsome youth, Reuben. And you're kind. You're much the biggest and the strongest, but you never hurt the younger ones. You're never mean. One day you will make a woman happy. Don't fret about the way things are now. It will pass."

I had always loved Bilhah, fairer even than Zilpah, with hair that reached almost to her knees.

When I was younger and fell and scraped my knees it was only Bilhah who paid any attention. Zilpah, my mother's maid, knew that my mother did not love me because my birth had not made her find favor in my father's eyes, so she pushed me away. But Bilhah would wipe away my tears and kiss my hurt to make it better.

If I had a nightmare and woke up screaming, it was Bilhah who came hurrying through the night to comfort me, who stroked my forehead until I stopped being afraid and could go back to sleep.

One evening, after I had found the mandrakes and given them to my mother and so, inadvertently, been the cause of yet two more brothers, I followed Bilhah as she left the noisy cluster of tents. I watched her as she passed the place where the animals were tethered, stroking the mangy-looking camel she usually rode, and giving it a handful of mashed lentils. Then she headed for a sandy hill with palmettos and tawny grasses blowing in the desert wind. She sat down, digging her toes into the sand and putting her head down on her knees so that her hair fell about her like a golden curtain. With one hand she picked up some sand and let it dribble out of her fingers.

Bilhah wanted to be alone, and so did I, but I felt I could be alone better with Bilhah. I made a noise so that I wouldn't surprise her, approached her, and sat down beside her. She smiled at me, sidewise, without lifting her head, pushing her hair away from her face. Without thinking I raised my hand and stroked her hair, feeling the fine silkiness, soft as rain. To my surprise a great shudder ran through her, and I drew away before she did.

"You grow into a handsome man, my Reuben," she said.

I touched my upper lip and chin where curling hair was beginning to grow.

She stood up, slowly, gracefully, stretching her arms starwards. "I must go tend to little Joseph or my mistress will be angry."

Why was it that both my mother and my Aunt Rachel were far more demanding of Zilpah and Bilhah after they had given my father man-children than they had been before?

It came to pass that my father and my Grandfather Laban parted company over some striped and speckled cattle, and my father packed up all our tents and all our goods and took all our animals and ran off to the hill country of Gilead, where there was to be no balm for me.

Grandfather Laban found us there, and he and my father shouted at each other, and the little children all huddled in the tents. But my father and grandfather made up, hugging and kissing each other, and we set off again, heading towards Mamre, where my Grandfather Isaac, my father's father, whom I had never seen, had his tents.

I had spent my entire life in one place, on Grandfather Laban's land, going no further from home than to tend the flocks. And now we were on a journey across alien lands, to a place and people I had never seen.

It was a terrible journey.

We came to the land of the Hivites, in Canaan, and Dinah, our sister, but no longer our *little* sister, went out to visit the women of the land.

Dinah, I was beginning to realize, was far more beautiful than our mother, easily as beautiful as Aunt Rachel, and looked, in fact, more like her daughter than our mother's. This displeased our mother. I suspect it equally displeased Aunt Rachel.

Bilhah said to me, "It is hard on your mother, to be surpassed first by her sister and now by her daughter."

And by you, too, Bilhah – I thought, but did not say it.

Dinah met the young prince of that land, Shechem, and they lay together before betrothal, which is against all our customs. Some of my brothers said that he seized her against her will, and defiled her. To lie with a man before betrothal is, of course, defiling, but I do not believe it was against her will.

Prince Shechem was not only honorable, he was wild to marry Dinah, willing to do anything to have her as his wife. She was the sun and the moon and the stars to him.

My brothers Simeon and Levi, next to me in line, said that she had been disgraced. "Should our sister be treated like a whore?" they demanded.

They were very loud. They did not listen to Dinah. They did not listen to me, although I was the eldest.

Prince Shechem, and Hamor, his father, showed us great hospitality, offering us their land, suggesting that we marry their daughters, and it was apparent that Shechem was utterly dazzled by Dinah. He readily agreed to Simeon's and Levi's suggestion that he and all of the men of their tribe be circumcised, according to our custom, if that was what we wanted, before he married Dinah.

And then, when Shechem and all the men of that place were weak and sore from circumcision, my brothers Simeon and Levi slaughtered Shechem, and his father, Hamor, and all the Hivites. It was to avenge Dinah's honor, they said, but they also took all the gold and earrings and jewels they could lay their hands on.

And Dinah screamed and screamed and clawed at them but could not stop them, and she flung herself upon the body of Shechem and was covered with his blood.

"Defiled!" Simeon and Levi shouted. I picked Dinah up in my arms, her poor bloody young body quivering like a plucked bow string, and Bilhah and Zilpah and our mother took her away.

We had to flee that place. My father made everybody give back all the gold and earrings and jewels they had taken. If Simeon and Levi were the killers, the others lost no time in scavenging from the dead. Ah, God, what an un-human lot we were! My father hid all the loot under an oak, and we took up our tents in haste and got on our camels and left.

Who were Simeon and Levi to take the honor of Dinah onto their shoulders without consulting with me, the eldest?

I never wanted to see blood again.

So we went our way, with Bilhah and Zilpah trying to clean Shechem's blood from Dinah, who had stopped screaming, and had become silent and still as a stone. Simeon and Levi rode together, whispering. And our father turned his back on all of us except Aunt Rachel.

El. It was a sad journey.

When we came to Bethel, Aunt Rachel's old nurse, Deborah, died, and was buried there. Aunt Rachel wept and wept. She was heavy with child and had counted on her nurse to assist in the delivery.

Why did Deborah, with all her skill, have to die just then? Was the journey too hard for her old bones, the assassination of Shechem and all his people too shocking, Dinah's grief more than she could bear?

Aunt Rachel started her labor and we stopped and pitched the tents when we were still some distance from Ephrath. It was a hard labor, and all the women were in the tent with her to help with the delivery, and there was no Deborah to clear them away and give Aunt Rachel space to breathe, and none had the skill of Deborah, and suddenly Aunt Rachel screamed, as Dinah had screamed when Shechem was slaughtered before her eyes, and then there was a long and terribly empty silence broken, at last, by a baby's cry. And then there was laughter and joy and then silence again, a long silence. And then much sobbing from the women.

Bilhah came out of the tent, carrying a swaddled baby to give to our father.

It was Leah, my mother, who had to tell him that Rachel was dead.

It was a journey of storms and tears, and I longed for home and the land around Grandfather Laban's tents where I had been born and brought up. I knew that Grandfather Isaac was very old, and wondered if we'd make it to his tents before he died.

We buried Aunt Rachel and set up a pillar of stones upon her grave, and then we journeyed on, because there seemed nothing else to do, and pitched our tents beyond the tower of Eder.

My soul was dark. Our father mourned and groaned in grief. Dinah was still as stone, except when she took care of the baby, Benjamin, whose birthing had killed his mother, and I wondered if Benjamin would pull Dinah out of the frozen darkness into which she had been plunged since Shechem's murder. Simeon and Levi kept away from me and that was just as well.

I went into the tent where Bilhah was, combing her moon-bright hair. Her breasts were like roses. She looked at me, and her eyes were pools of calm. She opened her arms and I moved to her and into her and knew her.

I knew her.

And I felt loved. For the first time in my life I felt loved in a way that was very different from Dinah's baby love of me. El, it was good.

I was too drowned in love to hear the tent flap lifted, but someone must have peered in, because whoever that someone was told our father what I had done. What Bilhah and I had done.

If Dinah broke a taboo in letting Shechem come in to her before they were married, I broke an equally rigid one by sleeping with my father's concubine. At least he paid attention to me for awhile, the first time he had ever done that, even if it was to berate me. He was still mad with grief for Rachel and hardly knew what he was saying.

I left him and went to the tent where Dinah was sitting on the camel's furniture, rocking our baby brother, Benjamin.

"I paid, Reuben," she whispered, "and so will you."

I left her with the baby. I wanted to go to Bilhah, regardless of my father's wrath, but she shook her head.

"No, my Reuben. It will only bring more trouble."

I did not go in to her. There was trouble anyhow.

2

Simeon

are brethren; instruments of cruelty are in their habitations. O my soul, come not thou into their secret; unto their assembly, mine honour, be not thou united: for in their anger they slew a man, and in their selfwill they digged down a wall. Cursed be their anger, for it was fierce; and their wrath, for it was cruel: I will divide them in Jacob, and scatter them in Israel.

Genesis 49:5–7

SIMEON AND LEVI sulked because they were not praised for avenging Dinah's honor. It was a time of trouble and it was a time of grief. Reuben grieved. Bilhah grieved. They were a large group traveling to Mamre to find Isaac, but their grief was solitary. Jacob kept apart, angry with all his sons – except Joseph. Reuben and Judah walked together, not talking. Dinah was white and silent as a stone. Simeon blamed Levi, and Levi blamed Simeon. Only Rachel, her pregnancy blooming, smiled as she rode along on her donkey. They were all together, but all more separate than they had ever been before.

So was I. After Hugh's death the phone rang constantly. Mail poured in. I was surrounded by love. But my grief itself was still solitary.

I kept to my lecturing schedule because that was what Hugh would have wanted me to do, going, the first month, from Portland, Maine to Denver, Colorado. In Portland it was the phone that almost undid me, looking at the phone and knowing that I couldn't pick it up and call Hugh to tell him that I'd arrived safely. But the work went well. I wrote in my journal, "Both yesterday and today the response was warm and generous. In a way, when people expect me to be 'good' they do half the work for me."

After Hugh's death Crosswicks was my base while I struggled to learn about grief, to learn to live with loss, drawing strength from the ancient hills. I knew that I would be moving back to my apartment in New York after Christmas, where my granddaughter, Charlotte, was living with one of her classmates. But for those first months I needed to be at Crosswicks, to feel a part of the rhythm of the land, the turning of the season, the coming of winter and snow and short days and long nights. The first weeks of grief are weeks when one is in shock. I functioned, kept my lecturing schedule. I think I functioned moderately well, but I was, as it were, on automatic pilot.

Christmas was at Crosswicks, with family and friends to surround me with warmth, and then I moved back to our (yes, in my mind, still Hugh's and mine) apartment on the upper west side of New York. How very blessed I was to have

Charlotte and her classmate living with me. And Lena, Charlotte's fourteen-month-older sister, was just a few blocks away in a Barnard dorm, and the girls, by their very existence, kept me in life. Charlotte's and Lena's parents had moved from New York to San Francisco the year before, where Alan is dean of Episcopal Grace Cathedral, and his and Josephine's distance is made bearable by Charlotte's and Lena's closeness to me. It also meant that my children didn't have to worry about my moving back alone to an apartment I had shared with Hugh for so many years.

Jacob took his tent with him wherever he went. He was always, therefore, "home." I had to make the move from Crosswicks to the apartment in Manhattan. I wrote, "Despite the visibility of two college students the apartment is very strange without Hugh. I am not sure where I am going to sleep tonight. I had thought the back room with my desk, but I'm inclining more and more to our own bed. We'll see." "Our own bed" it was, the king-size bed Hugh and I had bought together while we were still living at Crosswicks. Both boxspring and mattress are worn and old enough to need replacing. But not quite yet.

The Colorado trip was for a group of Christian writers gathered together by Richard Foster. Most of the writers I knew and respected; many were already my friends. But that first night I said firmly, "I am not a Christian writer. I am a writer who is a Christian." There is a big difference. Journal: " 'Christian' writing still makes me irritable, because a 'Christian' writer does not necessarily have to be a good writer, and so does not have to serve the work." And, as I understand the Gospel, the Good News is to be spread, not kept for the in-group who already have it.

Again, I wrote in my journal: "Night before last I dreamed that I was on a freighter-sized boat, and Michael [one of Hugh's doctors] was the captain. He explained that he captained a ship half the time in order to be an oncologist the other half.

"Last night I dreamed that Hugh was being given a transfusion, but the visual part of the dream was not Hugh, but the crumply, dark red, plastic transfusion bags. Mostly I haven't been remembering my dreams this summer – and why am I still calling it 'this summer' when not only is there snow on the ground here, but summer is fully over and the trees fast losing their leaves in northwest Connecticut?"

And then, "Last Sunday or Monday morning Clyde Kilby died, simply, quietly, in his sleep. Martha went to wake him with a kiss and lo, he was dead. A terrible shock for her, but how good for Clyde, past his mid-eighties, with lung problems which could have given him a suffocating death." Clyde Kilby, a dear friend, the person responsible for the wonderful collection at Wheaton College of the papers of C.S. Lewis, George Macdonald, Tolkien, G.K. Chesterton, Dorothy Sayers, among others. The person responsible for my own papers going to Wheaton Library's Special Collection. Clyde, gone from us. Another in a long line of griefs, though Clyde, like the patriarchs, died *full of years*.

"Friday night towards morning I slipped into sleep and dreamed that Hugh and I were driving along a country road at night and I thought that the doctors were wrong, that he was in remission, that he was going to be all right. Then I felt something warm and wet, and realized blood was flowing from him, and said, 'Darling, are you all right?' and realized that his life blood was flowing from him, and reached over to grab the wheel. It was the first time I have dreamed about him and was, I suppose, a dream of acceptance of his death."

But later that day I wrote, "And yet today I am incredulous. It is not possible that Hugh is gone, that if I play the piano he won't come in to me at seven with ice clinking in a glass, that he won't come out to the kitchen to talk while I make dinner, cutting up celery and tomatoes and lettuce and other goodies to fix the salad. That we won't travel together, give readings together. No, it is incredible."

At my next job I went to dinner with a group of librarians and was asked what my life is like, "And I had to say that I don't know, that without Hugh it is going to be very different. Lecture trips like this give it a kind of consistency. I was thinking last night as I got into bed that I have done this same bedtime routine many a time after a lecture, so it is familiar and comfortable. The only difference is that I can't pick up the phone and hear Hugh's voice on the other end of the wire."

Moving back to the apartment was difficult. Simeon felt displaced picking up his tent and moving from Grandfather Laban's land. I felt displaced in my own apartment. In order to have my desk in my bedroom, which was essential with the girls in the other two rooms, I had to get rid of the king-size bed. Our building was covered with scaffolding, as it had been for over four years, with the old stonework all being pointed, which hadn't been done since the apartment was built in 1912. Hugh and I had planned to redecorate as soon as the scaffolding came down. Now I would have to do it alone – but the scaffolding was still up. I moved the guest room bed and my desk into Hugh's and my bedroom with the help of young friends who did all the physical labor.

The scaffolding remained, but old traditions were gone forever. New ones came in to take their place. One evening I wanted to have some friends in for dinner. So did the girls. So we had a combined dinner party. To my joy the girls loved this chronological mix, and we got in the habit of multigenerational dinner parties, assembling together as many decades as possible. As has always been my bargain, I did the cooking, and the girls cleaned up. I'll cook for almost any number (my record as of now is fifty-eight) as long as the kitchen is taken care of after dinner.

How wonderful it is for me to have these splendid young women doing a good job of "bringing me up."

What would have happened to Jacob after Rachel's death if he hadn't had the support of and the responsibility for his large family?

My granddaughters and their friends keep me in the midst of things, help me to live in the chaos that comes when we rearrange beds and desks, and try to clean and polish the old apartment.

Jacob didn't have any such citified problems. His home was his tent wherever it was pitched. He had no phone. No warm bathtub in which to relax and ease sore muscles. No beds with sheets and blankets. What must the smell have been like?

But grief is grief, in the desert, in the city, in a tent or in a hotel.

And Jacob came to his father in Mamre, where Abraham and Isaac sojourned. And Isaac was a hundred and eighty years old. And Isaac gave up the ghost and died, and was gathered unto his people, being old and full of days, and his sons Esau and Jacob buried him. And Jacob dwelt in the land where his father was a stranger, in the land of Canaan.

Another death, another grief. But Jacob and his family settled down in Canaan, and there the younger children, Joseph and Benjamin, grew up. It was home to them, as Grandfather Laban's land had been to the others.

One day Jacob asked Joseph to go check on his brothers who were tending their father's flock in Shechem.

Where? I thought, startled as I read that. Yes, it appears to be the same place where Simeon and Levi murdered young Shechem, the prince of that land. There are many things in Scripture that are not to be understood, perhaps because so many years have passed that things have been left out, or added to, or shifted around. Or perhaps we are simply expected to understand, as Jesus expected his listeners to understand when he referred to passages in the Old Testament.

Joseph went to do his father's bidding, but he could not find his brothers. A man asked him, *"What are you looking for?"*

And he said, "I'm looking for my brothers. Do you know where they're feeding their flocks?" And the man said, "They've left here. I heard them say, 'Let's go to Dothan.'" So Joseph went after his brothers and found them in Dothan.

And when they saw him from a distance, before he came near them, they conspired together to slay him. And they said to one another, "Behold, here comes the dreamer. Let us slay him and cast him into some pit, and we will say, 'Some evil beast has devoured him, and we shall see what will become of his dreams.' "

When Reuben heard this he was deeply disturbed. Was more murder going to be piled on top of the murder of Shechem and his people? He said, *"Shed no blood, but cast him into this pit that is in the wilderness, and lay no hand on him."* Reuben's plan was to rescue his brother from the pit later, and return him to his father.

We are not told which of Joseph's brothers were in on the conspiracy to kill him. It is easy to suspect Simeon and Levi who were already killers, and perhaps the place itself reminded them of murder: Shechem. But only Reuben opposed them.

Surely the sons of the two maids would have been jealous of Jacob's rank favoritism of Rachel's son. Benjamin was too young to have been with the older brothers, wandering with their flocks far from their home tents to find fresh pasture.

There seems to have been little discussion about whether or not to kill Joseph. Only Reuben pulled back in horror. Surely we should remember him well because he tried to save the adolescent boy. But when it came time for the ancient Jacob to give his blessing to his sons, Reuben still had to pay for having gone in to Bilhah, Rachel's maid, Jacob's concubine. A taboo broken is a taboo broken, and throughout the legends of many cultures this appears an implacable law: break the taboo, and no matter how ignorant you are, no matter whether or not the taboo was broken inadvertently, whether or not you meant well, retribution will surely follow.

So Reuben was to suffer.

It happened that *when Joseph reached his brothers, they stripped him out of his coat, his coat of many colors that he wore, and they took him, and cast him into a pit; the pit was empty; there was no water in it.*

They sat down to eat bread, and looked up, and saw a company of Ishmaelites coming from Gilead with their camels, bearing spices and balm and myrrh, on their way to carry it all to Egypt.

The Ishmaelites, descendants of their Grandfather Isaac's half-brother, Ishmael. It was a small world. Wherever you turned you were apt to encounter at least a distant cousin.

Judah, Leah's fourth son, the younger brother of Simeon and Levi who slaughtered Shechem, *said to his brothers, "What profit is it to us if we slay our brother and conceal his blood?*

Come, let us sell him to the Ishmaelites, and let not our hand be upon him, for he is our brother, and our flesh." Judah's suggestion was pragmatic rather than compassionate.

And his brethren were content. Then the Midianite merchants came by, and the brothers drew and lifted Joseph up out of the pit, and sold Joseph to the Ishmaelites for twenty pieces of silver, and they took him with them to Egypt.

Where was Reuben during this transaction? The next verse of Scripture says,

And Reuben returned to the pit, and behold, Joseph was not in the pit, and Reuben rent his clothes And he returned to his brothers and said, "The child is not! And I, where shall I go?"

The other brothers paid little attention to Reuben's anguish. The next verse is:

And they took Joseph's coat, and killed a kid from their flock of goats, and dipped the coat in the blood. And they took the coat of many colors and brought it to their father, and said, "This we have found. Tell us whether it is your son's coat or not."

And Jacob knew it and said, "It is my son's coat. An evil beast has devoured him. Joseph is without doubt rent in pieces."

And Jacob rent his clothes (as Reuben had done) *and put on sack cloth and mourned for his son many days.*

He would not be comforted, but said, "I will go down into the grave mourning for my son." And his father wept for him.

It is not a pretty story, but we are so overfamiliar with it that repetition has blunted the ugliness of what the brothers did.

Joseph was a spoiled adolescent; they had cause to be jealous, but not cause to do what they did. And had it not been for Reuben and Judah, they would certainly have had Joseph's blood on their hands. Had they forgotten Cain?

What a rude awakening for young Joseph. Had he suspected the depths of his older brothers' resentment? What a shock to the pampered adolescent, first to be flung into a pit, then to be sold into the hand of strangers. Who kept the money?

Sometimes terrible things are redeemed in unexpected ways. This sudden and violent separation from everything known and loved and familiar was the beginning of Joseph's growing-up. This beginning of the breaking of the pampered pet was essential to his development into a mature human being. Likely the Ishmaelites were rough with him. He was, after all, a purchase, a commercial property, and that made him a slave. At least his life was spared.

But to Jacob, to the women, Joseph was dead. Now a new and terrible grief was added to Jacob's grief over Rachel. In my journal I wrote, "Grief is different from unhappiness. In unhappiness one is stuck in time. In grief time is totally askew. Christmas at Crosswicks was only three days ago and it was years ago. Coming to Maplewood to Maria and John and the babies is a parenthesis in time .... It is time I started saying 'this winter' and stopped saying 'this summer.' 'This summer' was so fiercely intense it's hard to get out of its grip. Especially since *out of its grip* means *out of my life with Hugh* and into a new life where I'm still groping my way."

So Jacob, too, because of Joseph's death, moved into a new way of loss. How could his other sons comfort him? Did he turn to little Benjamin?

The older brothers carried the burden of what they had done, but how painfully it weighted their consciences we do not know. Reuben, it would seem, was filled with pain and regret for having failed to rescue Joseph and return him to his father. The others may have felt that they were fine fellows for having spared the braggart's life, for having sold him into Egypt rather than murdering him. In any case, life had to go on, there was work to do, flocks to tend.

And where was God, the Maker of the Universe who took Abraham out to ask him if he could count the stars, who sent the ram in the bush to spare Isaac, who wrestled with Jacob, during all this? Thoughts of God seem to be singularly absent in Jacob's sons, and if there is any sense of God at all it is the tribal god, the one god among many gods, the masculine deity who is around to help his tribe. To the casual reader this rather chauvinist figure appears to be the God of the Old Testament. Our visions of God are partial and incomplete at best. But the God who shines through the Old Testament is the mighty Creator who made the brilliance of all those stars he showed Abraham, the God of the universe.

There have been many times in history when people must have wondered what kind of God we Christians have – for instance, when crusaders slaughtered Orthodox Christians in Greece; when the Spanish Inquisitors burned people at the stake for tiny differences in interpretation of faith; in Salem where a woman could be hanged as a witch if an angry neighbor accused her out of spite. Perhaps God needs less of our fierce protectiveness for his cause, and more of our love to El, to each other.

Did Simeon and Levi think they were doing God's will when they slaughtered Shechem? Did the brothers even consider what God would think of their selling Joseph into Egypt?

Did Reuben turn over his anguish to God when he was unable to save his brother? Perhaps he wanted to unburden himself to Bilhah, but whenever he even turned in the direction of Bilhah's tent his father's suspicious eyes were fixed on him. Bilhah's consolations were denied him forever.

* * *

BILHAH

There are advantages to being a woman and a slave, a foreigner with gentler gods than the harsh man-god of my mistress, a warrior god who helped them slaughter my people, take over our land, leaving the ground slippery with blood lapped up by their wild dogs.

Those few of us who were left were taken into captivity, and because I was young, my courses having started only a few moons before, and comely, I was chosen to be a slave girl for the master's favored wife. Not much older than I am is she, and beautiful, with heavy curling hair the color of dark honey, and amber eyes made darker by the long black fringe of her lashes. She treats me kindly, if casually, and I am no cause of jealousy to her; my own beauty, prized by my tribe, not being as appealing to the men who killed my father and brothers as to those slain men who were dazzled by my pale curtain of hair bright against copper skin, my firm young breasts, and long straight thighs.

It has not been bad here. There are servants under me, not slaves, yet less free than I, who must do my bidding or feel the lash, though I discourage that.

No whip has touched me in my long years among these strange people. And I have had hours of precious solitude, particularly during those two nine-moons when my body held my master's sons.

Ish, how she wept, my mistress, she, the younger, the more beautiful, the more desired of the two sisters. But it was the elder one, with her strange eyes looking in different directions so that you never knew what she was seeing, who gave birth to sons.

My mistress sent me to the master to have sons for her. The custom was strange to me. But she explained how the master's grandfather, one Abraham, had had his first son by his wife's maid, and that it was the way of their people. The master took me moderately kindly, for if my fair beauty is strange to these rough people my body can still awaken desire. He was gentle, but quick. And when my body filled with his child I was given milk of goat and camel to drink, allowed to stay away from the cook tent with its rank smells of oil and garlic, given whatever I asked for to eat, the fruits of home, pomegranate and wild pear.

The birthing times, especially the first, were beyond my comprehension. The midwives were there, the most skilled my mistress's old nurse. I longed simply to squat, with one woman of my tribe experienced in deliveries to urge me along. But no, my mistress was there, trying to make her body part of mine, and when, after the hours of anguish, the child burst forth she claimed it as her own.

Strange people. Strange customs. However, it was my breasts that had the milk, and I was allowed the child at feeding times, allowed, too, to keep him clean, then hand his tiny perfection back to waiting Rachel.

Twice I did this for her, twice bore sons in her place, willing because she was kind and full of sorrow and shame, because Jacob was a fair lover, and because I enjoyed the freedom from the heavier burdens, freedom to take time to think what it means to be a woman.

If I had the choice, would I be a man in this strange tribe whose god is a man, rough and wild, leaping on my master in the dark and striking him on the thigh so that he limps, and will forever move that one leg with difficulty and pain?

My goddess does not come so close, though she, too, is wild, as are the deities of all the tribes. The goddess orders the courses of the moon as well as women, and the turning of the seasons and the tides tells us when to sow and when to harvest, when to plant and when to lie fallow. Tells the women to rejoice in our slender wrists which, no matter how much we labor in the fields, will never be as strong as a man's, but are more deft and delicate.

When we are children we play together, boy and girl, not paying attention to our differences which are merely genital. Our bodies for the first years are otherwise indistinguishable. Then what hardens in the boys softens in the girls. Our breasts bloom like small flowers and our hips curve into roundness. We can no longer run as far or jump as high, or wrestle friend or brother to the ground, though we may try, unwilling to give up our wild freedom, even after we have become women.

But we and the boys are no longer the same. The difference used to be no more than a matter of standing or squatting to let out our water. Now our women's bodies are warm and full like new wineskins. And when they empty of a child, our breasts in turn are full, bursting with milk. When the child can toddle, our hips are small shelves on which we carry them, sitting astride us in comfort. Let a man try to hold a child this way and it slides down his thigh.

There are tribes where women proclaim themselves to be the same as men, sit astride wild horses, throw spears, gnaw meat off bones. Their hair is full of lice. They stink, and yet the stink is not a man's. It is folly, I think, for a woman to try to be a man.

And why? When I was a child it was the women who were wise. The oldest ones could listen to the goddess in the moon, the angels in the stars, listen well enough to warn us of earthquake or of drought. It was the old wise women who were heeded, honored by the men. When a child was born, male or female, it was not merely a source of pride for the man or prestige for the woman but of joy for us all, and the goddess laughed her pleasure with us.

Here my sons were hardly mine once they were weaned, but possessions of Jacob's pride. Even after Rachel had a child of her own my sons were still more hers than mine.

Sons. How greedy Jacob was for sons! Leah with her strange eyes, gave him four. Then her maid, Zilpah, gave her two more to add to Jacob's quiver, and then Leah filled it further, with two more sons and a daughter.

I still remember how good it is to be a woman, to give an offering of love, as I gave to Reuben, Jacob's first son – to give, instead of being taken.

It is the calling of women to give. Men believe that it is their prerogative to take. I would rather be a giver than a taker.

If it is thought less to be a woman than a man, how can a woman give? It is in the nature of a woman to give love. Ish! Will I ever give again?

3
Levi

WHAT VISION DID LEVI HAVE of the universe? Was he awed by the magnificence of the stars at night? Or was he so tired by the day's work that he retreated to his tent? Certainly, if he thought about it at all, his understanding of the universe and his place in it was simpler than ours.

Simpler than ours. The planet was still sparsely populated. When flocks had eaten the pastureland bare, the nomadic Hebrews moved on to fresher fields, even if it meant pushing out people who were already there. But that was all right, because God wanted them, his people, to have the land, so the heathen didn't matter. *"He hath shewed his people the power of his works, that he may give them the heritage of the heathen."* Alas, these words of the psalmist have been behind our treatment of the native Americans, and England's Empire. Is this what God really wants?

But God, El, the God of Joseph and the Patriarchs, seems to be almost two separate gods, the tribal god whom Bilhah found so offensive, and who still offends many people today, and the God who was the Maker of the Universe, Creator of the Stars, the All in All, the God of Love who still lights our hearts.

The tribal god can be described and defined. The God of love, the God of beginnings, cannot. And we have the desire to define, to encompass, to understand with our minds, rather than our hearts, the God we proclaim.

For Joseph and his brothers, this little planet was, of course, the center of all things, with the stars glistening in the sky for our pleasure, the sun and the moon for our sole benefit. When the Creator had created the universe in a brilliant burst of love, had seen what had been made, he called it good, very good, but it had been assumed that nothing was really very important until God had achieved the pinnacle of Creation in the persons of two human beings, Adam and Eve.

This anthropic point of view continued, basically unchanged, until well into the Middle Ages. Even after the birth of Jesus most people saw the universe very much as Joseph and his brothers saw it, despite the fact that God had come to us as Jesus of Nazareth in the most extraordinary outpouring of love that can be imagined – though, alas, it *cannot* be imagined. How can we understand that God cared so much about this sorry planet that the Creator Elself came to visit? To be with us as the Lord Jesus who lived and died and rose for us? And then, after the Ascension we were sent the Holy Spirit to give us strength.

But as far as the physical understanding of the universe went, this planet was still the center of all things. Joseph in Egypt was able and willing to change his way of looking at the world. He may have been spoiled, but he was also bright and flexible. Throughout the centuries many individuals have been willing to be flexible, while their institutions have not. All institutions resist change, and whenever anything happens to alter what the institution has decided is the right picture of God and the universe – not only the right picture but the only picture – they resist. It is frightening to be told that the "truth" that the institution has been teaching is not the "truth" after all. But it isn't the truth that changes, only our knowledge. Truth is eternal, but our knowledge is always flawed and partial.

The way we look at the making of the universe is inevitably an *image,* an *icon.* Joseph, standing out in the desert at night and looking at the sun sliding down behind the western horizon, turning to see the moon coming up in the east, understandably saw the sun and the moon as heavenly bodies that revolved around the earth. That, indeed, is how it looks to all of us. We may know that it is not the sun that is setting, but rather our planet that is turning, nevertheless the evidence of our eyes is that *the sun sets.*

As our knowledge changes, our images, our icons, must change, too, or they become idols. Our understanding of the universe today is very different from Joseph's understanding, but we, too, must be willing to allow our understanding to change and grow as we learn more about God's glorious work. We still tend to cling to our own ideas, or what we have been taught, or told, and to feel threatened if anything new is revealed. What we know now is probably as far from the way God really created as the patriarch's limited vision and version. How do we stay open to revelation?

It must have been a cozy feeling to believe that the earth was Creation's center, with everything else revolving around it for our pleasure. The self-satisfied human ego got a terrible blow in the sixteenth century with the Copernican Revolution which displaced earth as the center of the universe. But finally it had to be acknowledged that the sun, not the earth, was the center of the solar system, and that instead of the sun revolving around us, we revolve around the sun.

Human pride and self-satisfaction got yet another blow when it was seen that our sun is only one of many in our great galaxy the Milky Way – so gorgeous to look at when I am at Crosswicks, our house in the Litchfield hills, and I walk the dogs at night and see it flowing across the sky. I look up and try to understand that our solar system is a tiny pinprick in that great river of stars, and a relatively unimportant one in the exurbs of our spiral galaxy. It is the way we now understand God's Creation, but it is still only partial understanding. The truth I hold to is that it is all God's, joyfully created, and that it is good.

After it had been accepted that our planet was part of a solar system in the Milky Way, then came the even more humbling realization that the Milky Way itself is not unique, but is an ordinary spiral galaxy among hundreds of billions of galaxies all rushing away from each other to the distant reaches of space.

It was no doubt a good thing for the human ego to learn about the immensity of the universe. And in this century we have discovered not only the vastness of the macrocosm, but the equal vastness of the microcosm, the almost unimaginably small world of subatomic particles. It gives some idea of the smallness when we realize that subatomic particles are as much smaller than we are as the galaxies are larger than we are.

But this knowledge also had the effect of making the thinking, questioning human creature seem pretty unimportant. Who are we that God should be mindful of us? Worse than that, to some people it seemed that we are God's biggest mistake, with our unending wars, our terrorism, our greed which has caused us to be poor stewards of the land given us to nurture. How do we account for man's inhumanity to men? What has happened to God's image in us?

Even when we list our great saints and artists, Teresa, Julian of Norwich, Bach, Shakespeare, Rembrandt, nothing we do seems very important, set against the enormity of Creation.

The God I believe in is greater than anything I or anybody else can conceive. But part of my faith is that the Creator who made human beings with at least an iota of free will does not diminish that marvelous and terrible gift by manipulating us. God is not a Great Dictator. Every once in a while when life seems nearly unbearable I might long, fleetingly, for such a God who has already, as it were, written the story, but I do not want to be part of a tale that has already been told. God calls us to work with our Maker on the fulfilling of Creation. What we do either moves us towards the Second Coming, the reconciliation of all things, or holds us back.

Yes, each of us is that important, and this can be very frightening. With our abuse of free will we have increased the ravages of disease; our polluted planet is causing more people to die of cancer than when the skies and seas and earth were clean. But this does not mean that we have to throw out the idea of a God who loves and cares.

What kind of a God of love can we believe in at this point in the human endeavor? How do we reconcile God's love and the strange gift of free will?

As a human parent I have had to learn to allow my children to make their own mistakes, to become free adults and so, truly human. I cannot rush in and correct every error in judgment, or fix everything that goes wrong. The children of parents who attempt to do that usually end up as emotional cripples. The message of the Incarnation underlines the message that is all through Scripture: God cares about Creation.

If we abuse our free will, we hurt God. If we really cared about God and Creation, how could we continue to cut down the rain forests? To tear apart the ozone layer? To forget that our grandchildren will suffer from the results of our greed? What is happening to us human beings? Have all our icons become idols?

An icon is the opposite of an idol. An icon is an open window to the love of God. An idol is a closed door in the face of God's love. We must be sure that our symbols remain icons, rather than walls, like the Berlin Wall, or the Maginot Line, or the Iron Curtain – all of which have shown their fallibility.

Whenever we get too sure of ourselves we get a comeuppance. The Church Establishment stubbornly resisted giving up the Aristotelian idea that the earth is flat, with heaven above, hell below, a sort of cosmic sandwich. It was a blow to human pride to discover that the earth was not in fact a sandwich, but a slightly pear-shaped sphere. What did that do to the ideas of heaven and hell? It staggered some people for a while. Where, indeed, are heaven and hell? Have we been able to move beyond the literalism of the Middle Ages?

When Copernicus died in 1543 he had started what came to be known as the Copernican Revolution. This Polish doctor and church administrator displaced the earth as the center of the universe. Instead, from his observations he deduced that the earth is a planet, and this denigration of our place in the scheme of things was a bitter blow to human self-satisfaction. When Joseph dreamed of the sun and the moon and the eleven stars bowing down before him his cosmology was the old one of the earth as the center. But finally, in the sixteenth century, we had to acknowledge the falsity of the old image and adopt a new one.

What a terrible shock to the establishment that had taught its people that we are the center of everything and the reason for everything else! No wonder the Church went through the furious and futile process of denial. The closed, comfortable system had been burst asunder, and this produced anger and panic, rather than joy and wonder.

Giordano Bruno, one of Copernicus's disciples, shocked the establishment further when he conceived of the universe as infinite, and filled with countless stars which were suns. And then Johannes Kepler came up with the distressing realization that the orbits of the planets were not circles, but ellipses. The circle was considered perfect. How could planets travel a course that was less than perfect? What did this do to God, and Creation?

Nothing, of course, but we creatures have often confused protecting God with protecting our own ideas. We get frightened, and so we focus on peripheral ideas instead of on the glory of God and all that has been made. We cling to our untenable position and are afraid of changing it, unable to laugh at our grand statements and move on.

Throughout the centuries many grandiose statements have been made, both by scientists and theologians, yet most of these statements have had to be revised and expanded, if not discarded. How difficult it was for the Church to let go the image of planet earth as the center of the universe! Now it no longer upsets most people that our planet is in an ordinary solar system in the Milky Way. The important thing is that we still belong to the One who created it all.

When Darwin's discoveries indicated that perhaps the world had taken more than seven earth days to make and that it was considerably older than anybody had expected, this shook many people so badly that they felt that they had to choose between God and evolution, with a terrible misunderstanding of the beautiful interdependence of religion and science. A while ago when I was at Berea College in Kentucky I was asked the usual earnest questions about creationism vs. evolution.

I laughed and said that I really couldn't get very excited about it. The only question worth asking is whether or not the universe is God's. If the answer is YES! then why get so excited about how? The important thing is that we are God's, created in love. And what about those seven days? In whose time are they? Eastern Standard Time? My daughter in San Francisco lives in a time zone three hours earlier than mine. In Australia, what time is it? Did God create in human time? Solar time? Galactic time? What about God's time? What matter if the first day took a few billennia in our time, and the second day a few billennia more?

I told the student at Berea that some form of evolution seems consistent with our present knowledge, and that I didn't think that God put the fossil skeletons of fish in the mountains of Nepal to test our faith, as some creationists teach. But if I should find out tomorrow that God's method of creation was something quite different from either creationism or evolution, that would in no way shake my faith, because that is not where my faith is centered.

Thank God. If my faith were based on anything so fragile, how would I have lived through my husband's dying and death? How would I continue to live a full and loving life? My faith is based on the wonder that everything is contained in the mind of God, all that we can see, all that we cannot see, all that is visible and all that – like subatomic particles – is invisible. All the laughter, all the pain, all the birthing and living and dying and glory, all our stories, without exception, are given dignity by God's awareness and concern.

But we get frightened, and we begin to wonder if all this explosion of knowledge doesn't make us so tiny and insignificant that we don't even count in the vastness of Creation. In the enormity of existence, we ask, Is there really a point to it all?

That there is, indeed, a point is something that all who believe in Christ affirm. We may not always know what the point is, but we base our lives on God's knowing. When we say that Christ is Lord we are affirming that God cares so much that we get the point, that the Second Person of the Trinity came to live with us, to be one of us, just to show us the point.

But we keep losing it. It's all too complex. Life is unjust. Illness and death strike seemingly at random. Our planet reels dizzily, rocked by war and suspicion and hate – hate like that of Levi for Shechem. How do we make any reasonable sense of the big things, the little things, of Levi slaughtering Shechem?

A flicker of understanding came to me many years ago when Hugh and I were living on a small dairy farm and raising our children. We went through several years when we, and the village, had more death and tragedy than is statistically normal. The theologians I was reading didn't help me, but the small community of our Congregational Church did. Anglican Madeleine and Baptist Hugh found a loving church home in the white spired church across the street from the General Store. But I was still asking a lot of big, cosmic questions to which I was finding no satisfactory answers.

Was it a coincidence that just as I was ready to start writing *A Wrinkle in Time* I came across a book of Einstein's and discovered the new physics? Einstein, with his theories of relativity, Planck, with his quantum theory, the astrophysicists and particle physicists opened for me a new world in which I glimpsed the glory of God.

I'm often asked about my great science background. My great science background is zilch. When I was in school and college the scientists were pretty arrogant. Adam's and Eve's eating of the fruit of the tree of the knowledge of good and evil was about to pay off. What we didn't know, we would know shortly. Most scientists found science and religion as irreconcilable as did most religionists. I took as little science as I possibly could. In high school I had to take chemistry in order to get into college. Our chemistry lab was an old greenhouse, and one day I was pretending I was Madame Curie and blew the place up. That was the most exciting thing that happened to me in chemistry. In college we had to take a science course, so I took psychology.

But then we penetrated to the heart of the atom and the scientists discovered that they really didn't know very much after all. For every question they answered, two more questions arose.

As I began to read more and more of the world of particle physics I found myself more and more willing to ask questions. I had been trying to understand and to define God and the marvelous mystery of the Incarnation with my intellect. But that doesn't work. The Incarnation is God's act of total love for us, but it is not to be understood as algebra is understood. It is in the realm of faith, and faith is not for the provable, but for that which is beyond proof.

I was nourished by the vision of the universe as being totally interrelated, with nothing happening in isolation. Everything affects everything else. *Ask not for whom the bell tolls. It tolls for thee.* Indeed, we live in a *uni*verse.

The theologians I was reading were not the right ones for me, with their proofs of the unprovable, their isolationism, their judgmentalism. Granted, I was reading the wrong theologians. But I began to find my theology in my reading of the physicists. These men and women, studying the makeup of the universe as it has developed through the billennia, see it as designed in such a way that life, sentient life, is inevitable, is part of a plan (God's plan), not an accidental occurrence in the development of our galaxy. Of course, we've known that all along, as have Bach and John the Evangelist and Lady Julian of Norwich and the other rejoicers, but it seems a new thought to the physicists. I'm pleased that they've caught up with it.

These ideas are beautifully expressed in one of my favorite hymns, an ancient one from the fourth century,

Of the father's love begotten
E'er the worlds began to be,
He is Alpha and Omega,
He the source, the ending he,
Of the things that are, that have been,
And that future years shall see,
Evermore and evermore.

John Wheeler, one of the important physicists of this century, suggests that the principles of quantum mechanics point to a need for the universe to produce a phenomenon like us human creatures to observe and contemplate all that has been created.

To observe and to contemplate! Indeed, that seems as much a theological as a scientific thought. The great mystics throughout the centuries have been observers and contemplators of God's glory. The psalmist asks in Psalm 113,

"*Who is like our God?*" and it is answered, "*Who humbles himself to behold (observe and contemplate) the things that are in heaven and in the earth.*"

It takes humility for us to stop and behold, to observe and contemplate. Humility, and courage.

What we observe changes us, and we change what we observe. I think of the game we used to play, of looking steadily at someone's foot, in a classroom, on the subway. After a short time the foot would begin to move.

The physicists tell us that objectivity is an illusion. We cannot observe anything objectively, because to observe something is to change it. And, often, to be changed.

So what does our calling to be observers and contemplators imply? Does the universe really need us? Is this truly part of God's plan for Creation? Doesn't it plummet us right back into the ego-centered, planet-centered universe that Copernicus and Bruno and Galileo overturned?

Well, no, not necessarily. But it does bring up old questions I haven't thought about since college: When a tree falls in the forest, if nobody is there to hear it, does it make a sound?

Of course it makes a sound, I said. The tree falls, and sound waves are made, whether they are heard or not. But according to the new physics the sound waves have to be realized by being heard.

In the survey of philosophy I took freshman year, we read some of Bishop Berkeley, and his theory that the stairs outside his study weren't there if he didn't know that they were there. Things have to be apprehended in order to *be.*

During the years when I was writing and not getting published I had the feeling that a book could not be born until it was read and responded to. The reader has to create along with the writer if the book is to come to life.

And what about we, ourselves? I have seen myself growing and changing and developing as my husband and children drew me out of my shell and into being. Surely forty years with Hugh have changed me beyond recognition from the shy, gawky girl he married. Surely his death is going to push me into further growing, further understanding.

If we are responsible for the *being* of things, if we are, as this new theory implies, co-creators with God, this gives the sentient, questioning human being an enormous responsibility. Rather than swelling our egos, it should awaken in us an awed sense of vocation. We human creatures are called to be the eyes and ears and nose and mouth and fingers of this planet. We are called to observe all that is around us, to contemplate it, and to make it real.

Martin Buber expresses it this way:

The world is not something which must be overcome. It is created reality, but reality created to be hallowed. Everything created has a need to be hallowed and is capable of receiving it: all created corporeality, all created urges and elemental forces of the body. Hallowing enables the body to fulfill the meaning for which it was created.

Hallowing means being made whole and holy by the grace of the Holy Spirit, not by our own effort. It is heaven's gift. So our observing and contemplating needs to be hallowed, or we will fail in that for which we have been called.

This hallowing enables us to have a sense of our planet's place in the universe, to understand that it is part of a magnificent whole, part of the microscopic world of subatomic particles, part of the macrocosmic world of galaxies, and that everything in Creation affects the whole. If we are willing to contemplate all that is around us, to love it, to help make it real, we are adding to the health and beauty and reality of the entire universe.

But we live in a society which seems less and less concerned with reality. True and enduring love is replaced by multiple marriages or the shallow pursuit of physical pleasure. Our standards fall. And as I think of the word *standards* I think of a knight on his horse, holding aloft his standard.

Probably the worst thing that has happened to our understanding of reality has been our acceptance of ourselves as consumers. Our greed is consuming the planet, so that we may quite easily kill this beautiful earth by daily pollution without ever having nuclear warfare. Sex without love consumes, making another person an *object,* not a *subject.* Can we change our vocabulary and our thinking? To do so may well be a matter of life and death. Consumers do not understand that we must live not by greed and self-indulgence but by observing and contemplating the wonder of God's universe as it is continually being revealed to us.

Joseph and his brothers lived in a small universe. There was no church establishment, no educational establishment, no scientific establishment. Establishments, by their very nature, resist change. The Church resisted the change from the ego-centered view of the universe, and I am not sure that our broken Christendom has yet come to terms with this. Nor has the educational establishment of today come to terms with the fact that it is currently inadequate, and that we are becoming a vocabulary-deprived nation. The scientific establishment only a few years ago drew back in shock and resistance to the idea of plate tectonics and continental drift, which seems so obvious now.

But Joseph and his brothers had no such institutions to grapple with. Their God was with them, and they were with God, although there is little mention of God or what they thought of the Creator in the early chapters of Joseph's story.

Did Simeon and Levi have any compunction about their slaughter of Shechem and his people? Did it worry them that they were murderers? Did they care about what God thought of what they had done? We don't know. We are not told. We do know that when Jacob, on his deathbed, gave out his blessings to his sons, Simeon and Levi were condemned. Actions have consequences.

Jacob's words to them were:

Simeon and Levi are brethren; instruments of cruelty are in their habitations ... Cursed be their anger, for it was fierce; and their wrath, for it was cruel ... I will scatter them in Israel.

Harsh words from Jacob. But they were fulfilled; the tribes of both Simeon and Levi were scattered. We don't even know what happened to the tribe of Simeon. And the Levites became not a tribe but a priestly clan.

Dinah, the only female in the family, is not included in Jacob's deathbed blessing.

How did Dinah feel about all this, Dinah who had not been a woman for long when she met Shechem?

* * *

DINAH

Blessed art thou, O Lord our God, King of the universe, who has not made me a woman.

Oh, yes, that is their favorite benediction, my father and my twelve brothers. You can guess how that makes me feel, the one girl child. After she had me, my mother didn't have any more children. She had, after all, given my father six sons. So there I was, the youngest for a while, the eleventh child for my father, the seventh for my mother, but I was anything but special in her eyes. Or anybody's.

It wasn't that I had an unhappy childhood. We lived with my Grandfather Laban, my mother's and Aunt Rachel's father. We were well fed and cared for, and the older brothers played with me, especially Reuben, and made me feel that they were fond of me, even if my father and his wives and concubines had little use for a girl in their male-oriented world. And then Joseph was born, and then Benjamin, and I wasn't the baby anymore.

By the time Benjamin was born I hadn't been a baby for a long time. I had given myself to a man and seen him and his father and all the people of their tribe murdered in front of my eyes, by two of my brothers, my real brothers, my own mother's sons. They were defending my honor, they said. They didn't want me treated like a whore, they said. Did anybody ask me how I felt, or if I had been treated like a whore? Did anybody ask me whether I wanted to marry Shechem (Oh, my beautiful Shechem)? No. Nobody asked me. They cut him down and I flung myself on his bleeding body, and I don't think they even noticed me, they were so busy slaughtering everybody else.

The ground shrieks with his blood. If they were, as they say, obeying the will of their God, I want no part of that God.

Blessed art thou, O Lord our God, King of the universe who hast not made me a woman.

They can have their god, their bloody god. Bloody as far back as I can remember. I think of my grandfather, Isaac. His father was willing to sacrifice his only child, his son, in a holocaust on Mount Moriah. Even if there was a reprieve at the last minute, a ram to be substituted in Isaac's place, what kind of an erratic and unreasonable god would have made such a demand in the first place? Bloody. Greedy. Only a man would order or carry out that kind of sacrifice.

Where can I turn?

I am lonely. Lonely on earth. In heaven.

How can I turn to my father's and brothers' god?

As for my father, he was still terrified, twenty years after he had foxed him, of Uncle Esau. We were leaving Grandfather Laban's, to go who knows where, nobody told me. Father separated us into two groups so that if Uncle Esau should attack us – if he should, after all these years, still want vengeance – at least half of us might escape. And he, my father, stood alone near the river Jabbok, and someone – God, he said – jumped on him and started wrestling with him. Why? They wrestled, the two of them, all night, and neither one won over the other. If it had really been God, wouldn't God have won?

Anyhow, whoever he was, he gave in to my father's insistence that he be blessed, and for this blessing wounded him on the thigh. My father limps from it still, and will always limp.

Why did this God-creature attack my father, and ask him, "What is your name?" It makes no sense.

They fought all night and nobody won and my father was still terrified of his brother. Why be afraid of Uncle Esau, funny-looking, and hairy, but kind? I didn't meet my uncle until he came to Grandfather Isaac's deathbed. Grandfather Isaac was my father's father, and I never really knew him, not the way I knew Grandfather Laban, with whom I grew up. We all grew up with Grandfather Laban, except Benjamin, who was born on the road between grandfather and grandfather. A bloody road, with my Aunt Rachel bleeding to death after the baby's birth. We could not stop the blood. The ground was red.

I was not close to my Aunt Rachel, though I took after her in looks, rather than my mother. I had my mother's long eyelashes, but I had my Aunt Rachel's beauty, and more, because I was younger. She did not care for me. But it was still a terrible thing to watch the blood gush from her.

I took the baby, tiny, scrawny, red. One of our slave girls was nearly ready to wean her son, and she took Benjamin to nurse. But I rocked him and sang to him, wanting to and not being able to give him for love what she could give for duty.

If only Shechem's seed had flowered within me. Would my brothers have tried to kill that child, too?

He was gentle with me, Shechem, far gentler than my brothers, the gentlest man I'd ever met. The customs of his tribe were different from ours. He wanted to marry me. I would have married him and taken his god for mine, though he and all his tribe were dead before I ever found out about Shechem's god, dead because my brothers said that Shechem could have me for his wife only if he and his father and all the men of his tribe would agree to be circumcised, as my father's and brothers' god requires.

More bloodiness. But Shechem wanted me that much. And so it was done, and while Shechem and the other men were sore and weak my brothers slaughtered them before my eyes.

My father was not pleased.

Oh, no, he was not concerned for me, grieving, weeping my anguish. He was concerned for his own reputation. He said my brothers' murdering ways would make him stink. And we had to leave that place, take up our tents and move. My father's god told him to go to Beth-el, that strange place of his dream of angels. Too many dreams my father had; now Joseph is dreaming, too.

I had dreams, but no one cared.

I would not move from Shechem's body.

Simeon and Levi came to me, those murderers, and I screamed and spat and scratched until they left me alone.

Reuben, the kindest of all my brothers, came quietly and lifted me in his arms and took me away. My mother and Aunt Rachel (who would die so soon) and the concubines washed Shechem's blood from me. It was all that I had of him. Oh, I would that his seed had flowered, would that it had flowered ...

We journeyed, and Rachel's old nurse died along the way, and then Rachel, and at last we came to Hebron, and I saw my grandfather Isaac, old and dying; and Esau, Uncle Esau, came to help my father bury him.

Uncle Esau was red of hair, on his head, his beard, his body. He wept as he greeted my father and my brothers, and then he came to me and touched my cheek and said, "Do not be sad. He was full of days, my father. It is time for him to be gathered to his people."

How could I be sad for this grandfather I had never known?

Why should I weep for the death of an old man who has lived a life full of years? I weep for Shechem. I weep for the children we will never have (and I would they had been girls). I weep for myself and for my lost life because now, my brothers say, no man will ever want me. Very well. I want no man, not with their bloody gods.

Where are Shechem's gods? If I knew who they were I would turn to them, and perhaps find more gentleness. Were they – are they – gods of war, gods of anger? I think they could not have been, or perhaps they would have protected Shechem and his people.

I would rather have a helpless god than a bloody one.

Unknown gods, I call on you. I do not ask you to do anything to change that which has been done. It has been done.

But would you love me, please? Would you love me?

4

Judah

thou art he whom thy brethren shall praise: thy hand shall be in the neck of thine enemies; thy father's children shall bow down before thee.

Judah is a lion's whelp: from the prey, my son, thou art gone up: he stooped down, he couched as a lion, and as an old lion; who shall rouse him up?

The sceptre shall not depart from Judah, nor a lawgiver from between his feet, until Shiloh come; and unto him shall the gathering of the people be.

Binding his foal unto the vine, and his ass's colt unto the choice vine; he washed his garments in wine, and his clothes in the blood of grapes.

His eyes shall be red with wine, and his teeth white with milk.

Genesis 49:8–12

IN THE END, Judah came out pretty well. His name was even given to Jesus – the "lion of Judah." But before that he proved himself to be as complex and flawed as all the major scriptural characters.

Judah, for pragmatic reasons, stopped his brothers from killing Joseph, but was perfectly willing to sell him into Egypt. Joseph, betrayed by his brothers, by his own flesh and blood – Joseph, the spoiled, pampered boy, moved from being a boy to a man on the journey down to Egypt – what "culture shock" for the young Hebrew! The Egyptians were dark of skin, they were not nomads, and they spoke an unfamiliar language.

The Ishmaelites sold Joseph to Potiphar, who was an officer of the ruling Pharaoh of Egypt, and captain of the guard. He was an important man who would be careful of what – or who – he bought. But Joseph, sold and then resold, must have felt like a mere marketplace commodity, sold as casually as an animal is sold. This dehumanization has been the fate of slaves throughout the centuries.

About that time, Scripture says, *Judah left his brothers and went south and pitched his tent in company with an Adullamite named Hirah. There he saw Bathshua the daughter of a Canaanite and married her.*

And now follows a story which, like the story of Dinah, many people have found convenient to forget because it reminds us of our human fallibility. But because it is there, part of Scripture, we are unwise to ignore it, troublesome though it may be.

Judah, Leah's fourth son, is to become important in Hebrew history. When Jacob blesses his sons it is Judah whom he appoints as ruler and progenitor of a royal line rather than the firstborn son, Reuben. In the New Testament in the seventh chapter of Hebrews, the fourteenth verse reads: *For it is evident that our Lord sprang out of Judah.*

In the 78th psalm we read,

"He rejected the tent of Joseph and did not choose the tribe of Ephraim. He chose instead the tribe of Judah, and Mount Zion, which he loved."

And in the seventh chapter of John's Revelation we read,

From all the tribes of Israel there were a hundred and forty-four thousand: twelve thousand from the tribe of Judah,

the tribe of Judah being the first mentioned. And *Judaism* is known as the religion of the Jewish people who, according to my research, believe in one eternal, asexual, caring God.

Why Judah and not Reuben, the firstborn? Was it only because Reuben had broken the ancient taboo that he lost his place as head of the family, the firstborn? What was so special about Judah?

The first story about Judah is a strange one for a man who is to become as important as this fourth son of Jacob.

Judah married Shuah, as she was called, and went in to her. So she conceived and bore a son, and called his name Er. She conceived again and bore a son, and she called his name Onan. And she conceived again and bore a son, and called his name Shelah.

Judah, according to the custom, took a wife for his first son, Er, a young woman called Tamar. And then what happens? *Er, Judah's firstborn, was wicked in the sight of the Lord, and the Lord slew him.*

Despite the bloody god Dinah's brothers had shown her, the true God of Scripture never killed casually, or without reason. What do you suppose Er did that was so terrible that the Maker of the Universe had to wipe him out? We are not told. Nor are we told whether or not Tamar loved her husband, Er.

In scriptural times it was the custom that when a man died, childless, the brother should then marry the widow and have children by her for his dead brother. This was the custom (known as "levirate marriage") that was referred to when the Sadducees were trying to trap Jesus, and he was asked about the man who had died without issue, and whose six brothers, one after the other, had married the widow, and all died without issue. Who, in heaven, asked the Sadducees, would her husband be?

They were missing the point, Jesus said. For the Sadducees did not believe in the Resurrection at the coming of the Messiah, as did the Pharisees, and as did Martha of Bethany when she said of her dead brother, "I know that he shall rise again at the resurrection at the last day."

So, when Er died, Judah told his second son, Onan, to marry Tamar and beget children for his brother. But Onan knew that the children would not really belong to him, and he was jealous that his seed would belong to his dead brother, so when he went in to Tamar he spilled his seed on the ground, *lest he should give seed to his brother.* And the Lord considered this a travesty of marriage, and destroyed Onan as well as Er. At least we know *why* Onan displeased the Lord – onanism, it is called – "the spilling of the seed." The names of many sexual deviations ("sodomy" is another) come from someone or someplace in Scripture, though sometimes the words have changed their meanings through history. But the seed, as it were, arose in the Old Testament.

Judah told Tamar to return to her father's house and to remain a widow there until Shelah, his youngest son, was an adult old enough to marry her. So Tamar did as Judah bade her and went to her father's house to wait for Shelah to be grown. And waited. And waited.

Time passed, and Judah's wife died, and after he had finished mourning Judah went up with his friend Hirah to check on his sheep shearers. And Tamar was told, *"Your father-in-law is going to Timnath to shear his sheep."* Although Shelah was grown, Judah had not given him Tamar to be his wife. Was it that he was afraid that God was going to kill anyone who married Tamar?

But Tamar knew that the time was overdue for Shelah to marry her. She took off her widow's clothes, put on a veil to cover her face and, according to some translations, perfumed herself and dressed like a prostitute, then sat at a fork in the road on the way to Timnath. Some of the prostitutes at that time and place were temple prostitutes, an integral part of local fertility cults. In any case, Judah saw Tamar, took her for a harlot, and asked her to lie with him, having, of course, no idea that she was his daughter-in-law. And she asked him what he would pay her for her services. He told her,

"I'll give you a kid from my flock."

"Will you give me a pledge until you send me the kid?" she requested.

"What pledge shall I give you?" he asked.

And she asked him for his signet ring, and his bracelets, and the staff that was in his hand.

When he had given them to her he lay with her, and she conceived by him.

Harlotry. The oldest profession. Prostitutes, while accepted, were considered an underclass, because they took money for what should be given for love. However, when Dinah's brothers complained that Dinah had been treated as a harlot by Shechem, they were talking about a violation of the proprieties, not about selling their sister's body.

Judah hadn't kept his promise to Tamar when Shelah was grown. Therefore, to Tamar, anything she did to get children for Er was justified.

There is a lot to be wondered about here. Had Tamar loved Er so deeply, that she was willing to go to such lengths to get children for him? Did she feel that Er had been stricken down unjustly? Was she angry at God as well as Judah? Not much is told us in these early Scriptures about the feelings of the women. I wonder if Tamar and Dinah ever met and talked about the men they loved, both cut down young and seemingly without good reason.

In those days an unmarried or childless woman was stigmatized. Shelah would have been remedy for both of these problems. So Tamar went away and put back on her widow's clothes.

Judah kept his promise and sent a kid by his friend, Hirah, who had gone with him to the sheep shearing. But Hirah's search was fruitless. He asked, *"Where is the prostitute who sat here?"*

And he was told, *"There was no prostitute in this place."* And so he had to tell Judah that he had not found the prostitute.

About three months later Judah was told, *"Your daughter-in-law Tamar has played the harlot, and she is pregnant."*

Judah, adhering to the law, asked that Tamar be brought to him and be punished by being burned to death.

But when she was brought to her father-in-law she said, *"The father of my child is the one whose ring and bracelets and staff these are."*

When he saw them, Judah recognized what she showed him, acknowledged them, and admitted, *"She is more in the right than I am, because I did not give Shelah, my son, to her."*

The primitive thinking of a primitive people, perhaps. But it does show that Judah was willing to admit a fault.

And he did not sleep with her again, but as a result of their earlier liaison Tamar had twins in her womb. *As she was giving birth, one infant put out his hand, and the midwife tied a scarlet thread around it, saying, "This one came out first."*

But in fact it was the other baby who was the firstborn, so he was called Perez, which means *breaking out*; the other baby's name was Zerah, which means *redness*, because of the scarlet cord, or, according to another source it can mean *east*, or *brightness*. Was Perez the first breech birth? From him came the Perezite branch of the tribe of Judah; David was a Perezite, and since Tamar is reckoned to be the ancestor of King David (as in the genealogy in 1 Chronicles and in the story of Ruth, as well as in the genealogy at the beginning of Matthew), she is also considered to be the ancestor of Jesus.

What a strange story, interpolated between the selling of Joseph into Egypt, and his early years there. And yet there are no stories in Scripture that do not have a purpose, a proper place. The story of Judah and Tamar tells us something of the customs of the time when the twelve sons of Jacob lived, and something of Judah. Human, as all scriptural characters are human, he was also pragmatic. He was the one who felt that killing Joseph wouldn't accomplish anything. He didn't want blood on his hands, not from any particular compassion for the boy, but because it was not expedient. Better to sell Joseph and at least get some money from the transaction.

When Tamar was accused of harlotry, Judah immediately accepted the customary penalty; she was to be killed; burned, in those days; stoned, later on at the time that Mary was pregnant with Jesus. An odd contradiction, since prostitution was an accepted practice; you just avoided getting caught.

But when Judah discovered that he was the father of Tamar's child, he immediately accepted the responsibility. Yes, he had been tempted by the beauty of the prostitute, and if she was pretending to be a temple prostitute, Tamar represented a religion which was disapproved of by the Hebrews and which they wanted to wipe out. Judah did not try to deny what he had done. Granted, the evidence was laid out before him, his ring and bracelets and staff, but he did not try to rationalize or excuse himself, but said immediately that he was more to blame than Tamar, because he had not given Shelah to her to be her husband.

The judgments of what we consider ordinary morality simply do not work when they are applied to the characters of Scripture. In *A Mixture of Frailties* Robertson Davies writes,

> *Moral judgments belong to God, and it is part of God's mercy that we do not have to undertake that heavy part of his work, even when the judgment concerns ourselves.*

And what happened to Tamar and Shelah? That we are not told. Did they eventually marry? Did she have a full life as woman, wife, mother?

And what, again, about Er? What about Tamar's grief for the loss of a husband? How long had they been married before Er was struck down? Not very long, it would seem. Certainly nowhere near the forty years I was married to Hugh, so that my life with him has been far longer than my life before our marriage. But what a shocking grief for Tamar to have her husband wiped out by God!

Our God is a consuming fire, we read. *God is like a refiner's fire.* Moses saw God in a burning bush, a bush which burned and yet was not consumed. We are to be refined in the fire like silver. Shadrach, Meshach, and Abednego walked through the flames. Jesus promised a baptism "with the Spirit and with fire." The Spirit descended and descends in tongues of fire.

Satan has tried to take fire over as his own image, teasing, tormenting us with the idea of the flames of hell. Dante understood the wrongness of the metaphor; in his *Inferno*, the most terrible circle of fire is *cold*. The purifying fire comes not from Satan, but from God.

T.S. Eliot writes of the Holy Spirit,

The dove descending breaks the air
With flame of incandescent terror …
Who then devised the torment? Love.
Love is the unfamiliar Name
Behind the hands that wove
The intolerable shirt of flame
Which human power cannot remove.
We only live, only suspire
Consumed by either fire or fire.

The purifying fire of God, or the deadly cold fire of Satan. Tamar, a woman of great courage, went through the fire of suffering. I wish we had been told more of her story.

But through Tamar the genealogy of David is traced, and then, Jesus.

And here is an interesting thing: Jesus's genealogy is traced through his *adoptive* father, Joseph, who was of the tribe of David, emphasizing that to the Hebrew an adopted child is a real child and part of the blood line.

The earlier Joseph, having been sold into Egypt, knew nothing of all this.

❖ ❖ ❖

JUDAH

Blessed art thou, O Lord our God, King of the universe, who hast not made me a woman.

Trouble. That's all that women have brought us. Trouble. My mother was not loved by my father, though she gave him six sons. It was our Aunt Rachel he loved, and that brought trouble to us all. Rachel, so sure of herself and her beauty. So sure that she was loved. Is still loved, for she still troubles my father's heart, so that he cannot see straight, not even as straight as my mother. He has eyes only for Joseph, who lords it over us all from his pedestal of favoritism.

Enough of Joseph. May we never again hear from Joseph. May we never again hear of Joseph.

My wife. She was my wife, but she brought me nothing but trouble. My sons, the children of my loins, are dead because of a woman. Tamar. Beautiful. Oh, yes, though while Shuah was alive she saw to it that I noticed nobody but Shuah. But Tamar was death to my sons. How could I give her Shelah, when she had killed Er and Onan?

And then she tricked me, dressing like a temple prostitute, serving alien gods – gods who are women, tricksters, with their moon playing tricks on our hearts, so that I fell for the tricksters' wiles.

It is taboo to lie with your son's wife, but because I was tricked into it God was not displeased with me, nor with these two new sons.

Blessed art thou, O Lord our God, King of the Universe. I do not understand your ways. I am only grateful that you accept me as I am, without tricks, and bless me with two young sons.

5

Dan

shall judge his people, as one of the tribes of Israel.

Dan shall be a serpent by the way, an adder in the path, that biteth the horse heels, so that his rider shall fall backward.

Genesis 49:16–17

WE DON'T KNOW MUCH ABOUT DAN, except that he was Jacob's fifth son, Bilhah's first child, and that he was the head of the tribe of Dan, one of the twelve tribes of Israel. He conspired with his brothers to sell Joseph into Egypt. Dan was blessed by his father, and blessed by Moses, and his children took in battle a place called Laish, *a people that were quiet and secure, and they smote them with the edge of the sword and burned the city with fire.* Once again land was simply taken from the people who lived there. *And they called the name of the city Dan, after Dan, their father.*

Then, as we read on, in *Judges*, they set up a graven image (though of what, we do not know), and in doing that, alas, they were not unusual.

In Joseph's eyes Egypt must have been full of graven images, for the Pharaohs, with the exception of Ikhnaton, worshiped a pantheon of gods, and the temples were painted with their likenesses, and sphinxes and lions and elephants were carved to line the avenues of temples and palaces.

Not only were there strange gods in Egypt, but strange people, darker in color than Joseph, and speaking a strange language. In their knowledge of astronomy, they were far more sophisticated than the nomadic Hebrews. And Joseph was sold to a man who lived in a palace, and not a tent. He was extraordinarily adaptable, Joseph, toughened by the rough trip into Egypt, where he was sold to Potiphar, who was in the service of the Pharaoh.

Joseph had the perceptiveness to look around him, to observe and contemplate all that he saw.

If we human beings are called to be observers and contemplators, this calling is given reality because it is God's gift to us (as it was to Joseph), and this is what hallows it. It is nothing we can take pride in. At the end of this twentieth century since the birth of Jesus we cannot return to the old arrogance of considering ourselves to be the only focus of God's interest. We are called to observe the wonders of creation, to contemplate them, and then to make an appropriate response.

Our understanding of the stars in their courses and our own little planet has changed and expanded enormously since Copernicus and Galileo and Newton and Einstein and Hawking. And it will go right on changing; we must rejoice in it, rather than turning our backs in fear. Perhaps on his long journey south, Joseph also learned to move without fear from one way of looking at creation to a far different way, to let his images move and expand with his knowledge. We must learn that same openness.

The discoveries made since the heart of the atom was opened have irrevocably changed our view of the universe and creation. Our great radio telescopes are picking up echoes of that primal act of creation which expanded to become all the stars in their courses. It would seem that the beginning of all things came from something so incredibly tiny as to be nothing, a sub-sub-atomic particle so infinitesimal that it is difficult even to imagine. So science brings us back to a God who created *ex nihilo*. And who then took that early primordial soup, that chaos, and made from it night and day and galaxies and solar systems and all creatures great and small.

There are many theories today which I find immensely exciting theologically, but I want to sit lightly enough on it all so that if something new and perhaps contradictory is revealed I won't be thrown off-center, as were Darwin's frightened opponents, but will go on being excited about the marvelousness of being – of snowflake and starfish and geranium and galaxy. There is nothing too small or unimportant (and surely when he was sold into Egypt, Joseph was small and unimportant) to make a difference.

Much of what I read in the way of quantum mechanics and particle physics and the new theories of chaos and topology and fractals is over my head. Never mind. The fact that they are difficult doesn't stop me from continuing to grapple with new ideas, because all ideas ultimately come from God who made it all. There's a fascinating and as yet still unexplained little mathematical problem noticed first by Paul Dirac (and there's a joke about Dirac: "There is no god, and Dirac is his prophet"): numbers with the order of magnitude of one followed by forty zeroes keep appearing, to everybody's surprise. For instance, the ratio of the huge electromagnetic force between two particles to the much weaker gravitational force between them is one, followed by forty zeroes. The number that would equal the mass of the universe is one followed by forty zeroes multiplied by itself. The present temperature of space requires the expansion rate at the birth of the universe to be one followed by forty zeroes. Now, that is all certainly above my non-mathematical head, but it still intrigues me.

Why forty? At this point nobody seems to have any idea. I have never before thought of forty as being a number of any particular significance. But wait. After Noah boarded the ark it rained for forty days and forty nights. Moses and the Hebrew children took forty years to cross the desert to the Promised Land. Moses on Mt. Sinai talked with God for forty days. Elijah was fed for forty days by a big, black bird. Jesus, after his baptism, fasted for forty days. And after the Resurrection he stayed with his friends for forty days before the Ascension. Paul, evidently impressed by the potency of forty, said that he had received forty stripes but one.

And in Pharaonic Egypt, the period of mourning was forty days. In the Middle Ages in Europe someone seeking sanctuary was protected for forty days.

And I was married for forty years.

A potent number. One day we may understand why it is turning up so frequently in the mathematics of the universe, unless we try to hang onto our present state of knowledge as the church tried to hang onto the old theory of planet earth as the center of the universe.

It was pointed out to me by a young astrophysicist friend that gravity, too, plays a significant part in planetary life. Our gravity is at exactly the fine-tuned strength that will permit the evolution of planets which are capable of supporting life. If gravity were a fraction weaker, all stars would be red dwarfs; if it were a fraction stronger, all stars would be blue giants; and suns like ours, strong young suns with planetary systems, would not be possible, and there would be no sentient life whatsoever.

Does this seem to be in conflict with creationism? Why? If God is omnipotent and all powerful, can't the Creator create in any way that Love chooses, and so expand our metaphor? The important thing is that the universe was made by Love, and belongs to Love.

My astrophysicist friend showed me some complex scientific charts which he was taking with him to Amsterdam, where he was in charge of a planetology conference. At the bottom of one of these charts, black with equations like c=2.998 X 1010 cm s-1 (and that's one of the simpler ones) he had typed out, "He showed me a little thing, the quantity of an hazelnut, in the palm of my hand; and it was round as a ball. I looked thereupon with the eye of my understanding, and thought: what may this be? And was answered generally thus: It is all that is made."

It is a great comfort to me to find a highly respected astrophysicist quoting Lady Julian of Norwich in a series of scientific diagrams to be presented to other scientists.

Sometimes it is the acuteness of pain or anxiety that heightens our awareness of God's creation. Not long before Hugh died I went on a walk with two young friends who were planning their wedding, and who were deeply affected by Hugh's illness. One of them picked up a tiny blue eggshell, recently vacated by a fledgling. And for us there in the little shell was all of creation. A hazelnut. A robin's egg. The Milky Way.

Paul Dirac believes that all of the seeming coincidences in the makeup of the universe reveal a deep connection between microcosm and macrocosm, between astrophysics and particle physics. And physicists are actually asking, "May it be that life is of real importance to the universe?" John Wheeler takes an extreme anthropic view, feeling that we human beings are needed by the universe, that there has to be "observer participation" in order for the universe to be sustained.

Are we as important as that? It could be a pretty ego-swelling thought, plunging us back into the smugness of the old sandwich theory, with the universe totally earth-centered. Or is the anthropic theory, instead, ego-shattering? What have we human beings done with our participation in the great work of Creation? Are we being co-creators with God? Or are we being destroyers – consumers? Can a consumer co-create? Are we honoring God's Creation, when our greed causes us to pollute our planet?

And here is an extraordinary thing: among some right-wing, fundamentalist Christians it is seen as a sign of atheism or communism to care about the ecology of the planet God has given us to live on. I find that difficult to comprehend. How can Christians view stewardship of what God called good, very good, as being unChristian?

A longing for peace, too, is seen as atheist or communist. God help us! I have lived in a century of war, and I long for peace. The psalmist cries out, *"My soul hath long dwelt with him that hateth peace. I am for peace; but when I speak, they are for war."*

"Peace I leave with you," Jesus said. *"My peace I give unto you."*

How can we reject that peace?

Perhaps those who view as atheist or communistic a concern for the planet or a longing for peace are also unable to see God's creation as greater than we expected. In a book on particle physics the writer, a physicist, remarked that the universe seems to be far more "imaginary" than formerly had been believed.

Which leads to the question: Whose imagination?

If it is the scientists', if it is our human imaginations alone, then I don't think I trust it. But if it is God's, if *everything* that is is held in the mind of God, then our "observer participation" makes considerable sense. There are hints all through Scripture that God calls us to work with El on the great story of Creation, because the Maker of the story is constantly coming in and being part of it, helping us along in the great drama, and going to such lengths to be part of the story that the Power that created the universe willingly limited Elself to the form of a tiny baby.

The Word: the Word that loved us so much that it enfleshed itself for us at Christmas, hallowing our humanness, strengthening us to be what we are called to be.

Christmas fills me with utter awe. The incredible sacrifice of all Power and Glory in coming to be part of the human endeavor leaves me breathless. How can we have trivialized this amazing action of love by letting the media turn us into consumers! Christmas should be greeted with the silence of awe and wonder, since the great and mighty Word leaped into the womb of a human girl, and was born as all of us are born.

In my Goody Book I've copied out these unattributed words:

"Trumpets! Lightnings! The earth trembles! But into the Virgin's womb thou didst descend with noiseless tread."

And, again, "No longer do the Magi bring presents to Fire and Sun, for this child made Sun and Fire."

This is a story so wildly incredible that the world has tried to tame it, but it cannot be tamed, and we, like the Magi, are called to observe, contemplate, stand there, bring our gifts, and offer them. At our best, our offerings make us more human. At our worst, they make us less human. When religion causes judgmentalism, suspicion, and hate, there is something wrong with religion. It has become dehumanizing, and therefore it is bad religion, and we become once more a horror and a hissing and an everlasting reproach.

War dehumanizes. Hate, fear, revenge dehumanize. There has been too much dehumanization in this century. Two thousand years ago Jesus came and called people to become more human, to pull us back to the Image in which we were created. And that is still our calling.

It is our very humanness which enables us to observe and contemplate and, ultimately, to hallow or to affirm holiness. The more human we are, the better we are able to understand who is doing the calling. It is not an abstract principle of creation. It bears no resemblance to that "humanism" which puts man back in the center and has no need for God. Were not Adam and Eve called to observe and contemplate? Yet after they ate the forbidden fruit, they became self-conscious, thinking only of their nakedness rather than the loveliness around them.

Why did it matter to them that they were naked? Why didn't they look at their beautiful created bodies with joy? What caused them to feel shame? Shame was not an appropriate response. How did the tempter manage to stir up guilt feelings? Guilt for their nakedness, rather than for dishonoring their Maker's request. It was false guilt, certainly, blinding them to the real. What God made was perfect and to be rejoiced in. Was their shame the beginning of all our sexual confusions and repressions and lusts?

When they stopped responding to God's calling them to observe and contemplate all that had been created, they could no longer hallow.

To observe and contemplate what God has made is an act of joy. The moment Adam and Eve felt shame they lost the joy. Where there is no joy the presence of God is obscured.

Thomas Traherne writes,

You never enjoy the world aright, till the sea itself floweth in your veins, till you are clothed with the heavens, and crowned with the stars; and perceive yourself to be the sole heir of the whole world, and more so, because men [male and female] are in it who are every one sole heirs as well as you. Till you can sing and rejoice and delight in God and in good as coming from God ... you never enjoy the world.

This is a perfect description of how we human creatures are called to observe and contemplate. To enjoy thus is to shout, "This is holy!" To enjoy thus is to be enjoyed by God!

It seems odd that those who take the anthropic view seem not to have noticed that we have made a mess of it, with our lack of joy, our overblown sense of self-importance. How could human creatures who have truly observed and contemplated a child, any child, then blast that child with napalm? How could anyone who has ever loved anybody plant a bomb in a plane and wantonly kill several hundred people? How could human creatures who have truly observed the beauty of the planet, who have enjoyed the world aright then proceed to foul it with greed and stupidity and pollution? With the ugliness of inner cities which surely bear no resemblance to the Celestial City? With strip mining and deforestation and smoke belching from factory chimneys – and how much of the increase in cancer comes from polluted food and air and water?

How did we get a Pentagon and a stock market and state

mental institutions? (When I was a child there was no Pentagon.) Have we people of this planet gone mad?

But it is not too late. We are given a second chance, a whole series of second chances. God is indeed merciful. It is not too late to mend the terrible damage we have done – not single-handedly, but simply in our own lives, in our own living and in our dying. We have cleaned up the dying Hudson River and a dead Great Lake. If we will, we can.

What have the advances in technocracy done to our humanness? I am all for technology when it is used with wisdom. It is technology which enabled the eye surgeon to give me sight. But it is technocracy that dehumanizes.

There has been more change in this century than in all the preceding centuries put together. It is difficult to be observers and contemplators in the face of constant movement, of shift and flux. On the news not long ago I heard that a third of our purchases in the next decade will be objects which have not yet been invented. This produces uncertainty, and uncertainty produces fear, and fear produces rage. Young school-age friends of mine in New York have been beaten up, more than once, by other boys – not for money, just for anger, as racial unrest grows.

The last Christmas Hugh and I had together I wrote this poem for our Christmas letter:

Observe and contemplate.
Make real. Bring to be.
Because we note the falling tree
The sound is truly heard.
Look! The sunrise! Wait –
It needs us to look, to see,
To hear, and speak the Word.

Observe and contemplate
The cosmos and our little earth.
Observing, we affirm the worth
Of sun and stars and light unfurled.
So, let us, seeing, celebrate
The glory of God's incarnate birth
And sing its joy to all the world.

Observe and contemplate.
Make real. Affirm. Say Yes,
And in this season sing and bless
Wind, ice, snow; rabbit and bird;
Comet and quark; things small and great.
Oh, observe and joyfully confess
The birth of Love's most lovely Word.

We need to take time to step back, to observe, to contemplate. We need to acknowledge with as much honesty as Judah that Christianity has been so judgmental and so unloving that it has turned many people away. Where are our heroes and heroines? What do we call "role models" today? How do we stop being a horror and a hissing and an everlasting reproach, and instead become a joy to our Creator and to each other?

John Heuss, in his article, "The True Function of a Christian Church" writes, "It is customary for all of us to lay the blame for public indifference to religion at the door of the secularism and materialism of our age," of our longing for the fleshpots of Egypt. But then he goes on to say that the church is no longer offering a living, loving alternative. "Perhaps our contribution in these days is not so much the evangelizing of the world as it is the Christianizing of the Church itself."

Let us never forget that *Christianizing* starts all the way back at the beginning of Genesis, when Christ, the Word, shouted the galaxies into being. Jesus lived with us for a short lifetime, but Christ is with us always – was, in the beginning, is now, and always will be.

In *Daniel*, when Shadrach, Meshach, and Abednego are in the fiery furnace, King Nebuchadnezzar says, "But I see four men in the furnace! And one of them looks like the son of God!" So there was Christ, in the furnace with the three young men, although Christ was not yet known by that name. God did not take them out of the fiery furnace. God was in there with them.

As God was with Joseph in Egypt.

Immediately after the birth of Tamar's twins we read:

And Joseph was brought down to Egypt, and Potiphar, an officer of Pharaoh, captain of the guard, an Egyptian, bought him from the hands of the Ishmaelites who had brought him there.

And the Lord was with Joseph, and he was a prosperous man; and he was in the house of his master the Egyptian. And his master saw that the Lord was with him, and that the Lord made all that he did to prosper in his hand.

And Joseph found grace in Potiphar's sight, and he served him, and he made him overseer over his house, and all that he had he put into his hand.

And it came to pass from the time that he had made him overseer in his house, and over all that he had, that the Lord blessed the Egyptian's house for Joseph's sake, and the blessing of the Lord was upon all that he had in the house, and in the field.

The Joseph who could successfully manage Potiphar's large estate had certainly matured from the conceited child whose only duty was to go check on his brothers when they were tending their flocks. He had learned a great deal.

It must have taken considerable time from the moment when Potiphar bought himself another slave, to the time when Joseph was put in charge of everything that Potiphar had: months, perhaps years.

Joseph had to observe and contemplate. For him, Egypt must have been what is now called "culture shock." He had grown up as a nomad, with a tent for his home. Potiphar lived in a stone palace. Potiphar who, as an Egyptian, probably worshiped many gods, was not only tolerant of Joseph's God, but saw that this God was taking care of Joseph. Perhaps he was willing to accept Joseph's God into his pantheon of gods. We are not told what Joseph thought, only that God blessed him.

From our small hotel balcony in Cairo Hugh and I looked down at the modern city, dazzled at the view of the Nile, and even more dazzled as we looked across the city to the silhouettes of the pyramids – shadowy triangles in the distance. Below us on the street we heard the constant honking of horns, from cars caught in a never-ending traffic jam, made worse by an occasional horse or donkey cart moving at its own deliberate pace. The ancient and modern worlds seemed as tangled as the traffic.

There's a great fascination to Egypt, with its rich history, largely known because of its complex religion. When I was a child growing up in New York on 82nd Street, my short cut to the park to play hopscotch or skip rope was through the Metropolitan Museum. This was in a gentler day when museum security could afford to be loose, and it often took me an hour or more to get to the park. My favorite place was the Egyptian wing where I was free to wander through the reconstructed tombs. At that time one of my most reread Bible stories was that of Joseph and his dreams and his experiences in Egypt, and the Egyptian section of the museum made it more real for me.

But seeing Egypt with Hugh was a revelation to my understanding of Scripture. Abraham, Isaac, Jacob, all made trips to Egypt, which was as different from their desert setting as another planet. And yet Egypt was bordered by desert. Wherever the Nile flood waters did not reach was desert. The fertile valley was little more than a narrow strip kept fruitful by the spring flooding of the river.

I am grateful to have the memory of Egypt with Hugh, for what we have had can never be taken away from us. The sand blew in our faces as it must have blown when Joseph was there. The smells, too, took me back many centuries, smells of donkey and camel dung and cooking food and many bodies. Sound is different. The new sounds obscure the old. Horns honking: that will always be Cairo for me. And there is the sound of loud speakers amplifying the recording of the muezzin calling the faithful to prayer. Once upon a time (but long after Joseph) it would have been a real man up in the minaret making the strange and beautiful call. The mechanical voice has lost the resonance of life.

Then there are sounds of cars backfiring and sometimes the sounds of gunshots. Sounds of war, of people divided against each other. Joseph's brothers divided him from the home tents and sold him (and what would have happened if they hadn't?).

But they did, and Joseph learned. He was a handsome young man, and honest, and he honored his master. Somewhere on the journey between Canaan and Egypt he had developed integrity. He did well. Potiphar trusted him, and Joseph did not betray that trust.

Potiphar's wife, who lusted after him, is one of the nastiest women one could imagine. As soon as she looked at the young Hebrew she wanted him.

In the French Jerusalem Bible Potiphar is referred to as a eunuch, which I find both confusing and suggestive. Why would a woman marry a man who was a eunuch? Historically, eunuchs did not marry. On the other hand, if Potiphar were a eunuch, it would explain, if not excuse, the behavior of Potiphar's wife. It is more likely that Potiphar was an officer of Pharaoh, and an ordinary man, who needed someone in his household he could trust implicitly. And that someone was Joseph.

Potiphar's wife (we are never given her name) would have been well-dressed according to the Egyptian fashion, wearing jewels, and heavy makeup which was as much a protection from the sun as an aid to beauty. The deep black around women's eyes was originally to diffuse the sun's rays, and the red paint on the lips was to protect them from dryness. But they soon became symbols of beauty.

Egyptian men were also dressed ornately, and to an over-sophisticated woman Joseph must have seemed simple and earthy. Potiphar's wife wanted Joseph, and she ordered him bluntly, "Lie with me."

But Joseph refused, telling Potiphar's wife that his master trusted him with everything. *"Nor has he kept anything back from me but you, because you are his wife. How then can I do this great wickedness and sin against God?"*

Potiphar's wife knew nothing about Joseph's God, and his refusal made her want him more than ever, and whenever Potiphar was away she tried to tempt him. *One day when they were alone in the house she caught him by his garment, saying "Lie with me." But he left his garment in her hand and fled and ran outside.*

That gave the scorned woman her chance for revenge. She called all the other servants and told them that her husband had *"brought in a Hebrew to mock us. He came in to me to lie with me, and I cried out with a loud voice. And it happened, when he heard that I lifted my voice and cried out, that he left his garment with me and fled outside."*

She kept Joseph's garment and told the same lie to Potiphar when he came home. *"The Hebrew servant whom you brought to us came in to me to mock me,"* and she told her husband that she had screamed, and that Joseph had run away, leaving his garment with her.

And Potiphar, believing his wife, was outraged, and put Joseph in prison.

Again Joseph was betrayed, this time by a woman who felt herself scorned and had to lash out and see to it that Joseph was punished. She was not a nice woman, Potiphar's wife.

And Joseph lay in prison where he had plenty of time to observe and contemplate.

* * *

POTIPHAR'S WIFE

He is fat, fat and lazy, the old Pot. His belly is as big as though he is pregnant. But he does not produce. He lets others do his work for him. Just as well. They do better than he could.

I was given to him in marriage. Given to a man old enough to be my father, and who was willing to pay a large bride price and to ask little from my parents, who had little to give. I did not expect him to be as greedy for me, for my young body. I had thought that since he was old, our bed would be a quiet place. But his lust was, it seemed, insatiable, as night after night he drove himself into me, hurting me with his violence, and with never a thought for my pleasure or pain. No wonder he was exhausted by day and let others do for him any work he could escape.

I found love, then, with one of the young servants who was

gentle with me, concerned for my needs, waking in me undreamed-of pleasure. But he left, moving away from our household, leaving me aroused but, after his leaving, with no way to satisfy my need. And Potiphar grew more and more demanding. I do not know whether or not he suspected the young servant, or whether or not his suspicion caused my lover's departure.

I am beautiful. I could have anyone I wanted, and I sometimes did. But I was no longer satisfied.

Then the young Hebrew came, bought from some wandering Ishmaelites. Oh, he was beautiful, with his curling hair and beard, his lean young body, his dark, exciting eyes. At first he simply did his work, quietly, not speaking, for he did not know our language. Then, as he began to be able to speak, Potiphar gave him more and more responsibility until he was managing first our household, and, at last, the entire estate.

Why, I thought, had Potiphar bought him, if not for me?

So I turned to him, the young Hebrew. I offered myself to him.

And he said No. Something about his god and honoring Potiphar or not dishonoring Potiphar or some such nonsense.

He has only one god, so I went to the temple of Isis, or Osiris, and On, to temples whose gods are vultures, or crocodiles, or great, venomous snakes. Surely all our gods can override his one god.

And still he said No. I rimmed my eyes with more than the usual kohl, rouged my lips and cheeks and the lobes of my ears, oiled and perfumed my hair.

And all I got for my pains was his garment, and with it I destroyed him. Potiphar has thrown him into jail, and that will be the end of him.

But oh! I wish he had not gone.

6

Naphtali

is a hind let loose, he giveth goodly words.
Genesis 49:21

NAPHTALI WAS BILHAH'S SECOND SON, Jacob's sixth, and we don't know much more about him than we do about Dan. He was the head of the tribe that bore his name, and he shared his territory with the Canaanites. Twice his tribe answered the call of Gideon to battle against invading Midianites.

Jacob blesses this son, but tells him that although he was born a mountain ewe, wild and free, he would give birth to lambs in the fold, a veiled warning that Naphtali's land would lose its independence. Moses, too, blesses him, saying, *"Naphtali, sated with favor, and filled with Yahweh's blessing, possesses the sea and the high lands."* And, in the Song of Deborah, Naphtali is lauded with Zebulun for helping in the bloody battle against Sisera.

Otherwise we know little about him. He went along with most of the other brothers in selling Joseph into Egypt as a slave.

Joseph had done so well in Potiphar's house that again he was specially favored (much as Jacob had favored him). Yet once again he was betrayed. It must have been bitter indeed for Joseph to be put in jail by Potiphar because he had refused to betray his master. And perhaps Potiphar did not escape a tug of jealousy; Joseph was younger than he, handsome, and in the full strength of his youth.

What must Joseph have thought about as he lay in prison? There were as yet no Psalms to comfort him, no written Scripture to give him guidance and hope. Again, he was plunged into the darkness of betrayal, alone with his thoughts, in a strange land among strange people. And this time he had been slandered as well as betrayed.

Slander from the mouth of a selfish and greedy woman is more understandable than slander from those who loudly proclaim themselves as Christians. Potiphar's wife slandered because she didn't get her own way. "Christians" often appear to slander for love of slander. "Christian" groups – or individuals – read books *looking for* key words which will enable them to say the book is not Christian, or that it is pornographic.

I have received a good bit of this treatment. When *A Wrinkle in Time* was yet again attacked during Hugh's last summer, at a time when he was at home between hospital stays, he said, "They are afraid," and I suspect that he was right. It is particularly ironic that this book should come under fire since it was the book – my seventh – with which I realized that my work is vocation, not career. My work is God's gift to me, and I try to serve it, and in *Wrinkle* I was writing about that perfect love that casts out fear.

One night when I had received a gratuitous attack on one of my books by a woman concerned with smelling out books she considered unChristian – and her tools for condemnation did not include either reading the book or knowing what it was about – I turned to Scripture for comfort and perspective and opened to the Beatitudes and read, suddenly in a completely new and different way,

"Blessed are you when men shall revile you and persecute you, and shall say all manner of evil against you falsely, for my sake. Rejoice, and be exceeding glad, for great is your reward in heaven; for so persecuted they the prophets which were before you."

This did not mean that I was thinking of myself as one of the prophets, but that I was reading about the present, rather than about the long past. Holding the Bible in my hands, I knew that I was hoping to turn all my writing towards my Maker, to write for the sake of the Creator, and not for this small servant who struggles with words in order to serve the Word.

Thank God we do not have to make moral judgments, that this is God's prerogative, not ours. Hugh again pointed out that the attackers are afraid, afraid that their safe little God-in-a-box may not be safe at all – loving, perfectly loving, but not safe in a finite sense. Or afraid that their cozy and exclusive beliefs may possibly be too narrow. But when we truly have faith in God's love, then the wideness of God's mercy does not terrify. And Hugh's pointing out the fear of the censors was witness to his own courage in the face of terrible illness.

I would not knowingly or willingly read a blasphemous or pornographic book, though I have found some on the bestseller lists. But such books do not hurt me, because I am safe in God's love. I may be made uncomfortable or unhappy or angry by such a book because it is worthless or ugly, but it is not going to hurt me or shake my faith in the joyous power of love. And maybe it will have lessons to teach me, even if they are only to let me know what not to do. But it will not frighten me, because there is no place too dark for Love's light to shine, no place of filth without a spot where Love can come in and clean.

Then I came across these words of Brother Andrew, an Episcopal monk:

... fear can lead us to a compulsion to try to convert others to our point of view. We feel threatened by the possibility of our being wrong. [Oh, yes, I understand this. Hugh warned me of this.] Or we dread the possible changes that might enter our lives if we changed our minds about an important issue.

So I must be very careful not to fear the stinging accusations, but to look at them objectively and compassionately without imposing moral judgments.

I turn to the Psalms not only when I need comfort, but as a daily *devoir,* reading the Psalms each day so that at the end of a month I have read all one hundred and fifty. One evening I was reading in Coverdale's translation, and came to the verses about Joseph's imprisonment, and read, *The iron entered his soul.* In most other translations it reads, *They put an iron collar on his neck.* But I like better the implications of *the iron entered his soul.* Joseph was still in the process of maturing, developing from the pampered boy to the strong man.

We are not told how Joseph felt about the God of Abraham, Isaac, and Jacob while he was in prison. We do not know whether or not he prayed, whether or not he was angry at those who betrayed him and forsook him, whether or not he remembered his dreams of grandeur. What could have seemed more remote to him as he lay in prison?

But, just as Joseph had done well in the house of Potiphar, so he did well in prison,

for the Lord was with Joseph, and shewed mercy, and gave him favor in the sight of the keeper of the prison. And the keeper of the prison committed to Joseph's hand all the prisoners that were in the prison; and the keeper of the prison no longer had to do anything because the Lord was with Joseph and made everything he did to prosper.

We are not told of Joseph's own dreams while he was in prison. But when the butler and the baker offended Pharaoh, and he put them in the prison where Joseph was now in charge, we learn about their dreams.

The butcher, the baker, the candlestick maker were all there in jail with Joseph. No television, no radio, no newspapers, nothing to keep them in touch with the outside world except the gossip of the jailer.

But Joseph was a dreamer, and so he must have dreamed. Perhaps by now he had learned to keep his dreams to himself.

Most of us dream, even if we don't remember our dreams. I have several every night, and I don't bother to write them down unless they seem to have special significance, otherwise I wouldn't write anything else. The dreams come in three categories – ordinary, easily translated dreams; dreams that are story, in which I may be only an observer, not a participant, but stories which are enough on their own (only twice have I used a dream in something I was writing); and the special dreams, which are pure gifts of grace.

I had one of the golden dreams shortly before Hugh got ill. It started out grey. I was with a great many people in a wasteland of mud and dirt. We could look through a high hurricane fence into a large sunny garden full of flowers and trees, and brightly dressed people singing and laughing together. But the great gates were closed against us. And someone told me that it was my responsibility to speak to the people with me outside the garden and to warn them of their hardness of heart. And I cried out, "How can I possibly be the one to do that when there is still coldness in my own heart, when I have not yet learned fully to forgive, when I haven't learned nearly enough about love ... ?"

Then I looked up and the gates were swinging open.

While Hugh was dying my dreams were mostly garbled, neither good nor bad, jumbles of color and confusion. I was tired, bone weary. I would take out some of my frustration over what was happening to Hugh by taking the whacker and going after the weedy sumac trees which were springing up and obscuring my view of the western hills. Weeds were profuse in the vegetable garden, and I made great piles of them. Almost every evening we ate out of the garden, medleys of green and yellow beans, peas, broccoli, baby beets and carrots, reminding me of the harvest psalms where the hills dance for joy.

What was Joseph given to eat in prison? Nothing like the tender green bounty of our vegetable garden.

How long was he there before the butcher and the baker told him their dreams and things once again changed for him? Not a short time. Months, at the very least. Was he ever afraid? Did he turn to the God of his fathers for courage and strength? We are told that God was with him, but we are not told of his own awareness of God.

While Hugh was dying I was acutely aware of God, far more than when things go on in the ordinary way. Without that awareness how would I have survived? I wondered, as the weeks dragged on, if I was being faithful enough in prayer. I went through the motions, said the words, read the Scripture passages, but I was not always there.

And the wonderful thing is that this is all right. We don't have to be perpetually and flawlessly faithful. Only God is that. In God's love I may be angry, I may be anguished, I may be exhausted, but I am not afraid, because God is love and Love casts out fear.

Perhaps Joseph was closer to God in prison than when he was bragging about his dreams.

And the butler and the baker each dreamed a dream, and the dreams disturbed them.

Joseph came in to them in the morning and looked at them, and saw that they were sad. So he asked them, "Why do you look so sad today?"

And they said to him, "We have each dreamed a dream, and there is no interpreter of it."

And Joseph said, "Do not interpretations belong to God? Tell me your dreams."

Joseph had learned that dreams belong to God, and that the interpretation of dreams belongs to God. During the long nights in jail he must have pondered his own grand dreams which seemed far indeed from the possibility of fulfillment. And yet he still believed in them, and that they came from God. But now, rather than having a swelled head, he was increasing in probity and trustworthiness.

The chief butler told his dream to Joseph and said to him, "In my dream I saw a vine set before me, and in the vine were three branches, and it was as though the vine budded, and the blossoms shot forth, and from their clusters came ripe grapes. And

Pharaoh's cup was in my hand, and I took the grapes and pressed them into Pharaoh's cup, and I gave the cup into Pharaoh's hand."

And Joseph said to him, "This is the interpretation of it: the three branches are three days, yet within these three days shall Pharaoh lift up your head and restore you into your place, and you shall deliver Pharaoh's cup into his hand, and once again you will be as you were when you were his chief butler. But remember me when it is well with you, and show kindness to me, I beg you, and mention me to Pharaoh, and bring me out of this prison. For indeed I was stolen away out of the land of the Hebrews, and here in Egypt also I have done nothing that they should put me into this dungeon."

When the chief baker saw that the interpretation was good, he said to Joseph, "In my dream, behold I had three white baskets on my head, and in the uppermost basket there was all manner of sweetmeats for Pharaoh, and the birds ate them out of the basket on my head."

And Joseph answered and said, "This is the interpretation of your dream. The three baskets are three days, and within three days Pharaoh will lift up your head from off you, and he will hang you on a tree, and the birds shall eat your flesh."

And it came to pass the third day, which was Pharaoh's birthday, that he made a feast for all his servants, and he lifted up the head of the chief butler and the chief baker among his servants. And he restored the chief butler unto his butlership again, and he gave the cup into Pharaoh's hand. But he hanged the chief baker, as Joseph had interpreted to him. Yet the chief butler did not remember Joseph, but forgot him.

So it goes. Once the chief butler became chief butler again, once things were going well for him, he forgot the man who had predicted this.

And the chief baker was dead, and we do not know why. Were there good reasons? Or was it the arbitrary, irrational whim of a ruler with enormous power? Monarchs don't always behave rationally. Power sometimes causes the powerful to treat other humans as mere objects. But the record doesn't tell us why one man was promoted, and another was terminated.

And time passed. Joseph was incarcerated in Pharaoh's prison for two more years, two more long years. By now his adolescence was behind him. He was a fully grown man, and though he had been immature beyond his years when he was a lad, he was mature beyond his years now that he was a man.

His brothers were far away, and even though he was in charge of everything in the prison, no one was bowing to him yet.

And the chief butler had forgotten him. Why does it seem so often to be a human quality to forget those who have done good things for us, and to remember those who have hurt us?

To remember Joseph would have been for the chief butler to recollect his time in prison, and it is a human tendency to turn away from reminders of pain or difficulty. I had a letter from a young friend telling me of her father's death and that one of the hardest things for her was her friends who said nothing. They did not know what to say, she wrote, and so they didn't say anything, and she found that she desperately needed some kind of response from them, any kind of response, but they were silent, and so she felt betrayed.

What is there to say? Only, "I love you, and I care," and sometimes we are afraid to say even that.

One of the hardest things for me after Hugh's death was meeting people for the first time and finding that they did not know what to say; they felt terribly uncomfortable, and I had to say the words for them, start talking naturally about Hugh. When people die they are not wiped out of our lives as though they had never been; they are still and always part of our history.

My friend's friends (and mine) were not being willingly insensitive to her needs. But we are embarrassed. Someone else's death is a *memento mori*, and we do not want to remember that we, too, will die. Most of us no longer have the old belief in literal pearly gates and golden streets. We no longer know what death means.

Last January I took my nineteen-year-old granddaughter, Charlotte, to north Florida with me, to stay with my friend, Pat, on one of the great tidal lakes. I wanted Charlotte to know something of her Florida roots, which go very deep. My mother's family settled in north Florida in the late fifteen hundreds with that first wave of French Huguenots – the very first settlers on this North American continent.

One day we drove out to Fleming's Island – and Fleming is one of my family names. There we went to Saint Margaret's Church, one of the charming little Carpenter Gothic churches to be found all over the South. To the side of and behind the church is an old cemetery, where some of my forbears are buried. It is a peaceful place, shaded from the sun by the great live oak trees, hung with Spanish moss. Azalea bushes were beginning to bud. The air was moist and warm. We wandered around, reading the inscriptions on the old tombstones. I had been there many times before, but it suddenly struck me that each one who had been buried there had been planted in the earth with the sure and certain assurance that the very body that had died would rise up again from the grave at the last day.

My grandfather, who died when he was 101, would not want to be resurrected in that ancient body. And I don't believe that he will be, nor that the specific bones, the flesh now long gone, will leap from the grave. When literalism about the resurrection of the body was what the Church taught, people could not be cremated, because God was not powerful enough to recreate anything from ashes.

Hugh was cremated because that was his wish, and I know that God is quite capable of doing anything the Creator wishes to do with Hugh's ashes, which are now scattered over his beloved garden. But the Church, by and large, has not grown into an understanding of a God who is not limited in what Love can do. So many people do not know what death means, and that is the cause of their embarrassment. My faith affirms that it means something, and I don't have to know what. I am confident in Paul's paradoxical phrase, "a spiritual body." Perhaps my "golden dreams" are a foretaste of what it may be like after death. I do not know. I only know that God will not forsake us, not now, not at the time of our death, not afterwards. Love does not create only to abandon or annihilate.

But the Church has not moved beyond the old literalism. In the Episcopal Church there are sometimes what are called "white funerals" where a white pall is used, and Easter hymns are sung, and it is all alleluia, alleluia, as though the crucifixion had never happened and we could jump right into Easter. After Hugh died it was a long time before I was able to say "Alleluia!" No matter how strong my faith that Hugh was still Hugh, growing in God's love, my grief still had to be gone through. Life without my beloved spouse was something I was not ready to shout "Alleluia" about.

My faith tells me that Hugh has gone on to a new challenge, to something new that God wants him to learn. We all have so much to learn – it can't possibly all be learned in one lifetime. That God has new lessons to teach us in one manner or other seems completely consistent with what Jesus taught. We don't have to know how God is going to do this; we only have to have faith.

For the ancient Hebrew the terror of Sheol was that it was outside God's memory, and if you are not in God's memory, you *are not*. Nothing is told us of what Jacob believed about Rachel after she died. Perhaps Jacob's grief continued so unremittingly because he did not believe in God's continuing concern for his creatures after death (it was a long time before the Hebrew began to conceive of the Resurrection when the Messiah should come, very much as we believe in it when Christ will come again).

But my faith about Rachel, about Hugh, must now be consistent with the metaphor of the universe as we understand it today (though our understanding of our metaphor may change or be made anew tomorrow), and that means that I have to be willing to live with open-ended questions. Many of the old certainties have been washed away. I think of that ancient Florida graveyard, and particularly of the small tombstones. Diphtheria, scarlet fever, and measles were great killers of small children, and it must have been comforting to believe that those beloved little bodies would one day rise again. I believe that, too, but with an unanswered question about how.

While Hugh was dying of cancer, so were two of my close friends, young women, in mid-life. Now Hugh's sister is dead from cancer. We seem to be surrounded by death.

But that has always been true. It was as true for Joseph as it is for any of us today. And there is more than one kind of death. Joseph had to die to his life as a pampered pet, and live a new life as a slave. He had to die to his life as Potiphar's overseer, and live in prison. I have had to die to my life as a married woman with a dearly loved husband, and live a new life which, while it is full and rich, is different, totally different.

Joseph's life as a prisoner came to an end.

And it came to pass at the end of two full years, that Pharaoh dreamed: and behold, he stood by the river. And behold, there came up out of the river seven well-favored kine and fat-fleshed, and they fed in a meadow. And behold, seven other kine came up after them out of the river, ill-favored and lean-fleshed; and stood by the other kine upon the brink of the river. And the ill-favored and lean-fleshed kine did eat up the seven well-favored and fat kine. So Pharaoh awoke.

And he slept and dreamed the second time, and behold, seven ears of corn came up upon one stalk, full and good. And behold, seven thin ears blasted with the east wind sprang up after them. And the seven thin ears devoured the seven full and good ears.

Pharaoh was troubled by these dreams, and he called for all his magicians and wise men, but nobody was able to interpret the dreams for him.

Then the chief butler, who had been in prison with Joseph, suddenly remembered him, and his interpretation of dreams, and told the Pharaoh about him. Pharaoh immediately sent for Joseph, who shaved himself, and changed his clothing, and was brought from the prison to Pharaoh.

Pharaoh told Joseph about his dream, and that no one could interpret it. *"But I have heard said of you that you can understand a dream and interpret it."*

Joseph answered Pharaoh as he had answered the butcher and the baker. *"It is not in me; it is God."* In this way we are told a good deal about what Joseph thought of God. Joseph in his short life had been through as much radical change as we have gone through in our understanding of Creation, and had been able to accept the change and learn from it.

Pharaoh told Joseph his dreams, and Joseph said,

"God has showed Pharaoh what he is about to do. The seven good kine are seven good years, and the seven good ears are seven years: the dream is one. And then seven thin and ill-favored kine that came up after the seven years, and the seven empty ears blasted with the east wind shall be seven years of famine. This is the thing I have told Pharaoh: what God is going to do he has shown Pharaoh. There will be seven years of great plenty throughout all the land of Egypt, and after them shall arise seven years of famine, and the plenty shall be forgotten in the land of Egypt, and the famine will consume the land."

Joseph continued by telling Pharaoh that because the dream was dreamed twice, it was a sign that it was established by God, and God would bring it to pass. So Joseph suggested that Pharaoh

"look for a man discreet and wise, and set him over the land of Egypt. Let Pharaoh do this, and let him appoint officers over the land, and take up the fifth part of the land of Egypt in the seven plenteous years. And let them gather all the food of those good years, and lay up corn under the hand of Pharaoh, and let them keep food in the cities. And that food shall be for store to the land against the seven years of famine which shall be in the land of Egypt, that the land perish not through the famine."

We all know the familiar story. What Joseph said was appreciated by Pharaoh, who set Joseph over his house, as Potiphar had set Joseph over his house. But this time Joseph had authority over an entire land, the powerful land of Egypt. Pharaoh took off his own ring and put it on Joseph's hand, and dressed him royally, with a gold chain around his neck. He gave Joseph an Egyptian name, Zaphenath-Paneah (which fortunately we don't need to remember); he also gave him an Egyptian wife, Asenath, the daughter of the priest of On. So Joseph went out and surveyed all the land of Egypt.

And Joseph was thirty years old when he stood before Pharaoh, king of Egypt.

From prison to palace. Again it had happened.

From the favored son of an old man to the victim of his brothers. From being sold into Egypt to Potiphar's steward. From steward to being the imprisoned victim of Potiphar's wife's lust. From prison to palace. Incredible reversals.

Most of our reversals are not nearly so dramatic.

Drama is easier than dailiness. Drama lends us a surge of adrenalin that gives us energy we didn't know we had. In the midst of crisis we are too busy to worry about ourselves or to indulge in self-pity.

It is never even hinted that Joseph whined or despaired during his long years in prison. The iron that was in his soul strengthened him. If ever he was in an iron collar it can't have been for long, since he took care of all the prisoners and all that went on in the prison. He managed to remain strong in spite of what must have been a tedious dailiness that we can hardly imagine.

In one of my reference books I read that Abraham left Ur in Chaldea around 2100 B.C. So if we go from Abraham to Isaac to Jacob to Joseph, Joseph must have lived around four thousand years ago. Two thousand years from Joseph to Jesus, two thousand years from Jesus to our own time.

* * *

A PRISONER

I know why I am here. I stole. I got in a fight and I killed a man. If ever it is right to take a man out of the light of day and put him in the dark of prison, it was right to put me here.

At night I dream, but I do not tell my dreams, for there is a man here (a prisoner, but in charge of us) who interprets dreams and says the interpreter is God. The butler, he said, would be restored to his former position, and the baker, he said, would lose his head.

And so I do not tell my dreams. I have lost enough without losing my head, too. But I have told him that I killed a man in a stupid quarrel.

I was punished justly, because I was getting what my deed deserved. But this man, this Joseph, has done nothing wrong.

I told him my story: I did not mean to kill. When I stole, I stole knowingly. I am an excellent thief. But knowingly I did not kill. It seems my hands still bear the stain of blood.

He listens to me. Quietly. He speaks words of neither condemnation nor excuse. He gives me work to do, to help him in the prison. I scrub the stone floors, and the water helps wash the blood from my hands. One night when a prisoner, an old man, is coughing his life away, Joseph has me stay with him. I hold the man high against my chest to ease his breathing. Why is he in prison, so fragile and so old? At dawn he dies in my arms and I hold him until his limbs begin to stiffen. After that, I am the one whom Joseph calls whenever death is near. Sometimes he stays with me, talking quietly to the prisoner leaving life. Sometimes I am alone.

I know that I will never kill again, and when Joseph leaves, sent for by Pharaoh, and does not return, I am given his place, put in charge of the prison.

I hope that Pharaoh treats him kindly.

7

Gad

a troop shall overcome him: but he shall overcome at the last.
Genesis 49:19

BY GAD, there's not much to be known about Gad! How did his name get taken over as an expletive? Or was it simply a British pretense that one was not taking God's name in vain?

Gad was Zilpah's first son, Jacob's seventh. Moses describes Gad as a lioness and praises him for performing Yahweh's ordinances. But in the song of Deborah his tribe is chided for failing to participate in the war against Sisera. But Jacob encourages his son Gad, saying, *"he shall overcome at the last."*

By the time Joseph was established as principal ruler in Egypt, most of his older brothers would have been married and the fathers of children. But this story is Joseph's, and the others come into the story only because, at certain times, they affected Joseph.

Egypt stands in our minds for the fleshpots, the quick, good things of this life, instant gratification, fine foods, and wines, and clothing, and luxurious housing. Four hundred years later, the Hebrew children escaped Pharaoh and were heading back to the Promised Land, and God sustained them with manna, the sweet, flaky substance that fell each day from the sky. But they complained that they were tired of this manna, that they longed for their onions and garlic and all the fresh foods they were accustomed to in Egypt. Slavery began to seem preferable to freedom as long as slavery kept them comfortable.

It is all right to enjoy the "creature comforts" as long as they are not paramount, as long as they do not become little gods, as long as we do not become slaves to them. What God created is good, very good, and to be enjoyed, as long as we never forget the Source.

Joseph never scorned the fleshpots when they were offered to him. He wore with flair his coat of many colors, though it became a sign of favoritism rather than simply a beautiful and comfortable garment. More honestly, he enjoyed the luxuries of Potiphar's palace and the far greater luxuries showered on him by Pharaoh. But when his luxuries were taken away he did not whine and whimper. The fact that he told both the baker and the Pharaoh that the interpretation of dreams comes from God, not from himself, tells us clearly that Joseph had not forgotten God, that the fleshpots were not of prime importance in his life.

Jesus enjoyed eating with his friends, enjoyed the good things (and was criticized for it by the moral majority). And it is all right for us to enjoy them, too, as long as we remember that all good and lovely things come from our Maker, even if we have prepared or crafted them: well-cooked meals, finely-carved furniture, embroidered linens. And our enjoyment should be an act of worship. My friend Tallis was talking to a Quaker friend about the Eucharist, and how important it was to him. The Eucharist and the other sacraments are not part of Quaker worship, yet the old lady gently replied that she never sat down to a meal without thinking of the body and blood of the Lord, and giving thanks.

The evening meal, the table set with the best china and crystal, and lit by candles, has always been sacramental for me, the focal point of the day. It is when the family gathers together, shares the day's events, and God's bounty. When our children were little I did not mind when we ate as long as we ate together. If Hugh was previewing a Broadway play we sometimes ate at five o'clock. If someone had an after-school project we ate at eight or eight thirty. The family dinner table is no longer tradition in many families today; it is a great loss.

Now the dinner table is very different. In New York, where I stay during the academic year, I am living with my granddaughter, Charlotte, who is in college. Often one of her friends is living with us, too, for months at a time. But the dinner table, the candles, the food prepared with love, are still important.

When I am at Crosswicks, my son, Bion, is the cook. His wife, Laurie, is a busy physician and never knows when she is going to get home, so Bion has taken over the cooking, and a marvelous and inventive cook he is, coming up with delicious new recipes for the late summer overflow from the garden. As the days grow shorter towards summer's end we still eat out, by kerosene lamp light, and we stay out to watch the stars. Across the fields are the woods and then the ancient hills *"from whence cometh my help."*

When I was in Jerusalem it was the hills which deeply moved me, helping me to understand better than ever before the 121st psalm. How many people throughout the centuries have looked towards the hills for help, hills that are a metaphor of the strong, steadfast love of God. Hills are also a metaphor for the right and proper expression of grief, of directing our loss and anguish to God. All during my life I have slowly learned about grief, and the appropriate expression of it. Wearing mourning in the old days was not such a bad idea, because it took into visible account the fact of death, which we now try to hide (even in the Church we try to hide it) so that it won't embarrass others.

Joseph, despite all his power and prestige, despite his Egyptian wife, still had loss and grief to work through. He was still far from home and family, and from the familiar. He had had to learn a new language, a new way of daily living, which included being isolated when he ate. In spite of all his power and wealth, there was still discrimination, for the Egyptians would not eat with a Hebrew. How lonely for him to have to eat alone, always alone! Is this not something like Southerners allowing their children to be suckled by a black wet nurse, and yet refusing to eat at the same table with the woman who nourished their little ones?

Perhaps this is one reason that Joseph's immense secular power did not go to his head. Perhaps, despite wealth and luxury, he knew moments of feeling forsaken. Like all the biblical heroes (like all of us human creatures) he was complex, capable of feeling opposite emotions simultaneously.

Meanwhile there were, as Joseph had told Pharaoh there would be, seven years of plenty, and during this time of prosperity Joseph laid up food from the countryside for all the cities, storing it so that there would be enough laid by for the seven years of famine. Certainly he had enough work to do, and little time to brood. We are not told a great deal about his home life, whether or not he loved and was loved by the wife Pharaoh had chosen for him. Despite the love stories of Isaac and Rebecca, Jacob and Rachel, arranged marriages were then the custom for both Hebrew and Egyptian. Joseph had two sons by Asenath; the first son was called Manasseh, who remains a mysterious character throughout Scripture. The second son Joseph named Ephraim, saying, *"For God has called me to be fruitful in the land of my affliction."*

So, even in the midst of his worldly success, Joseph still thought of Egypt as the land of his affliction. Did he ever, on the journey into Egypt, or during his years in prison, cry out, *"My God, my God, why have you forsaken me!"?* That has been the human cry of anguish throughout the centuries. The psalmist cries it in the 22nd psalm. Jesus cried it out on the cross, and in so doing freed us all to cry it in moments of deepest pain and loss.

The night of the day we learned that Hugh had cancer I turned, as always, to the strength-giving of Evening Prayer, and the first psalm for that evening was the 22nd, *"My God, my God, why have you forsaken me?"*

I was not at home, but a few miles away, at a conference centre. The onset of Hugh's illness was so sudden that there was no time to find a replacement for me, and the center was close enough to the hospital that I could commute. But the blow that it was cancer had come only that afternoon, and I felt raw with shock. I read those anguished words in a strange room, with my world turned upside down, those words that Jesus, too, cried out. And so, despite the pain, they brought me strength.

The words of the psalmist. The words of Jesus. They are incredibly personal words, and they cannot be spoken by one who is not there.

But Joseph, as far as we know, did not question but accepted the afflictions that came upon him as he accepted the power.

So he laid up provision for the time of dearth, knew his wife, begat sons, ate alone, did what had to be done.

And the seven years of plenteousness in the land of Egypt were ended. And the seven years of dearth began to come, as Joseph had said they would, but in all the land of Egypt there was bread.

And when all the land of Egypt was famished, the people cried to Pharaoh for bread, and Pharaoh said to all the Egyptians, "Go to Joseph and do whatever he tells you to do."

And the famine was over all the face of the earth, and Joseph opened all the storehouses and sold to the Egyptians. And all countries came into Egypt to Joseph to buy corn, because the famine was terrible in all lands.

Our planet is once again suffering from famine. Not only is there drought and famine in Africa, with the dry sand of the Sahara gradually taking over more and more of the fertile land, but our own southeast and western states have experienced terrible drought. We may not have had a Joseph, but perhaps he taught us something, for, in a gesture of fraternal compassion, farmers whose crops produced grain and wheat in abundance sent to those whose crops were withering. The response of the world to the horrible plight of the Armenians after the earthquake and to Bangladesh after its flood, is proof that our human hearts are still warm, despite the coldness which presses in on every side.

Famine and disease. Yes, there was famine, but there is little mention of disease in Genesis. People died of old age; women too often died in childbirth. There is no mention of cancer, or even of head colds. Men and women were sexually and healthily active, enjoying each other into old age.

But today AIDS is reaching disastrously epidemic proportions in Africa, hitting men, women, children. Someone told me that the virus has been found in mosquitoes – a terrifying thought. It is increasing in this country. Although contaminated hypodermic needles account for many cases, the most common cause is intercourse.

The sexual revolution has backfired. We needed to move from the old repressions, the unscriptural idea that nice women did not enjoy sex, and that therefore men had to have a separate standard. But, as almost always happens, the pendulum has swung too far, swinging from repression to undisciplined lust.

How do we find love, that love which God showed us in Jesus? How do we return to ourselves as observers and contemplators of God's Creation? Not only can men not have a separate standard, but not one of us can separate ourselves from any part of God's Creation.

Perhaps the Egypt into which Joseph was sold needed a new morality as much as we do, but it must be a new morality, not a return to the old, which wasn't very moral. Some pretty scandalous things happened among those eminent Victorians. And in our own time scandal has soiled the souls and reputations of prominent Christians. We need to understand that love never treats subject as object. Indeed, treating subject as object is the beginning of pornography.

As I observe and contemplate love, it is never self-righteous. It does not condemn. It is a sacrifice, a sacred and hallowed giving. I have received this love and been allowed to give it, and this is why, rather than by accident of birth, I am a Christian.

And Joseph, despite the pantheon of gods with which he was surrounded, was able to retain his faith in the One God of his people.

But such faith is a mystery. The phrase about God which means the most to me is the *mysterium tremendum et fascinans.* It doesn't translate well: the tremendous and fascinating mystery. It does better in Latin.

Joseph, having been purged in the fire, knew God to be a total mystery. There was a purity, a directness, to faith in the Creator before the coming of the Law; it was a smaller world than that of the Exodus and the journey to the Promised Land. And by the time of Jesus both the world and the law had become overcomplicated. The law was by now so cumbersome that it was almost impossible to get through a day without inadvertently breaking some jot or tittle of it, and John the Baptist, with his cry for repentance, was offering relief from the tangled web of Law that had become laws.

But for Joseph there were the stars at night, the sands of the desert, the wild winds, and mystery. We, too, are mysteries, and we cannot be explained, we creatures who are born to observe and contemplate, any more than the Maker of it all can be explained.

Hugo Rahner writes,

Without mystery all religion must wither into barren rationalism. The church alone has retained the element of mystery: by her sacraments she has consecrated sun, moon, water, bread, wine, and oil, and also the love of the flesh, nor will it ever be permitted to her to cease teaching mankind that behind the veils of the visible the eternal secrets lie concealed, and that it is only through the word of God which lives on in the church that we can recognize the true meaning of earthly things.

Because I do not believe that Jesus ever had denominations or a divided Christendom in mind, when I speak of "the Church" I refer to all of us, from the sects to the fundamentalists to the Pentecostals to the mainline Protestants to the Catholics to – to all of us. That we are still one Church despite all our divisions is also a mystery.

Unless we are able to accept mystery we will not be able to move beyond literalism into a living faith, a trusting that a God of love will not create and then abandon or annihilate.

Carrying my babies was a marvelous mystery, lives growing unseen except by the slow swelling of my belly and the delightful stirrings within. Death is an even greater mystery.

After Hugh's death many people asked me if I still talk to him. And my reply is always, "No, I don't want to hold him back." For I think we can do that, clinging to the beloved who has died, rather than allowing freedom to go on and do whatever it is that God has waiting and prepared for husband, or wife, or child, or friend.

Hugh will always be with me, part of me. There is no way I can talk without including him. Inevitably he comes up in daily conversation. There is no way I can talk without including him. We were together for well over half our lives. But his mortal body is gone and I don't know what God has in store for him now.

But it is even more mysterious than that. In God's universe we are never completely separated from any part of it.

So while I do not want to hold Hugh back (from whatever God is calling him to do and be and become) so I also know that he is still part of God's purpose.

On the anniversary of his death I was carefully scheduled to be away from home, having accepted three speaking jobs in Michigan. This, I hoped, would keep my children from worrying about me, and I knew that I would be better off if I was busy, and doing work I hoped had some value.

The first stop was Calvin College. My friend Marilyn from Niles, Michigan was with me, and we were put up in the Harley Hotel in Grand Rapids, where there were real glasses to drink out of, not plastic, and good quality tissues. I stay in many hotels on my travels and that is one way of grading them.

The second stop, the "two-night stand," was Spring Arbor College, and we were put up at a Knight's Inn in Jackson. Marilyn got out of her car, went into the room she had been assigned, and came out with a strange look on her face. Then she went into my room, which was next door, and came out, still with that strange look, and called me to come.

I went into a room smelling heavily of sweetish antiseptic. There was bright red carpeting on the floor, a bright purple velvet bedspread on the bed, bright purple velvet curtains at the windows, and on the walls were murals of windows with chartreuse shutters. Marilyn assured me that her room was identical. There were only two things to do in that room when we weren't at the college: sleep, and write. I had with me the manuscript of this book, and I was working on it dutifully, and without enthusiasm. I had promised the book to Luci Shaw, and I care about keeping promises. But working without enthusiasm is not my usual way.

And then it was as though I heard Hugh saying to me, "You know you don't want to work on *Sold Into Egypt* right now. What you want to work on is that fantasy you've been thinking about. Go ahead and write it." So I put *Sold Into Egypt* aside, and that day, and the next, I wrote at white heat whenever I was free to be in the room. I wrote twenty-eight pages. And continued when we went on to Sturgess and were radically upgraded to a Holiday Inn.

An Acceptable Time was the book I had to write then.

I didn't hear Hugh's physical voice. I didn't see him. But I felt him, his *is*ness, with me, at a time when my grief was raw. The night before, sitting in that red and purple room and reading Evening Prayer with Marilyn, the words of the Psalms almost made me break down. My body, my spirit, all of me was aware of and open to Hugh. I don't want to make too much of this. All I know was that it happened and it was a great and beneficent gift.

Perhaps a mere year after my husband's death was too soon for me to be thinking about all the theological issues of life and death that the story of Joseph demands. Certainly I believed that Hugh still *was*, *is*, and I still believe that. Perhaps I needed to work on the fantasy, with its themes of love and sacrifice, to help me understand Joseph, and to relax in the promise of Jesus' love and sacrifice.

Several people said to me, "At least you know that Hugh is happy now."

How do I know that? Happiness is not always for our greatest good. It may be that God has more joyful or more difficult or more challenging and wonderful work for Hugh to do. I don't have to know whether or not Hugh is *happy*. I need to know only that he is growing in God's love.

This past year almost everywhere I have spoken, someone has asked me, "What do you think of reincarnation?" The question is asked sometimes with fear, sometimes with hope, sometimes accusingly.

Perhaps the question of reincarnation has come to the forefront of people's thinking about life and death because the Church has held back, unable to move from the thinking of my forbears in St. Margaret's graveyard on Fleming's Island in north Florida. Some churches remain stuck in the old literal representations of heaven and hell, so graphically painted by Hieronymus Bosch. They are still good metaphors, but no longer to be taken literally, anymore than the Aristotelian sandwich of heaven, earth, hell, is to be taken literally.

When the Church is silent, other voices inevitably are heard.

Thoughts about what life after death holds for us should never be a refuge from the fear of death. Who knows what the God of love has in store for us? There are many important lessons to be learned before we are ready for the unveiled glory of the Presence.

But is this one life we are given not enough? Hugh lived the biblical three score years and ten. Surely we need not ask for more. But what about God's children who do not have lives of any real quality? What about the ten-year-old o.d.ed on drugs? The raped and murdered adolescent? The children starving in Africa, or India, or South America? Or the little ones in St. Margaret's graveyard, dead at only a few years of age from scarlet fever or diphtheria? Doesn't God want more for them than that?

In the 22nd psalm we read, *"To him (God) alone all who sleep in the earth bow down in worship; all who go down to the dust fall before him."* So even in the dust of the grave we worship God. What God created will not be left unfinished.

Why are so many Christians afraid of the idea that the God of love will continue to care for us? There are hints all through Scripture. In the Psalms: *"Before you were formed in the womb I knew you,"* (echoing Jeremiah). *"In my house are many mansions,"* Jesus assured, each one prepared to meet the need of each person after death. There is nothing inconsistent with Christianity in such considerations as long as we don't fall into idolatry.

I hope this does not sound like what is called New Ageism, of which many Christians seem to be terribly afraid. I am not a New Ager, and I don't know a great deal about this movement. The chief problem seems to me to be that old heresy, Pelagianism – thinking we can do it all ourselves. At its worst it is the belief that because we can do it ourselves we don't need God.

And it is, perhaps, an indictment of the Church which has allowed God's wonder to be tarnished, which is fearful rather than joyful, and which has forgotten the wonderful wildness of Jesus, who could spit on the dust and make a blind man see, who could tell a little girl to arise from death, and who loved his disciples despite their betrayal of him, as Joseph also was called to love his brothers.

I know that I need God, and that if we are to care for the precarious ecology of this planet it will only be with our hands in the hand of God. That we do nothing, accomplish nothing, without God. After I had spent several days speaking in Fort Wayne, Indiana, first for the Friends of the Library, then for the Episcopal Church, a man who had not come to any of my talks wrote a letter to the editor of the local paper accusing me of being "a self-professed New Ager." What made him tell this bald-faced lie, after which he went on to accuse my books (without having read them) of being unChristian, leading children down the path to perdition? What is this fear that causes "Christians" to vilify and attack other Christians blindly? Aren't Christians supposed to act out of love, not fear? Aren't we supposed to be recognized by our love for one another? Does not our faith in the Lord of the universe keep us safe in Christ? Does not perfect love banish fear?

And what am I to do about my instinctive reaction towards people who are judgmental? How do I, in my turn, keep from being judgmental? I know that I frequently err. But at least I don't want those who disagree with me damned to eternal hell. I do want us all to meet with love at the Heavenly Banquet.

I don't worry much about reincarnation one way or another. It is enough for me to believe that God's love never ends. I don't need to know how God is caring for Hugh now, only that Hugh is still alive in God, as much as I am alive in God.

Elisabeth Kübler-Ross says that the subconscious mind cannot conceive of its own extinction. Most of the time the conscious mind cannot, either. We know that we are going to die, but most of the time we don't believe it.

There is a theory that people have to finish working out unresolved relations with each other until love is perfected. How that is going to be brought about is in the hands of the Maker, and I am willing to leave it in the realm of mystery, in the design of the *mysterium tremendum et fascinans.* Faith is not for the things we can prove, but for the things we cannot prove.

The medical profession is in a time of crisis because of its amazing new technology. There are instruments and techniques that are wonderful lifesavers; some of them are also terrible death prolongers. The church is in its own time of crisis, seeming to fall into the same trap as the scientists, that of attempting to prolong the life of the body even when the spirit is gone.

The early people of Genesis did not have to face such ethical dilemmas. They lived to ripe old ages without the benefit of medicine. They were robust and healthy as long as the land yielded to them its grain and wine and oil, its milk and honey and olives. In times of famine people died of starvation – but not as many as are dying of starvation today, because it was a much less crowded planet.

The famine against which Joseph had stored up great reserves of grain spread far beyond Egypt, and when Jacob learned that there was food to be bought in Egypt he sent his ten eldest sons to go buy corn. Benjamin, his youngest son, he kept at home, fearing something might happen to him, as he believed had happened to Joseph.

And the irony of it was that it was Joseph himself who was in complete charge of dispensing food to the hungry, so it was to their own brother (though of course they had no idea of this, thinking Joseph long dead) that Jacob's sons applied. After the long trek to Egypt, the ten of them prostrated themselves before him, like the sheaves of corn, like the stars of his dreams. They prostrated themselves before this magnificent stranger dressed in fine clothes and wearing all the emblems of power.

And Joseph saw his brothers and he knew them, but made himself strange to them, and spoke roughly to them, and said to them, "From where do you come?"

And they said, "From the land of Canaan to buy food."

And Joseph recognized his brothers, but they did not recognize him.

Did Joseph have any expectation that his brothers would come to Egypt, looking for food? How strange, after all these years, to see these ten men, some of them middle-aged by now. How did he recognize them? From a family resemblance to Jacob? If he suspected that they might come, for the famine was bad in Canaan, that very expectation would have made it easier for Joseph to recognize them, those brothers who had been so jealous of him that they had plotted against him; some of them had even been eager to kill him. Paradoxically, he had both suffered and prospered because of them. But surely by now he would have seen and acknowledged his own part in what had happened, his arrogance, his insufferable bragging. He had brought at least some of his problems upon himself.

And Joseph (seeing his brothers prostrate before him) *remembered the dreams which he had dreamed and he said to them, "You are spies, and have come to see the nakedness of this land."*

And they said, "No, my Lord, your servants are twelve brothers, the sons of one man in Canaan, and the youngest is at home with our father, and one of us is not."

But Joseph repeated the accusation that they were spies, and said that the only way that they could prove that they were honest men was to bring their youngest brother to him. He would keep one of them hostage in Egypt, in prison, as surety, while they went back to Canaan for Benjamin. Meanwhile, he locked them all up for three days.

To have time to think. To decide what to do. Was revenge totally sweet, or was it bittersweet? Egypt was still the land of his exile. He longed for home.

At the end of three days Joseph brought his brothers out of prison, and again told them that one of them should be bound in prison (as Joseph had been bound). The others were to go and buy corn to relieve the famine at home, then go back and give food to their father. Then they were to bring Benjamin to Joseph.

"So shall your story be verified, and you shall not die."

The ten brothers huddled in consternation, admitting one to another that they had been truly guilty about Joseph and that was why this present distress had fallen upon them, with this strange lord standing by, darting glances at them.

And Reuben answered them, saying, "Didn't I beg you not to sin against the child? And you would not hear. Therefore his blood must be avenged." And they did not know that Joseph understood them, because he spoke to them through an interpreter.

At last Joseph was hearing his own language, words that must have shaken him, but he held himself back, speaking only in the language of Egypt. By now he would have been completely fluent in Egyptian, perhaps even dreaming in that language (as occasionally I used to dream in French), but the language of his birth, coming from his brothers, must have pierced him with homesickness. *And he turned himself away from them and wept.*

He was to do considerably more weeping before finally the twelve brothers were reconciled, and Jacob was to see all his sons together again.

Men in Joseph's day were not afraid to weep, had not yet been forced by society to repress honest emotion. I am glad that Joseph wept, because it meant that he was not concerned only with revenge, but also for his brothers, concerned for little Benjamin, not so little any more, concerned for his father, who must be an old man by now.

I have wept for the loss of my husband, wept with our children, wept alone, wept in my bed at home, and sometimes in strange beds in hotel rooms. During the years of our marriage Hugh and I sometimes wept together, holding each other, not tears of self-indulgence or self-pity, but tears which are an appropriate response to the sorrows and losses of this world.

Joseph wept.

Jesus wept.

The shortest verse in the Bible is *Jesus wept.*

Why did he weep?

He wept after his friend, Lazarus, had died, and before he had raised him from the dead. The people said that he wept because he loved Lazarus so, and that was probably one of the reasons.

My friend Tallis says that Jesus wept from sheer anguished frustration, because nobody understood what he was about, nobody, not one of his disciples, not one of his friends. He may have held on to the hope that Mary would understand, Mary who had washed his feet with rare oil and wiped them with her hair. But even Mary did not understand.

And perhaps, because of the paradox of Jesus being human as well as God, he wept because of the anguish of his mission. He knew that he was the Messiah, and yet he also knew that when he went to Jerusalem he would be captured and killed.

And he wept because of Lazarus, but not because Lazarus was dead. He had stayed away from Bethany to be sure that Lazarus was indeed dead. By the time Jesus got there Lazarus had been dead for four days. Martha, that blunt woman, put it graphically: *"Lord, by this time he stinketh."*

Lazarus had been dead for four days, had been for four days in the Presence, and Jesus had to bring him back from that bliss. And so he wept for Lazarus. Then he had the stone rolled away and called him back to mortality.

We don't know much about Lazarus after his raising. Once when Jesus came to Bethany Lazarus was there at dinner with Mary and Martha, and people came to stare. But it would seem that he was different after Jesus brought him back to life, still partly in the presence of God, homesick for heaven. And it was likely that he had to go into hiding because he, like Jesus, was sought by the confused and angry authorities.

Jesus wept.

The tears of Jesus dignify our own tears. I am grateful for that brief, two-word verse of Scripture, because it frees us to weep our own legitimate tears. When we are alone with God there is no need to put on a front.

Jesus wept.

Joseph wept.

Gad. We don't know what Gad thought about God. But Gad grew up in the over-arching shadow of the patriarchs, Abraham, Isaac, and Jacob, the father of the twelve sons. They knew themselves to be called, specially called.

And one thing I learned in working on the fantasy which needed to be written before this book is that Gad was never separated from Christ; that Christ, the second Person of the Trinity, has always been, is always, and always will be available to all people and at all times. We are so focussed on the Incarnation, on Jesus of Nazareth, that sometimes we forget that the Second Person of the Trinity didn't just arrive two thousand years ago, but has always been. Christ was the Word that shouted all of Creation into being, all the galaxies and solar systems, all the subatomic particles, and the wonderful mix of Creation that is what makes up each one of us.

Jesus said, to the horror of the establishment people, *"Before Abraham was, I am."*

In Chapter 20 of Luke's gospel Jesus has been questioned by the elders of the temple, who are trying to trick him. Finally he says,

"How is it that they say the Christ is the Son of David? David himself declares in the Book of Psalms, 'The Lord said to my Lord, Sit at my right hand, until I make your enemies a footstool for your feet.' David calls him 'Lord.' How can he then be his son?"

Another heresy down the drain, I hope. How can we blithely assign all those who lived before Jesus to the flames of eternal hell when they never denied Christ? Their way of knowing was inevitably different from ours, but God cannot be limited, and a God of love does not casually wipe out the prophets and the people who found Christ in the love of the Creator.

Paul talks about the journey from Egypt to the Promised Land, and the Rock that went before the people, *and that rock was Christ.*

So, for Gad, for Joseph, for Moses, for all of us, Christ always is.

My Christmas poem for this year runs:

He came, quietly impossible,
Out of a young girl's womb,
A love as amazingly marvelous
As his bursting from the tomb.

This child was fully human,
This child was wholly God.
The hands of All Love fashioned him
Of mortal flesh and bone and blood,

The ordinary so extraordinary
The stars shook in the sky
As the Lord of all the universe
Was born to live, to love, to die.

He came, quietly impossible:
Nothing will ever be the same:
esus, the Light of every heart –
The God we know by Name.

But we find it hard to hold on to the impossible, so we tend to settle for the limited possible. And our vision of God dwindles, and we become selfish and hard of heart as we close ourselves off from love.

* * *

GAD'S WIFE

Had I known what a strange family I was marrying into I would have fought the match all the way. I thought I was marrying Gad. Instead I married Gad and his eleven brothers, including the one who was dead, torn into pieces by wild beasts – though I thought Gad's expression strange as I was told this.

I do not mean that the brothers came to our tent or did anything unseemly. In fact, Simeon and Levi scarcely spoke to me, as though the wives of the sons of the slaves were less important than the wives of the other brothers. What I mean is that Gad was not Gad except as part of his brothers. The father, Jacob, and the brothers and their wives were the tribe. There was nobody else. They had their tribal god, and I was expected to abandon my home goddess and obey their god. Since their god never bothered me, that was all right, and nobody knew what I was doing when I left the tent to watch the moon rise, or suggested the best times for plantings.

My prayers were answered, and I gave Gad sons. And then, for myself and my own joy, I had daughters. I do not mean to complain. Gad was good to me, a vigorous lover and a good provider. And though his pride was in his sons he loved our little girls and played with them and made them laugh. But sons were what counted. How strange! How could a man have sons without a woman? But if Gad and his brothers thought of women at all, it was because they were useful as producers of men. And, of course, to keep tent, draw water, be available whenever desire arose.

We had, I suppose, a good life. My children had plenty of cousins as playmates as well as each other, and in their games no difference was made between the grandchildren of the two slave women and the grandchildren of the two wives.

Gad was the first son of Zilpah, the slave who was unloved Leah's maid. She was less well thought of than Bilhah, dead Rachel's maid.

Dead Rachel. Dead Joseph. Not dead to Father Jacob! They were ever present in his brooding eyes, in the down-twist of his mouth when he thought he was alone. Sometimes he would clutch Benjamin – my youngest brother-in-law, still smooth of cheek – clutch him so hard that the poor lad would squirm and try to break away. Benjamin, the beloved. The rest of the brothers are sons. Father Jacob has sons, as he has camels and goats and sheep. He knows how to breed well, both man and beast.

He has grandsons. Oh, yes, he has grandsons. Between us, we have given him plenty, and granddaughters, too, and Reuben's children are old enough to give their grandfather great-grandsons and daughters. He will like that. Sometimes I wonder why he does not collect gods as he collects the rest of his livestock. Between us, we would give him quite a few.

But I do not mean to be unkind. He is good to us, the old patriarch.

But what, I wonder, happened to Dinah, the one sister? Where is she? Benjamin asked me about her, once, telling me she had been his mother – or like his mother – after Rachel died giving birth to him. He loved Dinah, but even he does not know where she is, or why she is not with the rest of the family.

When I leave the tent to watch the moon rise I pray for Dinah. I pray that she was not sent away from home by men who do not understand the ways of women. There is a mystery about Dinah that in some way touches on Simeon and Levi, whose faces close in on the rare occasions that her name is spoken. I pray that she may have left the home tents for love of some man who will be good to her, and let her have her own home god, if that is what she wants.

But I will never know.

8

Asher

his bread is rich; he provides fruit fit for a king.
Genesis 49:20

WHEN JACOB GIVES HIS BLESSINGS to his sons, he says, "*Asher, his bread is rich, he provides fruit fit for a king.*" Asher's land was lush and productive, and he benefited from his geography.

Moses, in his blessing, says, "*Most blessed of the sons may Asher be! Let him be privileged among his brothers and bathe his feet in oil!*"

And after all this we still don't know a great deal about Asher, Zilpah's second son, Jacob's eighth. In Egypt, how did Asher feel when Joseph wept? Did he see that the great man was turning away because he had tears in his eyes? Or were the brothers too terrified by all that was happening to notice anything except that the great man thought they were spies, and was holding one of them in Egypt while the others went to fetch Benjamin? It was fearful and confusing. Why did the most powerful man in Egypt want their little brother? (Not so little any more. By now, Benjamin was fully grown.)

Joseph wept.

One of the most important things we can do for each other in times of grief is to weep together. Words are useless. We are in the realm of ultimate mystery. Nothing speaks except touch and tears.

And, sometimes, anger. When Mrs. Pat Campbell's son was killed in the trenches in World War I, George Bernard Shaw wrote to her, his beloved friend, starting the letter with "Damn damn damn damn damn." That was compassionate understanding, outrage at the blasphemy of war. It was not sacrilegious, and was far more acceptable to God, I believe, than pious utterances about its being God's will. Such "piosity" is an obscenity, not a comfort. Terrible things are not God's will, but God can enter them with redemptive love, that is the promise of the Incarnation.

Was Joseph ever able to weep with his wife, Asenath? He was not allowed to eat with her, since she was an Egyptian and he a Hebrew, although he was allowed to sleep with her, know her, give her children. Did he ever weep in her arms?

I visualize Joseph turned away from his brothers, his shoulders shaking a little (did they think he was laughing at them?), his hand covering his face until he could turn and look at them again.

A formidable figure, this Joseph, with the power to hold Simeon in Egypt. (Since Simeon was one of the two brothers who had murdered Shechem, that may have had something to do with Joseph's choice of hostage.)

Joseph sent off the other nine brothers for home, ordering his servants to make sure that not only should their sacks be filled with corn, but that their money should be returned to them – the money with which they had paid for the corn – and put in their sacks.

On their way home, when one of the brothers, we are not told which one, *opened his sack to give his ass provender at the inn, he saw the money, because it was right in the mouth of the sack.*

And he said to his brothers, "My money is returned; look, it is in my sack!" and their hearts failed them, and they were afraid, saying one to another, what is this that God has done to us?"

Was it Levi who found the money? Did he and Simeon think of God when they slaughtered Shechem and his tribe? Were the brothers thinking of God when they planned to kill Joseph? When they sold him into Egypt?

When they got home they told their father all that had happened, how the lord of the land spoke roughly to them and accused them of being spies, despite their protestations that they were simply *"twelve brothers, sons of our father; one is not, and the youngest is this day with our father in the land of Canaan."*

They also told their father that the lord of Egypt had informed them that the only way they could prove their innocence was by leaving Simeon in jail until they brought their youngest brother, Benjamin, to Egypt. Then and then only would the great lord believe that the brothers were not spies, and Simeon would be restored to them.

Jacob put his arms around Benjamin in anguish, holding, shielding the beloved flesh of his youngest son.

The brothers had opened only one of their sacks on their way home. Now they opened the others, and each one of them found that his bag of money was in his sack, and they were afraid, and so was Jacob. He wailed,

"You are robbing me of my children. Joseph is no more. Simeon is no more. And now you want to take Benjamin. All this I must bear."

Again it was Reuben who intervened. He promised his father the lives of his own two sons if he did not bring Benjamin back to him. *"Put him in my care and I will bring him back to you."*

It was a generous and rash offer. Reuben did not ask his wife, he simply made this wild promise. But it was not enough for Jacob. He cried

"My son is not going down with you, for now his brother is dead and he is the only one left to me. If anything should happen to him on the way, you would bring down my grey hairs with sorrow to the grave."

Benjamin alone is left to me!

Reuben turned away. Benjamin alone? What about the other ten? Was it only for his beloved Rachel's children that Jacob truly cared?

Jacob was too involved in his own grief to understand what he was doing to his sons. And by now perhaps they were used to being second-best. They all lived near their father, with their wives and children, and they lived well. Their flocks had increased, and, until the famine struck their gardens had grown, their fields and flocks had prospered. They knew themselves to have a goodly heritage.

But Jacob was still immersed in grief, grief for Rachel, for Joseph he thought to be dead. He could not bear any more death. What did he believe about Rachel? About Joseph? About his fathers, Isaac and Abraham?

In the creed, as I say it each day, I affirm that "I believe in the resurrection of the body." I don't need to belabor my expressed belief that we don't know how that body is going to be resurrected, or what it is going to be like. If Paul could believe in a *spiritual body* so, most of the time, can I. It is yet another mystery of the Word made flesh.

The Episcopal Church is a credal church. When I go to the Congregational Church near Crosswicks there is no creed, but there is an "Affirmation of Faith." Wheaton College requires its faculty to sign a "Statement of Faith," and I can't see much difference between creeds and affirmations and statements. By whatever name it is called, most religious establishments express what they believe in one way or another. And these expressions are all inadequate. What we hold in common is the affirmation of our faith in the mystery of the Word made flesh.

If that Word should come to another planet in another galaxy with different life forms, and be made manifest according to the flesh of that planet, this different incarnation would still be the same original Word made flesh. That Word may express itself in many images, many languages, each equally the true Word.

We are given a unique glimpse of the mystery of the Word in the wonder of the Transfiguration, when briefly James and John and Peter were allowed to see the radiance of their Lord, bright and glistening and wholly other. Is that how we will appear at our resurrection?

We are given further glimpses when we remember that after the Resurrection Jesus was never recognized by sight, though he ate fish with his disciples, shared their bread and wine, to prove that the resurrection body was true body.

David Steindl-Rast reminds us that the word *spirit* means *breath*, and that breath stands for life, so to be spiritual means to be alive. The spiritual body that Paul talks about is a real body that is truly alive – truly aware, truly being – as most of us are alive only occasionally.

Did Jacob have any such hope? We don't know. But he rebelled categorically at the idea of letting Benjamin go to Egypt.

His roars are like that of the psalmist many generations later. *"I will say to the God of my strength, 'Why have you forsaken me? All day long they mock me and say, Where is now your God?'*

I, too, have cried out with the psalmist, *"You are the God of my strength; why have you put me away from you?"*

There was no hesitation in Old Testament days about crying out to the Lord in times of trouble.

"Awake, O Lord! Why are you sleeping? Arise! Do not reject us forever. Why have you hidden your face and forgotten our affliction and oppression?"

In the 13th psalm the appeal is even stronger:

"How long, O LORD? Will you forget me forever? How long will you hide your face from me? How long must I wrestle with my thoughts and every day have sorrow in my heart? How long will my enemy triumph over me?"

I do not believe that God is ever absent from us. There may be times when God's face seems hidden, but if we know where to look, it's always there.

There have been many times, such as the captivity out of which the psalmist was crying, and often in the world's history, and in our own personal histories, when we cry out like the psalmist. And in our crying out we try to come to terms with whatever it is that is troubling us ("No! Benjamin shall not go!"), and we struggle to be human.

We make a terrible error when we think that to be human means to be perfect, some kind of unerring Christian model that cannot exist in reality. Only God is perfect. To be human is to be able to laugh, to cry, to live fully, to be aware of our lives as we are living them. We are the creatures *who know that we know*, unlike insects who live by unthinking instinct. That ability to think, to know, to reflect, to question, marks us as human beings. And our humanness includes an awareness that we are mortal. To be a human being is to be born, to live, to die. We have a life span. George Macdonald reminds us that Jesus came to us in a human body not so that he would be like us, but so that we would be like Jesus. Jesus died to his human life, and what he demands of us is equally hard, never sentimental or easy, and it is always part of that call to be human.

We don't know what Jesus looked like, but it's a pretty safe guess that he didn't look like most greeting-card representations of him; it is not likely that he was a blue-eyed blond. He was a Jew, and he was a carpenter. He was a strong, rough-hewn man.

Dr. Paul Brand tells of a time when he was a student in England and his aunt went in to London to hear a famous speaker. She came back absolutely shattered because the speaker had talked about an historian, the only historian we know of who was writing at the time of Jesus, and recorded Jesus as an historical figure. And the historian referred to Jesus as a hunchback. This news shook Paul Brand's aunt badly. Brand himself was less upset. He remarked that because there was a great deal of TB of the spine in those days it was quite possible that Jesus' back wasn't quite straight. And he said, "I don't mind. I really don't mind." Well, I don't, either.

Among the early church fathers were those who talked of Jesus as being small, frail, long-faced, with eyebrows that joined, dark-skinned, a beautiful and ugly hunchback. In the apocryphal *The Acts of John* is this passage:

"What does this youth want of us? Why is he calling us from the shore?" said my brother James to me. I said, "My brother James, your eyes must be dimmed by the many sleepless nights we have spent on the lake. Do you not see that the man standing on the shore is a tall man with a joyful face of great beauty?" My brother said, "I do not see him like that. But let us row ashore and we shall see." When we hauled up the boat, Jesus himself helped us to make it fast. When we left the place to follow him, he appeared to me as a bald man with a thick-growing beard while to my brother James he seemed a youth with but a faint down on his cheeks, and we could not understand and were amazed. And so it often happened, and he would appear in forms even more marvelous, sometimes small of stature with crooked limbs, sometimes as a giant reaching for the heavens.

Perhaps he appears to each of us according to our need and according to what God wants of us. We are not to get stuck with any one image, no matter how dear.

If you will notice, the great novelists describe their secondary characters in far more detail than their protagonists. One reason for this is that if the protagonist is not too closely described, it is easier for us to identify with whoever the hero or heroine is – to put ourselves in that person's body.

But another reason is that we see those we love with far more than the outer eye. Think of someone you care about most dearly. Close your eyes and try to visualize that person. It isn't easy, because what we love in someone is far more than just what that person looks like. It is much easier to visualize an acquaintance – someone you do not know with your heart.

So we do not know what Jesus *looked like* any more than we know what those dearest to us *look like*. But we do know what they *are like*. We know them in movement, with their funny little idiosyncrasies that can sometimes irritate us but are basically lovable. We know the humanness in them, so that at the very best we know Christ in them. Jesus came to us to call us to be fully human, and Christ is still calling us to that fullness of humanity.

All of the heresies about Jesus Christ come about because we overemphasize the divinity at the expense of the humanity, or overemphasize the humanity at the expense of the divinity. Jesus was equally human and divine, and that has always been difficult for us to accept, much less comprehend.

The great hoo-hah about *The Last Temptation of Christ* a while ago came about because of this. I did not see it because I heard it wasn't a very good movie, and Jesus, as usual, was not cast strongly enough. But many of the movie's detractors also had not seen it, and what they were upset about was Jesus' temptations, because these people are (once again) emphasizing his divinity at the expense of his humanity. But we are told that Jesus was tempted in everything, just as we are, but that he did not give in to the temptations.

When Satan tempted Jesus after his baptism, and Jesus rejected the temptations, Satan *left him for a time*. Satan did not let go easily. Immediately after Peter recognized Jesus as the Messiah, the Promised One, Jesus talked of his return to Jerusalem and the trials he must suffer, and Peter protested that this must never happen, and Jesus cried fiercely, *"Get behind me, Satan!"* Of course he did not look forward to the betrayal, the pain, the cross. But he did not give in to the temptation to emphasize his divinity and to forget his humanness.

The more human we become, the more closely we follow Jesus, the less will Satan be able to tempt us.

One of Satan's temptations is *virtue* – making us believe that not only can we be virtuous, but that we can be virtuous by our own merit. And Satan confuses virtue with moralism and legalism. But virtue in Scripture is power, loving power. When the woman with the issue of blood touched the hem of his garment, Jesus felt the *virtue* drain from him.

Satan tempts us to make our virtue a matter of pride. And indeed, pride goes before a fall. Recently we have had several examples of this in Christendom. These people who fell from their pinnacles of virtuous pride were not bad people. They were, on the outside, moral. They tithed, they conducted services, they proclaimed themselves models of what people ought to be, and their very goodness produced pride, and the pride, in some cases, produced a terrible fall. Perhaps if they had preached less about the anger of God and dwelt more on God's forgiveness they would not have done what they did.

Jesus was never proud. He simply *was*. It was the pride of the Pharisees which made Jesus such a threat to them, because he challenged them to let go of their pride and be human. Being human was too frightening – too demanding. And so they tried to trap Jesus.

Recently I read the galleys of a book in which the author rather casually referred to Jesus as a wimp who was into sin, punishment, fear of life, denial of the flesh. Seeing Jesus that way seems to be a human tendency. We are not able to handle the Scriptural character who was robust and open. His first miracle was at a Jewish wedding feast where the guests had already had plenty to drink. But he went ahead and turned water into wine anyhow. Lavishly. And just as lavishly he poured out his own blood for us.

Jesus was lavish in all ways. He loved to laugh, to make jokes. He had a short temper; he occasionally blew his stack. His friends were not "the right people." Most, though not all of them, were from the wrong side of the railroad tracks, and those who belonged to the establishment were often afraid to be seen with him; Nicodemus came to visit him at night, lest he be seen in Jesus' company by his powerful friends at the Sanhedrin. The things that bothered Jesus most in people were hardness of heart, coldness of spirit, self-righteousness, judgmentalness. And he made it very clear that separating people into "us" and "them" was not a good idea. But he did demand that we be human (and remember, to be human does not mean to be perfect; indeed, to be perfect is inhuman). Though we are all called to bear within us the image of God, that image is expressed not through perfection, but through faith, love, passion.

What about the mandate *to be perfect as your Father in heaven is perfect?* The word *perfect* comes from the Latin and means *to do thoroughly.* So, if we understand the word that way, we might say that it means to be human, perfectly human, and perhaps that is what we are meant to understand by this command which is on the surface a contradiction to Jesus' emphasis that only his Father was good, only his Father was perfect. We human beings are to be human – to be perfectly human, not indefectible or impeccable or faultless or superhuman, but complete, right, with integrity undivided. I looked that up in my old thesaurus given me by my father when I was in high school. But no dictionary or thesaurus is going to define humanness for us. The storyteller comes closer.

We tell stories, listen to stories, go to plays, to be amused, to be edified, but mostly so that we can understand what it means to be a human being. Jesus was a storyteller. Indeed, according to Matthew, he taught entirely by telling stories. One of the great triumphs of Satan has been to lead us to believe that "story" isn't true. I don't know if all the facts of the story of Joseph are true, but it is a true story. That is very important to understand. Jesus did not tell his parables in order to give us facts and information, but to show us *truth*. What is the truth of the story of the man with the great plank in his eye? Doesn't it tell us very clearly that we must not judge others more stringently than ourselves?

And Joseph's story tells us much about what it means to be human. More important than whether or not Potiphar's wife actually tried to seduce him is the truth of his integrity in refusing to betray his master. Story is the closest we human beings can come to truth. God is truth. God is beyond the realm of provable fact. We can neither prove nor disprove God. God is for faith.

When I was a child, story helped me find out who I was in a world staggering from the effects of that war which was meant to end war but which, alas, was the beginning of a century of continuing war. Story helped me to accept that human beings do terrible things to other human beings, but that human beings also do marvelous things. Story was a mirror in which I could be helped to find the image of God in myself.

The image of God in ourselves is often obscured, and we surely don't find it in the bathroom mirror. Better mirrors are our friends, those we love and trust most deeply. That image is never found in competition with our neighbors or colleagues; rather, in not wanting to let down those who believe in us and in God's image in us. Each one of us is probably as varied as the Jesus in *The Acts of John*, and which aspect is the more true? Probably the whole bundle together.

Certainly the more human we are, the more varied and contradictory we are. And that is as it should be. God often reveals the infinite Presence to us through paradox and contradiction, and Scripture is full of both. Through paradox and contradiction we are enabled to sift for truth, that truth which will set us free, that truth which is not limited by literalism. What confuses many people about Scripture is that some of it is history, and some of it is story. The story of Joseph may be part history, and part story, but it is *true*.

Is it legalistic literalism which is behind the wave of censorship that is rolling across the land? Are people so afraid of the truth of story that they have to look for some way to deny it? If people look for key words (magic; witch; occult) does that excuse them for disregarding content? In Frances Hodgson Burnett's beautiful book, *The Secret Garden*, the children not only bring a dead garden back to life, but cold hearts are opened in love. Dickon looks at the wonders they have wrought, saying, "It's magic!" and then bursts into song: "Praise God from whom all blessings flow, praise him all creatures here below, praise him above ye heavenly host, praise Father, Son, and Holy Ghost." But because he has used the word *magic* the book is being censored, removed from the shelves as being unChristian. No regard has been paid to content, to what the book is *saying*. The truth underlying the book is beautifully Christian. Censorship is dangerous because there is something inhuman, or mechanical, about it. Jesus couldn't stand inhumanness. Hitler began by burning books and ended by burning people.

However, if I'm upset by the judgmentalism of the extreme Christian right, I'm equally upset at the permissiveness of the more liberal left where, it would seem, almost anything goes. Some of our jargon reflects this. "Lifestyle," for instance, is a word which came into the vocabulary only a decade or so ago, and seems to imply that we can choose any old way of life, as long as we call it our "lifestyle," and that we are permitted – even encouraged – to act out all our feelings, no matter what they are. Believe me, if I acted out all my feelings I'd end in jail.

Relationship is another of my unfavorite overworked, current words. Before it came into the vocabulary we had *friendship* and we had *love*. You can have a relationship without being committed, but not friendship or love. Relationships aren't considered fulfilled unless they end in bed; love involves every part of us, mind and spirit and body, an inseparable trinity. We need to revive friendship and love because these are human emotions. Joseph, being human, refused to have a relationship with Potiphar's wife. Relationships help us avoid being human. But it is our human emotions which help us to face all the joys and sorrows of being human – being betrayed by one's brothers and one's master's wife, being unjustly accused, working through grief, knowing moments of joy, the satisfaction of work well done, the true pleasure of being with friends, of a meal with friends (and Joseph had to eat alone).

Probably my most unfavorite word is *consumer.* How did we ever let the media get away with calling us consumers!? What an ugly noun to use for a human being. Last summer forest fires consumed vast acres of forest. Greedy developers and thoughtless farmers are consuming the great Rain Forests in South America. Drugs consume human beings. So does disease. Consumerism connotes greed, lust, gluttony, avarice, excess, self-centeredness. Can one be a Christian and be a consumer? I doubt it.

Do consumers ever contemplate mortality? I suspect that they shun the thought. But to be human is to be mortal. When Jesus was born in Bethlehem, he was born as all of us are born, to die. He didn't live a long life, but in his three decades he packed all the humanness that any of us need. Of those three decades in Jesus' life we know very little – only the stories of his birth, his visit to the Temple when he was twelve, and the short years of his ministry. But we don't need to know more. The story is there. It is complete. And it shows us the truth about Jesus.

My friend Tallis remarked that the synoptic Gospels, Matthew, Mark, and Luke, are snapshots of Jesus, and that John's gospel is a portrait. Between them they tell us the whole story, and it is a marvelous one.

In the four Gospels it is clear that Jesus was steeped in Hebrew Scripture, in what we call the Old Testament. He quoted from it, referred to it, and expected his hearers to understand it without explanation. We miss much of the New Testament if we are not thoroughly grounded in the Old. For the Old Testament, beginning with Genesis, is the beginning of the story, and we need to understand the beginning in order to understand that there is triumph at the end.

* * *

ASHER

We lived simply, but well, we sons of our father. Yes, we all had one father – four mothers, but one father, and though my mother was a concubine, I was as much a son of my father as was Reuben, his firstborn. Not as much, however, as Joseph and Benjamin, the favored two.

Joseph. He was intolerable. I do not miss him. Benjamin is sweet and undemanding and seems not to be aware that our father favors him over the rest of us. He does not brag, nor boast of dreams.

He is the one most at home here in Canaan, for this is all the land he knows as home, whereas the rest of us grew up on our Grandfather Laban's land. But here we are, where our Grandfather Isaac lived and died. Here we are, and have taken wives, sired children, prospered. This land is now our land. El, how I love this land! My land. The mountains bring peace to my soul. The valleys are lush with corn and grapes and grain.

Our wives are sometimes jealous of the fact that we brothers are the sons of our father, that we are together in this land, that we share one God, while they have many. They call on their gods to bring the spring rains, the growing times for fruits and grains, the birth times for the young animals, and for our own children. Perhaps their gods hear.

But now the rains have not come. The sun burns hot with death, not life. We go further and further afield with our flocks to find pasture. The grapes shrivel on the vine. We have grain stored, but it is not enough.

At night the wives leave our tents and join together to sing and dance and call on their goddesses, but in the morning the sun rises again, hot as molten brass. Our father says that we must stop our wives from praying to alien gods. Alien to us, they say, but not to them. And our one God has sent no rain.

The young animals die. We salt down the meat, but it is stringy and tough.

Is God angry with us? Angry that we married wives who have other gods? Is our God not more powerful than those other gods? Did not our God make the stars that shine at night, and the moon that touches our women every month, and the sun that is now brutal in the sky by day? Can he not send rain? We have made sacrifices of our best from the flocks and from the fields. What does El want?

I love my wife and children. My brothers and I work hard. What is wrong? Levi and Simeon scowl. Are we being punished for what they did? Or for what we did, all of us – well, not Reuben, perhaps not Judah, but all the rest of us – to Joseph? We have not told our father that it was not a wild beast who bloodied Joseph's coat. We cannot tell our father.

Can we tell God? Would that make a difference? To say that we sinned, sinned against our own flesh and blood? O God, we have sinned against heaven and before you and are no longer worthy to be called your sons.

9

Issachar

is a strong ass couching down between the sheepfolds: And he saw that rest was good, and the land that it was pleasant; and bowed his shoulder to bear, and became a servant under taskwork.

Genesis 49:14–15

ISSACHAR WAS JACOB'S NINTH SON, Leah's fifth. We know that after the brothers were reconciled, Issachar and his four sons emigrated to Egypt with Jacob's family. But so did Joseph's other brothers. And as with most of them, we know little about Issachar.

It is frustrating to have so little information about Joseph's brothers. We know more about Leah's first sons – Reuben, the compassionate one; Simeon and Levi, who slaughtered Shechem; Judah, who was honest and pragmatic. Of Dan and Naphtali, Gad and Asher, Issachar and Zebulun, our knowledge is scanty. Joseph is the one who engages our attention, whose progress we follow, as he moved through vicissitude and the foibles of fortune into full humanness.

And little Benjamin: even when he is a grown man he is referred to as little Benjamin, the youngest, the baby. When Joseph kept Simeon hostage in Egypt, and sent for Benjamin, the boy would hardly have been a boy any longer, but we still think of him as little Benjamin.

Little Benjamin was rooted in the land of Canaan with his father. Born on the way there, he had never known the land of his grandfather Laban, where the other brothers had been born and grown up. We do well not to worry too much about the chronology of the twelve brothers. The story of Joseph is as much story as history. Jacob thought of little Benjamin as a child, and so should we – little Benjamin, Jacob's last treasure, precious, probably overprotected. His trip to Egypt, at the command of some great, unknown lord in that distant land, was the strangest thing that had ever happened to him.

But for his father, Jacob, it was a terrible wrench, an acute fear that he would lose Benjamin as he had lost Rachel, as he had lost (he thought) Joseph.

Rachel was buried on the way from Laban's land to Isaac's. Jacob knew the place where her bones lay. Fairly frequently in my journal I referred to St. Margaret's graveyard and the bones of my forbears buried there. I wrote, "What does a cemetery mean nowadays? Every once in a while I have a fleeting wish that Hugh was buried over in the Goshen graveyard and that I could go visit the place of his mortal remains. But I don't need a cemetery. His garden is the right place for his ashes; and our life together in Crosswicks, in the apartment in New York, is more than enough of a 'memorial' marker. Every room is full of his presence. I can't believe that our bodies are anything but *gone* when they are gone, and my hope that our soul, our *us*, for want of a better word, is not annihilated, is a hope, not a rigid or legalistic system of belief."

My parents are buried side by side in a graveyard in Florida, not little St. Margaret's graveyard, but a larger one, along with many of my aunts, uncles, cousins, relations, ancestors. One of my cousins, a retired physician, visits the cemetery regularly, and I know that he makes sure that the family plots are properly tended, and I am grateful, for when I go south I do not go to the graveyard. That is not where my parents are. I touch my mother when I put on the piano music she played; when I serve dinner in bowls she used; when I put flowers in her vases. My father is with me when I sit at my desk which was his desk, when I touch his books, when I look at his portrait, painted before I was born, before the war which destroyed his health, a portrait of a vibrant young man in an apple orchard in Brittany, who had just come back from an assignment in Egypt and was wearing a dashing hat he had bought there, and whose eyes are full of life and fun and depth. That portrait is an icon, as my mother's music is an icon.

So we come back again to the question of the soul. Where is Hugh's *Hugh*? I remember looking at my father lying in his coffin when I was seventeen and thinking, "That is not Father. He is not there." And then asking myself – and God – "Where is he?" And believing then, as I do now, deep in my inmost heart, that God still has work for us to do, and the reality of my father, of Hugh, of all that cloud of witnesses, is still real, alive in a way we can't even begin to understand.

But how often God speaks to us in the darkness.

The March after Hugh's death was bleak. I wrote, "It has been a long, cold winter (it is snowing again today), a winter of inner and outer chill. A winter of hard work (too much out-of-town lecturing), revising the book; being grateful beyond words for family and friends. A winter of absences: Hugh's absence; God's absence.

"Then last week came an experience where God's hand was so visible that it was impossible not to recognize it, and out of tragedy came shining affirmation.

"Last Friday I was scheduled to take the shuttle to Boston to speak at Simmons College Friday night and Saturday morning. I planned to spend Saturday afternoon with Danna."

Danna was a young friend who had cancer. She had come through a double mastectomy and chemotherapy with shining faith. She lived near Boston and was a member of a prayer group that was very dear to me, young women, all of the age to have children still at home, who met together to pray, and who had avoided the many pitfalls to which prayer groups are prone.

One of Danna's amusing but apt suggestions was that all prayer groups should read John Updike's *The Witches of Eastwick*. A creative idea. That book certainly points out the pitfalls of spiritual pride!

Danna and I wrote regularly. In one letter she quoted Woody Allen. I can't remember the exact quote, but it was something like, "Life is full of anxiety, trouble, and misery, and it is over too soon." She added, "I love Woody."

In the early autumn she learned that her cancer, which was thought to be cured, had metastasized to the liver. We all knew that things were not good, but it looked as though she might have a year or so more of full living.

So I planned, after my Saturday morning talk, to spend the afternoon with Danna, and then I was to stay over to preach on Sunday morning and take the shuttle home. I was staying with Ethel and Paul Heins, who for so many years were, one after the other, editors of Horn Book, and friends of children's literature and its writers.

On Wednesday I got a call saying that Danna's condition had deteriorated, and she was in Massachusetts General Hospital, but was still looking forward to Saturday afternoon.

On Thursday at two in the afternoon I got a call saying that Danna's blood pressure was dropping rapidly and could I come. *Now.*

I walked home, stuffed a few clothes in an overnight bag, and somehow managed to catch the 3:30 shuttle. I was met by one of the prayer group and her husband and taken directly to the hospital, where I was able to be with Danna and her husband and eldest son, and the members of the prayer group, all of whom were there, caring, praying, and all of whom mentioned God's amazing timing in having me scheduled to be in Boston just at this time.

Ethel and Paul were gracious and kind about having me arrive a day early – and concerned about the reason. It had been planned that Danna's son would pick me up around ten o'clock Friday morning, but he arrived much earlier, while Ethel and Paul and I were having breakfast and we drove right to the hospital. It was apparent that Danna was dying.

I wrote, "It was, in a powerful way, like living through Hugh's death all over again. But I am grateful indeed to have been privileged to have been with Danna as she left this world, and to be with her husband and son.

"I did the jobs at Simmons, preached on Sunday, and stayed to preach at Danna's funeral on Monday. The timing was so incredible that it is impossible to put it down to coincidence. Suddenly, in death and tragedy, God was revealed.

"Danna was a person with a shining spirit, a deep gift of prayer, a merry, bubbling laugh. It is somehow right and proper that God should have chosen her dying as a vessel to reveal the love of the Maker to us all."

Timing. We all saw God's hand in the timing of my trip to Boston. Months later I wrote in my journal: "Each time I write the date I am aware of the passage of time, swift as white water. Time in which strange and irrational things happen, like the deaths of Danna, Gloria, Jean. Cynth had a timely death." I had just come from the memorial for a beloved ninety-two-year-old cousin. "The house in West Price Street (in Philadelphia) is full of memories. I wrote large chunks of *The Small Rain* sitting in the downstairs window seat. Before Hugh and I were married I could always call, 'Is it all right if I come down for a while?' I left Touché [my dog] there while I went to be with Hugh in Washington. Sleeping in 'the little room' where I have so often slept was poignant. Up early, and off to the airport. And here I am in San Antonio.

"The time in each day is precious and precarious. No one knows when some accident will shatter time, some tornado, or heart attack, or gunshot. Perhaps that is why music is so necessary, with its ordered building and structuring of time, and even when there are dissonances or odd chromatics or modulations, they emphasize the exquisite ordering of time.

"Cynth had twenty-two years more than Hugh did. Hugh had twenty years more than Danna or Jean, and well over a decade more than Gloria. How many people get ninety plus years of time that is rich and full of quality as Cynth did? Yes, we can truly say that it is quality and not duration of time that matters – and yet untimeliness is a warping of the music, or a violin string breaking in the midst of playing.

"I had expected that going back to the house on Price Street, so full of memories, that Jean's untimely death might send another wave of grief breaking over me. But no wild sobs have come, no torrent of tears, only a few dry little grunts and groans as I am getting ready for bed. Maybe it's that the emotions of a year ago are too intense, that they would let loose a storm, a rushing waterfall too violent to be poured through the fragile body. I am very carefully not remembering exactly what was happening a year ago today. Something deep in my body is doing the remembering that is too painful for my conscious mind."

A friend struggling with depression said to me, "I just want things to be normal." And I thought: What is normal? Normal is the reality of living with precariousness, of never knowing what is around the corner, when accident or death are going to strike. Normal is cooking dinner for friends in the midst of this precariousness, lighting the candles, laughing, being together. Normal is trusting that God will make meaning out of everything that happens.

So Jacob had to let Benjamin go.

He took the boy in his arms, holding him so tightly that the boy thought his ribs would break, and it was a long time before he understood that his father was weeping for Joseph, the brother who had so long ago been killed by some wild beast. The older brothers had brought home his bright coat stained dark with blood.

They had lived well in Canaan. Jacob's tents were large and comfortable. His flocks and herds had increased. The older brothers were married; their tents with their wives and children stood nearby. They were not prepared for the failure of the crops, for animals dying from hunger and thirst because the pasture land was brown and sere and wells were running dry. Benjamin had never been hungry before.

The corn the brothers had brought back with them from Egypt was soon gone. Jacob instructed his sons to return to Egypt to buy more. But there was one condition, Judah protested – they had been told that the lord of the land would not even see them unless they brought Benjamin. "We must take Benjamin, but I will be surety for him," Judah promised.

So, weeping, Jacob sent them off, bearing gifts (bribes) for the great man in Egypt.

What a strange adventure for Benjamin – his first time away from the home tents, not quite sure what had happened to his brothers in Egypt, or why they had been accused of being spies, or why Simeon was jailed there, or what the money in the bags was all about, or why the great man wanted to see him. But the anxiety of his brothers was palpable.

To leave home, to go into the unknown, is a kind of death. Did Benjamin know that? Are all these other little deaths in life preparation for the death of the body?

Joseph was not yet through playing cat and mouse with his brothers. Was it merely revenge, to pay them back for their betrayal of him? Or was Joseph, too, unsettled and disturbed, seeing his brothers unexpectedly after all these years? Did he, remembering his dreams of the stalks of corn bowing down before him, find the fulfilling of these dreams irresistible?

Cat and mouse. While Hugh was dying, while one thing went wrong after another, to the consternation of his doctors, it seemed that some malign power was playing cat and mouse. Cat and mouse all over the planet. Terrorist attacks in Paris. Strange, deranged men stalking and killing young women. A horrible fire in a South African gold mine – a terrible disaster in an already beleaguered country. We seem to be surrounded by a horror and a hissing and an everlasting reproach.

What is that *normal* my friend was looking for?

The powers of darkness are at work. Another word for them is *echthroi*, Greek for "the enemy," and the echthroi, too, are fighting the light.

Lady Julian of Norwich wrote,

He said not, *"Thou shalt not be troubled, thou shalt not be travailed, thou shalt not be distressed," but he said, "Thou shalt not be overcome." It is God's will that we take heed to these words, that we may be ever mighty in faithful trust in weal and woe.*

How were Benjamin's brothers to be faithful, taking the youngest away from their father, to a strange lord who had already shown himself to be erratic and unpredictable? As soon as the brothers arrived they were taken to Joseph's house, and again they were terrified. Benjamin was dazzled with what seemed to him to be a palace. His brothers were again speaking all at once, explaining that they had returned the money they had found in their sacks.

And Joseph's chief steward said, *"Peace be to you. Fear not,"* speaking in the familiar words of angels all through the Bible, *"Fear not!"* He went on, *"Your God, and the God of your father, has given you treasure in your sacks." And then he brought Simeon out to them.*

Then they were given water, and their feet were washed (prefiguring Jesus' washing of his friends' feet), *and their animals were given provender.*

When Joseph came home, the brothers gave him the presents they had brought, and bowed themselves to the earth before him. How many of them remembered Joseph's dream, and that this was the fulfillment of it?

Joseph asked them how they were. Then he questioned, "Is your father well, the old man of whom you spoke? Is he still alive?"

And they answered, "Your servant, our father, is in good health. He is yet alive." And they bowed down their heads and made obeisance.

And Joseph lifted up his eyes and saw his brother Benjamin, his mother's son, and said, "Is this your younger brother, of whom you spoke?" And he said to Benjamin, "God be gracious to you, my son."

Joseph was overcome with emotion and left them, because he ached to embrace his brother; so he went into his chamber and wept there. Then he washed his face and controlled himself, and the meal was brought in.

Joseph was served by himself, and the brothers were served by themselves, and Asenath, Joseph's wife, was served by herself, *because the Egyptians might not eat bread with the Hebrews, for that is an abomination unto the Egyptians.*

And later it became an abomination for the orthodox Jew to eat with the unorthodox.

How strange human customs are! When my daughter, Josephine, and her husband, Alan, an Episcopal priest, visited acquaintances in Israel, they were served food and drink, but their host and hostess would not eat with them, because that would have been an abomination to these orthodox Jews!

In my church, the Episcopal Church, it is only in recent decades that God's table has been opened to people of other denominations. And half a century ago a convicted murderer could confess, repent, and then be welcome at the altar rail, but a divorced person could not. In many places we still hold to the kind of division into differing denominations that my Baptist mother-in-law grew up with.

Not long ago I talked with a friend and he told me about reading a Metropolitan Opera bulletin and checking the names of all the singers he knew to be Christians. His question was not, Are they good singers, serving their art to the best of their ability? But, Are they *Christian*? And as we ate at a table with a group of people there was a conversation about whether or not a certain doctor was a Christian – not was he a good doctor, but was he a Christian? Isn't this reversed way of looking at things the reason that so much Christian art isn't very good art? That if you're a Christian that is all that matters? Christian or no, if you are a pianist you have to practise eight hours a day or you won't be a good pianist – or a good Christian. We are not very rational, we human beings who are called to observe and contemplate, but who often get wound up in customs and laws and dogmas and are blinded to that which we are supposed to see.

And Asenath, too, ate alone.

* * *

ASENATH

And who is the God of the gods?

Is there a God who orders the gods, chastises them for their jealousies and their outrageous demands?

My husband would say that his one god is this god, but his god, too, has limits – is the god of the Hebrew people only. Does he not care for all the rest of us, whether we live or die? This god my husband obeys does not hear the cry of anguish of the Egyptian mother whose child is caught by the crocodile. Only his own people matter to him.

So, he, too, is a god among many gods.

Is there a God whose mercy is over all?

I did not think these thoughts until I was given by my father, Potiphar, to be Joseph's wife. My father is priest of On, and his god is Ra, the sun god. My father is high priest, and has served Ra all his life, Ra who gives both life and death. It was a strange thing to me that I was given to the Hebrew, and it was a mark of how highly the Pharaoh regarded this strange man.

At night we lie together, we know each other. We have our sons, and what must they think about all these strange gods, each one more important (in someone's eyes) than another? There are many gods in Egypt, many priests who serve them, but Ra is the sun. Without Ra it would be perpetual night. Without Ra the Nile would not know when to flood and fertilize the land.

What did it mean to my father, the high priest, to give me to a man whose god was not his god?

My husband is a good man. He is fair. He is just. But he is seldom merry. Sometimes he has laughed when he has played with our sons, tossing them in the air, delighting to hear them shriek with pleasure, knowing themselves safe in his strong arms. With me he is always courteous. At night, when Ra has turned away, my husband brings up from me strange depths of delight, and I please him, too. This I know by his sighs of fulfillment, by his arms that remain around me as he falls into a deep sleep of contentment.

Do our gods know each other? Are they friends? In the darkness when Ra is behind the earth does he laugh with Joseph's god at our lack of understanding? It is not just Ra – this god of Joseph's whose name is unwritten, unspoken, and unpronounceable. In Egypt we have many gods, gods of the underworld, gods to lead us in this life and to lead us in the afterlife. Vultures and crocodiles and the strange black dog, Anubis. A jackal, some say. And there are the goddesses, too, of fertility, fertility for the crops, and for the people, too. Too many gods.

But it was a strong and strange thing for me to be given to Joseph – the Hebrew, the one with the most alien of gods – a tribute to his power, to his ability to rule with justice and not with pride. One might suppose he would have been a threat to the Pharaoh, but he was not. He did what needed to be done and at the end of the day came quietly home to play with our sons, to eat alone, to sleep with me.

10

Zebulun

shall dwell at the haven of the sea; and he shall be for an haven of ships; and his border shall be by Zidon.

Genesis 49:13

ZEBULUN WAS THE HEAD of the tenth tribe of Israel. His inherited land was mountainous, but within it was Gath Hepher, where Jonah came from, and Nazareth, Jesus' "home town."

Isaiah writes,

Nevertheless there will be no more gloom for those who were in distress. In the past he humbled the land of Zebulun and the land of Naphtali, but in the future he will honor Galilee of the Gentiles, by way of the sea, along the Jordan.

And then follow some of Isaiah's most beautiful verses, *The people walking in darkness have seen a great light, on those living in the land of the shadow of death a light has dawned.* And Matthew quotes Isaiah in the fourth chapter of his Gospel:

Leaving Nazareth, he [Jesus] went and lived in Capernaum, which was by the lake in the area of Zebulun and Naphtali, to fulfill what was said through the prophet Isaiah,
"Land of Zebulun and land of Naphtali, the way to the sea, along the Jordan, Galilee of the Gentiles – the people living in darkness have seen a great light; on those living in the land of the shadow of death a light has dawned."

The Old Testament so often nourishes and informs the New.
Zebulun, meanwhile, came with the brothers from Canaan, to Egypt, to the great lord's palace, was reunited with Simeon, and when they were seated in order of age – Reuben first, then Simeon, and on down to Benjamin – they looked at each other in wonder.

And Joseph put food before them, but Benjamin got five times as much food as any of the others. They ate and were merry with him.

Did Benjamin wonder at this favoritism, or was he used to it? Did it, perhaps, embarrass him? But he was the youngest, so he did not speak. How strange it must have been for Benjamin, receiving special and inexplicable favors from the great lord of Egypt. How strange was Egypt itself, with its buildings of stone, rather than tents of skins, with its huge palaces and temples and tombs – edifices that were built to last forever.
How strange the Pharaonic Egyptian language, into which the brothers' words were translated for the great lord. And how overwhelming for Joseph, to hear them murmuring in his

own familiar language, and yet to have to wait to respond until the interpreter gave him the words in Egyptian.

Words have incredible power to heal or to harm. The Name of Jesus is a word of love, and one which I hear misused daily, thoughtlessly, with no evil intent, but weakened and debased by misuse. Words of prayer can be words of healing. It frightens me very much to know that people not only those in "primitive" tribes, but even people who call themselves Christian, can pray against other people. But prayer that is not for love is not truly prayer.

In Joseph's story we note over and over again the power of words. Joseph abuses words by bragging, and pays for his abuse. His brothers use words with murderous intent, and are kept from acting out those words only by Reuben and Judah. Potiphar's wife uses words of false accusation against Joseph, so that he is cast into prison. Malicious gossip can cause terrible harm. Casual, thoughtless words, too, can cause grave damage. More than once it has come to my ears that someone has reported, "Madeleine said ..." something that Madeleine never said or even thought at all, but the damage has been done.

How powerful words are, and how we seem to forget that power today, with our radical loss of vocabulary. I was horrified to read that the textbook publishing houses are having to simplify the language of the college textbooks because today these books are too difficult for college students, who had no difficulty with them a few decades ago.

As our vocabulary dwindles, so does our ability to think, and so does our theology, and what is theology but the word about God?

Would we quarrel so much about God if we were able to think more clearly about our Maker? I worry about what we are doing to the story God has told about Elself in the greatest story ever told, that of Jesus of Nazareth.

It is easier to see what we are doing to our story in the credal churches, such as my own, where, after great committee effort and expense we have come up with a new *Book of Common Prayer.* Now I don't want to go back to the 1928 *Prayer Book.* We needed to think about what we believe in terms of the disturbed twentieth century in which we are living. But we haven't done well by the language, and when we do not do well by the language, we do not do well by our faith. What distresses me most acutely is that we have changed our story, that greatest story ever told, and without so much as a "by your leave." It is a strange, powerful, difficult story, but it has been our story for nearly two thousand years. If we are going to change it, we should at the very least call a Council of Houston or Omaha or Chicago and do it publicly.

My dearest friend, who is an Episcopalian, senior warden of her church, said to me, "I can't say the creed anymore."

I asked her, "Have you noticed that the language has been changed on you?"

"No."

"Well, it has."

Radically changed. I can't say it anymore, either. In the language of the media I don't believe a word of it. God is a greater storyteller than our recent committees, and we need to reflect back the glory with the greatest language of which we are capable.

I believe in One God, the Father almighty, maker of heaven and earth, and in all things visible and invisible.

Visible and invisible has been replaced with *seen and unseen*, and that's not the same thing at all. If I close my eyes I can't physically see the page in front of me, but it's still visible. I love the idea of the great invisible world that we cannot see, but God can – the world of subatomic particles, the world of the galaxies beyond the reach of our greatest telescopes.

Well, it gets worse. We've taken out *Begotten of his Father before all worlds.* That's a terrible omission, because it allows people to forget that Christ *was*, was before the beginning, *was* the Power that shouted all things into being, *was* incarnate for us, and still *is*.

Oh, and even worse. We used to say, *And was incarnate BY the Holy Ghost of the Virgin Mary.* Or, *who was conceived BY the Holy Ghost.* Oh, yes, that's the story, the greatest story ever told. But now we say, weakly, *by the power of the Holy Spirit.* We were all conceived by the power of the Holy Spirit. I was. My babies were. That's the Trinity, shining forth in love: two human beings and the Holy Spirit, and the miracle of a baby. But Jesus was conceived BY the Holy Spirit, and that's a very different story. That's what we used to say.

I have never been particularly hung up over the Virgin Birth. It hasn't been the focus of my faith one way or another. But it has been a significant part of our story and what it truly means is that Jesus' humanity came from his mother, Mary, and that his divinity came from his father, who is God the Holy Spirit. Take away the Virgin Birth and you take away Jesus' divinity.

And now the Virgin Birth has vanished into the lost world of the visible and the invisible. No one has even had the courtesy to ask those of us who go faithfully to church every Sunday, "Do you mind?" I mind.

I mind very much indeed. I can't say the creed in the new, impoverished language either. I don't believe that God is sitting on a golden throne with Jesus at his right hand on a smaller throne. I believe the creed in the language of high poetry that is the language of truth, not the language of fact. I think we need to do something about this, not to go backwards, but to admit humbly to ourselves that we have served language poorly, which means serving God poorly. Perhaps the men – they were men, weren't they? – who wrote the new version of the Creed didn't mean to change the story, didn't even know they were changing the story, but that is what, in fact, they did.

The story that got changed is a wonderful story. My friend, Canon Tallis, said that the Virgin Birth was embarrassing to the early Christians. They wouldn't have kept it in if it hadn't happened. God came to us through the womb of a fourteen-year-old girl who had the courage to say to the angel, *"Be it unto me according to your word."*

And what about the angel? What do Scriptural angels say when they come to anyone? *"Fear not!"* That gives us a clue about what angels look like – that the first thing they have to cry out to us is, *"Fear not!"* We've prettied up angels; no longer are they seen as flaming fires, and that's a weakening, too.

The Christian belief is that Jesus was wholly human and Jesus was wholly God. His humanness is his birthing by a young girl, so that Jesus was born as all of us are born. His Godness is that his father is God Elself. That is how the paradox that Jesus is wholly human and Jesus is wholly God is reconciled. If the Virgin Birth is taken away, isn't Jesus' Godness taken away, too?

I sense a kind of limiting chauvinism here. Did the men doing the translation feel that Mary couldn't have done it without one of them – Joseph, or whoever? Jesus was conceived *by* the Holy Spirit – condescending in total love. That is an extraordinary story, and when it got taken away from me, I found that I believe it passionately.

"And it came to pass." "Once upon a time." Wonderful words! To be a human being is to be able to listen to a story, to tell a story, and to know that story is the most perfect vehicle of truth available to the human being. What is so remarkable about the stories of ancient cultures is not their radical diversity, but their unity. We tell basically the same story in all parts of the world, over and over again in varying ways, but it is always the same story, of a universe created by God. We can tell more about God through the words of a story than through any amount of theology.

Joseph was forced to look low for the Creator, dumped into a pit, sold to strangers, sold again in Egypt, thrown into prison, catapulted into power. And with each strange reversal he grew, grew into a human being. To grow into a human being is not to grow into *humanism*, for humanists believe only in man, able to do it on his own without the help of God. To be a human being is to know clearly that anything good we do is sheer gift of grace, that God's image in us shines so brightly that its light is visible.

While Joseph's brothers ate the feast prepared for them he looked at them, his heart full, but he was not yet ready to reveal himself to them, and so he could not touch them. Men were not afraid to touch each other in those days, to fling their arms around each other in hilarity or grief or forgiveness, and Joseph must have longed particularly to touch Benjamin, his full brother, now grown to a comely young man.

After the brothers had eaten, Joseph ordered their bags to be filled with corn, and they bade him farewell with much gratitude, if considerable perplexity, and set off for Canaan. This time Simeon was with them and their hearts were light.

But then again they were faced with the unexpected, and further terror. The cat was not through playing with the mice. Was that all it was for Joseph? Mere cat play? Or was there anguish in his heart, too? We human beings are often unaware of our deepest motives, and our motives, at their best, are usually mixed. Joseph was settled in Egypt, in a position of power

– power that involved incredibly hard work, but still power. He was married to Asenath. He had sons. He had put Canaan and his family behind him, perforce. His brothers had betrayed him with "a horror and a hissing and an everlasting reproach." There was no point in looking back. He had to make his home in Egypt, to live as a stranger in a strange land.

Now he sent his steward riding after his brothers, and the steward stopped them and accused them of taking his master's silver cup.

They were horrified.

"No, no!" Reuben cried.

"How can you say such things to us? Why would we take your lord's silver cup after his great kindness to us?"

All the brothers protested their innocence loudly, and Reuben continued,

"You know that the money which we found in our sacks we brought again to you from the land of Canaan. How, then, should we steal silver or gold out of your lord's house? If any among us has anything of your master's, he will surely die."

All the bags were opened. And there, in Benjamin's sack of grain, the silver cup was found.

The brothers looked at each other, and at Benjamin. There was terror in their eyes, in their voices.

Wordlessly, Reuben picked Benjamin up and helped him onto his donkey, and the brothers turned back towards Egypt.

Benjamin was silent, terrified. Reuben had said that whoever took the silver cup would surely die, and Benjamin felt a great weight of horror. He had not taken the cup; why was it in his bag? Why? Why did the great lord heap his plate with more food than any of the brothers? What did he want?

It was a heavy and silent ride back to Joseph's palace, where he was waiting for them. He confronted them,

"What deed is this that you have done? Did you not know that a man such as I am can certainly divine?"

And Judah said, hopelessly,

"What shall we say to my lord? What shall we speak? God has found out the iniquity of your servants. Behold, we are my lord's servants, both we, and he also with whom the cup is found."

Judah's dark eyes were bleak. It was apparent to Benjamin that this older brother believed that they were all going to be killed for this thing that not one of them had done.

Joseph looked at Benjamin, and his eyes were surprisingly mild. He told them that the one in whose sack the cup was found would be his servant. Then he said to the others, *"As for you, get you up in peace to your father."*

In peace, without Benjamin?

Judah approached Joseph and said, *"Oh, my lord, let your servant speak a word in my lord's ears, and let not your anger burn against your servant."* And he pleaded with Joseph not to take Benjamin away from his father.

"Do not be angry with your servant, though you are equal to Pharaoh himself. My lord has asked his servants if we have a father or a brother. And we answered, 'We have an aged father, and there is a young son born to him in his old age. His

brother is dead, and he is the only one of his mother's sons left, and his father loves him.' After we had told you this, my lord told your servants to bring our young brother to him, and we said to my lord that we could not take our brother away from our father, for if we did so, our father would die. But you told your servants that unless we brought our youngest brother to you we would never see Simeon again."

And so he went on, an impassioned speech, a brave speech, because Judah had to acknowledge openly that the sons of Rachel were more dear to their father than the sons of the other wives. Judah ended by crying,

"If the boy is not with us when we go back to our father, and if our father, whose life is closely bound up with the boy's life, sees that we do not have the boy with us, he will die. Your servants will bring the grey head of our father down to the grave in sorrow. Your servant guaranteed the boy's safety to our father. I said, 'If I do not bring him back to you, I will bear the blame before you, my father, all my life.' Now then, please let your servant remain here as my lord's slave in place of the boy, and let the boy return with his brothers. How can I go back to my father if the boy is not with me? No! Do not let me see the misery that would come upon my father!"

At these words of anguish Joseph could no longer control himself in front of all his attendants, and, interrupting the interpreter he cried out, "Go away!" His servants and attendants looked at him wonderingly.

"Leave me!"

And they left him. At last he was alone with his brothers.

* * *

BENJAMIN

"Go away!" the great man orders all his servants. He heaves with sobs like a child, and all his retinue hurry to leave him. My brothers and I are frozen. Rooted to the spot. We cannot move.

And the great man weeps, and then he lifts me in his arms as though I were a small child – how strong he is! – and then he cries out, "I am Joseph! And does my father yet live?"

And no one dares answer him. They are all still afraid. But he holds me as once my sister Dinah held me, and I put my arms about his neck as though I were still a child, and I say, "Yes. Our father lives."

And now I know why he seemed familiar to me: he is my one full brother, my mother's son.

"And our mother," I breathe, "do you remember our mother?"

He holds me even more closely. "Yes. I remember our mother." And he tells me about her, how beautiful she was, and always sweet-smelling. In a land of tents made of skins, and of dust, and camel dung, always she smelled sweet. And when she knew that she was with child, with me, how happy she was, and how happy he was, too, and our father – and then, in birthing me, she died.

And again he wept, and I wept, too, for the mother I had never known. Oh, I wasn't lonely, and I wasn't unmothered. I had, you might say, mothers to spare. Too many mothers. But I was loved; I did not lack for love. And yet I wept, for loss of my mother, for gain of my brother.

And our brothers stood and their eyes were full of sorrow and full of anxiety.

"Come near to me," Joseph said to our brothers, and slowly, one by one, they came near. And he said, *"I am Joseph, your brother, whom you sold into Egypt."*

And they bowed their heads, and their eyes were downcast and they mumbled.

And Joseph said, speaking kindly, his arm still about me as I stood beside him, *"Do not be grieved, or angry with yourselves, that you sold me, because God sent me before you to preserve life. You meant it for evil, but Yahweh meant it for good."*

God's plan. Did God send Joseph to Egypt? If my brother had stayed in Canaan, he would not have saved the corn and grain to avert famine.

Was my mother's death part of God's plan? Was there some good purpose that it served that I do not yet know about?

Joseph told us that the famine would continue for five more years. And he said,

"God sent me before you to preserve you a posterity in the earth, and to save your lives by a great deliverance. So it was not you who sold me into Egypt, but God, and he has made me a father to Pharaoh and lord of all his house, and ruler throughout all the land of Egypt."

"Sold into Egypt? Who sold someone into Egypt?" I ask.

Joseph turns away. Simeon and Levi turn away. The others stare down at their feet, those feet washed by Joseph's servants after the dirty and dusty trip from Canaan. No one speaks.

I ask again.

Reuben and Judah draw me aside. Try to explain. Neither one tries to clear himself, but each one says that it was the other who did not want Joseph killed.

Killed.

My brother killed by his own brothers. My heart beats with new fear.

Only Reuben and Judah had held back from killing. Reuben wanted to rescue Joseph from the pit and bring him back to our father. But the others – and Judah did not stop them – sold him to a group of traveling merchants on their way to Egypt.

How can I ever feel safe with my brothers again?

What will our father –

But Joseph turns then and comes to me and tells me I must never, ever, say anything to our father. It would kill him, Joseph says, and Reuben and Judah nod agreement.

I am made to promise.

So I do. What purpose would it serve to grieve our father, when we can bring him such joy? And how he will rejoice that Joseph is alive!

I think again about what Joseph said about God's plan.

"Do you truly think it was God's plan for our brothers to sell you into Egypt?" I demand.

He nods.

"I do not understand."

"You do not need to understand," Joseph says gravely. "Nor do I. I only know that where there was great hurt, there is now great good, and that our God can come into all our pain and make use of it, as he has done with me." And he opens wide his arms to all the brothers, all of them.

And there are tears. And there is joy.

11

Joseph

is a fruitful bough, even a fruitful bough by a well, whose branches run over the wall: The archers have sorely grieved him, and shot at him, and persecuted him: But his bow abode in strength, and the arms of his hands were made strong by the hands of the mighty God of Jacob; Even by the God of thy father, who shall help thee; and by the Almighty, who shall bless thee with blessings of heaven above, blessings of the deep that lieth under, blessings of the breasts, and of the womb: The blessings of thy father have prevailed above the blessings of my progenitors unto the utmost bound of the everlasting hills: they shall be on the head of Joseph, and on the crown of the head of him that was separate from his brethren.

Genesis 49:22–26

OF COURSE Benjamin would not have known of his brothers' treachery, and his reaction would have awakened Joseph's pain.

Pain, lying long dormant, can rise up and be as acute as when it was first felt. The wonderful letters I have received since the publication of *Two-Part Invention: The Story of a Marriage* have reawakened my pain at Hugh's illness and death. The letters speak affirmation and joy; yet grief that had been drowsing, if not sleeping, is suddenly wide awake.

We don't "get over" the deepest pains of life, nor should we. "Are you over it?" is a question that cannot be asked by someone who has been through "it," whatever "it" is. It is an anxious question, an asking for reassurance that cannot be given. During an average lifetime there are many pains, many griefs to be borne. We don't "get over" them; we learn to live with them, to go on growing and deepening, and understanding, as Joseph understood, that God can come into all our pain and make something creative out of it.

Through his pain Joseph had learned to be a human being. And he had learned that to be human is to be fallible, and therefore in the end he harbored no hate nor held a grudge against his brothers.

To be human is, yes, to be fallible. We are the creatures who *know*, and we know that we know. We are also the creatures who know that we don't know. When I was a child, I used to think that being grown up meant that you would know. Grown-ups had the answers. This is an illusion that a lot of people don't lose when they grow up. But our very fallibility is one of our human glories. If we are fallible we are free to grow and develop. If we are infallible we are rigid, stuck in one position, as immobile as those who could not let go the idea that planet earth is the center of all things.

I was talking about this to a friend, and she said, "You don't think the pope is infallible?" And I laughed, because that wasn't what I was thinking at all. The pope is the pope. The Church has always tended to make absolute statements, and absolutism has always caused trouble. It was absolutism that caused the disastrous split between the Eastern and Western Churches, which was the beginning of the continuous and devastating fragmentation of Christendom.

When I was speaking at a Mennonite college I was told that the split between the Mennonites and the Amish in the fifteenth century came about because of buttons. *Buttons.* One group, I forget which, decided it was all right to wear buttons because they were useful. The other said, no, buttons are a decoration and are sinful. And they split over buttons.

Peripheral. And each fragment of the church, from the extreme evangelical right to the extreme permissive liberal left is convinced of the Bible's infallibility or the pope's infallibility or the infallibility of the creeds or the infallibility of not having creeds.

Wait! Did I imply that Scripture is not infallible? Scripture is true, and fallibility and infallibility is not what Scripture is about. According to Scripture it is perfectly all right to have slaves as long as you treat them kindly. Slaves are told to be diligent and loyal to their masters. The psalmist says that he never saw the good man go hungry or his children begging for bread. Yet we know that good men do go hungry and their children do beg for bread every day. In his letter to the people of Thessalonica Paul's harsh words about the Jews have encouraged the ugliness of anti-Semitism: *"It was the Jews who killed their own prophets, the Jews who killed the Lord, Jesus, the Jews who drove us out, his messengers."* Taken out of the context in which Paul was writing to the suffering Thessalonians, his words can do untold harm, and they have often done so.

So what do I believe about Scripture? I believe that it is true. What is true is alive and capable of movement and growth.

Scripture is full of paradox and contradiction, but it is true, and if we fallible human creatures look regularly and humbly at the great pages and people of Scripture, if we are willing to accept truth rather than rigidly infallible statements, we will be given life, and life more abundantly. And we, like Joseph, will make progress towards becoming human.

There are some creatures which are not given the blessing of infallibility – those insects that live totally by instinct. The instinct of an insect has to be infallible or it will perish. Every ant in an ant colony knows exactly what to do, when to do it, and how to do it. And an ant which deviates from the infallible pattern is a goner.

An ant has superb instincts, but precious little free will. Free will involves fallibility. An ant approached by Potiphar's wife would not have had the free will to say, *No* – or *Yes*.

With free will, we are able to try something new. Maybe it doesn't work, or we make mistakes and learn from them. We try something else. That doesn't work, either. So we try yet something else again. When I study the working processes of the great artists I am awed at the hundreds and hundreds of sketches made before the painter begins to be ready to put anything on the canvas. It gives me fresh courage to know of the massive revision Dostoevsky made of all his books – the hundreds of pages that got written and thrown out before one was kept. A performer must rehearse and rehearse and rehearse, making mistakes, discarding, trying again and again.

One of my favorite stories when I was a child was that of the Scottish leader Robert Bruce and the spider. Bruce had lost yet another battle. He had crawled into a cave, wounded and defeated. He was giving up. And while he lay there he watched a spider spinning her web. To make its perfection complete she had to throw a strand of silk to the center of the web. She threw and missed. Threw and missed. Six times she missed. But the seventh time she threw, the silk flew to its perfect place.

So Robert Bruce left the cave, gathered his people together, and together they fought one more battle. And this time they won.

The memory of that story, read when I was a small child, has stayed with me all these years. I, too, like most of us, have had to throw that strand of silk over and over again.

Infallibility and perfectionism go hand in hand. Perfectionism is a great crippler. We must be willing to try, to make mistakes, to try not to make the same mistakes too often, but to keep on trying. If I were a perfectionist I couldn't get the pleasure I do out of playing the piano, because there isn't any way that I can play like Rubenstein. But I don't have to be perfect. I have to listen to my fingers and hear what I want them to do perhaps more than what they are actually doing. But I don't have to be perfect. I just have to enjoy.

Joseph was a great mathematician. He had to be, in order to figure out the complicated logistics of storing food for seven years for the great land of Egypt, of distributing it, not only to the Egyptians, but to those who came from Canaan and other lands, of knowing how much to give and how much to keep in order that the supply might last until the time of famine was over. And, like all great mathematicians, he was an artist. The artist cannot be an artist without believing in the goodness of matter, of all that has been made; the artist cannot be an artist without having faith that what God has created is delightful and to be rejoiced in. Sometimes the man of business can fall into the Manichaean heresy of assuming that only spirit is good and all matter is evil. Is it coincidence that Puritans denigrated the joys of sex but were successful in business? Joseph refused

Potiphar's wife's advances because he would not betray his master, but he knew and enjoyed his own wife, Asenath.

Joseph, as a great mathematician, managed to combine a cool business sense with the *art* of numbers, and this combination is what business too often lacks. One of the horrors of the Industrial Revolution was that its factories reduced many of the workers to a state little better than bees in a hive or ants in a hill, and along with this denigration of the value of our humanness came the suspicion of the arts as being a "tool of the devil."

In this very century – not now, but in the early years – an actor could not be buried in consecrated ground. I was married to an actor for forty years, and I know that in his acting he was true, not infallible, but true. Many Christians have either tended to toss the arts off as unreal and unimportant, or as being sinful. And that is to miss the point. Anything good – and all that God made is good – can be distorted and made ugly and bad. That does not change the original good. I am glad that Joseph refused Potiphar's wife, even though it meant his going to jail. I am glad that he enjoyed Asenath.

If we have to be infallible we are not free to seek truth. We are not free to say *No*, this time, and *Yes*, that time. Truth often comes by revelation when we least expect it. It was in the middle of the night that I realized that Benjamin would have no idea that his brothers, his own brothers, had sold Joseph into Egypt.

My writing teaches me. It gives me truths I didn't know and could never have thought of by myself. Truth is given us when we are enabled to believe the contradictory and impossible. Jesus is wholly God? Jesus is wholly human? That's impossible. But it is the conjunction of these two impossibilities that make light.

Stagehands refer to light plugs as female plugs and male plugs.

I remember hearing a stagehand yell, "Give me a male plug." You have to have a male plug and a female plug to get light.

Light itself is a particle, and light is a wave. It is not that difficult to believe in the impossible because it is the impossible that gives us joy. The possible really isn't worth bothering about.

One of the bits of dogma that used to concern me was that Jesus is exactly like us – except he's sinless. Well, of course if he's sinless he's not exactly like us; he's not like us at all. And then I arrived at a totally different definition of sin. Sin is not child abuse or rape or murder, terrible though these may be. Sin is separation from God, and Jesus was never separate from the Source. Of course if we were close to our Source, if we were not separated from God, it would be impossible for us to commit child abuse or rape or murder. But when we are separated from God, that sin makes all sins possible.

Far too often we drift away from the Creator even if we don't deliberately turn away. We fall into self-satisfaction or self-indulgence. And we want above all things to be right. To insist on being infallible is to turn away from our Source, for only the Creator is infallible. And whenever we look for infallibility in any one of us, or in ourselves, we are putting ourselves in the place of God. *Hubris:* pride. That, of course, is the great danger of idolatry, of idolizing another human being. We are turning that human being into God, and of course no human being can be God – and disaster follows.

When we are without sin, we are totally in communion with the Creator who made us, along with galaxies, and quasars, and quail eggs, and quarks.

All I have to know is that I do not have to know in limited, finite terms of provable fact that which I believe. Infallibility has led to schisms in the Church, to atheism, to deep misery.

All I have to know is that God is love, and that love will not let us go, not any of us. When I say that I believe in the resurrection of the body, and I do, I am saying what I believe to be true, not literal, but true. Literalism and infallibility go hand in hand, but mercy and truth have kissed each other. To be human is to be fallible, but it is also to be capable of love and to be able to retain that childlike openness which enables us to go bravely into the darkness and towards that life of love and truth which will set us free.

Sometimes when I think about us human beings with all of our quirks, all of our flaws, all of our strangeness, our hilariousness, I wonder why God chose to make us this way. I have to assume that God knows better than I do, that this is indeed the way we are supposed to be, human beings bearing God's image within us. In the same way that we don't *see* those we love, but *know* those we love, we don't *see* God's image, but we *know* God's image. It is not a matter of sight but a matter of insight.

We human beings are creatures who live with questions that lead to new questions. What few answers there are come in the form of paradox and contradiction. I believe in the power of prayer. I believe in miracles, although Spinoza felt that a miracle was a denial of God's existence. Spinoza says,

Now, as nothing is true save only by Divine decree, it is plain that the universal laws of Nature are decrees of God following from the necessity and perfection of the Divine nature. Hence, any event happening in nature which contravened Nature's universal laws, would necessarily also contravene the Divine decree ... Therefore, Miracles, in the sense of events contrary to the laws of Nature, so far from demonstrating to us the existence of God, would, on the contrary, lead us to doubt it.

Since the universe is God's, I don't see why love can't alter any law which Love demands. Jesus made it very clear that love comes before law. So I have no trouble with miracles. The problem is: Why is *this* miracle granted, and *this* miracle withheld? Why does this child live and this child die? Why is one person cured and not another? Why is this prayer answered with a wonderful *Yes*, and other prayers with silence, or a *No*?

We don't understand the "no" answers, and probably we are not going to understand many of them in this life. But we will understand ultimately that the "no" always has a reason. When we say *No* to our children, we say *No* because there is a reason for saying *No*, a reason for their greater good. When my kids were little I'd say, "Do what I tell you to do when I tell you to do it. *Then* I'll explain to you that there's a truck coming down the road." Quite often we simply do not see the truck on the road that God is warning us against. We may never in this life know that it was about to run us down.

Surely when Joseph was sold into Egypt he knew only the ugliness of what his brothers had done, and had no inkling of how God was going to use it for good.

To be human is to be able to change, knowing full well that some change is good and some change is bad; some change is progressive and some is regressive, and we often cannot discern which is which. But if we lose the ability to change we stultify, we turn to stone, we die.

Remember, yesterday's heresy is tomorrow's dogma. Nowadays even the most avid creationists don't burn those who believe in the possibility of evolution. Giordano Bruno was burned at the stake because he had moved on from the belief that planet earth is the center of all things to understanding that we are part of a universe – a glorious, exciting part, called on to observe and contemplate, but still only a part.

The Church with its reluctance to change helped, if not forced, scientists into a position of atheism, in which many of them remain stuck to this day, with the absurd idea that religion and science have nothing in common and are, indeed, in conflict. The Church insisted, and sometimes still insists, that if you do not believe in God in a certain, specific, rigid way, then you are not a Christian. And so you come to equal folly on the part of the scientists. An article in the *New York Times* quoted the Academy of Sciences as saying that "religion and science are separate and mutually exclusive realms of human thought." Here is another example of rigidity and short-sightedness. At their best and wisest, religion and science enrich each other.

When Moses asked God his name, God said, "I am. Tell them that I AM sent you. I am that I am." The better, more accurate translation is, "I will be what I will be." Free. Free to manifest the glory in more brilliant ways of revelation than we can conceive of.

All through Scripture, the revelation of God and the people's understanding of God change. In the early chapters there are two quite different ways of looking at God, as there are two Creation stories, and two stories of the forming of Adam and Eve. There was a tribal god, who was one god among many gods. This tribal god was the warrior god of the patriarchs, who would expel the heathen from their own land so that his own people could occupy it, because the heathen were "them" and the tribal god wanted "us" to have the land.

Shattered remnants of this tribal thinking were behind England's empire, and behind our own treatment of the American Indians as we moved into the American continents. This refusal to change in our understanding of the Creator has brought about some very dehumanizing results, one of the least of which was forcing "them" to eat alone.

But there is also in Genesis a vision of the One God, the Maker of the Universe, the stars, and all things. This One God, unlike the tribal god, is a God of love, the One Jesus called Father, Abba, Daddy. There are suggestions in the Old Testament that the tribal god has a bad temper and is likely to throw thunderbolts if we arouse his anger, but the One God, the Creator, is lovingly merciful, quick to forgive. As Alan Jones reminds us, God says, "All is forgiven! Come home!"

We human beings are less quick than God to forgive, and quite a few Old (and New) Testament characters complain about God's forgiveness, saying that it is not reliable of God to be so forgiving, to say, "Come home. Let's have a party. Get out the fatted calf . . ." But God is love, and that love keeps breaking through our elder-brotherism, our stiff-neckedness, our resentments, our unwillingness to change. It is interesting in the story of Joseph and his brothers that Reuben and Judah, two elder brothers, were willing to change.

An amazing number of physicists have discovered that a belief in evolution does not necessarily mean that the Creation of the universe was happenstance. It is quite possible that this is how God chose to create. But it is important to remember that our present knowledge is far from the whole truth, and we probably have as far to go as the old earth-centered establishments in understanding the working of the Creator.

John said to the people of Laodicea,

"I know what you are. You are neither hot nor cold. I wish you were hot or cold. But because you are neither hot nor cold but lukewarm I will spew you out of my mouth."

Let us not be lukewarm. If we are passionate (rather than fanatic) we may be totally wrong (fanatics are never wrong), but we are still capable of change, capable of saying, "I'm wrong. I'm sorry."

Computers are passionless. I can probably have a relationship with my computer, but it is not love. And computers at airports cannot cope with apostrophes, and I'm having a terrible time keeping the apostrophe in L'Engle. I don't plan to give in to the computer and give it up. Computers do not know how to change. But we are able to change because we have passion – or better, *compassion.*

To be willing to change is to be willing to let go our most cherished beliefs, be they religious or scientific. But no scientific discovery has ever shaken my faith in God as Creator and Lover of us all. That is central. The rest – Baptist or Episcopalian, creationist or evolutionist – is peripheral. We are at a time on our planet when we must return to the central things, to understanding that we are all human beings on a very small planet and that we have, as Gandhi said, "enough for everyone's need but not for everyone's greed."

God feels deep pain when any of creation is rebellious and has turned against the Power of Love which made it all. We have hospitals because people cared about taking care of people who were ill or injured. By and large hospitals are not very good right now, but the love that started them was right. It's just that our technological knowledge has grown too fast and our compassion can't keep up with it, and a resurgence of compassion is essential. We can't have the absolute magnificent feast until everyone is well, and until everybody – Simeon and Levi, all of the family – is there, until everyone has said, "I'm sorry, I want to come home." And then the golden gates will fling open and the party can start.

When we are in communion with the Creator we are less afraid, less afraid that the wrong people will come to the party, less afraid that we ourselves aren't good enough, less afraid of pain and alienation and death. Jesus, who comes across in the Gospels as extraordinarily strong, begged in the garden, with drops of sweat like blood running down his face, that he might be spared the terrible cup ahead of him, the betrayal and abandonment by his friends, death on the cross. Because Jesus cried out in anguish, we may, too. But our fear is less frequent and infinitely less if we are close to the Creator. Jesus, having cried out, then let his fear go, and moved on.

A few months after my husband's death I went to speak at Brigham Young University in Provo, Utah. One of the professors asked me, "What has your husband's death made you think about death?"

I answered, "It's made it seem much less important."

"What do you mean by that?" he asked.

I don't know what I meant by that. I just told him what was. Probably it had something to do with closeness – closeness to the Creator and therefore to all of Creation – past, present, future, not separated by time, but part of God's eternal is-ness.

Eternity is not a time concept. It is almost impossible for us to glimpse what eternity is like because we were born into time. Our bodies move through time. We will die in time. But eternity, that which we are promised, has nothing whatsoever to do with time. It is not time stretched out, on and on forever. It is something wholly different.

My forbears and their contemporaries in St. Margaret's graveyard on Fleming's Island knew during their lifetimes far more about death than we do, because death was far more present. There are not very many old people in that graveyard. There are many children a year, two years, three years old, cut down by diphtheria or scarlet fever. My cousin Myra, my mother's first cousin, told me that when she was a child, five of her brothers and sisters died of scarlet fever in a week. Those who managed to grow up faced malaria, yellow fever, and pneumonia – with no antibiotics. It was not possible to forget or hide death then as secular society today urges us to do. To lose five children in a week! How did the families endure such grief? They endured it because they had to, and such tragedies were not uncommon. Only faith kept the living going.

It is no longer possible – for me, at any rate – to have the same kind of literal faith that my ancestors did. We have acquired a lot of knowledge, as well as antibiotics, since then. Our knowledge has kept people alive today who would have died early deaths a century ago. When there were a few cases of scarlet fever in our village when my children were little my first reaction (remembering Cousin Myra) was panic. I was told to relax; with our new medications, scarlet fever was no longer a killer. A century ago I, myself, would have died twice in childbirth, hemorrhaging, like Rachel, with no way to staunch the blood. Our medical knowledge exploded during and after World War II, and our miracles of science are miracles indeed. But we have saved lives so successfully that we tend to forget that to be human is ultimately to die. Our thinking about death has atrophied to the point where we reject it as being a medical failure. People are put away in hospitals or nursing homes so that we don't have to be tainted by death and perhaps catch it.

We are all going to die, and I suppose whether it is sooner or later makes little difference in eternity, for eternity is total is-ness, immediacy, now-ness. Living in eternity is, in fact, the way we are supposed to live all the time, right now, in the immediate moment, not hanging onto the past, not projecting into the future. The past is the rock that is under our feet, that enables us to push off from it and move into the future. But we don't go bury ourselves in the past, nor should we worry too much about the future. "Sufficient unto the day ..." my grandmother was fond of quoting. God in Jesus came to be in time with us and to redeem human time for us – human time, wristwatch time (*chronos*), and God's time (*kairos*). But even *chronos is* variable. How long is a toothache? How long is a wonderful time? When I fly from New York to San Francisco to see my eldest daughter and her family, I have to set my watch back three hours and I always have jet lag. Even chronological time is full of surprises.

We know that we will never get out of the solar system as long as we have to travel at the speed of anything, even light, because the intergalactic distances are so enormous. Added to that, the faster a moving body moves, the more slowly time moves. So if we got into a spaceship and went to Alpha Centauri, which is seven light years away, and turned right around and came back, we'd have been away for fourteen years. But about a hundred and fifty years would have passed on earth while we were away. So travel at the speed of anything involves the whole space-time continuum which is still something we do not understand.

In the heart and spirit we are less restricted by time. We are given glimpses of *kairos* in our own living, moments that break free of time and simply are. It is fascinating that music is so bound up with time and yet some of the greatest moments of music are the silences between notes. We all have moments of *kairos*, though we seldom recognize them till afterwards. One such glimpse that I remember with particular delight came after a long and very difficult labor when my doctor and friend dropped a small wet creature between my breasts, saying, "Here's your son, Madeleine." And I heard the angels sing.

It can be far less cosmic. It can be dinner with friends. Last spring when I came home from the hospital after knee surgery, my bed became the dining room table. One evening five young friends brought in dinner, and afterwards were sitting on or around the bed, and we began to sing hymns and folk songs. One of the girls started "Patrick's breastplate," one of the longest hymns I know, and we sang it all, every single verse. And it took a fraction of a second. It is, as always, paradox.

And I rejoice.

I want my church to think about eternity. I want to hear preached from the pulpit the Good News of Christ coming into time for us in order to show us how to be human. I want to hear the affirmation that God is powerful enough to do something with ashes if, indeed, something needs to be done. I want to hear that my husband's soul (yes, let's call it that), and the souls of my parents, my friends, are safe in God's care, reclothed in the "spiritual body," growing in God's love. I want to be helped to understand that we are not always ready to receive God's love, that we turn away with selfishness, permissiveness, despair, but that God is always waiting for our cold hearts to turn warm, our anger to peace, our willfulness to love. When we truly love someone we do not want to let that person down. We want to please, not to get Brownie points, but because we love. I want to love God so much that I will no longer obscure the lovely light, but will let it burn brightly.

It took a long time for Joseph to turn from being spoiled and arrogant to being humble and loving. But that's all right. The promise is not that it will be easy but that it will be wonderful.

* * *

JOSEPH'S SERVANT

He is a strange man. Kind to me always. To all of us. There are no floggings in his house. We eat as well as he eats. Better, because we eat together and are merry while he, perforce, eats alone. He has more power than Pharaoh, but he is a Jew. He eats alone.

He is a strange man. In his house we are given an atmosphere for merriment. He likes to hear us laugh, though he seldom smiles. He likes to hear us make music; sometimes he even beats out the time, but he does not sing. He gives us freedom, but, despite his power, he is not free.

Asenath, his wife, is beautiful and loving. Their sons are bright and full of laughter. Are they Egyptians, or are they Jews? They go to the great stone temple with their grandfather, the priest of On. They watch the rising and the setting of the sun and sing the hymns. Sometimes I hear them talk about their father's God as of a distant stranger. Do they know who they are? They are still too young for such questions.

He is a strange man, their father. Always it is as though he is waiting, waiting but for what? He has everything a man could want. Always it is as though something is missing, but what could it be? He works hard, from sunrise to sunset, overseeing, supervising. He is fair. He cannot be bribed. I know, because when a man with heavy gold earrings and much wealth tried to buy, at a high price, more than his share of corn, I saw my master white with anger. He flung the proffered money at the man's feet, turned on his heel, and went into the counting house.

He is a strange man, attractive to women, though he does not seem to realize it, or, if he does, he will have none of their wiles. It is not unusual for the privileged and powerful to add a beautiful woman or two to their privilege and power. But not my master, Joseph, who each night retires with his wife

Asenath to their rooms. We servants are sent away, even the two body servants, that they may be alone.

He is a strange man. When he eats his meals alone, it is as though he is waiting for someone to join him. When he rides his beautiful black mare, it is as though he is looking for someone to ride beside him. He does not speak of what it is that is missing, not even to Asenath, I think. But there is always an unfilled space at his side, even when he plays with his boys.

And now that space is filled with ten strange men from Canaan, men with dark beards half hiding their faces, and with dark eyes, dark as my master's. He speaks to them roughly, as I have never before heard him speak to any of the hungry people coming to Egypt to buy food. Who are they, that they make him weep? Yet, after all his roughness, he sends them away with their sacks filled with corn and wheat, and, after they are gone, he is restless. He has, for what reason I cannot guess, kept one of these men behind as a prisoner. The man is treated well, given fine clothing to wear, the best of food and wine. But my master does not visit him. He gives orders that the man be treated as an honored guest, and he knows that no one would dream of disobeying. And the man asks no questions. He does not ask why he is being held in a single, though spacious, room, with guards to see that he does not leave. He does not ask why he is given silken garments and delicacies to eat. Why does he not ask? Strange, indeed.

Yes, he, too, with his lack of questions, is a strange man, as my master is strange. My master paces when he is not working, paces, back and forth as though waiting. Sometimes Asenath has to call him three times before he hears. His work goes on. He does not slacken. But he paces.

And then at last the bearded men return, and with them a younger one, and my master prepares a great feast for them, and heaps food on the young lad's plate, and looks at him with hungry eyes. And then, again, I see those great eyes fill with tears, and he shouts at us servants, raising his voice. "Leave us!" he cries. At first we are too terrified to move. "Leave us!" And so we go.

And now the empty space is filled. He waits for unseen guests no longer. For the men from Canaan are his brothers, and now I hear him sing, at last I hear him sing, thanks and praise to his God who makes patterns of the stars in the sky and patterns of the people on earth, and with his patterning has brought twelve brothers together.

12

Benjamin

is a wolf that raveneth: in the morning he shall devour the prey, and at night he shall divide the spoil.

Genesis 49:27

JESSE, THE FATHER OF DAVID. In Judah, Jesse is rooted and so, ultimately, is Jesus.

Benjamin was uprooted. Over and over throughout history the Jews have been uprooted, taken from one land, forced to live in another, in exile. By the waters of Babylon have they hung up their harps, strangers in a strange land.

Joseph's aloneness before the return of his brothers is almost as incomprehensible to us as it was to his servant.

We live in an uprooted society. For Hugh and me Crosswicks was a place to put down roots, to belong to a community, a community that was rooted in the white spired church at the crossroads.

Joseph, despite his feelings of alienation, despite being strange in a strange land, had nevertheless put down roots in Egypt. He was rooted by his work, which he could not leave. He was rooted by Asenath and his sons, whom he would not leave. He did not consider going back to Canaan and his father's house, the place of his coat of many colors, and of his grand dreams which were now being fulfilled.

Instead, he begged his brothers to go back to Canaan for their father, Jacob, and to bring him back to Egypt.

"And you shall dwell in the land of Goshen, and you shall be near me, you and your children, and your herds, and all that you have, and then I will nourish you, for there are yet five years of famine, lest you, and all your household, and all that you have, come to poverty. And behold, your eyes see, and the eyes of my brother, Benjamin, that it is my mouth that speaks to you. And you shall tell my father of all my glory in Egypt, and shall haste and bring my father here."

"All my glory in Egypt." Joseph wanted his father to know. How human was the great man!

And Joseph flung his arms around Benjamin's neck and wept again and then he kissed all of his brothers, until their eyes lost their terror and they were able to speak with him.

The land of Goshen. That was where Joseph asked Pharaoh to let him settle his father and his brothers. Crosswicks sits high on a ridge a mile from the village of Goshen in the Litchfield Hills. It is a land that was colonized in the very early eighteenth century by people deeply steeped in Scripture. Canaan is not far away from us, and Bethlehem not much further. But Goshen is our village, where the beautiful old colonial church stands with its white spire, the highest spire in the state, not because the spire is unusually tall, but because Goshen is the highest (and coldest, and windiest) spot in the state.

How different it is in every way from Goshen in Egypt, where Benjamin was to plant new roots. Even after two visits to Egypt I find it hard to visualize the land of Goshen in which Joseph settled his family, because our rolling green dairy farm hills are imprinted in my mind's eye.

Goshen, a land of welcome. In gratitude, Pharaoh opened wide his arms and invited all of Joseph's family to come to Egypt. Benjamin, who had lived in Canaan all his life, was journeying into the unknown. Hugh and I took our children and moved them from Goshen back to New York and the world of the theater where we all had to put down new roots. New York is the place of my birth, and so it will always be home, but in leaving Goshen and returning to the great city we were moving into the unknown, not knowing what the future would hold. Of course we never know. Futures are roughly and irrevocably altered by unexpected accidents, betrayals, illnesses. What we have is this day, this moment.

Joseph moved his family to Egypt, to the land of Goshen, and there Benjamin and his brothers were able to put down new roots. But all earthly roots are only fibers, tender and temporary. Ultimately, another pharaoh down the line would be threatened by the prosperity of the Jews, and then would begin the great epic of Moses and the Exodus.

After Hugh's death once again I moved into the unknown. I stayed in Crosswicks until after Christmas, then moved back to New York and the scaffolded apartment and a new life with college students, and how blessed I was to have them there.

Then, at last, the scaffolding came down, and I had to think about redecorating the apartment, something which Hugh and I knew would have to be done as soon as the scaffolding was gone, and the rain stopped seeping into the living room ceiling. Why does everything take at least twice as long as it is expected to take? Charlotte and I lived out of boxes and in chaos for well over a year. Redecorating was complicated by a leak in the washing machine in the apartment above us, a slow leak which declared itself by blowing out our kitchen lights. We had to wait for leprous looking walls to dry before we could do anything about the kitchen. But now it's done, and it is beautiful – or, at least, it's almost done. But it's finished enough to be comfortably livable, and for us to resume our multigenerational dinner parties. Perhaps the rooms, clean and light, do not look as they would if Hugh and I had done them together, but that's something that's no longer possible. It is perhaps more of a women's apartment than it was, but then, Charlotte and I are women.

One night as I was getting ready for bed after a dinner party, during which many people had commented on how lovely the apartment is, I thought to myself, "I hate the apartment this way. I want it all back exactly the way it was." I knew this was irrational. I knew the apartment was lovely. And suddenly I realized that of course what I wanted was not the apartment back the way it was. I wanted Hugh back. Once I realized that, I was able to let it all go and take a good hot bath and get into bed and read and relax before going to sleep.

It is helpful that sometimes we can understand the real motives underlying some of our irrationality. I think Joseph always knew that he would not feel complete until he had been reconciled with his brothers.

As I continue to move out into the unknown the only thing I know is that I still believe with Paul that *all things work together for good to them that love God* – not just in this mortal life, but in God's ultimate purpose for Creation which we are called on to observe and contemplate. It may be that our contemplation will involve great pain. And sometimes our pain will be deepened as we struggle to remember that its purpose is love.

I am grateful that I was able to honor my promise to Hugh all the way to the end, to be with him when he died. We had promised each other no death-prolonging machinery, and with all my heart I thank the doctors who allowed him to die when the time came for death, a good and holy death, a beginning of a new journey.

Paul goes on to ask,

Who shall separate us from the love of Christ? Shall tribulation, or distress, or persecution, or famine, or nakedness, or peril, or sword? ... Nay, in all these things we are more than conquerors through him that loved us. For I am persuaded that neither death, nor life, nor angels, nor principalities, nor powers, nor things present, nor things to come, nor height, nor depth, nor any other creature, shall be able to separate us from the love of God which is in Christ Jesus our Lord.

Powerful words. Words of high poetry and truth. Words to hold on to. Words which I have held to for many years.

When Paul speaks of angels and principalities and powers as trying to separate us from the love of God he is, of course, speaking of fallen angels, of the principalities and powers which have chosen to follow Satan rather than the Lord of Love. There are true angels, such as the three who came to Abraham; Gabriel, who appeared to young Mary; the angels who ministered to Jesus in the garden, and who have unfailingly followed their calling to be "ministering spirits." There are principalities and powers who eternally worship the Creator with hymns of joy. What God has created is good, and it is a part of the fallenness of all of Creation that some angels, as well as human beings, have turned in pride away from the Creator. But the good angels are more powerful, the great principalities and powers are more loving, than all the fallenness and pride put together. We cannot be separated from the love of God.

Ye watchers and ye holy ones,
Bright seraphs, cherubim, and thrones,
Raise the glad strain, Alleluia!
Cry out, dominions, princedoms, powers,
Virtues, archangels, angels' choirs,
Alleluia, alleluia, alleluia, alleluia, alleluia!

Crosswicks is a place of roots for me, but it is also a place where I have known great pain, where I have clung to the strength of Paul's words. Four times in two years the phone rang to tell us of the death of close friends, deaths which would alter the patterns of our lives. Whenever the phone rings at an unusual hour my heart catapults back into the cold white grief of those phone calls. On the fourth evening of every month when I read the first lines of the 22nd psalm, *"My God, my God, why have you forsaken me?"* I am back in that strange room in the conference center the night after I learned of Hugh's cancer.

I remember a long-gone winter night when I sat waiting by the fire until two in the morning while a blizzard raged outside, and I waited for Hugh to come home. He had set out in the early afternoon on an errand of mercy, to drive a friend at a time of crisis a hundred miles north, into the teeth of the blizzard. I fed our children, put them to bed with the usual stories and songs and prayers, fed and walked the dogs, put the cats in the cellar for the night, kept feeding the fire. A little after two the dogs jumped up, tails wagging, and Hugh staggered in, exhausted, hungry, needing to be fed, loved. And our roots went even deeper into the land of Goshen.

But no place is safe, not even an isolated, dairy farm village. In the late fifties it seemed that war with Russia, nuclear war, was imminent. At school in the village the children were taught to crouch under their little wooden desks, their hands over their heads, in case an atom bomb fell on the school. As if that would protect them! What insanity! In the spring when the lilacs bloomed I wondered if there would be another spring, if Goshen would still be there, if we would ever smell the spring fragrance again, hear the peepers singing in the marsh.

Nothing can separate us from the love of God. Whatever happened, God would be with us, as God was with Shadrach, Meshach, and Abednego in the fiery furnace.

There are happier, more placid memories. Seeing my daughter Josephine kneeling beside the old wooden cradle in which her baby brother lay. (A snapshot of that is framed and on the wall.) Meals around the table, holding hands as we sang grace. Watching my mother walk down the lane, picking an assortment of weeds and wildflowers with which she always managed to create a beautiful arrangement.

The old house, like most old houses, is full of the richness of living, of joy and tears, birth and death, marrying and burying.

Five years ago Bion and Laurie moved in. Laurie had finished her hospital internship and residency. There is an excellent hospital in the nearby town which has attracted a group of fine physicians. Our son said, "Well, Mother and Dad, you taught us about multi-generational living."

And what a blessing it is to have them there. After Hugh's death there was no way I could have kept Crosswicks on my own. It would have had to be sold. And now it is Bion's and

Laurie's home, and the pattern has changed as the pattern changed for Jacob when he moved with his sons from the land of Canaan to the land of Goshen. No mention is made of Dinah in this move. We do not know what happened to Dinah.

Jacob and his sons and their wives and their children and their flocks and their herds moved to the land of Goshen. But their roots, their hearts, were not in Egypt, but in the land from which they had come, from home. In his last days, Jacob asked to be taken home to be buried. And so, later on, did Joseph.

Years ago when my children were young, my mother did not want to come to us, to Crosswicks, for Christmas, and I did not understand. She loved us and the children. I was her only child, our three children were her only grandchildren. Why didn't she want to come?

After Hugh's death my daughters each urged me to come to them at Christmas. I love my daughters. I love my grandchildren. But I didn't want to go to them at Christmas. It was a strong, visceral feeling. I needed to be where my roots are. At last I understood my mother.

It was the famine that drove Jacob away from home and into the land of Goshen. He was an old man, and before he died in that foreign land he gathered his children about him. Jacob had not only his own twelve sons, but Joseph's two sons, Manasseh and Ephraim, who appear to have been favoured above the children of all the other sons, who are not even mentioned when Jacob dispenses his blessings.

When old Jacob saw Joseph's sons he asked who they were, and Joseph replied, *"They are my sons, whom God has given me here."*

Jacob was deeply moved, saying, *"I had not thought to see your face, and lo, God has let me see your children also."* And he called the boys to him to be blessed.

The blessing harks back a generation; just as Jacob replaced his elder brother, Esau, when Isaac blessed his sons, so Jacob gave primary blessing to Ephraim, the younger of the two boys, once again overturning the rule of primogeniture.

When Joseph saw his father placing his right hand on Ephraim's head he was displeased; so he took hold of his father's hand to move it from Ephraim's head to Manasseh's head. Joseph said to him, "No, my father, this one is the firstborn; put your right hand on his head."

And his father refused, and said, "I know, my son, I know. He also shall become a people, and he also shall be great; but truly his younger brother shall be greater than he, and his seed shall become a multitude of nations." And he blessed them that day, saying, "God made thee as Ephraim and Manasseh; and he made Ephraim before Manasseh."

Joseph was not pleased with this, but a blessing given cannot be withdrawn.

Jacob spoke to each of his twelve sons, in order of their birth, but he did not make his first-born Reuben the foremost of the brothers. Reuben still had to pay for his night with Bilhah.

It was Judah who was the favored son. *"The sceptre shall not depart from Judah,"* Jacob prophesied, *"nor the ruler's staff from between his feet."*

To Joseph he promised that God almighty would bless him

"with blessings of heaven above, blessings of the deep that couches beneath, blessings of the breasts, and of the womb. The blessings of your father are mighty beyond the blessings of the eternal mountains, the bounties of an everlasting life."

And his blessing of Benjamin seems strange indeed, little Benjamin who seems to have caused no one any trouble. *"Benjamin is like a vicious wolf. Morning and evening he kills and devours."*

There seems little indication that he did so, though God skips over him, and over Joseph, to choose Judah as the brother from whose tribe the great king David would spring. Perhaps in a prophetic way Jacob was seeing his son's fierce descendants – the Benjamite warriors like Ehud and Saul and Jonathan – famed for their archery.

When Jacob yielded up the ghost and was gathered unto his people, Joseph fell upon his father's face, and wept upon him, and kissed him. And Joseph commanded the physicians who served him to embalm his father, and the physicians embalmed Israel. And forty days were fulfilled for him, for so are fulfilled the days of those who are embalmed, and the Egyptians mourned for him threescore and ten days.

Again that extraordinary number, forty!

But when the days of his mourning were past, Joseph spoke unto the house of Pharaoh, saying, "If now I have found grace in your eyes, speak, I pray you, in the ears of Pharaoh, saying, My father made me swear, saying, Lo, I die. In my grave which I have digged for me in the land of Canaan, there shalt thou bury me. Now therefore let me go up, I pray thee, and bury my father, and I will come again." And Pharaoh said, "Go up, and bury thy father, according as he made thee swear."

So Joseph went to bury his father.

And when Joseph's brothers saw that their father was dead, they said, "Perhaps Joseph will hate us, and will certainly require us all the evil which we did to him."

Like many of us, they could not believe that they were forgiven for what they had done. Joseph had welcomed them into the land of Goshen, and treated them with love and kindness, once he had revealed himself to them as Joseph, and still they were afraid.

And they sent a messenger to Joseph, saying, So shall you say to Joseph, "Forgive, I beg you, forgive the trespasses the servants of your father's God have done."

And Joseph wept when he heard their words.

And his brothers fell down before his face, and they said, "Behold, we are your servants."

And Joseph said to them, "Do not be afraid, for am I in the place of God? But as for you, you thought evil against me, but God meant it for good, to bring to pass, as it happened, that many people have been saved alive from starvation. So do not fear: I will nourish you, and your little ones." And he comforted them, and spoke kindly to them.

All things worked together for good to Joseph, for he loved God. Terrible things happened to him, and wonderful things happened to him, and Joseph grew strong and compassionate, very different as a man from the spoiled bragging brat he had been as a child.

Indeed his brothers did bow down before him, but that was no longer what was important. What was important was that because Joseph had come to love God in this land of strangers, he no longer needed to brag, to thrust himself onto center stage. He had learned to love.

I know that all things work together for good as God ultimately works out the creative and loving purpose of the universe. Just as Joseph learned to understand that God could use the wickedness of his brothers – in selling him into Egypt – for the saving of many lives from the slow and agonizing death of starvation, so God can come into all that happens to us, our griefs and our joys, and use them for good towards the coming of the kingdom.

Simeon and Levi, who slaughtered Shechem and all his tribe, and all the brothers when they conspired to kill Joseph, and when they sold him into Egypt, were indeed a horror and a hissing and an everlasting reproach. But through the prophet Jeremiah God not only warns, he encourages,

"My people, do not be afraid, I will come to you and save you. I will make you well again; I will heal your wounds. People of Israel, I have always loved you, so I continue to show you my constant love. The time is coming when I will make a new covenant with the people of Israel. It will not be like the old covenant ... The new covenant will be this: I will put my law within you and write it in your hearts."

For God is indeed a God of mercy, waiting for us to say, "I'm sorry! I want to come home!" And then the Almighty arms are opened to receive us into joy.

Joseph's life, with its sudden reversals of fortune, was more dramatic than most of our lives. But I have learned much from him on my journey towards becoming human. Surely after his brothers sold him into Egypt he learned how to observe and contemplate, looking out on all that was around him, rather than in towards his own pride and arrogance. In Egypt he learned to see everything as belonging to God: his dreams; the stars at night; the prisoners under his care; Asenath, his wife, and their two sons; the starving people who, like the prisoners, were entrusted to his care, and for the appeasing of whose hunger he was responsible. He had learned to live in the moment, rather than in the projections of his grandiose dreams. It was only when he let his pride go that there was any possibility of the dreams being fulfilled.

We, too, are to live in the moment, the very now. Our roots are deep in the past, but our branches reach up into the future. In the present we observe and contemplate all that God has made, and all that we, with our stiff-necked pride and greed and judgmentalism, have made of what God has made. Are we not created to love and care for our planet, and to love each other enough to live in peace? If we love God, then the Source of Love can come into our lives with redemptive power.

This past Sunday when I knelt at the altar in church, the minister put the bread into my hands, and I took it into my mouth. That morsel of bread, my hands, the minister's hands on my head as he prayed for me, all the other people in church, in other churches, on the streets, alone, all, all, are made of the same stuff as the stars, that original stuff with which Jesus clothed himself when he came to live with us. I ate the bread, took the cup, and with it all the truth of the stories that tell us about ourselves as human beings. And I was as close to Joseph as I was to the people on either side of me.

After church I went home for lunch with a few of the people who had shared communion with me. I had made a mess of pottage, that mixture of lentils, onions, and rice, which Joseph's father, Jacob, sold to Esau for his birthright. It wasn't nice of

Jacob to sell it and defraud his brother, but the pottage was a tempting dish. Friends, food, the love of God, all calling us to be human – not infallible, but human.

We are amazing, we human beings. We do wonderful things, and we do terrible things – but, above all, we make marvelous stories.

* * *

JOSEPH

Sometimes at night, after Asenath and our boys are asleep, I go to the temple to speak to my father-in-law, the high priest of On. The temple is made of stones that gleam with the gold of the sun god he serves. The stones are fitted together so that not even the thinnest blade of knife or sword can slip between them. On the day when night and day are the same length, neither one shorter or longer than the other, the midday sun moves through the portals and strikes all the way through the chambers of the temple to touch the altar.

One night, because he knows that numbers are beautiful to me, he worked them out for me, the movement of the heavenly bodies and the days and nights and months, so that I understood the calculations, and how the temple had been built, just so, so that he could know the very moment when the rays of the sun would reach the altar. A holiest of holy days. He knows, he says; he can do the purest mathematics, he says, because the sun does not move around the earth, he says. Instead, the earth moves around the sun, and the moon around the earth. His beautiful numbers are very persuasive. Would it disturb the Maker of the Universe if this were so?

At night he takes me out and shows me stars that are not just pricks of light, he says, but heavenly bodies like our earth, that dance around the sun. It is a holy dance, he says, this circling of the sun who is his god.

How strange it seems to me. I can see that the heavenly bodies which he tells me are not stars are different from the stars – steadier, less sparkling. We watch the great night sky, and he asks me about my God. I tell him of my great-grandfather, Abraham, who was taken out into the desert at night.

"Count the stars if you can," my God told Abraham. "So shall your descendants be."

"And has it happened?" asked the priest of On.

"It is happening," I tell him rashly, and I think of my brothers at home, so far away, and I wonder about their wives and their children. What is happening at home I do not know, nor if my father is still alive, nor my little brother, Benjamin. And yet I know that God's promises are never empty, and that it is through God's promise that I have been brought to this alien land and given power far beyond anything I could have had at home. Power beyond my dreams.

My father-in-law, the priest of On, says, "Then if your great-grandfather's descendants are to be as many as the stars in the sky, there will be jealousy of them."

He may be right. I know all about jealousy.

Sometimes we talk about our dreams. I had a dream in which I watched my father bless the Pharaoh, and I and my father were together once again. Will that happen? My father blessing the Pharaoh? And I and my father together once again? It was a dream of comfort.

The priest of On nods, but sadly, for, he says, he will die before that time of fulfillment. He is old, old and wise. He tells me of his dreams. He dreams of strange chariots, bearing people, flying across the sky. He dreams of buildings towering higher than the highest temples. He dreams of a great cloud that is brighter than a million suns. These dreams, he says, may or may not come to pass, depending on the paths chosen. He tells me of his dreams, but they are in a strange language which does not lend itself to interpretation. And though God does not give me the interpretation, I sense that these dreams are not against the plan of God. And I am troubled.

He laughs and tells me that he has dreamed of a child of God who will come to save us. "But I will be long dead before he comes," he tells me, "and you, too, and your children, and your children's children."

He questions me about my life at home, and about my brothers, and about the journey to Egypt. He wags his head as I tell him about Potiphar's wife, and I cannot tell what he thinks. He asks me about my time in prison, and I tell him of a foreign sailor who came there with a ring in his nose. He had been captain of a ship and he talked of the four corners of the earth, and how his sailors had feared they would sail off the edge, where strange and fearful monsters waited, and they had rebelled and cast him out of his ship, and a sea god found him a log which carried him to shore. And the priest of On laughed deep in his throat and talked once more about the great dancing circles of the earth and stars.

I listen to many stories of gods who live in the sun, and in the sea, and in the moon, and also in strange beasts. I do not know whether my father-in-law, the priest of On, believes in these gods, or only in the sun.

His eyes are bright as he talks about the sun god who holds the heavenly bodies that dance around it, but never come close.

For them, to come close would be to burn. The sun god is fire, and fire burns, and does not care about what is burned.

The God who showed my great-grandfather Abraham the stars walks with us. That is the difference. The sun god shines with brilliance but does not touch its people. The God of my fathers, of Abraham, Isaac, and Jacob, is with us. When my brothers threw me into the pit, God was there, in the pit with me. When I ruled over Potiphar's household, God was there in my ruling. When I refused Potiphar's wife because I would not dishonor my master, God was there in my refusing. When I was in prison, God was there in my bondage. In my days of power, God is with me, guiding me.

And is God with my brothers and my father? When Simeon and Levi killed Shechem, did they escape God? Or when my brothers sold me into Egypt was not God there? with them? with me?

If my heart is cold towards my brothers, does not that also chill the heart of God?

The sun god looks down but is not part of the lives of those who worship the burning light. But my God – how can we bear a God who cares?

The high priest of On can turn away from those who disobey him or those who hurt him or those he does not love. He can condemn them to death.

Oh, my brothers, because God is with us, how can I turn away from you without turning away from God?

Oh, yes, my father-in-law, you who are the high priest of On, the sun burns, but it burns not because it is a god but because it was made by God, to burn me until I love my brothers once again.

Oh, my brothers, I thank you for all that you gave me when you sold me into Egypt. Because of you, it is my riches of understanding that I value, not my palace and my power. Yes, the sun burns, burns away anger and outrage, and my heart opens like a lotus flower.

And now my brothers have come, oh my brothers, and now that I love them, and they are freed to love me, joy will come again, and laughter.

And I will praise God.